A Guide to MATLAB®
Object-Oriented Programming

A Guide to MATLAB®
Object-Oriented Programming

Andy H. Register

Georgia Tech Research Institute
Atlanta, Georgia, U.S.A.

Chapman & Hall/CRC
Taylor & Francis Group
Boca Raton London New York

Chapman & Hall/CRC is an imprint of the
Taylor & Francis Group, an **informa** business

SCITECH
PUBLISHING, INC.

MATLAB* is a trademark of The Mathworks, Inc. and is used with permission. The MathWorks does not warrant the accuracy of the text or exercises in this book. This book's use or discussion of MATLAB software or related products does not constitute endorsement or sponsorship by The MathWorks of a particular pedagogical approach or particular use of the MATLAB software.

Chapman & Hall/CRC
Taylor & Francis Group
6000 Broken Sound Parkway NW, Suite 300
Boca Raton, FL 33487-2742

© 2007 by SciTech Publishing Inc.
Chapman & Hall/CRC is an imprint of Taylor & Francis Group, an Informa business

No claim to original U.S. Government works
Printed in the United States of America on acid-free paper
10 9 8 7 6 5 4 3 2 1

International Standard Book Number-13: 978-1-58488-911-3 (Softcover)

Library of Congress Cataloging-in-Publication Data

Register, Andy H.
   A guide to MATLAB object-oriented programming / Andy H. Register.
      p. cm.
   Includes index.
   ISBN-13: 978-1-58488-911-3 (alk. paper)
   ISBN-10: 1-58488-911-X (alk. paper)
   1. MATLAB. 2. Object-oriented programming (Computer science) 3. Numerical analysis--Data processing. I. Title.

QA76.64.R454 2007
005.1'17--dc22   2006100724

Visit the Taylor & Francis Web site at
http://www.taylorandfrancis.com

and the CRC Press Web site at
http://www.crcpress.com

Dedication

For Mickey

Table of Contents

Figures xv
Code Listings xvii
Tables xxi
About the Author xxiii
Preface xxv

Chapter 1 Introduction 1

1.1   Examples 2
1.2   Object-Oriented Software Development 2
    1.2.1   At the Top of Your Game 3
    1.2.2   Personal Development 3
    1.2.3   Wicked Problems 5
    1.2.4   Extreme Programming 6
    1.2.5   MATLAB, Object-Oriented Programming, and You 8
1.3   Attributes, Behavior, Objects, and Classes 9
    1.3.1   From MATLAB Heavyweight to Object-Oriented Thinker 9
    1.3.2   Object-Oriented Design 10
    1.3.3   Why Use Objects? 11
    1.3.4   A Quality Focus 12
        1.3.4.1   Reliability 12
        1.3.4.2   Reusability 13
        1.3.4.3   Extendibility 14
1.4   Summary 15

PART 1   Group of Eight *17*

Chapter 2 Meeting MATLAB's Requirements 19

2.1   Variables, Types, Classes, and Objects 19
2.2   What Is a MATLAB Class? 21
    2.2.1   Example: Class Requirements 21
        2.2.1.1   Class Directory 22
        2.2.1.2   Constructor 22
        2.2.1.3   The Test Drive 24
2.3   Summary 26
2.4   Independent Investigations 27

Chapter 3 Member Variables and Member Functions 29

3.1   Members 29
3.2   Accessors and Mutators 30
      3.2.1   A Short Side Trip to Examine Encapsulation 31
              3.2.1.1   cShape Variables 32
      3.2.2   cShape Members 33
              3.2.2.1   cShape Private Member Variables 33
              3.2.2.2   cShape Public Interface 34
      3.2.3   A Short Side Trip to Examine Function Search Priority 36
      3.2.4   Example Code: Accessors and Mutators, Round 1 37
              3.2.4.1   Constructor 37
              3.2.4.2   Accessors 37
              3.2.4.3   Mutators 38
              3.2.4.4   Combining an Accessor and a Mutator 39
              3.2.4.5   Member Functions 40
      3.2.5   Standardization 40
3.3   The Test Drive 41
3.4   Summary 42
3.5   Independent Investigations 43

Chapter 4 Changing the Rules ... in Appearance Only 45

4.1   A Special Accessor and a Special Mutator 45
      4.1.1   A Short Side Trip to Examine Overloading 45
              4.1.1.1   Superiorto and Inferiorto 47
              4.1.1.2   The Built-In Function 48
      4.1.2   Overloading the Operators subsref and subsasgn 48
              4.1.2.1   Dot-Reference Indexing 50
              4.1.2.2   subsref Dot-Reference, Attempt 1 51
              4.1.2.3   A New Interface Definition 52
              4.1.2.4   subsref Dot-Reference, Attempt 2: Separating Public and
                        Private Variables 53
              4.1.2.5   subsref Dot-Reference, Attempt 3: Beyond One-to-One,
                        Public-to-Private 53
              4.1.2.6   subsref Dot-Reference, Attempt 4: Multiple Indexing Levels 55
              4.1.2.7   subsref Dot-Reference, Attempt 5: Operator Conversion Anomaly 57
              4.1.2.8   subsasgn Dot-Reference 59
              4.1.2.9   Array-Reference Indexing 62
              4.1.2.10 subsref Array-Reference 63
              4.1.2.11 subsasgn Array-Reference 64
              4.1.2.12 Cell-Reference Indexing 65
      4.1.3   Initial Solution for subsref.m 66
      4.1.4   Initial Solution for subsasgn.m 68
      4.1.5   Operator Overload, mtimes 69
4.2   The Test Drive 70
      4.2.1   subsasgn Test Drive 70
      4.2.2   subsref Test Drive 72
4.3   Summary 74
4.4   Independent Investigations 75

Chapter 5   Displaying an Object's State 77

5.1   Displaying Objects 77
    5.1.1   What Should Be Displayed? 77
    5.1.2   Standard Structure Display 79
    5.1.3   Public Member Variable Display 80
        5.1.3.1   Implementing display.m, Attempt 1 80
        5.1.3.2   Implementing display.m, Attempt 2 81
5.2   Developer View 83
    5.2.1   Implementing display.m with Developer View Options 84
5.3   The Test Drive 86
5.4   Summary 88
5.5   Independent Investigations 88

Chapter 6   fieldnames.m 91

6.1   fieldnames 91
6.2   Code Development 91
6.3   The Test Drive 93
6.4   Summary 93
6.5   Independent Investigations 94

Chapter 7   struct.m 95

7.1   struct 95
7.2   Code Development 96
7.3   The Test Drive 97
7.4   Summary 98
7.5   Independent Investigations 98

Chapter 8   get.m, set.m 99

8.1   Arguments for the Member Functions get and set 99
    8.1.1   For Developers 99
    8.1.2   For Clients 100
    8.1.3   Tab Completion 101
8.2   Code Development 101
    8.2.1   Implementing get and set 102
    8.2.2   Initial get.m 104
    8.2.3   Initial set.m 107
8.3   The Test Drive 110
8.4   Summary 111
8.5   Independent Investigations 112

Chapter 9   Simplify Using get, set, fieldnames, and struct 113

9.1   Improving subsref.m 114
9.2   Improving subsasgn.m 115
9.3   Improving display.m 116
9.4   Test Drive 118
9.5   Summary 121
9.6   Independent Investigations 122

Chapter 10 Drawing a Shape 123

10.1 Ready, Set, Draw 123
    10.1.1 Implementation 123
        10.1.1.1 Modify the Constructor 124
        10.1.1.2 Modify fieldnames 125
        10.1.1.3 Modify get 125
        10.1.1.4 Modify set 128
        10.1.1.5 Modify mtimes 131
        10.1.1.6 Modify reset 132
        10.1.1.7 Adding Member Function draw 132
10.2 Test Drive 133
10.3 Summary 136
10.4 Independent Investigations 137

PART 2 Building a Hierarchy 139

Chapter 11 Constructor Redux 141

11.1 Specifying Initial Values 141
    11.1.1 Private Member Functions 142
11.2 Generalizing the Constructor 143
    11.2.1 Constructor Helper /private/ctor_ini.m 145
    11.2.2 Constructor Helper Example /private/ctor_1.m 146
11.3 Test Drive 147
11.4 Summary 150
11.5 Independent Investigations 151

Chapter 12 Constructing Simple Hierarchies with Inheritance 153

12.1 Simple Inheritance 154
    12.1.1 Constructor 154
    12.1.2 Other Standard Member Functions 157
        12.1.2.1 Child Class fieldnames 161
        12.1.2.2 Child Class get 162
        12.1.2.3 Child Class set 165
    12.1.3 Parent Slicing in Nonstandard Member Functions 167
        12.1.3.1 draw.m 168
        12.1.3.2 mtimes.m 168
        12.1.3.3 reset.m 169
12.2 Test Drive 169
12.3 Summary 173
12.4 Independent Investigations 174

Chapter 13 Object Arrays with Inheritance 175

13.1 When Is a cShape Not a cShape? 175
    13.1.1 Changes to subsasgn 176
    13.1.2 vertcat and horzcat 177
    13.1.3 Test Drive 178

13.2 Summary 182

13.3 Independent Investigations 182

Chapter 14 Child-Class Members 183

14.1 Function Redefinition 183

    14.1.1 /@cStar/private/ctor_ini.m with Private Member Variables 184

    14.1.2 /@cStar/fieldnames.m with Additional Public Members 184

    14.1.3 /@cStar/get.m with Additional Public Members 185

    14.1.4 /@cStar/set.m with Additional Public Members 186

    14.1.5 /@cStar/draw.m with a Title 187

14.2 Test Drive 187

14.3 Summary 189

14.4 Independent Investigations 190

Chapter 15 Constructing Simple Hierarchies with Composition 191

15.1 Composition 191

    15.1.1 The cLineStyle Class 192

        15.1.1.1 cLineStyle's private/ctor_ini 193

        15.1.1.2 cLineStyle's fieldnames 194

        15.1.1.3 cLineStyle's get 195

        15.1.1.4 cLineStyle's set 196

        15.1.1.5 cLineStyle's private/ctor_2 197

    15.1.2 Using a Primary cShape and a Secondary cLineStyle 198

        15.1.2.1 Composition Changes to cShape's ctor_ini.m 199

        15.1.2.2 Adding LineWeight to cShape's fieldnames.m 199

        15.1.2.3 Composition Changes to cShape's get.m 200

        15.1.2.4 Composition Changes to cShape's set.m 201

        15.1.2.5 Composition Changes to cShape's draw.m 202

        15.1.2.6 Composition Changes to cShape's Other Member Functions 202

15.2 Test Drive 203

15.3 Summary 204

15.4 Independent Investigations 206

Chapter 16 General Assignment and Mutator Helper Functions 209

16.1 Helper Function Strategy 209

    16.1.1 Direct-Link Public Variables 210

        16.1.1.1 get and subsref 210

        16.1.1.2 set and subsasgn 211

    16.1.2 get and set Helper Functions 212

        16.1.2.1 Helper functions, get, and set 212

        16.1.2.2 Final template for get.m 213

        16.1.2.3 Final Template for set.m 217

        16.1.2.4 Color Helper Function 221

        16.1.2.5 The Other Classes and Member Functions 222

16.2 Test Drive 222

16.3 Summary 223

16.4 Independent Investigations 224

Chapter 17 Class Wizard 225

17.1 File Dependencies 226
17.2 Data-Entry Dialog Boxes 226
     17.2.1 Main Class Wizard Dialog 227
          17.2.1.1   Header Information Dialog 229
          17.2.1.2   Parents ... Dialog 231
          17.2.1.3   Private Variable ... Dialog 232
          17.2.1.4   Concealed Variables ... Dialog 234
          17.2.1.5   Public Variables ... Dialog 235
          17.2.1.6   Constructors ... Dialog 237
          17.2.1.7   More ... Dialog 238
          17.2.1.8   Static Variables ... Dialog 239
          17.2.1.9   Private Functions ... Dialog 240
          17.2.1.10 Public Functions ... Dialog 242
          17.2.1.11 File Menu 243
          17.2.1.12 Data Menu 244
          17.2.1.13 Build Class Files Button 245
17.3 Summary 246
17.4 Independent Investigations 247

Chapter 18 Class Wizard Versions of the Shape Hierarchy 249

18.1 cLineStyle Class Wizard Definition Data 249
     18.1.1 cLineStyle Header Info 250
     18.1.2 cLineStyle Private Variables 251
     18.1.3 cLineStyle Public Variables 253
     18.1.4 cLineStyle Constructor Functions 255
     18.1.5 cLineStyle Data Dictionary 257
     18.1.6 cLineStyle Build Class Files 258
     18.1.7 cLineStyle Accessor and Mutator Helper Functions 259
18.2 cShape Class Wizard Definition Data 261
     18.2.1 cShape Header Info 261
     18.2.2 cShape Private Variables 261
     18.2.3 cShape Concealed Variables 262
     18.2.4 cShape Public Variables 263
     18.2.5 cShape Constructor Functions 264
     18.2.6 cShape Public Functions 265
     18.2.7 cShape Data Dictionary 265
     18.2.8 cShape Build Class Files 266
18.3 cStar Class Wizard Definition Data 268
     18.3.1 cStar Parent 268
     18.3.2 Other cStar Definition Data 269
18.4 cDiamond Class Wizard Definition Data 271
18.5 Test Drive 271
18.6 Summary 272
18.7 Independent Investigations 275

PART 3   Advanced Strategies *277*

Chapter 19 Composition and a Simple Container Class 279

19.1 Building Containers 279
19.2 Container Implementation 280
    19.2.1 The Standard Framework and the Group of Eight 280
        19.2.1.1 Container Modifications to fieldnames 281
        19.2.1.2 Container Modifications to subsref 283
        19.2.1.3 Container Modifications to subsasgn 285
        19.2.1.4 Container Modifications to get 287
        19.2.1.5 Container Modifications to set 289
    19.2.2 Tailoring Built-In Behavior 290
        19.2.2.1 Container-Tailored end 291
        19.2.2.2 Container-Tailored cat, horzcat, vertcat 291
        19.2.2.3 Container-Tailored length, ndims, reshape, and size 293
    19.2.3 cShapeArray and numel 294
        19.2.3.1 Container-Tailored num2cell and mat2cell 295
    19.2.4 Container Functions That Are Specific to cShape Objects 296
        19.2.4.1 cShapeArray times and mtimes 296
        19.2.4.2 cShapeArray draw 298
        19.2.4.3 cShapeArray reset 299
19.3 Test Drive 299
19.4 Summary 302
19.5 Independent Investigations 302

Chapter 20 Static Member Data and Singleton Objects 303

20.1 Adding Static Data to Our Framework 303
    20.1.1 Hooking Static Data into the Group of Eight 304
        20.1.1.1 Static Variables and the Constructor 305
        20.1.1.2 Static Variables in get and set 305
        20.1.1.3 Static Variables in display 306
    20.1.2 Overloading loadobj and saveobj 307
    20.1.3 Counting Assignments 308
20.2 Singleton Objects 308
20.3 Test Drive 309
20.4 Summary 311
20.5 Independent Investigations 312

Chapter 21 Pass-by-Reference Emulation 313

21.1 Assignment without Equal 313
21.2 Pass-by-Reference Functions 314
21.3 Pass-by-Reference Draw 315
21.4 Pass-by-Reference Member Variable: View 316
    21.4.1 Helpers, get, and subsref with Pass-by-Reference Behavior 316
        21.4.1.1 Pass-by-Reference Behavior in the Helper 317
        21.4.1.2 Pass-by-Reference Code in get.m 318
        21.4.1.3 Pass-by-Reference Code in subsref.m 321

        21.4.2 Other Group-of-Eight Considerations...321
21.5 Test Drive..322
21.6 Summary...324
21.7 Independent Investigations 324

Chapter 22 Dot Functions and Functors..327

22.1 When Dot-Reference Is Not a Reference...327
22.2 When Array-Reference Is Not a Reference..332
        22.2.1 Functors 333
        22.2.2 Functor Handles...334
        22.2.3 Functor feval..335
        22.2.4 Additional Remarks Concerning Functors..335
23.3 Test Drive..336
22.4 Summary...337
22.5 Independent Investigations 337

Chapter 23 Protected Member Variables and Functions 339

23.1 How Protected Is Different from Other Visibilities..339
23.2 Class Elements for Protected 339
        23.2.1 Protected Functions and Advanced Function Handle Techniques 340
        23.2.2 Passing Protected Handles from Parent to Child 340
        23.2.3 Accessing and Mutating Protected Variables...341
        23.2.4 Calling Protected Functions..343
23.3 Test Drive..344
23.4 Summary...345
23.5 Independent Investigations 346

Chapter 24 Potpourri for $100 347

24.1 A Small Assortment of Useful Commands 347
        24.1.1 objectdirectory 347
        24.1.2 methods and methodsview 347
        24.1.3 functions 348
24.2 Other Functions You Might Want to Overload...348
        24.2.1 Functions for Built-in Types 348
        24.2.2 subsindex 349
        24.2.3 isfield...349
24.3 Summary...350
24.4 Independent Investigations 350

Index 351

Figures

Figure 1.1 A simple hierarchy 14

Figure 1.2 Demonstration of the extendibility of a hierarchy: (a) original organization;
(b) parent–child relationship; and (c) general subset is reused 15

Figure 2.1 Puzzle with MATLAB-required pieces in place 27

Figure 3.1 Puzzle with member variable, member function, and encapsulation 43

Figure 4.1 Access operator organizational chart 50

Figure 4.2 Puzzle with subsref, subsasgn, builtin, and overloading................................74

Figure 5.1 Puzzle with display and function handles 89

Figure 8.1 get's functional block diagram 103

Figure 8.2 set's functional block diagram...104

Figure 8.3 All the pieces of the frame are in place 112

Figure 10.1 Default graphic for cShape object..134

Figure 10.2 cShape graphic after assigning an RGB color of [1; 0; 0] 134

Figure 10.3 cShape graphic scaled using the size mutator...135

Figure 10.4 cShape graphic scaled using the overloaded mtimes.................................135

Figure 10.5 Graphic for an array of cShape objects..136

Figure 11.1 Default constructor graphic for a cShape object..147

Figure 11.2 Example graphic of object constructed from a corner-point array 148

Figure 11.3 Example graphic for shape with no corner points 149

Figure 11.4 UML static structure diagram for cShape...151

Figure 12.1 The simple shape taxonomy 153

Figure 12.2 The inheritance structure of cStar and cDiamond......................................154

Figure 12.3 Call tree for cStar's default constructor 171

Figure 12.4 Call tree for cStar's dot-reference accessor..172

Figure 12.5 cStar graphic (simple inheritance) after setting the size to [2; 3] 173

Figure 12.6 cStar graphic (simple inheritance) after scaling via multiplication, 2 * star * 2 173

Figure 13.1 cStar graphic (simple inheritance plus an array of objects) after scaling
via multiplication, 1.5 * star(1)… 178

Figure 13.2 cDiamond graphic (simple inheritance plus an array of objects) after
setting the size of (2) to [0.75; 1.25]..179

Figure 13.3 Combined graphics for cStar and cDiamond 181

Figure 14.1 cStar graphic with a title...188

Figure 14.2 cDiamond graphic, no title 188

Figure 14.3 Combined cStar and cDiamond graphics, now with a title 189

Figure 14.4 cStar graphic, now with a new title...189

Figure 15.1 Combined graphic, now with shape {1}(1) changed to 'bold'....................204

Figure 15.2 Simplified UML static structure diagram with inheritance and composition 205

Figure 15.3 Puzzle, now with the inheritance pieces...206

Figure 16.1 cStar graphic after implementing helper-function syntax 223

Figure 17.1 Dependency diagram for a simple class..226

Figure 17.2 Dependency diagram with inheritance 227

Figure 17.3 Class Wizard, main dialog 228

Figure 17.4 Class Wizard, **Header Info** ... dialog...230
Figure 17.5 Class Wizard, **Parents** ... dialog...232
Figure 17.6 Class Wizard, **Private Variables** ... dialog 233
Figure 17.7 Class Wizard, **Concealed Variables** ... dialog 234
Figure 17.8 Class Wizard, **Public Variables** ... dialog..236
Figure 17.9 Class Wizard, **Constructors** ... dialog...237
Figure 17.10 Class Wizard, **More** ... dialog 239
Figure 17.11 Class Wizard, **Static Variables** ... dialog...240
Figure 17.12 Class Wizard, **Private Function** ... dialog..241
Figure 17.13 Class Wizard, **Public Function** ... dialog 242
Figure 17.14 Class Wizard, standard File::Open ... dialog 244
Figure 17.15 Class Wizard, standard File::Save As ... dialog 244
Figure 17.16 Class Wizard, Data File::Dictionary ... dialog 245
Figure 17.17 Class Wizard, **Build Class Files** dialog 246
Figure 18.1 Class Wizard, main dialog for cLineStyle..250
Figure 18.2 Class Wizard, cLineStyle header information dialog...251
Figure 18.3 Class Wizard, cLineStyle private variable dialog...252
Figure 18.4 Class Wizard, cLineStyle public variable dialog 254
Figure 18.5 Class Wizard, cLineStyle constructor function dialog......................................255
Figure 18.6 Class Wizard, cLineStyle data dictionary dialog 257
Figure 18.7 Class Wizard, cLineStyle directory-selection dialog 258
Figure 18.8 Class Wizard, cShape private variable dialog 262
Figure 18.9 Class Wizard, cShape concealed variable dialog 263
Figure 18.10 Class Wizard, cShape public variable dialog 264
Figure 18.11 Class Wizard, cShape constructor function dialog..265
Figure 18.12 Class Wizard, cShape public function dialog..266
Figure 18.13 Class Wizard, cShape data dictionary dialog 267
Figure 18.14 Class Wizard, cStar parents dialog...268
Figure 18.15 A double blue star drawn by the Class Wizard generated classes.........................272
Figure 19.1 Shapes in a container drawn together..301
Figure 23.1 The complete picture..346

Code Listings

Code Listing 1, Command Line Example to Illustrate *Class* and *Object* 19
Code Listing 2, Minimalist Constructor..23
Code Listing 3, Chapter 1 Test Drive Command Listing 24
Code Listing 4, A Very Simple Constructor 37
Code Listing 5, getSize.m Public Member Function 38
Code Listing 6, getScale.m Public Member Function 38
Code Listing 7, setSize.m Public Member Function..38
Code Listing 8, setScale.m Public Member Function..39
Code Listing 9, ColorRgb.m Public Member Function 39
Code Listing 10, reset.m Public Member Function 40
Code Listing 11, Chapter 3 Test-Drive Command Listing 41
Code Listing 12, Skeleton Switch Statement for subsref and subsasgn.................................49
Code Listing 13, By-the-Book Approach to subref's Dot-Reference Case 51
Code Listing 14, Public Variable Names in subref's Dot-Reference Case............................54
Code Listing 15, Modified Constructor Using mColorHsv Instead of mColorRgb 54
Code Listing 16, Converting HSV Values to RGB Values...54
Code Listing 17, An Improved Version of the subsref Dot-Reference Case 55
Code Listing 18, A Free Function That Returns Indexing Error Messages 58
Code Listing 19, Operator Syntax vs. subsref...58
Code Listing 20, Addressing the subsref nargout Anomaly 59
Code Listing 21, Initial Version of subsasgn's Dot Reference Case 60
Code Listing 22, Initial Version of subref's Array-Reference Case 63
Code Listing 23, Initial Version of subasgn's Array-Reference Case 64
Code Listing 24, Initial Solution for subsref..66
Code Listing 25, Initial Solution for subsasgn 68
Code Listing 26, Tailored Version of cShape's mtimes 70
Code Listing 27, Chapter 4 Test Drive Command Listing for subsasgn 71
Code Listing 28, Chapter 4 Test Drive Command Listing for subsref 72
Code Listing 29, The Normal Display for a Structure 79
Code Listing 30, Displaying the Object's Private Structure 80
Code Listing 31, Desired Format for the cShape Display Output 80
Code Listing 32, First Attempt at an Implementation for cShape's Tailored display.m 81
Code Listing 33, Second Attempt at an Implementation for cShape's Tailored display.m.............82
Code Listing 34, Example Display Output for the Tailored Version of display.m....................83
Code Listing 35, Improved Display Implementation with Developer View Options.....................84
Code Listing 36, Chapter 5 Test Drive Command Listing for Display 86
Code Listing 37, cShape Constructor with Developer View Enabled by Default 87
Code Listing 38, Chapter 5 Test Drive Command Listing Using the Alternate Display................87
Code Listing 39, Initial Design for fieldnames.m 92
Code Listing 40, Chapter 6 Test Drive Command Listing for fieldnames.m 93
Code Listing 41, Initial Implementation for struct.m..96
Code Listing 42, Chapter 7 Test Drive Command Listing for struct.m..................................97

Code Listing 43, Output Example for Built-In get and set 101
Code Listing 44, Initial Implementation for get.m...104
Code Listing 45, Initial Design for set.m 107
Code Listing 46, Chapter 8 Test Drive Command Listing for set.m 110
Code Listing 47, Chapter 8 Test Drive Command Listing for get.m...111
Code Listing 48, Improved Implementation for subsref.m..114
Code Listing 49, Improved Implementation for subsasgn.m...115
Code Listing 50, Improved Implementation for display.m..117
Code Listing 51, Chapter 9 Test Drive Command Listing:
A Repeat of the Commands from Chapter 4 119
Code Listing 52, Chapter 9 Additional Test-Drive Commands...120
Code Listing 53, Improving the Constructor Implementation 125
Code Listing 54, Improved Implementation of fieldnames.m..126
Code Listing 55, Improved Implementation of get.m...126
Code Listing 56, Improved Version of set.m..128
Code Listing 57, Improved Version of mtimes.m...131
Code Listing 58, Improved Version of reset.m...132
Code Listing 59, Improved Implementation of draw.m..133
Code Listing 60, Improved Constructor without Inheritance 143
Code Listing 61, Modular Code, Constructor Helper /private/ctor_ini.m 145
Code Listing 62, Modular Code, Constructor Helper /private/ctor_1.m Example 146
Code Listing 63, Chapter 11 Test-Drive Commands (Partial List)..148
Code Listing 64, Modular Code, Simple ctor_ini with Inheritance 155
Code Listing 65, Modular Code, cStar's Private parent_list Function 156
Code Listing 66, Main Constructor with Support for Parent–Child Inheritance 157
Code Listing 67, Implementing Parent Slicing in cStar's fieldnames.m 161
Code Listing 68, Implementing Parent Forwarding in cStar's get.m...162
Code Listing 69, Implementing Parent Forwarding in cStar's set.m 165
Code Listing 70, Parent Slice and Forward inside Child-Class draw.m......................................168
Code Listing 71, Parent Slice and Forward in Child-Class mtimes.m...169
Code Listing 72, Parent Slice and Forward in Child-Class reset.m...169
Code Listing 73, Chapter 12 Test Drive Command Listing:
Exercising the Interface for a cStar Object 169
Code Listing 74, Questionable Inheritance Syntax...175
Code Listing 75, Changes to subsasgn That Trap Mismatched Array Types 176
Code Listing 76, Implementing Input Type Checking for vertcat.m 177
Code Listing 77, Implementing Input Type Checking for cat.m 177
Code Listing 78, Modified Implementation of draw That Will Accept an Input Figure Handle....180
Code Listing 79, Adding a Private Variable to a Child-Class Constructor...................................184
Code Listing 80, Adding a Public Variable to a Child-Class fieldnames.m 184
Code Listing 81, Child-Class Public Member Variables in get.m 185
Code Listing 82, Child-Class Public Member Variables in set.m 186
Code Listing 83, Child-Class draw.m Using Additional Child-Class Members 187
Code Listing 84, Chapter 14 Test Drive Command Listing for Child-Class Member Variables ..187
Code Listing 85, Modular Code, cLineStyle's /private/ctor_ini.m..193
Code Listing 86, Modular Code, cLineStyle's fieldnames.m 194
Code Listing 87, Public Variable Implementation in cLineStyle's get.m 195
Code Listing 88, Public Variable Implementation in cLineStyle's set.m....................................196
Code Listing 89, Modular Code, cLineStyle Constructor, private/ctor_2.m 197
Code Listing 90, Modular Code, Modified Implementation of cShape's ctor_ini.m 199
Code Listing 91, Adding LineWeight to cShape's fieldnames.m...199

Code Listing 92, Adding ColorRgb and LineWeight Cases to cShape's get.m............................200
Code Listing 93, Adding ColorRgb and LineWeight Cases to cShape's set.m 201
Code Listing 94, Modified Implementation of cShape's draw.m...203
Code Listing 95, Chapter 15 Test Drive Command Listing for Composition 203
Code Listing 96, Standard Direct-Link-Variable Access Case for get.m 210
Code Listing 97, Varargout Size-Conversion Code..211
Code Listing 98, Handling Additional Indexing Levels in subsref.m 211
Code Listing 99, Standard Direct-Link-Variable Access Case for set.m.....................................211
Code Listing 100, Final Version of get.m Implemented for cLineStyle................................213
Code Listing 101, Final Version of set.m Implemented for cLineStyle 457
Code Listing 102, Final Version of cLineStyle's Color_helper.m 221
Code Listing 103, Chapter 16 Test Drive Command Listing: The cStar Interface.........................223
Code Listing 104, Header Comments Generated by Class Wizard 230
Code Listing 105, Constructor Helper from Class Wizard, @cLineStyle/private/ctor_ini.m 252
Code Listing 106, Two-Input Class Wizard Constructor, @cLineStyle/private/ctor_2.m
function this = ctor_2(this, color, width)..256
Code Listing 107, Public Variable Helper, as Generated by Class Wizard,
cLineStyle::Color_helper 259
Code Listing 108, Chapter 18 Test Drive Command Listing Based on Class
Wizard–Generated Member Functions 273
Code Listing 109, Modifications to the subsref Array-Reference Case for a Container Class......284
Code Listing 110, Modifications to subsasgn Array-Reference Case for a Container Class.........285
Code Listing 111, Modifications to the Public and Concealed Variable
Sections of get.m for a Container Class 287
Code Listing 112, Modifications to the Public Section of set.m for a Container Class.................289
Code Listing 113, Overloading end.m to Support Container Indexing 291
Code Listing 114, Overloading cat.m to Support Container Operations 292
Code Listing 115, Overloading length.m to Support Container Indexing 293
Code Listing 116, Overloading num2cell to Support Raw Output from a Container....................296
Code Listing 117, Overloading times.m for the cShape Container 296
Code Listing 118, Overloading draw.m for the cShape Container 298
Code Listing 119, Overloading reset.m for the cShape Container..299
Code Listing 120, Chapter 19 Test Drive Command Listing: cShape Container 300
Code Listing 121, Private static.m Used to Store and Manage Classwide Private Data 304
Code Listing 122, Additional ctor_ini.m Commands for Static Variable Initialization 305
Code Listing 123, Direct-Access get case for mLineWidthCounter...305
Code Listing 124, Direct-Access set case for mLineWidthCounter 306
Code Listing 125, Static Variable Additions to developer_view...306
Code Listing 126, Tailored saveobj That Includes Static Data..307
Code Listing 127, Tailored loadobj That Includes Static Data 307
Code Listing 128, A Modification to LineWidth_helper That Counts LineWidth Assignments ..308
Code Listing 129, Chapter 20 Test Drive Command Listing: Static Members 309
Code Listing 130, An Approximation to Call-by-Reference Behavior 315
Code Listing 131, Enabling a Helper with Call-by-Reference Behavior......................................317
Code Listing 132, Pass-by-Reference Code Block in get.m...319
Code Listing 133, Pass-by-Reference Parent Forward Assignment Commands 319
Code Listing 134, Array Reference Case in subsref.m with Pass-by-Reference Commands........321
Code Listing 135, Chapter 21 Test Drive Command Listing: Pass-by-Reference Emulation.......322
Code Listing 136, Helper Function to Experiment with input–substruct Contents 328
Code Listing 137, Chapter 22 Test Drive Commands for Dot Member Functions 329
Code Listing 138, cPolyFun Array-Reference Operator Implementation 333

Code Listing 139, Functor feval Listing 335
Code Listing 140, Chapter 22 Test Drive Command Listing: functor...........................336
Code Listing 141, Protected Function Modifications to the Constructor 341
Code Listing 142, Parent Forward Inside Protected pget..342
Code Listing 143, Parent Forward Inside Protected pget..344
Code Listing 144, Redefined Behavior for sqrt 349

Tables

Table 4.1 Overloadable Operators 46

Table 4.2 Array-Reference and Cell-Reference Index Conversion Examples.............62

Table 15.1 Member Functions Used to Draw a Scalar cShape Object 205

Table 18.1 cLineStyle Private Variable Dialog Fields..252

Table 18.2 cLineStyle Public Member Variable Field Values.......................................255

Table 18.3 cLineStyle Data Dictionary Field Values 258

Table 18.4 cShape Private Variable Dialog Fields 262

Table 18.5 cShape Concealed Variable Dialog Fields..263

Table 18.6 Public Member Variable Field Values..264

Table 18.7 Public Member Function Field Values...266

Table 18.8 cShape Data Dictionary Values 267

Table 18.9 cStar Private Variable Data..269

Table 18.10 cStar Public Variable Data 269

Table 18.11 cStar Public Member Function Data 270

Table 18.12 cStar Data Dictionary Values..270

Table 18.13 Executed Member Functions Are Highlighted 273

Table 19.1 cShapeArray Class Wizard Main Dialog Fields 281

Table 19.2 cShapeArray Private Variable Dialog Fields 281

Table 19.3 cShapeArray Public Function Field Values 282

Table 19.4 cShapeArray Data Dictionary Field Values...284

About the Author

Andy Register has been an admitted object-oriented fanatic since his first introduction to the concepts of object-oriented design in the late 1980s. At that time, he was working on his doctoral degree in electrical engineering at the Georgia Institute of Technology, Atlanta. His research involved the real-time control of nonminimum phase systems, human and hardware-in-the-loop simulations, state-of-the-art computer architectures, and low-level programming of multiple-instruction multiple-data (MIMD) parallel computers. Object-oriented programming was still in its infancy with a number of object-oriented contenders: Actor, C++, CLOS, Eiffel, Flavors, and Smalltalk, among others. Dr. Register needed a language that supported a close association between software and hardware, and he found the right combination of performance, utility, and elegance in C++. After using C++ for several years, he published his first two papers on object-oriented programming in 1994.

Fast-forward to the twenty-first century, and we find Dr. Register working at the Georgia Tech Research Institute in Atlanta on complex radar-tracking simulations. These simulations do not require a close association with hardware so that real-world interface requirements dictate much of the software design. In this environment, an object-oriented approach to MATLAB yields big advantages. Dr. Register brought his years of experience developing object-oriented C++ software to bear on MATLAB and developed a set of techniques and tools that allows a standard object-oriented design to peacefully coexist with MATLAB. In his day-to-day work, these techniques allow for interchangeable modules and the capability to add new features to a simulation. In this book, these techniques are described and Dr. Register's Class Wizard tool is explained and demonstrated.

Preface

I am an admitted object-oriented fanatic. I have been designing and implementing object-oriented software for more than twenty years. When I started designing and implementing object-oriented MATLAB®, I encountered many detractors. They would say things like "The object model isn't complete," "You can't have public variables," "The development environment doesn't work well with objects," "Objects and vector operations don't mix," "Object-oriented code is too hard to debug," and "MATLAB objects are too slow." None of these statements matched my experience with MATLAB objects. It quickly became obvious that MATLAB objects don't have a capability problem; rather, they have a public relations problem. Part of the public relations problem stems from the fact that the sheer genius behind the design and implementation of MATLAB's object-oriented extensions is masked by the abbreviated discussion in the user's guide. If you want to use MATLAB to develop object-oriented software, ignore the critics, study the examples in this book, and reap the benefits.

Mark Levedahl exposed me to the possibility of developing object-oriented MATLAB software in 2001. Both of us had written a lot of C++ code, and we spoke the same object-oriented dialect. MATLAB objects are seductive because they seem so easy. Without help, trying to get everything right is anything but easy. My first object-oriented implementation was terrible. Construction was dicey. Interfaces were terrible. Modules were slow. The code was very hard to maintain. Maybe the critics were right. I was still learning. The lessons improved the next implementation, but there still seemed to be a fundamental difference between, for example, object-oriented programming in C++ and object-oriented programming in MATLAB.

MATLAB object-oriented code always bumped up against the same limitation. The elements spelled out in the object-oriented design didn't map easily to an m-file implementation. Part of the reason for the poor match comes from the fact that each design element must be spread into more than one m-file: one module to get a value, another module to set it, and yet another to display it. In an evolving design, files can easily get out of synch. Couple this with the fact that a developer is free to define the mapping, and the result can be chaos. Faced with many competing alternatives, it is fair to ask, "Is one alternative better than the others?" After a lot of consideration and study, I believe the answer is yes. Following the best alternative improved the object-oriented implementations by orders of magnitude. Armed with the best mapping, a software tool to keep the modules and design in synch is a matter of design and implementation. Version 3 of the MATLAB Class Wizard will do this. The Class Wizard tool is included on this book's companion CD.

The first version of Class Wizard was not easy to use. George Brown, Kyle Harrigan, and Mike Baden used it with some success. Their comments helped shape the graphical user interface in the current version. At the same time, I was using my Class Wizard tool to create object-oriented code for a large MATLAB project. That project, the Target Tracking Benchmark, was primarily sponsored by the Missile Defense Agency and involved a cadre of accomplished MATLAB programmers from government, academia, and industry. Good techniques were allowed to blossom, and the bad were very quickly rooted out. Reactions to MATLAB objects were mixed. The ensuing debates improved everyone's understanding of the risks and benefits. Over time, the debate participants included Mark Levedahl, Steve Waugh, Laura Ritter, Dale Blair, Phil West, George Brown, Paul Miceli, Terry Ogle, Paul Burns, Chris Burton, Lisa Ehrman, Dan Leatherwood, Darin Dunham, Steve Kay, Al de Baroncelli, Ron Rothrock, Bob Isbell, Bruce Douglas, Greg Watson, Ben Slocumb,

Mike Klusman, Jim Van Zandt, and Joe Petruzzo. These gifted individuals improved my understanding of MATLAB objects and helped shape the second and current versions of Class Wizard.

The second version of Class Wizard was easier to use, and about three years ago I set out to write a user's guide for it. I quickly discovered that telling someone how to use a tool is a lot different from telling someone why. Many MATLAB programmers seem genuinely interested in learning why. For example, my half-day seminar on object-oriented MATLAB at the 2003 IEEE Southeastern Symposium on System Theory was the best-attended session by a wide margin. After that seminar, I started adding more detail to the Class Wizard user's guide. I also improved Class Wizard by adding a guide-based graphical interface and support for object arrays and multiple inheritance. Shortly after that, Mel Belcher and Dale Blair encouraged me to turn the user's guide into a book. I am very grateful for their insight and moral support. I would never have undertaken this project without their initial prodding and enthusiasm.

MATLAB is a registered trademark of The MathWorks, Inc. For product information, please contact:

The MathWorks, Inc.
3 Apple Hill Drive
Natick, MA 01760-2098 USA
Tel: 508-647-7000
Fax: 508-647-7001
E-mail: info@mathworks.com
Web: www.mathworks.com

1 Introduction

The organization of this book breaks MATLAB object-oriented programming into three sections. The first section covers the required elements and focuses on developing a set of functions that give MATLAB objects first-class status within the environment. In the first section, we will develop a group of eight indispensable functions. These functions provide object initialization, a simple intuitive interface, interaction with the environment's features, and array capability. Even more important, the group of eight is responsible for an object-oriented concept called encapsulation. Encapsulation is fundamental to using object-oriented programming as a better, safer alternative to structures. The default functions in MATLAB seem to be at odds with the information-hiding principle of encapsulation; but the group of eight brings MATLAB back under control. By the end of the first section, you will have an excellent working knowledge of MATLAB's object-oriented capability and be able to use object-oriented programming techniques to improve software development.

The second section builds on the first by developing strategies and implementations that allow the construction of hierarchies without compromises. Such hierarchies are important for achieving true object-oriented programming. The concept of building the next layer of functionality on a firm foundation of mature code is very compelling and often elusive. Encapsulation certainly helps, but another object-oriented concept called inheritance makes it much easier to build and traverse an organizational hierarchy. With inheritance, each successive layer simply builds up additional capability without changing code in the foundation. As the code matures, bug fixes simply make the foundation stronger. At first blush, the desire for both first-class status and an inheritance hierarchy appears incompatible. The section on building a hierarchy delivers a harmonious framework.

The third section discusses advanced strategies and introduces some useful utilities. Advanced strategies include, among others, type-based function selection, also known as polymorphism; passing arguments by reference instead of by value; replacing **feval's** function handle with an object; and a utility for rapid object-oriented code development. Do not expect to use all the advanced strategies in every software development. Instead, reserve the advanced techniques for difficult situations. Discussing these concepts is important because it opens the door to what are essentially limitless implementation options. It is also nice to know about advanced strategies when the uncommon need arises.

This book makes two assumptions about you, the reader. The first assumption is that you consider yourself an intermediate or better MATLAB programmer. At every opportunity, example code uses vector syntax. The example code also uses a few important but relatively obscure MATLAB functions. Example code also uses language features that some might consider to be advanced topics, for example, function handles and try-catch error handling. Even though code examples are described line by line, entry-level MATLAB programmers might find the example code somewhat vexing.

The second assumes only a cursory knowledge of object-oriented programming. I dedicate a significant amount of the discussion to the introduction of fundamental object-oriented programming concepts. MATLAB programmers new to object-oriented programming will be able to follow these discussions and thus gain the ability to implement object-oriented designs. Even so, there is also plenty of substance to keep seasoned object-oriented programmers on their toes. Going back to the basics will often reveal important design considerations or expose hidden object-oriented capability. It is my sincere hope that everyone reading this book will mutter the phrase "I didn't know you could do that" at least once.

Most of this book concentrates on MATLAB coding techniques; however, the introductory chapter gives me an opportunity to touch on a few topics critical to general software development that are somewhat peripheral to the mechanics of writing code. It also gives me a place to discuss some of the ideas that support object-oriented programming. I trust you are anxious to dive into the world of MATLAB object-oriented programming, so this introduction will be brief.

Some of you might decide to skip this chapter and dive right into the MATLAB implementation. You will be skipping background information on general object-oriented programming: topics like encapsulation, inheritance, and polymorphism. Nothing in this chapter is critical to the examples; however, if you decide to skip this chapter, you might want to come back and read §1.3 before diving into the second section on inheritance. I will remind you to come back when the time comes.

1.1 EXAMPLES

One of the easiest ways to learn is by example. I have tried to include examples of working source code for every new concept or iterative improvement. Each chapter is complete in that the example source code will run and produce results. Subsequent chapters will often add to or improve modules from earlier chapters, but by the end of the chapter everything should execute. You can work along by either typing in the example code or copying the source from the CD. Every chapter has its own directory. All of the examples are included on the CD that accompanies this book.

Interact with the examples. Type in the example source code or copy it from the CD and experiment. The descriptions that accompany the listings will guide you along by supplying command-line instructions. As an alternative to constantly setting MATLAB's path, it is more convenient to experiment with the examples from each chapter's directory. I will include a listing with the explicit **cd** command or the result **pwd** (print working directory) when it is important to move to a particular directory. That way, you will know where to navigate before typing the commands. The recommended location for the example files is **c:/oop_guide**.* Of course, the **cd** directory or **pwd** display will be different if you copy the example files to a different location.

To save a little space, displayed results use compact spacing. MATLAB displays results using a compact format when the **'FormatSpacing'** environment variable is set to **'compact'**. The following command can be used to set the environment variable.

```
>> set(0, 'FormatSpacing', 'compact')
```

Set **'FormatSpacing'** to **'loose'** to get back to the default display spacing.

1.2 OBJECT-ORIENTED SOFTWARE DEVELOPMENT

In lieu of a long discussion, I will instead refer you to authors, books, or websites that I have found to be particularly helpful. The referrals are of course not exhaustive because there are too many effective ways to attack software development. The cited references are simply some of the tools I have found to be effective for me. With time and experience, you will accumulate a set of tools that are effective for you. If you do not already have a favorite resource in some particular area, the citations are a good place to begin. I am confident that this book will find a place in your favored set of tools.

---

* The direction of the directory slash will depend on your operating system. In Windows you can navigate directories using either / or \, but **pwd** uses \ in its output. In Unix and Linux, only / may be used. In code, the variable **filesep** always returns the directory slash appropriate for the operating system; see **help filesep**.

1.2.1 At the Top of Your Game

As you are no doubt aware, software development is not just about implementation. Development involves an extensive set of activities that span a wide range of topics, and for any large project, the human element is vitally important. To attack increasingly difficult problems you will need to sharpen your own development ability. Successful software development also draws upon the collective abilities of individuals, teams, and organizations. As problems grow in size you need to be able to focus the development team and help improve the capability of your entire organization. Such continuous professional development at all levels is personally rewarding and directly leads to bigger, better, and faster software. It also leads to more responsibility and improved salaries.

First, recognize that the development of bulletproof software is an exceptionally difficult undertaking. You need to be at the top of your game, and you need to focus and organize your development team. There are a number of proven techniques that can improve both your personal effectiveness and that of your team. These techniques are not limited to coding but span the entire project scope from design through delivery.

Second, recognize that both MATLAB programming and object-oriented programming represent two areas that by themselves rely on a high level of hard-won expertise. Merging the two represents yet another challenge. The MathWorks software engineers did a very commendable job in adding object-oriented capability to MATLAB. Their object model seamlessly meets all of the basic requirements of object-oriented programming; however, this does come with a price. You must write efficient code or run-time performance will suffer. Gaining efficiency requires advanced MATLAB techniques. There are new functions to learn, and familiar functions will be used in entirely new ways. Even fundamental subjects like the function search path get new rules when objects are involved.

The various quirks of MATLAB's object-oriented model can tax the ability of even the most capable designers. MATLAB contains encapsulation and inheritance capability equal to any modern object-oriented language. Sometimes, however, it is difficult to use all of that capability. To clear that hurdle, simply expand and reuse the coding patterns presented in the various examples. The biggest difference between MATLAB and more typical object-oriented languages stems from one of the fundamental properties of MATLAB, untyped variables. The lack of strong variable typing represents a handicap. The rules that govern search-path searching help in some regard. Even so, minor concessions are usually required when implementing a complex object-oriented design in MATLAB. With very weak typing, MATLAB's use of polymorphism is similarly weak. You as the programmer are responsible for choosing correct functionality based on the data. MATLAB's polymorphism usually leads you to a function in the correct class, but the rest is up to you.

1.2.2 Personal Development

Evolving your personal skills is important, but how do you do this effectively? To paraphrase Watts Humphrey of the Software Engineering Institute,

> If you want to get to where you're going, you need a map;
>
> if you don't know where you are, a map won't help.

Following from this statement the general procedure for continuous improvement is not difficult to describe:

- Gauge your level of expertise; find that big, red "You are here" arrow.
- Identify the skills you want to acquire, that is, identify the destination.
- Plot a path from where you are now to where you want to be.
- Periodically check that you are indeed moving toward the destination.

This sounds simple enough, but as always, the devil is in the details.

One good resource where you can learn to sort out the details is a book by Watts Humphrey titled *Introduction to the Personal Software Process*sm.* The Personal Software Process (PSP) sets up an organized approach that allows you to gauge your existing skill set and control the introduction of new skills. By following the PSP's prescriptions, you can improve all phases of your personal development from planning through delivery. The PSP is particularly effective in helping to eliminate the introduction of errors in the critical design and coding stages. Errors eliminated early in the process cannot then affect later stages.

The PSP is a tailored, one-developer version of a software discipline used to improve team-based software engineering. A multiple-developer software discipline can be found in *The Capability Maturity Model (CMM)* by Mark Paulk et al.** The *CMM* is not unique in its objective. A large body of research on the introduction of structure and rigor to team-based software development certainly exists. Among the many resources available, the articles found at http://www.sei.cmu.edu are quite extensive and use the same language as that used in the PSP and *CMM*.

Aligned with personal improvement and software engineering rigor is the software development life cycle. Different software products benefit from using different life cycle models, and indeed, there are many different models. Each model supports a relatively unique development environment. The IEEE/EIA 12207 standard***,**** is a concession by both industry and government that no single development model works for every situation. This gives us the liberty to search for models that work well with both our intended applications and MATLAB.

MATLAB programs are successful across a variety of disciplines. The most successful use is when a small group of technical professionals attempts to solve an entirely new problem. This type of development usually contains an evolving set of interlocking constraints. The software is part of the evolution. Designing and writing one iteration increase problem awareness. The discipline involved in developing the software improves understanding and reveals new issues and constraints. Each new revelation folds back into the requirements and begins a new implementation. In the extreme, the revisions never end and it is difficult to complete one revision before discovering new requirements.

There is no definitive stopping rule. Answers to questions like "When is the software model close enough to reality?" or "When is the algorithm accurate enough?" are often difficult to know in advance because each revision uncovers the need for more detail. The software development process itself has become one method of problem discovery. Consequently, each revision extends the capability of the software. After several iterations, the code often evolves completely away from the initial design. We often refer to the result of this constant change as "spaghetti code" because of all the twisted connections among modules. It does not take too much iteration before continued development becomes painfully slow and protracted. Is this a familiar situation?

It turns out that this "typical" MATLAB project description fits the definition of a so-called wicked problem.***** The extreme-programming life cycle model****** is gaining traction as the preferred method for wicked-problem software development. The extreme-programming model is also increasing in popularity for general software development. Since the topic of this book is object-oriented programming, it should come as no surprise that object-oriented programming and the extreme-programming life cycle model are well suited for each other. In fact, certain protections

---

* Addison-Wesley Professional, 1999.

** Mark C. Paulk, Charles V. Weber, Bill Curtis, and Mary Beth Chrissis, principal eds., *The Capability Maturity Model*, Addison-Wesley Professional, 1995.

*** http://standards.ieee.org/reading/ieee/std_public/description/se/12207.0-1996_desc.html.

**** http://www.stsc.hill.af.mil/crosstalk/about.html.

***** P. DeGrace and L. Stahl, *Wicked Problems, Righteous Solutions: A Catalogue of Modern Software Engineering Paradigms,* Yourdon Click, 1990.

****** http://www.extremeprogramming.org.

afforded by object-oriented programming actually enable the extreme-programming life cycle model. There is more to say about wicked problems and extreme programming.

1.2.3 WICKED PROBLEMS

We can classify all problems into one of two categories: tame and wicked. Tame problems can be subdued using traditional linear thinking and thus lend themselves to traditional linear development method (e.g., a waterfall model). Wicked problems by contrast are not so easily domesticated. When dealing with wicked problems you need a different approach, and learning to identify them is a good place to begin.

If developers cannot agree on a shared description of the problem, it is probably wicked. Such consensus is difficult because the definition of the problem changes every time a new solution is considered. Individuals on the development team will be at different stages in problem discovery and thus have different opinions about the problem description. Lack of a shared vision often leads to constantly changing requirements, another bane of software development. When developers finally solve the problem, the solution leads to a shared description.

There are many other clues. Some of the most distinctive characteristics often associated with wicked problems are as follows*:

- You cannot understand the problems until you develop solutions, and unfortunately, every solution is expensive and has lasting unintended consequences.
- You find an evolving set of interlocking issues and constraints.
- Proposed solutions are not necessarily right or wrong but rather better or worse.
- There seems to be no definitive stopping rule aside from exhausting the available resources.
- The problem and the proposed solutions are novel or unique.
- The problem does not seem to provide an ultimate test whether the solution is correct or complete.

Anyone with experience in software development can certainly recall a project or two with some of these characteristics. Many of these projects get into trouble not because the wicked problem exists, but rather due to a failure to identify the problem as wicked and approach the solution with the appropriate tools and techniques. Software development has a dismal record where one third of software projects are canceled, and of those that remain half fail to meet the original budget.** The skill and dedication of developers are not at fault in this record. More likely, the whole methodology of approaching the solution of wicked problems is broken.

For example, the knee-jerk approach in dealing with a failing project is to apply more management scrutiny and impose processes that are more stringent. The hope is that a more detailed definition of the requirements, deeper analysis of the problem, in-depth planning, or more progress tracking will get the project back on track. With a so-called tame problem, this approach might actually work. With a wicked problem, this linear approach will almost certainly fail. Wicked problems are very resistant to up-front detailed analysis. The usual approach is failing so we must consider a new set of tools.

The most important part of the new strategy is to accept that wicked problems do indeed exist. After accepting their existence, we need a method of identification. A development team at odds with each other, at odds with management, or at odds with the customer over exactly what the software is supposed to do is a strong indication. A project that continues to spiral downward after

---

* Horst Rittel and Melvin Webber, "Dilemmas in a General Theory of Planning," Reprint no. 86, the Institute of Urban and Regional Development, University of California, Berkeley.
** Mary Poppendieck and Tom Poppendieck, *Lean Software Development: An Agile Toolkit for Software Development Managers*, Addison-Wesley, 2003.

adding more resources or swapping out key personnel is also waving a wicked flag. There are other more subtle indications, and a web search on the keywords "wicked problems" will result in a host of resources for both identifying wicked problems and dealing with them.

Accepting the fact that we must begin the solution before we have all the data is important in dealing with wicked problems. Accepting this allows development to focus on revealing more problem detail rather than trying to solve the complete, poorly defined problem. Additional detail refines the problem statement, which folds back into the next solution. Developers are not upset about modifying or scrapping code because neither the goal nor the schedule called for a solution on the first cycle. After several adaptive cycles, developers understand the problem and the software represents a good solution. The solution process for wicked problems concedes that bouncing among design, implementation, and test is the best way to solve poorly understood problems.

This type of iterative development usually runs counter to the current, generally accepted software development practices; however, the future of software development is iterative. This does not mean that software development will revert to the early days of no process maturity or an ill-defined process framework. Developing software in such a stop-and-go manner can result in an unwieldy design unless the iterative development follows a suitable development model. The current set of development processes go hand in hand with a procedural approach. The extendible power of object-oriented programming enables new development models capable of solving wicked problems.

Decades ago there were dire predictions made about the adoption of object-oriented programming. As we now know, most of these damning predictions turned out to be false. Now, the same voices are shouting warnings about iterative development. History appears to be repeating itself. In spite of such dire predictions, companies are obtaining good results using the combined power of object-oriented programming and iterative development.

1.2.4 EXTREME PROGRAMMING

The extreme-programming development model* is one of several models that embody precisely the kind of iterative development necessary to solve wicked problems. In brief, the extreme-programming model emphasizes the following:

- The use of test suites to define project milestones (fanatical testing)
- Frequent releases with small, stable additions to functionality
- A simple design that is iteratively refined
- Continuous code improvement (to make code faster and easier to maintain)
- Pair programming
- Collective code ownership
- Documented standards

The items in this list and object-oriented programming go hand in hand. Frequent releases and continuous code evolution require the use of a language that supports reliable, extendible, reusable code. Object-oriented languages support these goals, and in §1.3.4 we will see how. Items in the list also encourage more of a team-based approach compared to traditional methods. Collective ownership, pair programming, and documented standards make peer review and code walk through integral parts of code development rather than after-the-fact quality assurance steps. Individual effort is still valuable for innovation. The difference here is in bringing the result of individual innovation into the team-based environment.

Perhaps the only valid criticism of iterative methods like extreme programming involves documentation. With very little predevelopment emphasis on requirements and design, developers

---

* http://www.extremeprogramming.org.

write documentation concurrently as the code is developed or after the code is complete. Neither is ideal. The evolutionary nature of iterative development makes it extremely difficult to document revisions synchronized with code revisions. The community of developers must take collective ownership of the documentation, but supporting tools are not well established. Pushing the development of documentation to the end of the project yields the same poor results regardless of the life cycle model. The descriptions are often lacking in important detail because developers forget many of the nuances. The truth is that software documentation is a tough problem. Even with traditional methods, documentation is often out of date or incomplete. Iterative methods make some problems of documentation different, but the situation overall is neither better nor worse.

You have to relate the importance of documentation to your development team because good documentation relates to productivity. Effort spent analyzing undocumented code is effort that could have gone toward solving the real problem. Multiply this over several developers and many classes, and the consequences become clear. The iterative development community has adopted a posture that says documentation is not required, a posture that might actually have some merit. Instead of separate documentation, the code itself should be self-documenting. Any description other than code is simply a translation, and all translations are subject to error. Under some strict conditions the idea of self-documenting code might actually work. Generally, these conditions are not exclusive to extreme programming but are conditions of good software development in any environment.

Clearly written code is the first condition. Use variable names that represent the data in them and function names that represent the operation. All developers need to be on the same page with respect to the conventions. Community code ownership demands uniformity. Unfortunately, every problem domain seems to use a different vocabulary, making one universal convention impossible to establish. The convention must be somewhat flexible to change just like the code itself. Clearly written code also limits the number of operations carried out on each line. Sometimes run-time performance issues are at odds with such limiting. The 80–20 rule of thumb says that only 20 percent of the code consumes 80 percent of the run time. Surprisingly accurate, this rule allows you to be judicious in trading run time for code complexity. Where code syntax becomes unusually difficult, add a comment to aid in future maintenance. Code idioms and a modular implementation also improve clarity and quality. Document standard conventions and idioms in a coding standard, but allow the standard to evolve.

Taking advantage of MATLAB's help utility is the second condition. Use a **Contents.m** file to display a table-of-contents description of all the functions in a directory. Use a standard, compatible format for header comments. Format all the lines in a header as comments, and MATLAB displays the comments in response to **help** *function name*. These header comments should summarize the function's intent and cite important assumptions for input–output arguments. In an extreme-programming environment, the header should also include a list of test functions. The first comment line is particularly important because it plays a significant role. Known as the H1 line, MATLAB displays the first header line in response to a **lookfor** command.

Up-to-date requirements and at least a high-level design hierarchy form the minimum level of documentation for the third condition. Documented requirements are necessary because these represent the best view of the problem. Use the requirements to scope the problem and drive development in a particular direction. As the development progresses, requirements can and often do change. A formal update of the requirements keeps everyone's expectations on track. A high-level design hierarchy imposes a shared vision.

Align the design with the requirements and allow it to drive iteration goals. Like the requirements, the design hierarchy evolves with the development. In an ideal situation, the hierarchy simply expands its level of detail. Indeed this should be the goal for the design of the public interface. Sometimes entire branches of the hierarchy need reorganization. Allow this reorganization to set the stage for the next cycle of code refactoring. Documented requirements, an up-to-date high-level design, and a standard for self-documenting code are significant improvements over the typical status quo.

Finally, code specifically designed and developed for reuse needs a higher level of documentation. Presumably, the public interface is mature and the behavior is predictable. In short, the code has ceased to evolve so there is little danger of documentation becoming obsolete. Under this scenario, good documentation can improve productivity because even self-documenting code is harder to understand compared to a carefully written, peer-reviewed, cataloged document. With a documented reuse library, we are plainly trying to discourage a developer from redeveloping the same solution.

1.2.5 MATLAB, OBJECT-ORIENTED PROGRAMMING, AND YOU

Effectively dealing with MATLAB object-oriented programming means first effectively dealing with MATLAB. The included code examples and idioms rely on an advanced understanding of the MATLAB path, passing data using variable argument lists, and improving run time with vector syntax. Object-oriented techniques also require an expert's knowledge of both standard and obscure MATLAB functions. Object-oriented programming in MATLAB is an advanced topic, and the examples and idioms assume a certain level of MATLAB-language expertise. My goal is to increase your understanding of MATLAB in general, but this book is not a general language reference. The various manuals that come with MATLAB are one of the best general references. Although cryptic at times, they provide a very concise, complete description of almost every language feature. The help facility makes most of the manual information available from the desktop. Online resources at http://www.matlab.com supplement the manuals with up-to-the-minute documentation and user examples. The discussion groups and contributed utilities on the site are particularly valuable.

Programmers include a continuum of MATLAB expertise, but with respect to object-oriented programming, there are two divisions: *client* and *developer*. Client programmers use objects in their own software but do not develop "low-level" object code. Clients are vital to the development in other ways. Clients are important because they often represent the group of domain experts. Their expertise is not in object-oriented programming but rather is steeped in the real problem. As such, clients are an important resource for defining interfaces and functionality. If it were not for clients, developers would be out of a job. Clients, however, are not the target audience of this book.

Developers, on the other hand, are responsible for developing low-level object code. The remaining chapters develop examples, define idioms, and introduce a software tool specifically designed to ease the burden of object-oriented development in MATLAB. As your experience with object-oriented programming increases, you will be called on to both build the object-oriented foundation and use the foundation elements to build applications. The first role represents developer; and the second, client. Clients and developers use different mind-sets. and part of your job as a developer is being able to apply the client mind-set when playing that role.

Playing the role of developer requires a greater attention to detail because you will design both the outward appearance and the inner workings of each object. The outward appearance is important because this is the only part of the object seen by a client. Here, careful thought and attention to detail make the object easy to use. Indeed, this book describes a set of techniques that can be used to give objects an interface identical to that of a structure. A structure-like interface eases a client's use of objects but the structure-like interface is only half the equation. The other half involves the inner workings or private implementation. While the object interface might appear structure-like, your code is actually taking over and producing a result. You have to be diligent in anticipating every condition or the implementation will fail, usually at the worst possible time. Isn't that how Murphy's Law always works? MATLAB's model for object-oriented programming gives you powerful tools to thwart misuse by clients; but as a developer, you must learn how and when to use each tool. Some of these tools are pervasive across all object-oriented languages, while some are unique to MATLAB.

The remaining chapters and examples put you on the right track of becoming a MATLAB object-oriented developer. Same as with the MATLAB language itself, the examples presume a certain level of expertise in general programming and in object-oriented design. Unlike the treatment of the MATLAB language, objects in the examples remain relatively simple because the implementation methods for simple and complicated objects are essentially the same. There is no reason to cloud the discussion of implementation issues by trying to attack a difficult problem. Of course, this does put limits on how far we will delve into the problem of object-oriented design. As you try to attack increasingly difficult problems, you will undoubtedly need additional object-oriented design resources. A seminal book focusing on object-oriented design is Grady Booch's *Object-Oriented Analysis and Design with Applications**. Booch is one of the early pioneers and has a very intuitive approach to object-oriented design. Two other object-oriented pioneers are James Rumbaugh and Edward Yourdon.

These three object-oriented giants have put aside their differences to develop a graphical design format called the Unified Modeling Language (UML). UML is the standard development and documentation tool for object-oriented programs. The modeling environment provides a very rich and detailed approach, and the basics are easy to learn. The book by Booch et al. titled *The Unified Modeling Language User Guide*** is one of many UML references.

1.3 ATTRIBUTES, BEHAVIOR, OBJECTS, AND CLASSES

Before we try to answer the fundamental question "Why objects?" let's first discuss the difference between an object and a class. The two terms are closely related but are not interchangeable, even though that is how they are often used. In short, a class is a model that exists as lines of code, and an object is an instance of the model that exists in memory during program execution. A class is a user-defined type and an object is a variable of that type.

For tangible objects, we generally accept that they will have both attributes and behaviors. In addition, we usually know how to link attributes and behaviors depending on the object's type. For example, a hungry baby cries and an alarm clock rings. For tangible objects, an object-modeling approach is easy to rationalize because that is how we naturally organize them. In concept, software objects are not much different from tangible objects. Software objects represent tangible elements of the problem domain. Just like worldly objects, software objects have both attributes (data) and behaviors (functions). In a good design, these attributes and behaviors associate naturally and are inseparable from one another. Perform some thought exercises centered on this idea.

What image enters your mind at the mention of the word "shape"? Is it two-dimensional or three? What is its color? Are the sides straight or curved? If you describe your image, do you think I would agree that it is indeed a shape? It can be square, circular, or star shaped; red, blue, or rainbow colored; stationary, rotating, or zipping about; and it would still be a shape. From experience, we are able to abstract the idea of shape into a general collection of attributes and behaviors. In object-oriented terms, the abstraction is a *class* and any particular shape is an *object* of that class. This particular abstraction is easy because we practice it without even realizing. With practice and experience, abstraction into an object-oriented software design is almost as easy.

1.3.1 FROM MATLAB HEAVYWEIGHT TO OBJECT-ORIENTED THINKER

Until fairly recently universities taught most engineers, scientists, mathematicians, and technical professionals to decompose a problem into a series of actions. Converting these actions into a loosely organized set of functions yields a so-called procedural-based design. The procedural-based approach spawned a variety of other software-engineering techniques. Software development life

---

* Grady Booch, *Object-Oriented Analysis and Design with Applications*, Benjamin Cummings, 1991. The 3rd edition was released in 2004.

** Grady Booch, James Rumbaugh, and Ivar Jacobson, *The Unified Modeling Language User Guide*, Addison-Wesley Professional, 1998.

cycles are the most notable. In too many cases, the customer's project-planning tools assumed a so-called waterfall life cycle model. Project planning is much easier with a waterfall model.

Unfortunately, the procedural approach and the waterfall life cycle are showing their age. The amount of module-to-module coupling hinders the ability to maintain or extend many large programs. Adding a new feature or fixing an old one takes longer than expected and, far too often, introduces side effects unrelated to the new feature. The use of object-oriented methods can drastically reduce the amount of module-to-module coupling. Many in the software-engineering community believe that shifting to an object-oriented approach is the only way to achieve significant increases in program size and complexity.

The ready availability of commercial MATLAB toolboxes has allowed large increases in complexity even with the use of traditional, procedural methods. Invariably with time, software requirements will grow to the point where even the use of toolboxes will not be enough to offset the limitations of the procedural approach. No one can predict when the typical program size will outstrip the capacity of the current approach; however, some MATLAB projects have already crossed the threshold. Many MATLAB programmers recognize the early-warning signs. If we follow the lead of our software-engineering brethren, embracing object-oriented techniques appears to be the solution. Helping defend this position is the fact that MATLAB includes a very robust object model.

Where would the study of mathematics be without whole, real, and complex numbers? Biology would be equally difficult without taxonomy divisions among plants, animals, fungi, virus, protozoa, and bacteria. In these disciplines, properties rather than behavior drive the decompositions. Object-oriented programming is no different. User-defined types are the central focus of the software architecture. Just like other taxonomies, the types contain both properties and behavior but the decomposition emphasizes the properties. For someone steeped in procedural decomposition, the object-oriented approach appears backward. Instead of focusing on behavior (functions), object-oriented programming focuses on attributes (data). Along with this change in focus come big differences in life cycles, coding development, testing, and integration.

To many, object-oriented development represents a radically different way of thinking. Introducing changes of this scale into an organization can be difficult and protracted. By one estimate, the transition takes an average programmer about one year.* This book should help speed the transition by defining specific coding practices and by exposing potential problem areas. The Class Wizard tool also allows programmers to focus on design rather than implementation (see Chapter 18), further speeding the transition. Other techniques may also hasten the transition. For example, pair programming is a type of co-mentoring activity that should be helpful in shortening the transition time. There are also many more books, seminars, and short courses available today compared to 1994 when the estimate was made.

1.3.2 OBJECT-ORIENTED DESIGN

Think about shapes again. If asked to design a software representation of a shape, how would you begin? You might have a good idea about shapes but you still need to find out if your ideas match the needs of your clients. You can use client requirements, user stories, and domain experts to help pin down the set of attributes and behaviors required of your software shape. At first these attributes and behaviors might seem disconnected; however, with more analysis, patterns and dependencies usually emerge. First, arrange shapes with similar attributes in a loose taxonomy. Then use behavior differences to infer additional attributes. For example, it might be perfectly reasonable to combine a division between moving and stationary shapes by defining a speed attribute. This gives all shapes the same behavior; however, shapes with zero speed do not appear to move. It might also be perfectly reasonable to keep moving shapes separate from stationary ones. In that case, a moving

---

* B. Stroustrup, *The Design and Evolution of C++*, Addison-Wesley, 1994.

shape is still a shape but it has at least one additional attribute and behavior. The choice affects the software design and code, but the client's experience with the final design is the same. When the taxonomy stops changing, we establish the software architecture. Each leaf in the taxonomy represents a set of attributes that can be implemented as a class. Connections among leaves allow classes higher in the taxonomy to serve as the foundation for lower classes. Lower classes do not redeclare higher-level attributes because they can inherit the higher-level attributes by simply declaring a connection in the taxonomy. The same organization works for behaviors.

The process is similar in many respects to procedural design except that the final organization focuses on data rather than function. In theory, the process sounds reasonable, but in reality, some software problems are maddeningly difficult to organize. Sometimes developers do not have enough experience in the problem area to foster good organization. At other times, the special terms and notation used by the experts simply overwhelm the designer. Object-oriented designers have experienced these difficulties and have developed many techniques useful in difficult design environments. Unfortunately, a full treatment of object-oriented design is outside the scope of this book. If you are new to object-oriented programming, you will gain valuable experience by implementing and evolving someone else's design. When you are ready to design your own object-oriented architecture, a library of books and a wealth of articles and websites are available that fully develop object-oriented design. The authors and references already cited represent good starting points.

1.3.3 WHY USE OBJECTS?

Previously, I made the statement that the creation of objects seems to mirror the way we naturally view the world. A brief discussion about shapes was used to demonstrate the idea. If true, the idea that software development can reflect our typical worldview is nice but it certainly would not compel programmers to abandon their current practice. This is particularly true in light of the amount of effort involved in making a change. No, the argument has to be a lot more compelling.

The area of software development most influenced by object-oriented programming is software quality. Demonstrated quality improvements can make converts of even the most grizzled procedural programmers. Quality has many facets, but bug-free software that works correctly the first time it is used is a typical goal. It is hard to disagree that bug-free software somehow equates to high-quality software; however, if bug-free code takes too long to develop or runs too slowly, what then of quality?

In reality software quality is an elusive topic with a lot of "I'll know it when I see it" judgments. Running correctly without crashing is certainly one aspect of quality, but other areas are important too. Assuming the requirements correctly identify what is needed, software engineers generally agree that overall quality is influenced by the following:

- Reliability
- Reusability
- Extendibility

Specific features in object-oriented programming relate to every one of these factors. Another possible factor is productivity. Perhaps it would be better to emphasize productivity rather than quality. After all, we know that bug-free software is impossible to produce. Even if we could get all the bugs out, delivery times would be very long and the production cost would be astronomical. Besides, customers have learned to expect bugs, particularly in the first few versions.

I hope you were *not* nodding in agreement with the last few sentences. These often accepted assumptions are *wrong, wrong, wrong*. The fact that your competitors believe them gives you an enormous competitive advantage. Proven techniques can both reduce the number of coding errors and hasten the discovery of bugs that do manage to slip in. The introduction of fewer errors along with quicker discovery increases productivity by reducing the amount of unproductive time spent reworking broken code. With a lower error rate, testing reveals fewer bugs, thus allowing the entire development to run at a faster pace. In the manufacturing sector, Lean-Six-Sigma* techniques dramatically improve both quality *and* productivity. Proven false in the manufacturing sector is the notion that high quality equals low productivity. In fact, attaining both exceptional quality and high productivity can be the rule rather than the exception. There is nothing to prevent the introduction of Lean-Six-Sigma ideas into the software development process.

Customers can also be retrained. Once you start delivering high-quality products, the market-place will demand the same quality from all producers. The rise of the Japanese auto industry provides a clear example where a customer's appreciation for quality disrupted the marketplace. I predict that the same disruption will eventually occur in the software industry. Currently, India seems to be the likely winner, but China too is coming on strong. I urge you to consider the implications and work to drive your organization toward the delivery of world-class quality. Sooner than you imagine, customers will be demanding it.

1.3.4 A Quality Focus

Proven techniques can enhance software quality. Some techniques focus on one particular quality measure like reuse. Others cut across all measures. Object-oriented techniques belong in the latter group because they create a fundamentally different development environment. It is an environment with a proven ability to improve all areas of quality. Below we summarize the major factors contributing to quality.

1.3.4.1 Reliability

The most visible aspect of software quality is reliability. If the software crashes or produces the wrong result, customers consider the product unreliable. Even when most features work reliably, it follows from Murphy's Law that the one unreliable feature will be the most important to the customer. Contrary to opinion, highly reliable software is not impossible or prohibitively expensive to develop. Consider the selected observations about the state of general software development published in 2001**:

- Half the modules are defect free.
- Disciplined personal practices can reduce the initial defect rates by up to 75 percent.
- Avoidable rework constitutes 40 to 50 percent of the total effort on most software projects.
- It costs 50 percent more per line of code to develop high-dependability software.... However, the initial investment reduces overall cost if the project involves significant operations and maintenance costs.

The fact that on average half the modules are defect free provides strong evidence that it is possible to write defect-free software. Anything that can increase the defect-free percentage will have an enormous impact, and the second observation promises a huge improvement. Reducing initial defect rates by 75 percent means the typical rate of five defective lines out of ten improves to about one in ten. Extending the same improvement to well-implemented modular code means that close to 90 percent of the modules will be error free the first time a developer releases the code for test. At a minimum, this implies fewer trips between test and rework, but the implications on productivity are much deeper.

Examine the effect on resources. Spending 50 percent of your time on rework means that every four hours of programming require, on the average, another four hours to find and fix defects — defects that were *avoidable*. If four hours is the average debug time, how wide is the span around

---

* Michael L. George, *Lean Six Sigma: Combining Six Sigma Quality with Lean Speed*, McGraw-Hill, 2002.
** Barry Boehm and Victor R. Basili, "Software Defect Reduction Top 10 List," *IEEE Computer*, January 2001, 135–17.

the average? From experience, we know that some bugs are unbelievably hard to find. Consequently, it is very difficult to predict how long it will take to fix a broken module. The span around the average is very wide indeed. When you stop and consider the typical environment, it becomes obvious why workdays are long and slipped schedules are considered normal.

Now consider high-reliability practices. The previous four hours of programming time increase by 50 percent to six hours. Development is longer, true; but, there are now one fourth the number of defects. If on average the time to fix an error does not change, debugging should take one fourth as long as before. Now, debugging adds only one hour instead of four. The total time to bug-free software with high-reliability practices is seven hours. Compare that to eight hours without them. Both produced the same code; however, high-reliability practices give you extra time to learn new development techniques, keep your desk tidy, or be even more productive.

What about the span? It is extremely difficult to estimate how long it will take to find and fix a bug. If you dedicate four of every eight hours to a task that is extremely difficult to predict, how good is your predicted schedule? We know from experience that the schedule is often wrong. Bringing the debug time down to one of every eight hours fosters much more confidence in the schedule. As strange as this may sound, it is easier to estimate how long it will take to develop error-free code compared to developing sloppy code and debugging it. Reducing the expected span of the estimate has an enormous impact on planning, scheduling, and product rollout.

At the beginning of this subsection, we dismissed productivity in deference to quality. It is empowering to understand that quality and productivity are not at odds with one another. It might seem counterintuitive that the quest for high reliability results in on-time delivery, less stress on the development team, and cost reduction, but this is not a new revelation. Eliyahu Goldratt* wrote about it in his series of critical-chain, project-planning books. Andrew Carnegie understood the relationship and lived by the mantra "Quality is the most important factor in business." Japanese industry also understands the relationship: "When quality is pursued, productivity will follow" (K. Fujino, vice president, NEC).**

Now you too are a member of this august group.

Of course, high-quality techniques are not limited to object-oriented programming. In the short term, as you confirm the value of object-oriented programming and transition development to it, your current MATLAB projects can achieve a significant boost in quality and productivity.

1.3.4.2 Reusability

A software module is reusable when we can grab it from one project and use it, as is, in another project. Reusability does not happen automatically. Code intended for reuse must be designed, developed, and packaged in a form that promotes reuse. Good documentation, consistent conventions, and stellar code quality are a few of many aspects used to judge reuse potential.***

Over the long haul, software reuse improves quality and hence productivity in a number of ways. Reusable components can shorten development time or allow the production of more capable software in a given amount of time. With fewer new lines of code, there are fewer defects and a lower maintenance burden. As long as the reusable components are robust and high quality, most defects can be isolated to the new code. Toward that end, every reuse adds more test conditions and improves our confidence that the component library is defect free. Run-time optimization of reusable code also benefits every module reusing it. This is particularly true if the reusable code is an optimized MEX function. (A MEX file is a compiled C, C++, or Fortran function that can be called from a MATLAB module.) Code reuse also encourages the use of common code styles

* For example, Eliyahu Goldratt and Jeff Cox, *The Goal: A Process of Ongoing Improvement*, Gower, 1986.
** Fujino quoted Carlo Ghezzi, Mehdi Sazzjeri, and Dino Mandrioli, *Fundamentals of Software Engineering*, Prentice-Hall, 1991.
*** Bertrand Meyer, *Reusable Software: The Base Object-Oriented Component Libraries*, Prentice-Hall, 1994.

and conventions. The use of common styles and conventions is highly correlated with improvements in quality.

Imagine writing code in an environment where every variable is global. Now imagine trying to reuse a module. Reuse is difficult because every line of code depends on the same set of variable names. The first step toward improving reuse defines functions with formal parameters and local variables. The formal function definition creates a user interface that controls a client's use of the function. The function interface also hides local variables, thus preventing unintentional side effects. Client code no longer depends on the syntax of the function module, and vice versa. With function definitions, we protect the integrity of our functions. With object-oriented programming and encapsulation, we can take the next step: create a user interface that controls the use of data. The encapsulation interface divides data into public and private elements. Client code can use and thus depend on public elements; however, clients cannot create a dependency on private elements. Object-oriented rules enforce the integrity of the encapsulation and thus reduce dependency. The improvement in reuse from data encapsulation is equal in importance to improvements gained from using function definitions and local variables.

The proliferation of MATLAB toolboxes demonstrates that reuse is valuable. The fact that many toolboxes aren't object-oriented indicates that reuse, like reliability, does not depend on a particular development approach. Some development methods are more reuse friendly compared to others. Indeed, designing for reuse with the traditional approach requires an exceptional level of expertise. By contrast, object-oriented development includes certain design elements that allow code to adapt to reuse more easily. Encapsulation, also known as information hiding, is the main element.

Using a commercial toolbox is one thing, but developing a similar set of general-purpose modules is a long-term endeavor. Even accounting for the assistance object-oriented techniques bring, it takes time and effort to generalize project-specific modules into a set of general-purpose reusable ones. After that, it takes experience and patience to make them reliable. Finally, it takes time for others to reuse the modules in another project. The payback can be enormous, but selling object-oriented techniques as a quick fix for reuse is dangerous. If reuse takes longer than promised, people might give up and thus lose many of the long-term benefits.

1.3.4.3 Extendibility

A software module is extendible when we can grab it from one project, modify it slightly, and use it to do something the original author never envisioned. Designing for reuse and encapsulation improves extendibility by keeping a lid on dependency. Object-oriented techniques can also improve extendibility through a concept called inheritance. Inheritance gives us a convenient way to organize and store modules so they can be easily shared and suitably redefined.

Inheritance directly supports a hierarchy. For example, the diagram shown in Figure 1.1 suggests both similarities and differences between circles and squares. An object-oriented implementation collects the similarities in modules assigned to **cShape** and differences in modules assigned to

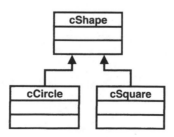

FIGURE 1.1 A simple hierarchy.

cCircle and **cSquare**. Inheritance gives circle objects access to modules defined for both **cShape** and **cCircle** classes. Similarly, square objects have access to both **cShape** and **cSquare** modules. Both circles and squares depend on modules defined for **cShape**. The opposite is not true: **cShape** does not depend on modules defined for **cCircle** or **cSquare**. The hierarchy permits one-way dependencies only.

This one-way dependency makes object-oriented code extendible along three fundamental directions: down the hierarchy (e.g., to all shapes), to individual classes (e.g., a specific shape like **cCircle**), and to the hierarchy itself. In this example, changes or additions to **cShape** automatically extend down the hierarchy to all shapes. Extending **cShape** has the effect of extending all classes inheriting from **cShape**. The one-way dependency isolates the effect of individual shape extensions. The branch of the hierarchy from the point of the extension down is affected, but inheritance prevents the change from extending back up. For example, extending **cCircle** will never change the behavior of **cSquare** objects. The same one-way isolation allows the creation of new shapes and the general reorganization of the hierarchy.

In an ideal world, we would always generalize to the best hierarchy. Unfortunately, the best hierarchy is not always initially apparent. As we develop the software solution, discovery leads to organizational changes and hierarchy extendibility becomes important. Otherwise, we are stuck with an inappropriate architecture. The one-way inheritance dependency allows new class creation with no effect on existing code. In the example, we could extend the hierarchy by creating a **cStar** class that inherits **cShape**. All existing classes and class code are unaffected by the addition.

The one-way dependency also allows us to split one class into a mini-hierarchy of two (or more) classes. As an example, Figure 1.2a shows the original hierarchy. At the outset, we knew we needed squares but did not realize we would need other shapes too. After writing some software and showing it to the customer, the need for other shapes became apparent. We could stick with the original architecture by adding an independent class for each additional shape, or we could create a hierarchy of shapes. The first step toward building a hierarchy organizes the **cSquare** class into two classes, as shown in Figure 1.2b. As long as the combined public interface doesn't change, modules developed for **cSquare** objects don't care whether the object is organized as a single class or as a parent←child hierarchy. The new combination **cShape←cSquare** behaves no different from the Figure 1.2a monolithic **cSquare** class. The reorganization had minimal impact on the operation of existing code and set the stage for the inheritance shown in Figure 1.2c. Both the hierarchy and the existing code are exhibiting a high degree of extendibility. Extendibility enabled by inheritance.

1.4 SUMMARY

Developing effective object-oriented software in any language involves a lot more than mastering the coding mechanics. Compared to structured programming, object-oriented programming

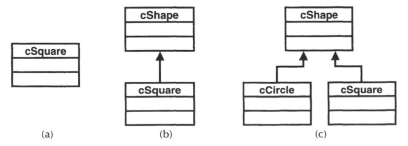

FIGURE 1.2 Demonstration of the extendibility of a hierarchy: (a) original organization; (b) parent–child relationship; and (c) general subset is reused.

introduces fundamental differences in discovering and stating requirements, in extracting and representing designs, in processes and life cycles, in unit testing and quality assurance, and of course in code syntax. In this chapter, we touched briefly on some of the differences. The way that object-oriented programming combines with the extreme programming model to solve so-called wicked problems is one of the more interesting differences. Use the various footnote references in this chapter as a starting point for further study.

We also touched on issues important to all software development. The most important and most urgent issue is quality. I cited reliability, extendibility, and reusability as three of the many facets of quality. We probably agree that high-quality software is desirable. Unfortunately, many also believe the notion that high-quality development practices are too expensive in terms of both time and effort. To help dispel this notion I briefly mentioned the way other industries have been able to improve productivity by targeting quality as a goal. I also presented arguments and cited references that describe a direct link between high quality and high productivity in software development. Achieving both requires discipline and practice, but is well within the grasp of every developer and organization.

We have not yet discussed differences in code syntax between typical MATLAB code and object-oriented MATLAB code because the rest of this book devotes itself to that topic. On the surface, the differences do not seem to run very deep. This is somewhat deceiving because the rules allow you to code very simple but very weak classes. Our goal is the development of strong, robust, bulletproof code capable of attaining the utmost quality. To achieve that goal, the following chapters introduce code idioms that use convention to augment the basic rules. Along the way, you get an introduction to the object-oriented terms and ideas behind the idioms. Taken together, the idioms form a cooperating set of reusable modules that can be used to repeatedly to develop world-class, object-oriented MATLAB programs.

Part 1

Group of Eight

MATLAB object-oriented rules dictate only one required function for each class. In practice, there are eight functions so fundamental to MATLAB object-oriented programming that each warrants its own chapter. Apart from each other, any one from this group of eight would be easy to describe, design, and code. Toy classes rarely use more than two or three of the eight, making their design easy. We are not interested in toy classes. In industrial-strength classes, the functions comprising this so-called *group of eight* always occur together, and each relies on functionality contained in the other members. In Chapter 1, we discussed dependency and coupling and concluded that such reliance requires careful attention to detail. Care is doubly important for the group of eight because these functions implement the most important part of any object, its interface. As you read along and consider the examples, keep the fact of coupling in mind. Sometimes it forces design decisions that become apparent only after the coupling partner is described, designed, and implemented.

As we will soon see, the notion of an interface goes hand in hand with the object-oriented concept of encapsulation. This first major section focuses on object-oriented encapsulation and develops an effective interface strategy. By the end of this section, the advantages of encapsulation along with the access rules enforced by MATLAB should be clear. Every function in the group of eight contributes to encapsulation. If you are wondering about the names of the group-of-eight functions, they are listed below. There are chapters in this section devoted to each member.

Functions belonging to the group of eight are

- **constructor**
- **subsref.m**
- **subsasgn.m**
- **display.m**
- **struct.m**
- **fieldnames.m**
- **get.m**
- **set.m**

The required elements are the best place to begin. First, there are not many; and, second, the required elements should exist in every class we write. After we cover the required elements, we will develop a set of optional elements that allow object-oriented variables to attain a status equal to built-in types. Without these optional elements, object-oriented code is difficult to use and maintain. After the optional elements, we examine strategies for atypical situations. This section covers all of the required and many of the optional object-oriented coding elements.

2 Meeting MATLAB's Requirements

MATLAB forces very little on us in the way of requirements. This is both good and bad. To the good, it means that we have a lot of freedom to make the implementation match our particular need. It also means that we do not have to devote a lot of time toward learning an intricate set of requirements, nor do we have to devote effort toward implementing the requirements with our code. To the bad, it means we must blaze our own trail without the benefit of requirements to keep us on track. Loose requirements provide enough rope to hang ourselves. It is too easy to weave a path that is difficult to maintain. In this chapter, we will learn how to meet requirements in a way that supports the needs of the group of eight. This helps keep MATLAB object-oriented programming on the straight and narrow.

2.1 VARIABLES, TYPES, CLASSES, AND OBJECTS

In every specialty, there are certain words that carry special meaning. At first glance, the sheer number of special words associated with object-oriented programming appears overwhelming. The sad fact that these words are sometimes misused does not help the situation. An additional burden comes in understanding slight differences among words that appear to be describing the same thing. Fortunately, mastering the vocabulary is not difficult. Most of the differences are anchored to the normal programming vocabulary.

In discussing object-oriented programming, the words *class* and *object* seem to suffer the most abuse. When you look closely at what these words actually represent, it is easy to understand why. After we carefully define both words, you will be able to follow discussions where the language is sloppy. This knowledge will also allow you to determine the competency of self-professed experts.

The easiest way to explain the differences between class and object is to relate them to things you probably already know. Look at the MATLAB command-line listing provided in Code Listing 1. First, let me reassure you. If the command syntax and results in Code Listing are familiar, you stand an excellent chance of taking full advantage of MATLAB object-oriented programming.

Code Listing 1, Command Line Example to Illustrate *Class* and *Object*

```
1    >> x = 10;
2    >> name = 'Wilbur';
3    >> whos
4      Name            Size                Bytes   Class
5
6      name            1x6                    12   char array
7      x               1x1                     8   double array
8
9    Grand total is 7 elements using 20 bytes
```

Look carefully at the information displayed by the **whos** command and you will notice, perhaps for the first time, a heading titled **Class**. I hope you find this particular word choice very interesting. You might complain that **char** and **double** are not classes but rather types. There's no cause for alarm. In this particular context, *class* and *type* mean almost the same thing. Class is a slightly more specific term, one with special meaning to object-oriented programmers. In fact, the connection between class and type is so close that the term *user-defined type* is often used as a substitute for *class*.

You might reasonably wonder why the object-oriented pioneers felt the need to coin a new term. The short answer is that class represents a new category of a variable's type in the same vein as array, cell, or structure. When we identify a variable as a double, its type attaches certain expectations to the variable. A class is more complicated than one of the simple types like double, char, or integer, but it still represents a type. We are comfortable with many of the simple or built-in types because we know what to expect. By comparison, identifying a variable's type as class is uncomfortable unless we already know what that means. Like me, you have probably forgotten that once upon a time, even the so-called simple types were not so simple. It took time and effort to arrive at a comfortable level of understanding for double, char, and cell. The same is true for class. Before long, the idea of class as simply another variable type will seem natural.

Learning about object-oriented programming will require some time and effort, and we certainly don't want to take on all of the special properties at once. After all, even with numbers we started with 1, 2, and 3 before moving on to π and e.

Before moving on, go back to the **whos** display in Code Listing 1 and examine the information associated with variable **x**. Think about the low-level details that you usually take for granted. Reading from left to right, **x** is the name of the variable. What is a variable name? The variable's name provides a human-readable reference to a value stored in memory. The variable's size is listed as **1×1**. From the size, we know that **x** is scalar. From the variable's type, **double**, we know that **x** is a member of the set of real numbers. The type establishes limits on which functions to use and on the expected accuracy. At a glance, we know how **x** should behave and we take many details for granted.

So, what is **x** exactly? Is it a variable? a memory location? a scalar? a real number? ... Of course, this is a trick question. Indeed, **x** represents all of those things and more. For algorithm design, the fact that **x** is **double** rather than **complex** or **char** is the primary focus. During code implementation, the variable's name, structure, and indices become increasingly more important. During execution, MATLAB's memory manager needs to know the physical address, the number of bytes, and so forth. No one is shocked that the meaning of **x** radically changes depending on context. This is exactly how we naturally cope with complexity. We avoid confusion by choosing to focus only on the features that are important to us right now.

Now I tell you that **x** is an *object*. Is it still a variable? Still located in memory? Still a scalar? ... Of course! The new information that identifies **x** as an *object* does not change the fact that it is still double precision. Saying that **x** is an object merely attaches yet another feature to the variable **x**. In the **whos** display, **Class** simply puts built-in types and user-defined types on an equal footing. Some programmers might bristle at the use of class to describe common built-in types, but with MATLAB this attitude is misguided. The fact that **double array** is a class and **x** is an object opens many interesting options. We will examine many of these options as we progress through the various examples.

Class is simply another description used to organize variables. The choice of the word "class" must imply something, or one of the more common terms would have been used. A class is a formal description of something general, possibly a reusable data structure, an abstract concept, or a tangible thing. While there are often other supporting documents, the ultimate class description exists as class' executable code. A class defines data elements and defines a set of functions used to operate on the elements. The data represent features or attributes and as a collection form the class' outward appearance. MATLAB uses a structure to define the data elements. The class' functions manipulate the data contained in the class' structure. Functions are implemented using m-files. What makes a class different from a normal structure and set of m-files are the object-oriented rules that associate the data structure and the m-files in a way that they always exist together as a whole. In short, a class defines a data structure and an inseparable set of m-files designed to operate on that structure.

There must also be a difference between a class and an object. Objects relate to classes in the same way variables relate to types. During the course of a program's execution, objects are created, used, and destroyed. The data structure for each object is unique and exists as a set of values stored in memory. Object **x** is different from object **y** because each occupies a different memory location. The structure of the data might be the same but the values can be different. All objects of the same class use the same set of class-specific m-files. The object's data are always passed into these functions. In this way, the behavior is always consistent with a particular object's data. In short, an object is a run-time entity that includes a type and individualized data.

2.2 WHAT IS A MATLAB CLASS?

What is a MATLAB class? Even though the MATLAB user's guide does a good job of answering it, I hear this question a lot. After numerous discussions and mentoring sessions, I now realize that this is not really the intended question. Askers are really searching for a framework on which they can build their own classes. Other languages provide this type of framework, so it is natural to expect MATLAB to provide one too. The user's guide doesn't define such a framework, probably for good reason. It would require more detail than is typical for a user's guide.

In C++ and Java, the framework is largely predefined by the language syntax. In MATLAB, no such framework exists and the few required elements allow for a lot of customization. Unfortunately, this also means there is no single answer to exactly what constitutes a MATLAB class or what constitutes an acceptable framework. There is a range of answers that depend on the desired level of customization. Classes designed to do one particular job in some specific application do not need an extensive framework. Classes that are nearly indistinguishable from built-in types or classes implemented with an extensive reuse goal require a sophisticated framework. Both need to include the required elements, but the first requires fewer "optional" elements.

Another thing to consider is change. The object-oriented framework in this book is tailored for MATLAB versions 6.5 through 7.1. When version 7 was released, a beta version containing several improvements to the object framework was also released. The framework in the version 7 beta release and the framework developed in this book can peacefully coexist. Future releases of MATLAB will undoubtedly contain framework elements that improve the performance or organization of this book's framework. This is a good thing, and from what I have seen, it should be easy to incorporate those improvements. Also, from what I have seen, there is a lot to like in the beta version of the framework. Future releases could also include elements that break this book's framework. So far, there is no hint of a problem. The detailed descriptions and examples in this book will allow you to adapt to any new framework.

2.2.1 EXAMPLE: CLASS REQUIREMENTS

Currently there are only two requirements for creating a class: a directory that identifies the class, and an m-file that defines the data structure and returns an object. Central to both requirements is the name of the class. All class files are stored in a directory with a name that is essentially the name of the class, and the name of the class' defining m-file is the same as the class name. Since the class name and the name of the defining m-file are the same, the naming restrictions for the class are identical to restrictions placed on functions: no punctuation, no spaces, cannot start with a number, and so on.

In this section, we will work on an implementation for an oversimplified version of a shape class. In the example, the name of the class will be **cShape**. As we will see, the class' directory will be named **@cShape** and the defining m-file will be named **cShape.m**.

2.2.1.1 Class Directory

MATLAB uses a distinctive directory-name syntax that includes an ampersand, "**@**," to identify class code versus nonclass code. For class **cShape**, MATLAB expects to find the class code in a directory named **/@cShape**. The class directory itself must *not* be added to the MATLAB path; however, the class directory's parent (i.e., the directory containing **/@cShape**) must be on the path.

> **Requirement:** The class directory name must begin with an @ symbol.

> **Requirement:** The class' parent directory must be on the function search path.

> **Requirement:** The class' @ directory must <u>not</u> be on the function search path.

There is one additional wrinkle regarding the class directory. There can be more than one directory named **/@cShape**. This requires more than one parent directory, but in such a setup, MATLAB will traverse the path and search all class directories it can locate. The search follows standard path-search rules. The **addpath** order resolves ambiguity. The first directory in the path with a **/@cShape** subdirectory is searched first, and so on. Usually this behavior is simply a curiosity. Under normal conditions, you should strive to avoid confusion by locating all of your class' m-files in one directory. Sometimes the application conspires against us and we need to break with convention. There are some special circumstances when this behavior is desirable. One such situation involves replacing default functions for built-in types. For example, you can add a **/@double** directory and add m-files to the directory. Now if you properly arrange the path-search order, you can force MATLAB to find functions in the new **/@double** before it finds the built-in version. This ability is very useful during debug because you can log values and temporarily change a function's behavior. Another situation involves class functions that are proprietary or classified. In those situations, you can provide nonproprietary functions in the standard **/@cShape** directory and keep proprietary functions in a second **/@cShape** directory located in a safe place. When you want to run the proprietary version, all you need to do is arrange the path so that the proprietary version is found before the default version. That way, you do not have to have multiple copies of nonproprietary files.

If you are familiar with the MATLAB search path, you know that the present working directory (**pwd**) is always on the path and is high up in the search priority. This makes **pwd** a convenient place to perform code experiments because you do not have to mess around with the path. Instead of manipulating the path, it is often easier to **cd** into a temporary directory and get to work. Of course, if you would rather manipulate the path that is okay too. You are free to use any convenient directory to experiment with the book's example code. If you don't have a preference, use the name **c:/oop_guide** and you will be in step with the text included in the example commands.

2.2.1.2 Constructor

MATLAB needs a way to create an object. While this might sound out of the ordinary, it is actually very common. Think about how you might normally use, for example, **ones(r, c)** or **complex(x, y)** or **struct**. MATLAB fills in default values for the built-in types that it understands. By providing a constructor, you are extending the list of types that MATLAB understands to types beyond the built-in types. Consequently, every class is required to have a function that both clients and MATLAB can use to create an object filled with default values.

In object-oriented terminology, the m-file that creates an object is called a *constructor*. The constructor defines the data structure and fills in element values. The so-called default constructor is called with no input arguments and is configured to fill the element values with reasonable default values. The m-file name for the constructor takes the same name as the class. The complete constructor code for the simplified shape class is given in Code Listing 2. You can type in the function from scratch or copy the file from the code disk. This file is on the code disk at **/oop_guide/chapter_1/@cShape/cShape.m**.

Code Listing 2, Minimalist Constructor

```
1    function this = cShape
2    this = struct('dummy', []);
3    this = class(this, 'cShape');
```

Code Listing 2 is very simple, yet this three-line constructor meets all of MATLAB's requirements:

- The function is located in the appropriate class-specific directory.
- The m-file's name identifies it as the **cShape** class constructor.
- The constructor can be called with no arguments.
- The data structure of the object is defined.
- Each field of the structure is assigned a default value.
- The return value is an object of class **cShape.**

These bullets can be expressed in terms of requirements.

Requirement: The constructor m-file must be located in the class' @ directory.

Requirement: The constructor m-file must use the same name as its directory without the leading @ symbol.

Requirement: A default constructor call, one with no required input arguments, must be available.

Requirement: The constructor must define a structure and assign default values to each element.

Requirement: The constructor must call **class** so that it can return an object instead of a structure.

Code Listing 2 is also easy to dissect. Line 1 is simply the normal syntax for the definition of a function. The function accepts no input arguments and returns one value. The default constructor by definition has no input arguments. When arguments are passed in, we are asking the constructor to do more than the minimum. Construction using input arguments is important; however, we will not need to go beyond default construction until Part 2 of this book. The single return argument is the constructed object. Returning more than the constructed object is possible but discouraged.

Line 2 defines the object's data structure and assigns the structure into the variable **this**. The data structure must be a **struct array**, and any conceivable structure can be used.* The structure can also be created using **struct**, by adding fields one at a time or by calling a function that returns a structure. The only real requirement is that the method must be able to reproduce the same structure every time. MATLAB enforces object consistency by requiring that all objects of the same class be based on the same structure. The values contained in the structure elements can be different, but the number and order of the structure's elements must be the same. If you try to construct two objects of the same class using two different structures, MATLAB will issue an error during the second attempt.

Requirement: All objects of the same class type must be based on the same structure.

There is nothing special about the variable name **this**. In MATLAB, **this** is not a reserved word, nor does it have any special properties. There is nothing but convention to compel you to use a standard name to identify the operated-on object. My advice is to always use the same name, and the example code follows this advice. A standard name makes coding, debugging, testing, and maintenance much easier. It is also a good idea to refrain from using the standard name outside of the class' m-files for similar reasons. Choosing the name **this** is nice because of its familiarity. Programmers with a C++ background already have an idea of what **this** represents.

Recommendation: Reserve the variable name **this** for exclusive use within class code.

Line 3 uses MATLAB's **class** function to convert the data structure into an object. The class function is multipurpose and you can use **help** to investigate the various options. In this context, the first input argument is the object's structure and the second input argument is a string containing the name of the class. During the execution of **class**, MATLAB uses the structure and class name to check consistency. If no errors occur, the structure is converted into an encapsulated object and returned. Convention reserves this particular use of **class** to the constructor function. Depending on the version, MATLAB will generate an error if you try to convert a structure outside of the constructor function. More recent versions strictly adhere to this rule.

2.2.1.3 The Test Drive

It may be hard to believe, but the development of our first class is complete. The **cShape** class includes all required functionality, and the code is ready for a test drive. If you already typed in the constructor, change into the directory that contains the **@cShape** directory. Otherwise, you can copy files from the code disk and change into the Chapter 2 directory. You are now ready to create your first object. The command-line entries included in Code Listing 3 demonstrate a sample of the class' current capability.

Code Listing 3, Chapter 1 Test Drive Command Listing

```
1    >> clear classes; clc
2    >> cd /oop_guide/chapter_2
3    >> set(0, 'FormatSpacing', 'compact');
4    >> shape = cShape
5    shape =
6      cshape object: 1-by-1
```

---

* Version 6.5 does not allow an object to be created from an empty structure, that is, **struct([])**.

```
7    >> disp(shape)
8      cshape object: 1-by-1
9    >> save test_shape shape;
10   >> clear all;
11   >> whos
12   >> load test_shape;
13   >> whos
14     Name          Size                      Bytes   Class
15
16     shape         1x1                         124   cshape object
17
18   Grand total is 1 element using 124 bytes
19
20   >> class(shape)
21   ans =
22   cShape
23   >> shape.dummy
24   ??? Access to an object's fields is only permitted within
       its methods.
```

Line 1 in Code Listing 3 clears the workspace and clears the command window. You are probably familiar with **clear all** but may not be familiar with **clear classes**. The **clear classes** command includes **clear all**'s functionality and adds the ability to clear the association between a class name and a specific structure. You don't need to **clear classes** every time, but there is no harm in using **clear classes** instead of **clear all**. You must call **clear classes** if you change a class' structure. If you change the structure but fail to call **clear classes**, MATLAB will remind you by displaying the following error:

??? Error using ==> class.

Line 2 changes the present working directory to the base directory for this chapter. If you copied files into a different location, change the command to suit your directory structure.

Line 3 is optional and tells MATLAB to display output values using the so-called compact format. The compact format displays fewer blank lines compared to the **'loose'** option.

Line 4 is the first object-oriented command. The assignment, **shape=cShape**, initiates a lot of behind-the-scenes work. First, MATLAB searches for a constructor by checking the right-hand side against all **@**-directory names that occur in directories on the path. In this case, MATLAB is looking for the **@cShape** directory. As long as we changed into the correct directory, there will be a **@cShape** directory in the present working directory. MATLAB now searches the **@cShape** directory, finds the **cShape.m** function, and runs it. Our constructor code builds the structure, converts the structure into an object, and returns the object as an output. On return, the object is assigned into the **shape** local variable. Since we conveniently left off the semicolon, MATLAB displays the variable. The display isn't informative. The result from **disp** in line 7 is not any better. We can certainly do better, but providing a cogent display is not a requirement.

Since we have met all the requirements, we can pass **cShape** objects in and out of functions, assign objects to structure fields, save objects to a mat file, and load them back into the workspace. The next few command lines demonstrate this capability. For example, the variable **shape** is saved to a mat file in line 9. Line 10 clears the workspace, and line 12 restores **shape** back into the workspace. In line 20, the **class** command returns **shape's** type. As expected, we see that **shape's** type is indeed **'cShape'**.

Emboldened by our success, line 23 tries to access the **dummy** value stored in the object's structure. We know the object has a **dummy** field because we included it in the constructor. The result is not a value but rather an error. MATLAB tells us we are not allowed to access the field. How can this be?

The answer lies in the fact that **shape** is not a structure but rather an object. As an object, MATLAB treats access to its fields differently. We already know that objects are associated with a particular **@** directory, that objects are created by a special m-file called a constructor, and that all objects of the same class use the same structure. Attempting to access **dummy** uncovers another important detail: the fields of the class' structure are not accessible. In object-oriented lingo, we would say that the fields are *encapsulated*. The general philosophy driving encapsulation was introduced in §1.3.

In §1.3, we said that encapsulation helps protect an object's integrity by hiding selected elements. Also in §1.3, we said that encapsulation includes various levels of visibility or access. From the error message in line 24, it appears that **dummy** must be one of the hidden elements. Being hidden means that **dummy** has private visibility and MATLAB is correctly denying us access to it. Now that we understand the source of the error, all we need to do is learn how to unhide **dummy**. There must be a way to make elements of the object public, right?

First the bad news: you cannot unhide elements and make them public. MATLAB treats the entire structure and everything stored in it as hidden, private data, period. You cannot make **dummy** public even if you want to. If that were the end of the story, this book would be very short. Now the good news: private variables are accessible; however, they are not accessible using normal techniques. Object-oriented programming and encapsulation define the concept of an interface and the hidden elements are indirectly accessible through the interface. The next chapter dives headlong into the issue of encapsulation and begins to develop techniques to deal with the inviolable fact that the object's structure is always private.

2.3 SUMMARY

All the requirements have now been met, and we know how to build classes that play well in MATLAB's environment. Having met the requirements, our budding **cShape** class represents a new data type with many of the properties we expect from any type. We can create a variable based on **cShape**, and once created we can display it, save its state to a mat file, and load it back into the environment. This variable is also called an object, and we demonstrated all of this in the test drive. We can pass the variable into and out of a function, assign it into the field of a structure, and create arrays of objects.

While this is indeed a great start, we really can't do much with a **cShape** object because we don't yet know how to access the private elements. Accessing private elements requires an interface, but before we can define an interface, we need to focus some attention on exactly how a user might want to use an object. Designing an interface to meet the user's expectations is the hardest part of MATLAB object-oriented programming.

In every object-oriented programming environment, various topics fit together like a jigsaw puzzle. The topics all relate to one another, and you can't see the whole picture until most of the pieces are in place. If you pick a piece at random, it's hard to find exactly where it fits in. Most people begin a puzzle by finding the corners. In our object-oriented puzzle, Figure 2.1, the required elements are the corners. Usually the frame pieces are added next. The chapters in the rest of this section piece together the frame by focusing on encapsulation and interface. Later sections bring the whole picture into focus.

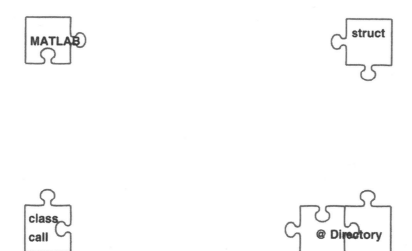

FIGURE 2.1 Puzzle with MATLAB-required pieces in place.

2.4 INDEPENDENT INVESTIGATIONS

Every chapter will conclude with a set of questions or exercises. You are encouraged to ponder the questions and attempt the exercises. Spending some time considering them will help cement the chapter's topics, introduce the next chapter's topics, and sometimes point out useful tricks or common pitfalls.

This book is not designed to be a textbook, and the questions or exercises are not intended as an exit exam. Sometimes answers will not be readily apparent until more pieces of the puzzle fall into place. Before moving to the next chapter, you should at least spend a few moments considering each of the proposed investigations. If any pique your interest, take a break from reading, fire up MATLAB, and attempt a solution. Also, keep in mind that the investigation topics will grow more challenging with each passing chapter. As you grow in the knowledge of object-oriented programming, you will be up to the challenge.

1. Examine the use of memory. Create a normal structure using the command

    ```
    ns = struct('dummy', []);
    ```

    and create an object using the command

    ```
    shape = cShape;
    ```

    Now use **whos** to display the size of each variable. Is there anything noteworthy about the sizes and number of bytes?

2. Experiment with the size of the constructed object by changing the structure that underlies each **cShape** object. In the constructor, replace line 2 with

    ```
    this = struct('dummy', {[] []});
    ```

    Next, save the file, and create a new **cShape** object. Don't forget to **clear classes** before creating the object. Use **whos** to display the object's size. Can you also use the **size** function to return the object's size? What is the modified constructor creating?

3. Investigate what kind of data the object can hold. Add additional fields along with default value assignment to the data structure. You might as well build an equivalent structure, too, and compare size and bytes. Can the object store strings, arrays, cell arrays, or structures?

4. The object's structure is fixed by calling **class**. Is each field's data type also fixed by **class**? (Answer: no.)

    If a field is assigned a structure value, is this structure fixed by **class**? (Answer: no, only the first level of field names is fixed.)

    If the default value of a field is a number, is it possible to assign a string into the field? (Answer: yes, but doing so usually results in a poor interface.)

5. Create a **cShape** object and name it **x**. See what happens when you type

    ```
    y=struct(x)
    ```

    What does **whos** tell you about **y**? Add some fields to the object's structure by modifying the constructor code, and repeat the same command. What is **struct** doing to the object?

    This exercise is included here so I can warn you about **struct**. In the context of object-oriented programming, **struct's** ability to convert an object into a structure is very dangerous. Until we discuss the specifics in Chapter 7, you should absolutely avoid calling **struct** with an object as its argument.

6. Try to create an array of **cShape** objects. One way to do this would be

    ```
    shape_array = [cShape cShape];
    ```

    Can you add a new element to the array? For example, what happens if you try the following command?

    ```
    shape_array(3) = cShape;
    ```

    Repeat this exercise, but properly replace **[]** or **()** with **{}**.

7. Explore how built-in types make use of object-oriented facilities. Create a **/@double** directory in the present working directory. Add a **rand.m** function inside the **/@double** directory that simply returns 0.5 instead of a random number. From the command line, enter **rand(1)**. What value do you get? The directory and code for this exercise are included in the example files for Chapter 2.

3 Member Variables and Member Functions

With the required elements covered, it is time to piece together the frame of the puzzle. The frame pieces include many features that make object-oriented programming different from procedural programming. These features rely on encapsulation, and the differences stem from the fact that procedural languages cannot exhibit encapsulation. These features also influence the interface. For ease of use, every class interface should include a common subset of behavior. Chapter 2 described the requirements, and now we are on our own. The rest of this book provides a coding framework that covers "everything else." While perhaps not perfect in every way, the framework and recommendations make good use of MATLAB's various peculiarities.

Similar to the requirements development in Chapter 2, framework development includes both discussions and example code. The example code forms the basis of every class implementation. Due to its ultimate importance, the example code needs to be compact and efficient. In most of the example code, the desire for efficiency pushes the code syntax into the realm of advanced coding techniques. The discussions around each example include a brief explanation of the syntax. I hope that these explanations offer enough detail. If not, many MATLAB references focus exclusively on language syntax. The discussions around each example also provide an in-depth explanation of the object-oriented aspects. The object-oriented discussions are the central focus because there is no other comprehensive reference source.

In §2.2.1.3 the command generated an error when we tried to inspect the value of **shape.dummy**. The reason for the error is the fact that MATLAB hides all object data. To access the data we need to add functions to the class directory. The group of eight represents the set of functions common to all classes, and most classes will include additional specialized functions. Taken together these functions form the class interface. The interface functions are fundamentally different from functions that exist outside the class directory. This chapter describes the differences, introduces some terms, and generally sets the stage for interface design. Chapters that follow will specifically address each function in the group of eight. By the end of Part 1 of this book, the initial implementations for all functions in the group of eight will be nearly complete.

Before moving on to the interface description, let's reexamine our attempt to inspect the value **shape.dummy**. This is the correct syntax if both **shape** is a structure and **dummy** is an element of the structure. In MATLAB terminology the operation is a *subscripted reference*. MATLAB also allows the use of subscripted references for objects. In general, subscripted references come in three flavors: dot, array ("()"), and cell ("{}"). All three can be included in an object's interface, and we need a standard, shorthand way to refer to each reference type. The discussions that follow use the following terms:

- *dot-reference*: subscripted reference with ' . ' (e.g., **shape.dummy**)
- *array-reference*: subscripted reference with ' ( ) ' (array indexing)
- *cell-reference*: subscripted reference with ' { } ' (cell indexing)

3.1 MEMBERS

A class is like an exclusive club, and membership has its privileges. The m-files stored in the class directory are members of the club. All other m-files are nonmembers. Standard object-oriented terminology uses the name *member functions* to identify the files in the class directory. In total, these functions are responsible for implementing the interface because they enjoy the privilege of accessing the object's private structure. This is exactly why we say that the private data are hidden behind the interface. As clients, we can't "see" the data unless we get them indirectly via one of the interface functions.

If you look in the **/chapter_2/@cShape** directory, you will find only one file, **cShape.m**. That means the constructor is currently the only member, and we all know it's no fun being the only member of a club. We need to expand the membership rolls, not because we are afraid the constructor will be lonely but because member functions are the only way for nonmembers to collaborate with an object.

The close association between member functions and an object's private structure is a very important feature in object-oriented programming. To help enforce the importance of the association, the fields of the private structure are collectively referred to as the *member variables*. Every object has the same member variables, but the values contained in the variables are unique from object to object. The functions are the same from object to object, but the values used by the functions are different. Every time a member function is called, the object's private structure is used to populate the variables in a private workspace.

It is this close association between member functions and member variables that requires every object of the same class have the same set of member variables. For MATLAB objects, this means that the private structure for each class' object must be identical to every other. MATLAB enforces this by two means. First, MATLAB saves the object's structure description and compares the structure of every subsequent **class** call to the initial description. If the structure in the **class** call does not match the previously stored description, MATLAB generates an error. Thus, the constructor must build the framework of the object's structure the same way every time. The values and even the types stored in each field can be different, but the fieldnames themselves must be identical. During class development, the structural description can be cleared using the command **clear classes**.

Second, after **class** transforms the structure into an object, it is illegal to add or remove a field. MATLAB will generate an error if you try. This behavior is actually very helpful in catching spelling or capitalization errors. Rather than silently creating a new field, MATLAB instantly alerts you to the error. This behavior also protects the integrity of every object in the environment.

3.2 ACCESSORS AND MUTATORS

Accessors and *mutators* are not horror-movie creatures waiting to drag unsuspecting programmers into the fire and brimstone. Accessors and mutators are simply two member function categories. Altogether, there are only three categories — constructor, accessor, and mutator — so it is easy to keep them straight.*

The constructor is mostly about defining the member variable organization. Accessors and mutators concern themselves with the values stored in each member variable. The terms accessor and mutator are descriptive of what the member function does to the object's data. An accessor returns one or more values but does not change any of the data already stored in the object. Changing the object's data is the job of the mutator. A mutator may also return values, but primarily it functions as an agent for change. Unlike the name "constructor," the names "accessor" and "mutator" are not universal. Other programmers and authors use a variety of names to describe the same thing.

Accessors are member functions that *return* values associated with an object. It is very common for the function name to indicate its role by including the word "get" somewhere in the name. For

---

* In some languages, but not in MATLAB, there is a fourth group named *destructor* that undoes the action of the constructor before a variable goes out of scope.

example, **cShape** might provide accessors with names like **getColor** or **getSize**. The association between the function name and the value accessed is obvious. The fact that the function is an accessor is also obvious.

Mutators are member functions used to *change* values associated with an object. Often the name of a mutator will include the word "set" somewhere in its name, for example **setSize** or **setColor**. Again, the association between the function name and the mutated value is obvious.

Now the real fun begins. If we choose to add these particular accessors and mutators, do we also need to add member variables with names like **color** or **size**? Well, sometimes yes and sometimes no. For simple member variables, a pair of get and set member functions might be appropriate. Attempting to match member variables with get and set member functions, and vice versa, reveals a strong bias toward structures. Once we eliminate the bias, restricting accessors and mutators to such a simple association is a limitation we can't live with. After all, it seems a bit silly to carefully hide all the data behind an interface and then write a bunch of "get" functions for every variable. If it doesn't seem so silly now, it will by the time you finish the book.

Individual get and set functions have their place, but they do not represent the real power behind object-oriented programming and the philosophy of encapsulation. They are an easy way to demonstrate some of the basic aspects of member functions, and this chapter uses them for that purpose. MATLAB gives us a much better way to handle such a mundane chore, so don't get too comfortable with the idea of always including individual get and set functions. I introduce the better way in Chapter 4 and improve on the initial version in later chapters.

3.2.1 A Short Side Trip to Examine Encapsulation

Up to this point, we have been dancing around the concept of encapsulation. To understand fully the connection between member functions and member variables, we need to examine encapsulation in more detail. In particular, we need to discuss MATLAB-specific details or the code in the examples will be difficult to follow. The two topics, encapsulation and members, are very closely related, making it hard to explain one before the other. The implementation details in the example should tie up any loose ends in the encapsulation discussion.

We have already introduced encapsulation as a way to both control the fields of an object's structure and hide member variables. As one of the three pillars of object-oriented programming, encapsulation includes a lot more. Principal to encapsulation is the idea of hidden members. Of course, not everything can be hidden or we couldn't do anything with an object. Consequently, encapsulation brings with it the idea of member visibility and provides a way to control what is hidden and what is not.

The object-oriented terminology defines two types of class members: *public* and *private*.* Private members are hidden and public members are not. In Chapter 2, I made a big deal out of the fact that all class variables are private. Indeed, from the class developer's perspective, this is always true. In Chapter 4, we will introduce a special technique that allows us to create classes that appear to have public variables. As developers, we know this must be an interface illusion.

Public and private visibility also applies to functions. By definition, all m-files located in the class directory are public functions. In its current condition, **cShape** contains one public function, the constructor. Standard MATLAB convention lets us create a **/private** directory inside the class directory. Ordinarily, we use a private directory to avoid path-search ambiguity when m-files share the same name. In object-oriented programming, the private directory has a different purpose because the object's type along with the class directory already resolve path-search ambiguity. M-files in the class' private directory are *private member functions*, callable only by the public members.

Visibility rules restrict the use of private members by functions outside the class. Recall the error that occurred when we tried to access a private variable in §2.2.1.3. Class member functions

---

* Some languages include a third type, *protected*. Currently MATLAB does not support protected members.

are not similarly restricted. Visibility rules allow member functions unrestricted use of public and private variables and functions. Of course, unrestricted access to private class members is available only to those functions that belong to the same class.

One important aspect of encapsulation is visibility control. Strong encapsulation absolutely prevents a client from observing private members. We always strive for strong encapsulation because we never want a client to develop code that depends on private members. Strong encapsulation extends to the object's structure, its fieldnames, and its values. MATLAB's default treatment of encapsulation is not strong because it allows clients to bypass the interface to observe private fieldnames and read private values. Fortunately, clients can't bypass the interface to change private variables; however, even unprotected read access opens the door for abuse. This chapter focuses on the properties of the default encapsulation. We can't achieve the strongest possible encapsulation until all functions in the group of eight are fully developed. Even then, there is one small crack where the encapsulation can't be protected. It is too early to go into all the details. If you are curious, look at **help builtin**, **help struct**, and **help fieldnames**.

3.2.1.1   cShape Variables

Let's try to tie the idea of encapsulation back to the **cShape** example. We didn't define shape-related member variables in Chapter 2 because we didn't need any. Now that we need variables, we need to sort out the requirements. Rather than defining all requirements at once, let's follow an incremental approach by introducing new requirements only when necessary. For many software projects, this approach mirrors reality. For the purposes of this chapter, the set of requirements is small. We only need enough requirements to continue the encapsulation discussion and demonstrate the general implementation for member functions.

Before you start screaming, "What kind of shape?" I need to tell you that I don't want to go in that direction until we start talking about an object-oriented concept called inheritance. If you are already familiar with inheritance, the rationale is clear. If you are not yet familiar with inheritance, rest assured: we deal with different kinds of shapes in Part 2 of this book. We certainly don't want to dive into inheritance now because encapsulation is both more important and forms its foundation.

Without the benefit of encapsulation, requirements exert a strong influence on data structures and functions. The influence is so strong that it is often difficult to separate the requirements from the implementation. This coupling occurs because clients and developers have no choice but to depend on the same organization, including name, type, and size. Encapsulation breaks this dependency by providing a public interface consistent with the requirements and a private implementation tailored to the task.

We will set four requirements:

- Get and set the size of the shape's bounding box.
- Get and set a scale factor value.
- Reset the shape's size back to its original value.
- Get and set the shape's border color.

Notice the implied dependency among this simple requirement set. The current bounding box size depends on both the original size and a scale factor.

In a structure-based design, this kind of dependency always forces a lesser-of-two-evils solution. Often the safest course eliminates the data dependency by pushing the dependency out to the client. In this simple example, we first create a structure containing **original_size** and **scale_factor**. By defining the structure this way, we force clients to calculate the current box size using the equation **shape.original_size * shape.scale_factor**. This works fine until a client needs to save a vector scale factor (i.e., a different scale value for horizontal versus vertical) rather than a scalar one. Every client module must be updated with a revised equation.

In the other structure-based course, we ask clients to interact with the structure using function calls rather than normal dot-reference syntax. The approach breaks down because we are asking clients to treat structure elements as if they were private, but there is no built-in support for this request. For example, clients can easily view the structure, but finding the associated function names is a lot harder. Clients are also comfortable with dot-reference syntax and usually prefer it. It doesn't take long before clients start bypassing the function interface. When that happens, the data are no longer under control and any number of errors can result. Even with this potential for disaster, the function-based approach is often the best approach.

An object-oriented design is safer. The property of encapsulation helps an object-oriented implementation avoid these problems. The fact that an object's structure and its data are private allows a lot more data flexibility. As long as we can support the interface requirements, we can store any combination of original size, current size, and scale factor. Built-in protection also means we can more easily support requirements that include dependency. It is usually safer to address these dependencies in the class functions rather than relying on every client to get it right. Encapsulation also allows us to be somewhat cavalier with the private organization. If we make a bad choice, at least we can be certain that any ill effects will be isolated to functions inside the class.

3.2.2 CSHAPE MEMBERS

Before we can investigate accessors and mutators, we need some member variables to, well, access and mutate. Here we refine the high-level requirements to produce a set of private member variables and public member functions. After that, the object-oriented implementation follows easily. Code for this example is included on the code disk in the following directory:

```
/oop_guide/chapter 3/@cShape
```

3.2.2.1 cShape Private Member Variables

The high-level requirements from §3.2.1.1 are repeated below.

- Get and set the size of the shape's bounding box.
- Get and set a scale factor value.
- Reset the shape's size back to its original value.
- Get and set the shape's border color.

These high-level requirements give us a lot of wiggle room in defining the interface. As a starting point, we will include **mSize, mScale**, and **mColorRgb** as elements in **cShape**'s class structure. It would then be correct to say that **mSize, mScale**, and **mColorRgb** are **cShape**'s private variables. Clients will never see these variables, so we can define them so they are convenient to the implementation.

Both **mSize** and **mScale** will be stored as 2×1 numeric vectors. The current size of the bounding box is stored in **mSize**. The multiplicative scale factor used to convert the original size to the current size is stored in **mScale**. Values at array indices (1) and (2) correspond respectively to the horizontal and vertical directions. We can reset the value of **mSize** using the following equation:

```
this.mSize = this.mSize ./ this.mScale;
```

The border color is stored as a 3×1 RGB array in **mColorRgb**. Values at array indices (1), (2), and (3) correspond respectively to red, green, and blue. Each color value ranges from zero to one.

Defining arrays as column vectors is convenient for concatenation and ultimately vectorization. When we add support for object arrays, the vectorized code dealing with column arrays will have an easier syntax. Proper concatenation of row arrays across an array of objects is possible, but it usually requires a call to **vertcat**. It is also convenient to store *N*-dimensional arrays as columns. In this case, use a **reshape** call to change the array into the desired shape. Finally, standardizing around column vectors as the default internal format makes maintenance much easier. Unless you have a good reason to the contrary, always store private arrays as columns.

You might also be wondering about the lowercase **m** at the beginning of each private member variable. The **m** serves several purposes. Beginning each fieldname with lowercase **m** identifies the variable as a member variable, and such identification is often helpful during code development. The syntax serves as a cue in the same vein as the variable name **this** and the lowercase **c** added to the beginning of the class name. It helps remind you that the variable belongs to an object and is private. As with the other cues, adding an **m** is not required. If you discover that it is not useful, leave it off.

3.2.2.2   cShape Public Interface

It is too early in our study of the MATLAB implementation to do anything fancy. In this chapter, we will define a set of member functions capable of implementing the interface; however, keep in mind that as we learn new techniques we will drop support for some of them. Presently we have two techniques that we can exploit: a get and set pair and a switch based on the number of input arguments obtained using nargin. To demonstrate both, we will implement the interface for size and scale with get and set pairs and border color with an internal switch. Since the requirements did not dictate names and formats, we will take the liberty to define them ourselves.

Object-oriented design advises a minimalist approach when creating the interface. Each accessor or mutator exposes a little more of the class' internal workings. If we expose too much of the implementation or if we expose it in an awkward way, our future options are limited. Remember, once advertised, a function is part of the interface forever. This locks you into supporting legacy areas of the interface that might have been better left hidden. Being prudent and miserly when defining the interface keeps our classes nimble.

Encapsulation along with a minimalist interface create a certain amount of tension between the data required to support normal operation and the data required to support development tasks like unit testing. A normal interface that exposes all hidden variables doesn't quite follow the philosophy of encapsulation; however, efficient testing sometimes mandates full exposure. For example, an accessor that calculates its output based on some combination of private variables is much easier to test if you can set private values and execute the member function. The problem here is that you now have more than one type of client. Each type has a different agenda and consequently needs a different interface. Indeed, this common situation is often included in books discussing object-oriented design.

You don't have to supply the entire public interface to every client. MATLAB has some very convenient ways to accommodate different clients. You can include relatively simple switches designed to turn certain features on and off. You can support different access syntax to reveal concealed elements. There are others but the full list includes topics we haven't yet discussed. Later, when you refer back to the list, some of the items will make more sense. The list includes the following:

- Selectively add special-purpose member functions for use by special-purpose clients by using secondary class directories and manipulating the path. The possibility of multiple-class directories was first described in §2.2.1.1. Technically, member functions in a secondary directory are part of the interface; however, their use is generally easier to control compared to the functions in the general interface.

- Temporarily modify the constructor so that it enables built-in support for special-purpose clients. For example, private logical values can easily guard debug displays. In another example, store a function handle in a private variable and let special-purpose clients reference a more capable function.

- Conceal certain variables by making their access or mutate syntax more difficult compared to public variable syntax. This is actually a good option when you want to maintain the general appearance of a simple interface yet still add advanced capability for sophisticated clients. So-called concealed variables might not be advertised as belonging to the public interface, but they need to be treated as public.

- Use private functions that don't require an object but still operate with member variables. Instead of passing an object, simplify the arguments by passing dot-referenced values. The resulting code will be modular and allows functions to be tested separately from the class.

- Allow a class to inherit a parent class that temporarily adds interface elements, or create a child class that includes an alternate interface. An inheritance-based solution is often difficult because, currently, MATLAB has no intrinsic support for protected visibility.

Most of these options result in challenging implementations. Serving two masters is inherently difficult. As the examples become more challenging, some of these techniques will be discussed further. We will not be able to develop a complete solution, but we will develop some of the options.

In the case of our simple example, there are not a lot of decisions to make regarding the interface. The client's view of the interface is functionally defined as follows:

```
shape = cShape;

shape_size = getSize(shape);

shape = setSize(shape, shape_size);

shape_scale = getScale(shape);

shape = setScale(shape, shape_scale);

shape_color = ColorRgb(shape);

shape = ColorRgb(shape, shape_color);

shape = reset(shape);
```

where

> **shape** is an object of type **cShape**.
> **shape_size** is the 2×1 numeric vector [**horizontal_size**; **vertical_size**] with an initial value of [1; 1].
> **shape_scale** is the 2×1 numeric vector [**horizontal_scale**; **vertical_scale**] with an initial value of [1; 1].
> **shape_color** is the 3×1 numeric vector [**red**; **green**; **blue**] with an initial value of [0; 0; 1].

All of these functions will be implemented as public member functions. The first function is the constructor. The constructor is one of the required elements, and we already understand what it needs to contain. The other member functions are the topic of this chapter.

First, notice that every mutator includes the mutated object as an output. MATLAB always uses a pass-by-value argument convention. The mutator must pass out the modified object and the client must assign the modified object to a variable or all changes will be lost. The syntax is simply a fact of programming under a pass-by-value convention. In many respects, the syntax used in object-oriented MATLAB programming would benefit from the addition of a pass-by-reference approach. The **assignin** function can be used to emulate a pass-by-reference calling syntax. Before you attempt this technique, you should consider the warnings mentioned in Chapter 21.

Second, notice that the input argument lists include a **cShape** object as the first argument. This is one of the hallmarks of a member function. The member function needs the object so that it operates on the correct data, and MATLAB needs the object's type so that it can locate the appropriate class-specific member function. MATLAB still uses the search path; however, an object in the input list triggers some additional priorities. Before we discuss the member function implementations, we need to take another brief side trip to examine this critical detail.

3.2.3 A SHORT SIDE TRIP TO EXAMINE FUNCTION SEARCH PRIORITY

MATLAB uses something called the search path to locate and execute functions. The search path is simply an ordered list of directories, and any function you want to run must exist in one of the search-path directories. Even though it does not show up in the ordered list, the present working directory is also included in the search. Private directories are also absent from the list, but search rules include them too. Of particular interest to us are the class directories. Class directories are also absent from the list, but we already know that MATLAB readily locates the constructor. MATLAB can also locate member functions. In most cases, you will not encounter problems with the search. For those rare occasions when a problem comes up, it is good to understand the rules. MATLAB documentation already includes a good description of the rules. For all the various conditions, I will refer you to those documents. Here, the emphasis is on the object-oriented aspects of the rules.

MATLAB always applies the same set of rules when it searches for a function. MATLAB can locate all files on the search path that have the same name; however, it only executes the first file that it finds. A determination of the first file can be made because locations are ordered according to a priority. The location of the class constructor and other public member functions has a very high priority. In order, from highest priority to lowest, the top few are summarized in the list below.

1. The function is defined as a subfunction in the caller's m-file.
2. The function exists in the caller's **/private** directory. There are two subtle exceptions to this rule. First, the rule does not extend to **/private/private** directories. Instead, functions that exist in a private function's directory are located with a priority of 2. The subtle nature of this rule can catch you if you are trying to call another class' overloaded function from within a private function of the same name.
3. The m-file is a constructor. That is, a class directory named **/@function_name** exists and contains the m-file named **function_name.m**. A free function on the path with the same name as a constructor will not be found before the constructor. In §2.2.1.1 we discussed the possibility of spreading member functions across multiple class directories. Like-named class directories are searched in the order that their parent directory appears in the path.
4. When the input argument list contains an object, the object's class directories are searched. In those cases when more than one object appears among the input arguments, only one type is selected and there is a procedure for determining which type. Under typical conditions, the first argument's type is used. Atypical conditions involve the use of **superiorto** and **inferiorto** commands. These commands and their use are described in §4.1.1. Inheritance also affects the search. The directories for the object's

most specific type are searched first. The search continues in the parent directories until all parent levels have been exhausted. Inheritance from multiple parents uses type superiority to decide which path to traverse.

5. An m-file for the function is located in the present working directory (i.e., **pwd**).
6. The function is a built-in MATLAB function.
7. The function is located elsewhere on the search path.

Items 3 and 4 are important in understanding how MATLAB treats objects, classes, and member functions. Inherent in the search is the notion of type. This is a little odd because we typically think of MATLAB variables as untyped. Once we accept typing, we note that locating an object's member functions is among the search path's highest priorities. Except for a few subtle situations, the member functions are usually located first.

3.2.4 EXAMPLE CODE: ACCESSORS AND MUTATORS, ROUND 1

In §3.2.2 we expanded the requirements into a set of public member functions supported by a private set of variables. This section implements conversion code. Accessors convert from the private variable set to the return values expected. Mutators accept input values and convert these values into a consistent, private, internal representation. As a demonstration of some of the power behind the interface, the mutators in this implementation check for input assignment errors.

3.2.4.1 Constructor

Recall from §2.2.1.2 the constructor's job: define the class structure and assign default values. The constructor shown in Code Listing 4 meets all the requirements; it has the right name, it creates a structure, and it calls **class** to convert the structure into an object. All we have to do is make sure the file is stored as **/@cShape/cShape.m**. The structure is no longer being constructed with a **dummy** field but rather includes the private variables identified in §3.2.2: **mSize**, **mScale**, and **mColorRgb**. By setting the private variables to reasonable initial values, we avoid member function errors and allow clients the luxury of omitting a lot of error-checking code.

```
Code Listing 4, A Very Simple Constructor
1    function this = cShape
2    this = struct( ...
3      'mSize', ones(2,1), ... % scaled [width height]' of bounding
       box
4      'mScale', ones(2,1), ... % [width height]' scale factor
5      'mColorRgb', [0 0 1]' ... % [R G B]' of border, default
       is blue
6      );
7    this = class(this, 'cShape');
```

3.2.4.2 Accessors

The class' various interface functions were identified and defined in §3.2.2. Clients have read access for every private variable. A get function from a get and set pair was defined as the interface to both **mSize** and **mScale**. Accessors do not come any simpler compared to those shown in Code Listing 5 and Code Listing 6 for **getSize.m** and **getScale.m**, respectively. The first line defines the function. The second line uses dot-reference syntax to assign the private variable value to the return argument. The simplicity of these functions relies on the operation of the constructor and the mutators. For the **cShape** class, the constructor and the mutators must carefully control what is assigned into the private variables.

Code Listing 5, getSize.m Public Member Function

```
1    function ShapeSize = getSize(this)
2    ShapeSize = this.mSize;
```

Code Listing 6, getScale.m Public Member Function

```
1    function ShapeScale = getScale(this)
2    ShapeScale = this.mScale;
```

The private variable **mColorRgb** also gets an accessor, but we will not implement its accessor using a get function. Instead, the implementation combines both accessor and mutator into a single function. The implementation is found in §3.2.4.4.

3.2.4.3 Mutators

Like the accessors, the mutators were identified and defined in §3.2.2. Clients have write access for every private variable. A set function from a **get** and **set** pair was defined as the interface to both **mSize** and **mScale**. Mutators rarely get any simpler compared to those shown in Code Listing 7 and Code Listing 8 for **setSize.m** and **setScale.m**, respectively.

Code Listing 7, setSize.m Public Member Function

```
1    function this = setSize(this, ShapeSize)
2    this.mScale = ones(2,1);      % reset scale to 1:1 when size
     is set
3    switch length(ShapeSize(:))
4      case 1
5        this.mSize = [ShapeSize; ShapeSize];
6      case 2
7        this.mSize = ShapeSize(:);   % ensure 2x1
8      otherwise
9        error('ShapeSize must be a scalar or length == 2');
10   end
```

In Code Listing 7, line 1 defines the function. Line 2 sets the horizontal and vertical scale factor to 1:1 whenever a new size is assigned. This behavior was not specified, but it seems to be a reasonable thing to do. The alternate behavior would simply leave the scale factor with its current value. Line 3 enters a switch based on the number of values passed via **ShapeSize**. Line 5 expands the size value to both directions when a scalar value is passed in. This behavior was not specified, but most MATLAB functions seem to provide this sort of flexibility. Line 7 performs the assignment when two values are passed in. These two values can occupy two elements of an array of any dimension, and they will still be correctly assigned into **mSize** as a 2×1 column. Again, this behavior was not specified, but such flexibility is generally expected. Finally, if any number of values other than 1 or 2 is passed in, an error is thrown.

In most respects, Code Listing 8 is equivalent to Code Listing 7. Line 2 is different because it calls the **reset** function. Since we are applying a new scale factor, we need to reset the shape

```
Code Listing 8, setScale.m Public Member Function
1   function this = setScale(this, ShapeScale)
2   this = reset(this);  % back to original size (see Code
    Listing 10)
3   switch length(ShapeScale(:))
4     case 1
5       this.mScale = [ShapeScale; ShapeScale];
6     case 2
7       this.mScale = ShapeScale(:);  % ensure 2x1
8     otherwise
9       error('ShapeScale must be a scalar or length == 2');
10  end
11  this.mSize = this.mSize .* this.mScale;  % apply new scale
```

back to its original size before we can apply and store the new scale. The details for **reset** can be found in §3.2.4.5. Line 11 resizes the shape by multiplying the reset size by the new scale value.

These two functions demonstrate the elegance of encapsulation by keeping **mSize** and **mScale** in synch. The two variables are coupled so that whenever one changes, the other must also change. Encapsulation enforces the use of the member functions, making it impossible for clients to change one without changing the other. The coupled values always maintain their proper relationships.

3.2.4.4 Combining an Accessor and a Mutator

So far, we have not defined an accessor or mutator for **mColorRgb**. We could of course define a get and set pair of functions, but we have already investigated that syntax. Instead, let's look at a syntax that combines the functionality of both accessor and mutator into a single member function. The combined implementation is shown in Code Listing 9.

```
Code Listing 9, ColorRgb.m Public Member Function
1   function return_val = ColorRgb(this, Color)
2   switch nargin  % get or set depending on number of arguments
3     case 1
4       return_val = getColorRgb(this);
5     case 2
6       return_val = setColorRgb(this, Color);
7   end
8     otherwise
9   % --------------------------------
10  function ColorRgb = getColorRgb(this)
11  ColorRgb = this.mColorRgb;
12
13  % --------------------------------
14  function this = setColorRgb(this, Color)
15  if length(Color(:)) ~= 3
16    error('Color must be length == 3');
17  end
18  if any(Color(:) > 1) | any(Color(:) < 0)
19    error('all RGB Color values must be between 0 and 1');
20  end
21  this.mColorRgb = Color(:);  % ensure 3x1
```

The **switch** in line 2 sorts out whether the member function is being called as an accessor or mutator. If **nargin** equals one, the lone input must be a **cShape** object. The function is not provided with an assignment value; therefore, the client must be requesting read access. Read access calls the subfunction **getColorRgb** and simply returns the value stored in **mColorRgb**.

If **nargin** equals two, the function operates as a mutator. In the two-argument case, the object and the assignment value are passed into the subfunction **setColorRgb**. Line 15 verifies the number of color values, and line 18 verifies their values. If the values are okay, they are assigned into the object as a 3×1 column. The modified object is passed back to the client.

The switch in line 2 doesn't need an **otherwise** case because MATLAB will never allow a member function other than the constructor to be called without an argument. Function-search rules allow MATLAB to locate a function inside a class directory only when an argument's type matches the type of a known class. With no argument, MATLAB has no type to check. MATLAB might find and execute a **ColorRgb** function, but it will not belong to any class.

3.2.4.5 Member Functions

With the current set of member functions, it is easy to get the wrong idea about accessors and mutators. Accessors and mutators are *not* limited to simply returning or assigning values one-to-one with private member variables. As we add capability to **cShape**, we will see that accessors and mutators are more varied. Member functions can do anything a normal MATLAB function can do because they are normal MATLAB functions. Just because they possess the special privilege of reading and writing private variables does not preclude them from doing other things. This includes calling member functions, calling general functions, graphing data, and accessing global data.

As an initial example, the expanded requirements stipulate a **reset** function. Unlike the other member functions, neither the function name nor the argument list implies a direct connection to a private variable. We know **reset** is a mutator because it passes the object back to the client. As long as **reset** behaves properly, clients do not need to worry about the private changes that take place. Behaving properly in the current context means resetting the shape's scale to 1:1 and adjusting the size back to the value assigned in the constructor or in **setSize**. The implementation is provided in Code Listing 10.

Code Listing 10, reset.m Public Member Function

```
1    function this = reset(this)
2    for k = 1:length(this(:))
3      this(k).mSize = this(k).mSize ./ this(k).mScale; % divide
         by scale
4      this(k).mScale = ones(2,1);   % reset scale to 1:1
5    end
```

Line 1 defines the function. The function is a mutator because the object, **this**, is passed in and out. Line 2 loops over all objects in **this**. We could vectorize the code with calls to **num2cell** and **deal**. Line 3 calculates the object's size by dividing the current size by the current scale. This calculation never needs to worry about a variable mismatch because the mutators work together in ensuring that data are always stored in the proper format. A simple addition to **setScale** could add protection from divide-by-zero warnings. Line 4 resets the scale back to 1:1.

3.2.5 STANDARDIZATION

The current implementation presents two equivalent implementation approaches that result in big differences in client syntax. One method uses a pair of get and set functions, while the other combines accessor and mutator capabilities into a single function. In my opinion, it is a bad idea to follow this example and mix the use of both methods in the interface for a single class. It is much better to choose one method and apply it consistently. In a similar vein, a library composed of many classes is simply easier to use when all member functions use the same syntax. This broadens the scope considerably because it typically means development teams should standardize around a single method.

It seems reasonable to ask which approach is better. Unfortunately, there is no clear-cut winner. The combined syntax is convenient because it results in fewer m-files overall. The combined syntax also collects code associated with the same variable into the same source file. In my experience, co-located accessor and mutator code is easier to maintain. On the other hand, get and set syntax inherently describes the interface. If a variable has no associated set function, it means the variable is not mutable, at least not directly. Identifying read-only versus read-write variables based on the member function list is easy. The function name used by the combined syntax does not provide this level of detail. In Chapter 8, when we will discuss a command-line feature called tab completion, we will see how to get a complete list of public member functions. Finally, some clients prefer get and set syntax.

Fortunately, MATLAB provides another alternative. Consider again our earlier attempt to inspect the value **shape.dummy**. We tried this approach because the syntax is universally recognized. It says there is a structure variable named **shape** and we think it has a field named **dummy**. Using dot-reference notation is elegant, easy, and entrenched. What if MATLAB included a way for objects to handle dot-reference notation? If such a feature exists, choosing get and set vs. a combined syntax is a lot less urgent. MATLAB does indeed support this capability. We will discuss dot-reference support in the next chapter. First, let's take the current **cShape** class for a test drive.

3.3 THE TEST DRIVE

Our class now has the beginnings of an interface and we can use the interface to interact with objects of the class. We need to construct some **cShape** objects and exercise the interface. We need to both demonstrate the syntax and make sure objects behave according to the requirements. The commands shown in Code Listing 11 provide a sample of **cShape**'s new capability.

```
Code Listing 11, Chapter 3 Test-Drive Command Listing

1    >> cd 'C:/oop_guide/chapter_3'
2    >> set(0, 'FormatSpacing', 'compact')
3    >> clear classes; clc;
4    >> shape = cShape;
5    >> shape = setSize(shape, [2 3]);
6    >> getSize(shape)'
7    ans =
8       2       3
9    >> shape = ColorRgb(shape, [1 0 1]);
10   >> ColorRgb(shape)'
11   ans =
12      1       0       1
13   >> getScale(shape)'
14   ans =
15      1       1
16   >> shape = setScale(shape, [2 4]);
17   >> getScale(shape)'
18   ans =
19      2       4
```

```
20  >> getSize(shape)
21  ans =
22    4       12
23  >> shape = reset(shape);
24  >> getSize(shape)
25  ans =
26    2       3
27  >> shape
28  shape =
29    cShape object: 1-by-1
```

From the command results, we see that objects of the class behave as we expect. Lines 1–3 move us into the correct directory, configure the display format, and clear the workspace. Line 4 calls the **cShape** constructor. Line 5 assigns a size, and line 6 shows that the size was correctly assigned.* Similarly, lines 9 and 10 mutate and access the shape's color using the dual-purpose function **ColorRgb**. Line 13 displays the default scale factor, and line 16 assigns a new scale. Lines 17–22 show that directly mutating the scale indirectly mutates the size. Lines 23–26 show that **reset** returns size back to its most recent **setSize** value. Finally, displaying the shape results in the same cryptic message we saw in Chapter 2. In Chapter 5, we will replace this cryptic output with an output tailored for the class.

3.4 SUMMARY

The primary topic in this chapter was encapsulation. Encapsulation is one of the three pillars of object-oriented programming and as such carries a heavy load. Therefore, it is impossible to cover every aspect in one chapter. This chapter did lay a solid foundation by including the most important aspects. Primarily, encapsulation includes the idea of an interface, and an interface brings with it a separation between so-called members and nonmembers. Membership has its privileges. For a class, membership means unrestricted access to hidden or private variables and functions. Non-members are restricted to public variables and functions.

Member functions are physically located inside a class directory. This allows MATLAB to find them by checking a variable's type. To do this, MATLAB follows the search path. We saw that additional object-oriented search locations are one of the many consequences of encapsulation. Now that we understand both path rules and encapsulation, locating the additional search directories is a simple matter of applying the rules.

Member functions come in three flavors: constructor, accessor, and mutator. These three types of member functions work in concert to provide object consistency. Each type serves a particular role in the client-to-object interface. Constructors create the object's private structure and assign default values. Accessors provide read access, while mutators provide assignment capability. Encapsulation supports different connection options between the interface and the private variables. The most straightforward connects private variables one-to-one with an interface function. The most powerful completely separates the interface from the implementation. The most common uses a combination of the two.

Even though the member functions in this chapter are basic, they reveal the potential power of encapsulation. By adding these pieces, our object-oriented puzzle is off to a good start. Figure 3.1 shows us that we are missing pieces, but it also shows us that we are well on our way toward filling out the frame.

---

* The member variable **mSize** should not be confused with the MATLAB function **size**. They represent different things. Now suppose we developed a combined accessor and mutator named **Size**. The potential for confusion is certainly high.

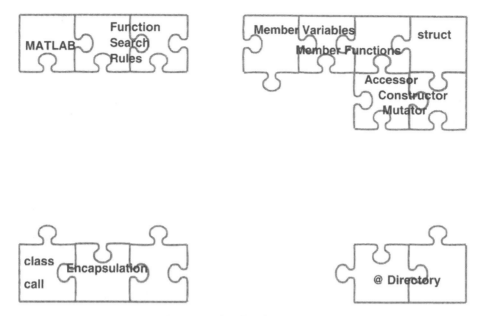

FIGURE 3.1 Puzzle with member variable, member function, and encapsulation.

3.5 INDEPENDENT INVESTIGATIONS

1. Modify **setScale** to protect other member functions from divide by zero errors.
2. Investigate path-search rules in action. Create functions with the same name, locate them in various directories, and call them with various arguments. Place a function in a **/private** directory in the class directory and see if MATLAB can find it. Try to get MATLAB to find a function located in a **/private/private** directory. Inside each function, you can use **mfilename('fullpath')** to display the complete search path. You can also use **keyboard** to prevent an infinite recursive loop.
3. Investigate more implementation alternatives. Instead of a series of **get** and **set** pairs tailored for each member variable, can you design a general accessor named **get.m** and a general mutator named **set.m**? (Hint: look at help for **getfield** and **setfield**.) If your implementation relies on a large **switch** statement, can you use dynamic-field-name syntax instead? Which implementation is more extendable and maintainable?
4. Try to enhance the interface. Most of your clients want to set the color using a string like **'red'** or **'blue'**. What do you do: eliminate the use of [r g b] values from the interface spec? Write a new member function? Modify **ColorRgb.m**? (Hint: look at help for **ischar** and **isnumeric**.) How does each choice influence quality measures?
5. Examine one benefit of encapsulation. Suppose you need to change the implementation and store colors in HSV (hue–saturation–value) format but you can't change the interface in any way. What changes are required inside **ColorRgb.m**? (Hint: look at help for **rgb2hsv** and **hsv2rgb**.) Do you need to change other member functions? Don't forget the constructor. You should be able to implement this change. Try it and see how well you can do.
6. Examine another encapsulation option. Half your member functions need an RGB format, and half need HSV. Clients always specify colors in terms of RGB. You have three options: store the color using RGB format, store the color using HSV format, or store both formats and rely on member functions to keep them synchronized. Which option do you choose? Suppose you know the color is rarely changed and the conversion from

RGB to HSV is very expensive. Does this additional information push you toward a different option? Without the benefit of encapsulation, keeping multiple copies of the same data is risky business. Does encapsulation change the level of risk involved?

4 Changing the Rules ... in Appearance Only

Near the end of the previous chapter, I alluded to the fact that MATLAB gives us a way to tailor standard dot-reference syntax to suit the needs of our objects. In the eyes of our clients, dot-reference tailoring makes an object look like a structure. This gives objects an enormous boost. If objects look like structures, using objects rather than structures is completely transparent. Transparency is a good thing because it gives us immediate access to a very powerful tool we can use to protect the integrity of our code, encapsulation.

The good news is that MATLAB allows dot-reference tailoring. In this chapter, we will develop a set of member functions that implement the tailoring in a way that allows objects to mimic structures. We will take advantage of a pair of standard, but relatively unknown, functions, **subsref.m** and **subsasgn.m**. The built-in versions operate on structures. Tailored versions, as long as MATLAB can find them, operate on objects. From Chapter 3, we know MATLAB will find them as long as they exist in the class directory as member functions. As tailored member functions, **subsref.m** and **subsasgn.m** are so critical to object-oriented programming that they share a place beside the constructor in the group of eight.

4.1 A SPECIAL ACCESSOR AND A SPECIAL MUTATOR

The reason these very important functions are not well-known is that outside the realm of object-oriented programming, they are almost never called by name. MATLAB classifies these functions as operators in the same way it classifies symbols like **+**, **-**, **/**, and **~=** as operators. There are many operators (see Table 4.1), but the distinguishing feature is syntax. When MATLAB encounters an operator, it orders the arguments and converts the operator's symbol into a function call. Unless you understand what it means to be an operator, you might not realize what is going on behind the scenes. Shortly we will specifically examine **subsref.m** and **subsasgn.m** operators. First, let's take a brief side trip to discuss operators and introduce a technique called operator overloading.

4.1.1 A Short Side Trip to Examine Overloading

Most of the symbols you can type from the keyboard have special meaning. The meanings behind **+**, **-**, **/**, and **~=** are clear. These special symbols are called operators. When MATLAB interprets a line of code, it maps every operator to an m-file. Table 4.1 lists the mapping from symbol to m-file. From the command line, you can display a similar list using **help ops**. If you look at the list you see conversions like **+** $\Rightarrow$ **plus.m** and **<=** $\Rightarrow$ **le.m**. We can call these functions by name, but we almost never do because operator syntax is a lot easier.

Stop for a minute and consider the implications. Every operator maps to an m-file, and the execution of every m-file is determined based on the search path. That means we can redefine the operation of any operator. All we have to do is create a new m-file with the same name as the operator and put it in a directory with a higher search-path priority. For objects, we simply put the tailored operator function in the class directory. Since MATLAB searches for member functions before it searches for built-in functions, the tailored function has higher priority. Clients use normal operator syntax, and MATLAB conveniently finds the appropriate function.

TABLE 4.1
Overloadable Operators

Operator Symbol	m-file Name
a & b	and.m
a:b	colon.m
a'	ctranspose.m
a(end)	end.m
a == b	eq.m
a >= b	ge.m
a > b	gt.m
[a b]	horzcat.m
a .\ b	ldivide.m
a <= b	le.m
loading object from .MAT file	loadobj.m
a < b	lt.m
a – b	minus.m
a \ b	mldivide.m
a ^ b	mpower.m
a / b	mrdivide.m
a * b	mtimes.m
a ~= b	ne.m
~a	not.m
a | b	or.m
a + b	plus.m
a .^ b	power.m
a ./ b	rdivide.m
saving object to .MAT file.	saveobj.m
a(k)=b, a{k}=b, or a.field=b	subsasgn.m
x(a)	subsindex.m
a(k), a{k}, and a.field	subsref.m
a .* b	times.m
a.'	transpose.m
-a	uminus.m
+a	uplus.m
[a; b]	vertcat.m

Object-oriented terminology calls this technique operator overloading, and every function in Table 4.1 can be overloaded. When MATLAB encounters operator syntax, it collects variables into argument lists and calls the operator's function. Once you know the name of the operator's function, you can display the function's help information to get a description of the arguments. For example, the statement **c = a + b;** converts to the function equivalent **c = plus(a, b);**.

Operator overloading represents an important subset of general function overloading. General function overloading allows a class to customize the operation of virtually any function by including a tailored copy of the function in the class directory. Thus, any discussion of overloading involves two functions, the function doing the overloading and the function being overloaded. Let's refer to the function doing the overloading as the tailored version and to the function being overloaded as the original version.

With very few exceptions, MATLAB allows a class to overload any function. The original function might exist as a built-in function or as a function on the path. If we jump ahead and consider inheritance, the original function might also exist as a parent-class function. In short, once a class overloads a function, the location of the original isn't too important.

Given the ability to overload almost any function, you are also given the responsibility of doing it wisely. Unfortunately, this is an area where experience is the best guide. There are few hard-and-fast rules, but there are some things to consider. Original functions are generally well understood, and overloading works best when the behavior of the tailored version can be inferred from the behavior of the original. The argument syntax of an original function is also well-known, and the tailored version should match the syntax very closely. This is particularly true for operator overloading because you can't control the conversion from operator syntax to function call. The implementation examples and the group of eight represent a good resource for examining operator and function overloading. As we progress through the example code, you will be building experience.

4.1.1.1 Superiorto and Inferiorto

In §3.2.3 the description of function-search rules conveniently assumed there was only one input argument. Finding the correct function is a simple matter of including the argument's class directory in the search. Most functions require more than one input argument. With the prospect of more than one type, we need to understand what MATLAB does to locate the correct function.

Some object-oriented languages select a function based on the combination of all input arguments; however, MATLAB always uses one input argument. For functions with more than one input, a priority scheme picks the argument with the highest priority. By default, **class** creates all classes at the same priority level. After that, user-defined types can increase their relative priority by calling **superiorto** and decrease it by calling **inferiorto**. Calls to these functions must occur inside the constructor, and that means built-in types cannot change their priority. When one argument clearly has the highest priority, its type is used in the search. When one argument is not the clear winner, argument order is used as a tiebreaker. In this case, the type of the first tied argument in the argument list is used.

If all arguments have the same type, MATLAB uses the type of the very first argument. This is convenient for a number of reasons. First, a single priority eliminates errors that occur due to unanticipated argument combinations. If you set up a complicated priority tree, it is easy to find yourself in an unexpected function call. Second, a single priority makes it easy to understand which class directory will be selected. It will always correspond to the first argument's type. Finally, with a single priority you never need to search the argument list to find **this**. The active object is always passed in the first position.

Classes that overload operators usually need to increase their priority relative to built-in types.* This is particularly true for commutative operators like + because the object can be passed using either argument. Relying on default priority will result in an error about half the time. When the object shows up on the left side of the operator, the tailored version executes and all is well; however, when the object shows up on the right-hand side, MATLAB will call the built-in version and the built-in version does not know what to do with an object. For example, **obj+1** is converted into the function call expressed as **plus(obj, 1)**. Here the **plus** function associated with **obj** correctly executes. Switch the argument order to **1+obj** and the conversion becomes **plus(1, obj)**. If **1** and **obj** have the same priority, the built-in **plus** will be called and the result will be an error. To remedy this situation, the constructor needs to include the command **superiorto('double')**.

Other than superiority over built-in types, the software design ultimately determines the complexity of the priority tree and thus represents a barrier to implementing some object-oriented designs in MATLAB. The barrier is not impossible to cross but does limit extendibility in some designs. When one of the design constraints is to limit the number of priority levels, the result is

---

* In version 7.1 (R14), this is no longer true. User-defined types are superior to the built-in types. Relative argument priority still applies to operations using user-defined types.

a better implementation. For designs with a small number of classes and a reasonably flat structure, the risk is low. By the time your designs approach that level of complexity, you will be well equipped to consider priority as a constraint.

4.1.1.2 The Built-In Function

More often than you might imagine, you need to call the original version of a function from inside the tailored version. For example, suppose you design a class interface that makes objects of the class look like a simple one-dimensional array of doubles. To implement the interface, you need to overload **length**, **ndims**, **numel**, and **size**. Depending on the private variable organization, all of these tailored functions might need to call the built-in version of **size**. We can't simply write **size(this)** because path rules insist on running the tailored version.

The **builtin** function solves this problem. The argument syntax for **builtin** uses the same syntax as **feval**. The name of the function is the first input argument, and the remaining inputs are passed into the function named in argument one. The output arguments are declared the same as if the function was being called directly. The prototype for this function is

```
[y1, …, yn] = builtin('function_name', x1, …, xn);
```

The availability of **builtin** solves one problem but creates another. Clients can use **builtin** to circumvent the interface and violate the integrity of the encapsulation. Unfortunately, we can't stop them. All we can reasonably do is dissuade them from using **builtin** and periodically search for its use.

4.1.2 OVERLOADING THE OPERATORS SUBSREF AND SUBSASGN

It may come as a surprise to realize that ., (), and {} are operators. If you scan Table 4.1, you will see that dot-reference, array-reference, and cell-reference syntax map to **subsref.m** and **subsasgn.m**. Thus, using one of these index operators on an object tells MATLAB to call that object's version of **subsref** or **subsasgn**. It is up to us to include the appropriate class-specific commands in the body of each. These functions are the most important operator functions we will encounter because they allow us to create an easy-to-use interface. This will become clear as we progress through the examples. The accessor is **subsref**, and the mutator is **subsasgn**. Each function can determine which operator triggered the call because MATLAB passes a specially formatted version of the operator along with the other arguments.

In Chapter 3 the only member function tools at our disposal consisted of a pair of **get** and **set** functions for each public member variable. With operator overloading and the availability of **subsref** and **subsasgn**, **get** and **set** syntax can be easily replaced by dot-reference syntax. Doing so makes the interface a lot more convenient because it looks like something very familiar, a structure.

In the test drive for Chapter 3, we wrote,

```
shape_size = getSize(shape);

shape = setSize(shape, [10; 20]);
```

In the test drive for this chapter, we will be able to write,

```
shape_size = shape.size;

shape.size = [10; 20];
```

Compared to the other operators, more code is required to implement tailored versions of **subsref** and **subsasgn**. For the most part the additional code results from the fact that each function must handle three operators. Using a switch statement to select the appropriate case is an easy approach. First, let's look at the function syntax.

The function definitions for **subsref.m** and **subsasgn.m** can be written as

```
function varargout = subsref(this, index)

function this = subsasgn(this, index, varargin)
```

In both cases the first argument is the active object **this**. Since MATLAB passes **this** as the first argument, these operator overloads don't require calls **superiorto** or **inferiorto**.

The second argument, **index**, is a specially packaged version of the operator and indices. In addition to supporting three different operators, **index** also supports multiple index levels. Another obscure function, **substruct**, can be used to create the special packaging, and because of this, the **index** format is also called **substruct**. All **substruct** indices are stored as a structure array with two fields:

index(k).type

index(k).subs

Each index level represented by **index(k)** contains a **type** field and a **subs** field. The **type** field is a string containing one of three string values: `'.'`, `()`, or `{}`. These three string values respectively represent a dot-reference, array-reference, and cell-reference operation. When MATLAB converts operator syntax into an **index**, only certain combinations of operators and levels are converted.

When the **type** field is `'.'`, the **subs** field will contain a character string that names the desired public member variable. When the **type** field is `()` or `{}`, the **subs** field will contain a cell array. Each cell index holds the index values for one dimension. The values in **index(k).subs{1}** are used to select values in the first dimension, values in **index(k).subs{2}** the second dimension, and so on. With one exception, the index values will be packaged as a fully expanded array. The lone exception occurs when the specified index was `':'`. In that case, the index value is equal to `':'`. Fortunately, when the **type** field is `()` or `{}`, we don't need to manage the contents of the **subs** field on our own. Instead, we can coerce MATLAB into performing all of the low-level work. We still have to process `'.'` and the public variable names; but, since there is only one format, that is the easy case.

The standard set of allowed values for **type** is well defined and small, making a **switch** statement ideal for implementation.* The **switch** skeleton is shown in Code Listing 12. This

---

Code Listing 12, Skeleton Switch Statement for subsref and subsasgn

```
1    switch index (1).type
2      case '.'
3        % code to deal with the fieldname in index(1).subs
4      case '()'
5        % code to deal with an array of index values
6      case '{}'
7        % code to deal with cell array of index values
8      otherwise
9        error(['Unexpected index.type of ' index(1).type]);
10   end
```

---

* It is possible to pass nonstandard operators into **subsref** and **subsasgn** but not via automatic operator conversion. A manually created **substruct** index can include an arbitrary **type** string, and this index can be passed into **substruct** or **subsasgn** if the functions are called by name. Adding new access categories might seem bizarre, but might actually be useful under the right set of circumstances. Nonstandard indices are not supported by the built-in versions of **subsref** and **subsasgn**, and they are not supported by Class Wizard.

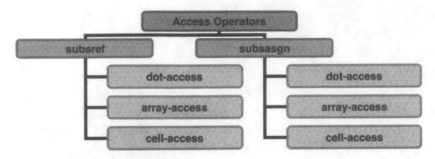

FIGURE 4.1 Access operator organizational chart.

skeleton is used inside both **subsref** and **subsasgn**. Before filling in code for each case, I need to outline an approach for discussing the boxes shown in Figure 4.1. One organization discusses all cases of **subsref** before moving on to all cases of **subsasgn**. The alternate organization discusses one operator **case** with respect to both access and mutation before moving on to the next. As you might expect, there is a lot of overlap between these alternate paths. The discussion seems to work better when access and mutation for a single **case** are covered together.

4.1.2.1 Dot-Reference Indexing

The dot-reference operator looks something like the following:

```
b = a.field;

a.field = b;
```

When MATLAB encounters these statements, it converts them into the equivalent function calls given respectively by

```
b = subsref(a, substruct('.', 'field'));

a = subsasgn(a, substruct('.', 'field'), b);
```

The two representations are exactly equivalent. You will probably agree that dot-reference operator syntax is much easier to read at a glance compared to the functional form. The functional form gives us some important details to use during the implementation of **subsref** and **subsasgn**.

With either conversion, the **index** variable passed into both **subsref** and **subsasgn** is composed using **substruct('.', 'field')**. The **type** field is of course **'.'** and the element name is represented here by the **subs** field value **'field'**. The **substruct** argument is a structure, and the MATLAB display looks like the following:

```
1    >> index = substruct('.',   'field')
2    index =
3        type: '.'
4        subs: 'field'
```

If all we want to do is provide a 1:1 mapping between public and private member variables, the **'.'** case of **subsref** would include just one line*:

---

* Dynamic fieldname indexing works for versions 7.0 and later. In some earlier versions, dynamic field syntax did not always work from inside a member function. If dynamic fieldname syntax generates an error, revert to the use of properly formatted calls to **getfield** or **setfield**.

```
varargout = {this.(index(1).subs)};
```

Similarly, the '.' case of **subsasgn** would include the following line:

```
this.(index(1).subs) = varargin{1};
```

The one-line 1:1 mapping code works well as an introduction but is too simplistic for most classes. For example, the one-line solution does not support multiple indexing levels, and it doesn't support argument checking. Even worse, the one-line solution maps every private member variable as public. It is easy to address each of these deficiencies by adding more code and checking more cases. By the end of this chapter, we will have a good working knowledge of **subsref** and **subsasgn**, but we will not yet arrive at their final implementation. The final implementation relies on first developing some of the other group-of-eight members.

4.1.2.2 subsref Dot-Reference, Attempt 1

One potential solution to the **subsref** challenge is shown in Code Listing 13. This solution is similar to the solution outlined in the MATLAB manuals and is more versatile than the previous one-liner. This approach might be okay for simple classes, but for classes that are more complicated it needs improvement. The biggest downfall of the implementation in Code Listing 13 is the coupling between the dot-reference name and private variable names. It also doesn't take care of multiple index levels and is not as modular as we might like. Such complaints are easily remedied. It just takes a little more work to push it over the top.

```
Code Listing 13, By-the-Book Approach to subref's Dot-Reference Case
1    switch index(1).type
2    case '.'
3      switch index(1).subs
4      case 'mSize'
5        varargout = {this.mSize};
6      case 'mScale'
7        varargout = {this.mScale};
8      case 'mColorRgb'
9        varargout = {this.mColorRgb};
10     otherwise
11       error(['??? Reference to non-existent field ' ...
12       index(1).subs '.']);
13     end
14   case '()'
15     % code to deal with cell array of index values
16   case '{}'
17     % code to deal with cell array of index values
18   otherwise
19     error(['??? Unexpected index.type of ' index(1).type]);
20   end
```

Line 1 references the operator's type. For dot-reference the type string is '.' and execution enters the case on line 2. Line 3 references the name included in the dot-reference index. This name, specified by the client, is part of the public interface. That is an important point that bears repeating. The string contained in **index(1).subs** is a public name. The situation in this code example can be very confusing because the client's interface and the private member variables share the same name. Lines 4, 6, and 8 assign the private member variable with the same dot-reference name into the output variable, **varargout**. We already know that object-oriented rules prohibit clients from directly accessing private variables, but the contents of this version of **sub-sref** seem like an attempt to get around the restriction. The source of the confusion comes from making the public dot-reference names identical to the private variable names. The client doesn't gain direct access to each private member variable but the names make it seem so. The specific cell-array assignment syntax in lines 5, 7, and 9 supports later extensions where **this** will exist as an array of structures. Finally, line 11 throws an error if the client asks for a dot-reference name not included in the list.

The **subsref** syntax is different compared to the **get** and **set** syntax from Chapter 3. Clients usually prefer **subsref** syntax because it is identical to accessing a structure. In Chapter 3, the only interface tool in our member function toolbox was **get** and **set**. With the addition of **subsref**, we can now define a friendly interface. In doing so we will deprecate some of Chapter 3's interface syntax.

4.1.2.3 A New Interface Definition

The initial interface syntax was defined in §3.2.2.2. Here we are going to make a couple of changes that both take advantage of dot-reference syntax and allow the investigation of specific implementation issues. The client's new view of the interface is defined as

```
shape = cShape;

shape_size = shape.Size;

shape.Size = shape_size;

shape = shape_scale * shape;

shape = shape * shape_scale;

shape_color = shape.ColorRgb;

shape.ColorRgb = shape_color;

shape = reset(shape);
```

where

> **shape** is an object of type **cShape**.
> **shape_size** is the 2×1 numeric vector [horizontal_size; vertical_size] with an initial value of [1; 1].
> **shape_scale** is the 2×1 numeric vector [horizontal_scale; vertical_scale] with an initial value of [1; 1].
> **shape_color** is the 3×1 numeric vector [red; green; blue] with an initial value of [0; 0; 1].

Notice that the only member functions implied by syntax are the constructor, **cShape.m**, and **reset**. The functions **getSize**, **setSize**, and **ColorRgb** have been completely replaced by **subsref**, **subsasgn**, and dot-reference syntax. Also, notice the abstraction of the client's use of a scale factor into multiplication and **reset**.

4.1.2.4 subsref Dot-Reference, Attempt 2: Separating Public and Private Variables

From the by-the-book approach in Code Listing 13, it would be easy to get the idea that objects are just encapsulated structures and that **subsref** and **subsasgn** simply avoid a collection of **get** and **set** functions. Nothing could be further from the truth. The real purpose of **subsref** and **subsasgn** is to support encapsulation by producing an easy-to-use interface.

Let's formalize some terminology that will simplify the discussions. To the client, values associated with **subsref**'s dot-reference names are not hidden. Furthermore, dot-reference syntax makes these values appear to be variables rather than functions. Based on appearances, we will refer to the collection of dot-reference names as *public member variables*. This will differentiate them from the fields in the private structure, that is, the *private member variables*. Even in Code Listing 13, where public member variables and private member variables shared the same names, clients could not directly access private variables. Cases inside **subsref** guard against direct access.

As we will soon see, **subsasgn** also uses a switch on the dot-reference name and cases inside **subsasgn** guard against direct mutation. The fact that MATLAB uses one function for access, **subsref**, and a different function for mutation, **subsasgn**, gives us added flexibility. At our option, we can include a public variable name in the switch of **subsref**, **subsasgn**, or both. If the public variable name is included in **subsref**, the variable is *readable*. If the public variable name is included in **subsasgn**, the public member variable is *writable*. A public variable is both readable and writable when the name is included in both **subsref** and **subsasgn**. Independently controlled read and write permissions also differentiate object-oriented programming from most procedural programming. A complete interface specification should include the restrictions read-only and write-only as appropriate, and these restrictions should be included in the implementations of **subsref** and **subsasgn**.

Use different names to reinforce the idea that private member variables are separate from public member variables. This is where the lowercase 'm' convention is useful. In one-to-one public-to-private associations, the 'm' makes the code more obvious. The variable with a leading 'm' is private, and the one without is public. There is a second part to the 'm' convention. If private variables are named using the 'm' convention, no public variable should include a leading 'm'. For coding standards that only allow lowercase characters in variable names, expand the convention from 'm' to 'm_' to avoid private names beginning with 'mm'.

The **subsref switch** in Code Listing 14 implements the replacement. The difference from the by-the-book approach occurs in lines 4 and 6, where the 'm' has been removed from the **case** strings. The **mScale** case has also been removed. Now, dot-reference names match the new interface definition from §4.1.2.3. Most variables in this example are still one-to-one, public-to-private. Let's remedy that situation next.

4.1.2.5 subsref Dot-Reference, Attempt 3: Beyond One-to-One, Public-to-Private

For an example of a general public variable implementation, let's change the internal color format. One of the exercises at the end of Chapter 3 asked you to consider this exact change. Instead of storing red-green-blue (RGB) values, we want to change the class implementation to store hue-saturation values (HSV). For this change, we are not allowed to change the interface defined in §4.1.2.3. According to the interface, the public variables use RGB values and the implementation change must not cause errors in client code. To help in this change, MATLAB provides two conversion functions, **hsv2rgb** and **rgb2hsv**. These functions allow us to convert between RGB and HSV color representations.

Code Listing 14, Public Variable Names in subref's Dot-Reference Case

```
1    switch index(1).type
2    case '.'
3      switch index(1).subs
4      case 'Size'
5        varargout = {this.mSize};
6      case 'ColorRgb'
7        varargout = {this.mColorRgb};
8      otherwise
9        error(['??? Reference to non-existent field ' ...
10       index(1).subs '.']);
11     end
12   case '()'
13     % code to deal with cell array of index values
14   case '{}'
15     % code to deal with cell array of index values
16   otherwise
17     error(['??? Unexpected index.type of ' index(1).type]);
18   end
```

Modify the constructor by replacing all occurrences of **mColorRgb** with **mColorHsv**. Also in the constructor, set the value for **mColorHsv** to **rgb2hsv([0 0 1])'**. The modified constructor code is shown in Code Listing 15. Line 5 replaces **mColorRgb** with **mColorHsv** and assigns blue as the default color. Line 8 also represents an addition over the earlier constructor. Here we increase the superiority of **cShape** with respect to **double** because the interface definition overloads the associative operator, **mtimes**.

The change to **subsref** is almost as simple and is completely isolated inside the **ColorRgb case**. The modified **ColorRgb case** code is shown in Code Listing 16. Line 2 uses **hsv2rgb**

Code Listing 15, Modified Constructor Using mColorHsv Instead of mColorRgb

```
1    function this = cShape
2    this = struct( ...
3      'mSize', ones(2,1),  ... % scaled [width height]' of
       bounding box
4      'mScale', ones(2,1), ... % [width height]' scale factor
5      'mColorHsv', rgb2hsv([0 0 1])' ... % [H S V]' of border,
       default, blue
6      );
7    this = class(this, 'cShape');
8    superiorto('double')
```

Code Listing 16, Converting HSV Values to RGB Values

```
1    case 'ColorRgb'
2      rgb = hsv2rgb([this.mColorHsv]')';
3      varargout = mat2cell(rgb, 3, ones(1, size(rgb,2)));
```

to convert private HSV values into public RGB values. The function will convert multiple HSV vectors by packaging each HSV 3-tuple as a row of the input matrix. Similarly, each output RGB 3-tuple is returned as a row of the output matrix. In Line 2, **[this.mColorHsv]** supports a nonscalar **this** by concatenating HSV columns. The concatenated columns are transposed before they are passed into **hsv2rgb**, and the result is transposed so that each column contains an RGB 3-tuple. Line 3 converts the combined RGB array into a cell array of 3×1 RGB vectors and assigns the cell array into **varargout**. Now, just like all the other cases, a nonscalar **this** returns multiple arguments.

To a client familiar with dot-reference and structures, dot-reference and objects looks identical. While the outward appearance is the same, inside the private implementation we can do whatever we want. As with **Size**, the public name might refer to a private member variable, but the public name can easily refer to a data conversion or a combination of several private variables. The public names are included in the interface specification and the client doesn't need to know what is really happening behind the interface.

4.1.2.6 subsref Dot-Reference, Attempt 4: Multiple Indexing Levels

If the length of the **substruct index** array is greater than one, **index** includes reference operators beyond the initial dot-reference operator. The length is unlimited; however, certain combinations of nested reference operators are illegal. For example, when the length of the indexed variable is greater than one, a second dot-reference operator generates an error. That is, when **a** is nonscalar, **a.level_1** is allowed but **a.level_1.level_2** is not. MATLAB already lives by these rules so it would be very convenient to coerce MATLAB to handle all of these details.

Code Listing 17 shows an improved version of the dot-reference **case** that can handle multiple indexing levels. This version is not as compact as before primarily due to the addition of error-checking code. Each public name case adds a check for an empty object... If the object is empty the function's return value is also empty. Lines 4–5 and 10–11 are examples. Exactly how an empty object can occur is discussed in the array-reference-operator section. When an empty object does appear, the correct return is an empty cell. The nonempty else code is identical to the code already discussed. Lines 20–35 implement multiple-level indexing.

Code Listing 17, An Improved Version of the subsref Dot-Reference Case

```
1    case '.'
2      switch index(1).subs
3        case 'Size'
4          if isempty(this)
5            varargout = {};
6          else
7            varargout = {this.mSize};
8          end
9        case 'ColorRgb'
10         if isempty(this)
11           varargout = {};
12         else
13           rgb = hsv2rgb([this.mColorHsv]')';
14           varargout = mat2cell(rgb, 3, ones(1, size(rgb,2)));
15         end
16     otherwise
```

```
17    error(['??? Reference to non-existent field '
        index(1).subs '.']);
18  end
19
20  if length(index) > 1
21    if length(varargout) == 1
22      varargout{1} = subsref(varargout{1}, index(2:end));
23    else
24      [err_id, err_msg] = array_reference_error
          (index(2).type);
25      error(err_id, err_msg);
26      switch index(2).type
27      case '.'
28        error('??? Dot name reference on non-scalar structure.');
29      case {'()' '{}'}
30        error(['??? Field reference for multiple structure ' ...
31                'elements that is followed by more reference ' ...
32                'blocks is an error.']);
33      otherwise
34        error(['??? Unexpected index type: ' index(2). type]);
35        end
36      end
```

Deeper indexing is needed when the length of the **index** array is more than one. In that case, the test in line 20 will be true. Now look at line 22 and the **subsref** call. The value that needs deeper indexing was assigned into **varargout** by the first dot-reference operation, and **index(2:end)** contains the remaining indices. Passing the initial value and the remaining indices into **subsref** will force the remaining indices to be evaluated; but which **subsref** is used?

To answer that question we need to apply function-search rules:

1. *The function is defined as a subfunction in the caller's m-file.* While this rule might seem true, the rule applies strictly to subfunctions. The primary function in the m-file is not considered as a subfunction. That eliminates **/@cShape/subsref.m.**
2. *An m-file for the function exists in the caller's /**private** directory.* There is not yet a **/@cShape/private** directory, so that rules out **/@cShape/private/subsref.m.**
3. *The m-file is a constructor.* MATLAB will not recognize a **subsref** class even if you define one. That rules out **/@subsref/subsref.m.**
4. *When the input argument is an object, the object's class directory is included in the search for the function.* The class type of the value in **varargout{1}** is used to steer MATLAB to a class-specific version of **subsref**. For user-defined types, this means a tailored version. For built-in types, this means the built-in version.

The path-search rules are beginning to make a lot of sense. Here, MATLAB saves us a lot of work by using the value's type to find the correct version of **subsref**. With every new value, the process repeats until all indices have been resolved.

The **else** clause for the test in line 21 restricts the level of indexing for nonscalar objects. For objects, the restriction is somewhat arbitrary because MATLAB will convert almost any arrangement of access-operator syntax into a **substruct index**. Code inside **subsref** gets to decide which particular arrangements it will support. In the case of structure arrays and dot-reference, the built-in version of **subsref** throws an error if the length of **index** is greater than one. In the case of object arrays and dot-reference, we could choose to process all additional indices; however, the **else** clause beginning on line 23 chooses instead to throw an error. This makes the dot-reference behavior for object arrays consistent with the dot-reference behavior of structure arrays. For scalar objects, all index levels are processed; and for nonscalar objects, the presence of index levels beyond the first dot-reference will throw an error. Line 24 selects the error message depending on the string in **index(2).type**.

The ability to detect array-indexing errors and throw an error with the correct message is something that other member functions will also need. Rather than repeating lines 24–33 in many places, it is much better to create a free function that will return the correct message. That way every class will issue the same message, thus providing a consistent look and feel. The function **array_reference_error** is shown in Code Listing 18. This function returns both the error identifier and the error message. To use this function, lines 20–35 in Code Listing 17 are replaced by the following,

```
if length(index) > 1

    if length(varargout) == 1

        varargout{1} = subsref(varargout{1}, index(2:end));

    else

      [err_id, err_msg] = array_reference_error(index(2).type);

        error(err_id, err_msg);

    end

end
```

This function must also exist on the path. Add **c:/oop_guide/utils/wizard_gui** to the MATLAB path or copy **array_reference_error.m** from the **utils/wizard_gui** directory to a directory that is already on the path.

4.1.2.7 subsref Dot-Reference, Attempt 5: Operator Conversion Anomaly

Look carefully at the answers to the various commands listed in Code Listing 19. The command in line 1 builds a regular 1×3 structure array with two dot-reference elements. The element names, sizes, and values correspond to the "shape" interface but **struct_shape** is not an object. Line 9 uses operator syntax to select two array indices and concatenate the **Size** elements from each. Exactly as we expect, the answer is **[[1;1] [2;2] [3;3]]**. Line 14 uses function syntax to request identical indexing, but the answer is not the same. For object arrays, this is a problem.

Ordinarily, you might think this is okay because the whole point of tailoring **subsref** is to allow clients the use of operator syntax and using operator syntax on line 9 produces the correct result. The problem is that access operator conversion is different for built-in types vs. user-defined types. For built-in types, MATLAB appears to interpret access-operator syntax without a call to **subsref** or **subsasgn**. For user-defined types, the only option is to convert the syntax into a call to **subsref** or **subsasgn**. This would be okay if **subsref** receives the correct value for **nargout**. Unfortunately, conversion from access-operator syntax into the equivalent function call doesn't always preserve the correct value of **nargout** ... or at least does not always preserve the same value for both built-in and user-defined types.

This behavior means that we cannot always trust the value of **nargout**. Based on the index, the tailored-version of **subsref** knows how many values to return regardless of the value in **nargout**. In fact, the syntax in each public member case has already filled in the correct number

---

Code Listing 18, A Free Function That Returns Indexing Error Messages

```
1   function [err_id, err_msg] =
    array_reference_error(index_type)
2   switch index_type
3     case '.'
4       err_id = 'MATLAB:dotRefOnNonScalar';
5       err_msg = '??? Dot name reference on non-scalar
        structure.';
6     case {'()' '{}'}
7       err_id = 'MATLAB:extraneousStrucRefBlocks';
8       err_msg = ['??? Field reference for multiple structure '
                    ...
9                   'elements that is followed by more reference '
                    ...
10                  'blocks is an error.'];
11    otherwise
12      err_id = 'OOP:unexpectedReferenceType';
13      err_msg = ['??? Unexpected index reference type: '
        index_type];
14  end
```

Code Listing 19, Operator Syntax vs. subsref

```
1   >> struct_shape = struct( ...
2   'Size', {[1;1] [2;2] [3;3]}, ...
3   'ColorRgb', {[0;0;1] [0;1;0] [1;0;0]})
4   struct_shape =
5   1x3 struct array with fields:
6     Size
7     ColorRgb
8
9   >> [struct_shape.Size]
10  ans =
11    1       2       3
12    1       2       3
13  >> [subsref(struct_shape, substruct('.', 'Size'))]
14  ans =
15    1
16    1
```

---

of cells. You might think that this would solve the problem; however, MATLAB will not deliver more than **nargout** outputs even when more have been assigned. The lone exception occurs when **nargout** equals zero but one return value is allowed.

The only available work-around for this anomaly is to repackage the individual cells of **varargout** into **varargout{1}**.* From inside the tailored **subsref** there is no way to tell

---

* **Inline** objects overload the **nargout** command; however, this approach does not work for other object types.

whether the client wants the values packaged as array or as a cell array. Since we can't tell, the strategy is to pick one and hope for the best. Admittedly this is not perfect, but currently it is the best we can do.

The code in Code Listing 20 represents a good approach. Line 1 decides if we really trust the value in **nargout**. Untrustworthy values for **nargout** are zero and one. Whenever more than one return value has been assigned and **nargout** is zero or one, we need to repackage the return. Line 2 looks for two conditions that usually dictate the use of a cell array: strings and an empty element. Strings are detected using **iscellstr**, and empty elements are detected using **cellfun** and **isempty**.* Strings default to a cell array because it is very difficult to undo the effect of string concatenation after the fact. Return values with empty elements default to a cell array because normal concatenation would make it impossible to determine which object index contained the empty element.

If the **cellstr** or **isempty** tests fail, the code tries simple array concatenation in line 6. If the concatenation is successful, the result is assigned into **varargout{1}**. If concatenation throws an error, the error is caught by line 8 and the entire cell array is assigned into **varargout{1}**. A client might not always get the desired result but the code in Code Listing 20 provides the data in a format that is easy to manipulate. (By the way, if you know of or discover a better solution to this problem, I would love to hear about it. One of my initial reviewers suggested redefining the behavior for **numel**. Unfortunately, a tailored version of **numel** didn't solve the problem.)

Code Listing 20, Addressing the subsref nargout Anomaly

```
1    if length(varargout) > 1 & nargout <= 1
2      if iscellstr(varargout)  ||  any([cellfun('isempty',
       varargout)])
3        varargout = {varargout};
4      else
5        try
6          varargout = {[varargout{:}]};
7        catch
8          varargout = {varargout};
9        end
10     end
11   end
```

4.1.2.8 subsasgn Dot-Reference

Many details that drove us through five attempts for **subsref** can be folded into the initial implementation of **subsasgn**. We will still use switch statements for both the operator and the public names. The primary differences are due to mutation versus access. For example, in **subsref**, the return value based on multilevel indexing could be refined incrementally. In **subsasgn,** the opposite has to happen because the value can't be assigned before all index levels have been resolved. Again, we will coerce MATLAB into doing most of the work. The initial code for the dot-reference case of **subsasgn** is shown in Code Listing 21.

The case on line 3 handles the assignment of the public variable **Size**. There are two situations, one when dot-reference **Size** is the only index and another when **Size** is the first of many. In the length-one-index situation, lines 9–17 error-check the new size values. Line 9 preallocates a 2 by number of inputs array, and the loop on line 10 fills up columns. Line 12 tries to assign each input value into a corresponding column. If the length of **varargin{k}** is one or two, there is

---

* Note that [] and `` are both empty; however, **ischar(``)** is **true** while **ischar([])** is **false**.

Code Listing 21, Initial Version of subasgn's Dot-Reference Case

```
1    case '.'
2      switch index(1).subs
3      case 'Size'
4        if length(index) > 1
5          this.mSize = ...
6            subsasgn(this.mSize, index(2:end), varargin{end:-
               1:1});
7          this.mScale = subsasgn(this.mScale, index(2:end), 1);
8        else
9          new_size = zeros(2, length(varargin));
10         for k = 1:size(new_size, 2)
11           try
12             new_size(:, k) = varargin{k}(:);
13           catch
14             error('Size must be a scalar or length == 2');
15           end
16         end
17         new_size = num2cell(new_size, 1);
18         [this.mSize] = deal(new_size{end:-1:1});
19         [this.mScale] = deal(ones(2,1));
20       end
21     case 'ColorRgb'
22       if length(index) > 1
23         rgb = hsv2rgb([this.mColorHsv]')';
24         rgb = subsasgn(rgb, index(2:end), varargin{end:-1:1});
25         this.mColorHsv = rgb2hsv(rgb')';
26       else
27         hsv = rgb2hsv([varargin{end:-1:1}]')';
28         hsv = num2cell(hsv, 1);
29         [this.mColorHsv] = deal(hsv{:});
30       end
31     otherwise
32       error(['??? Reference to non-existent field ' index(1).
             subs '.']);
33   end
```

no error. An error occurs if **varargin{k}** is larger than two, and execution jumps to line 14 and displays a meaningful error message. Line 17 makes assignment easier by converting the array into a cell array of columns. Line 18 assigns the error-checked values, and line 19 assigns **[1;1]** to **mScale**. For the function **subsasgn**, assignment values are passed into **subsasgn** through **varargin** and the error-checking code assigns **varargin** values into **new_size**. The argument order presents us with another conversion problem with no good work around. When the functional form is used, arguments in **varargin** occur in the same order that they appear in the call; however, when MATLAB converts operator syntax and calls **subsasgn**, it reverses the order of the **varargin** arguments. The only solution is to avoid using the functional form and always assume that operator conversion reversed the order of the assignment values. The reversed values are assigned into the appropriate object indices with **deal**.

In the more-than-one-index situation, lines 5–7 perform the assignment. As an example, client syntax might be

```
shape.Size(2) = 5;
```

For deeper indexing, we will allow MATLAB to do the assignment with a call to **subsasgn**. The target of the assignment is **this.mSize**, and its type determines which version of **subsasgn** to use. The **index** minus the first element is passed as the new index, and a reversed version of **varargin** is passed as the assignment values. The case completes by putting the return value back into **this.mSize**. Line 7 addresses the coupling between **mSize** and **mScale**. When a new value for **mSize** is assigned, we want to set **mScale** to one. Line 7 is particular about which values are set to one. By using **index(2:end)**, only scale factors associated with the modified size are set. No input-error-checking code was included, but it is probably needed. The **subsasgn** calls in lines 6 and 7 allow a client to expand the length of **mSize** and **mScale**. An unchecked example is

```
shape.Size(3) = 10;
```

Now that we understand the error mechanism, we could easily add code to error-check the input. Doing so is an exercise at the end of the chapter.

The obscure way this error occurs is one reason why an interface should be as simple as possible. With each interface feature comes the added burden of ensuring the integrity of the object. It is always prudent to ask whether all of the features we will discuss are always necessary. Do we really need to support multiple levels of indexing? If not, **subsref** and **subsasgn** can still inspect the index length and throw an error. Do we really need to support arrays of objects? If not, we can adjust **subsasgn** and overload the various concatenation functions. It is sometimes prudent to ask whether the class should accept the full burden for object integrity. Error checking has a negative impact on run time and results in functions that may be harder to maintain and extend. Many of these choices are difficult, and are usually decided on a case-by-case basis. It is nice to know there are alternatives.

The **ColorRgb case** is more complicated because **hsv2rgb** and **rgb2hsv** functions need to convert color formats before anything can be assigned. In the length-one-index situation, the client specifies a complete RGB 3-tuple that will completely replace the existing color. The strategy is to convert input RGB values to corresponding HSV values and assign the HSV 3-tuples into **mColorHsv**. Line 27 converts input RGB values into their equivalent HSV values. To do this the input RGB values are reversed, concatenated, and transposed before they are passed into **rgb2hsv**. HSV values from **rgb2hsv** are organized in rows and must be transposed before they are assigned into the local **hsv** variable. Line 28 splits the **hsv** array into a cell array of HSV columns, and line 29 deals cell elements into **this.mColorHsv**.

In the more-than-one index situation, clients specify a subset of the RGB color values. This subset cannot be converted to HSV format until the whole RGB 3-tuple is available. In this situation, the strategy is to (1) convert **mColorHsv** into RGB format; (2) assign the input RGB subset into the proper indices of the converted, current values; (3) convert the mutated RGB values back into HSV format; and (4) assign mutated HSV values back into **mColorHsv**. Line 23 assembles and converts a copy of the **mColorHsv** values into RGB values. The result is stored in the local variable **rgb**. Line 24 allows MATLAB to assign color subset values by calling **subsasgn**. Line 25 transposes **rgb**, converts values into HSV format, and assigns the transposed result into **this.mColorHsv**. We don't really need error-checking code in either case because the **rgb2hsv** function catches and throws errors for us.

4.1.2.9 Array-Reference Indexing

The array-reference operator looks something like the following:

```
b = a(k);

a(k) = b;
```

When MATLAB encounters these statements, it converts them into the equivalent function calls given respectively by

```
b = subsref(a, substruct('()', {k}));

a = subsasgn(a, substruct('()', {k}), b);
```

The two representations are exactly equivalent. You will probably agree that array-reference operator syntax is much easier to read at a glance compared to the functional form. The functional form gives us some important details to use during the implementation of **subsref** and **subsasgn**.

With either conversion, the **index** variable passed into both **subsref** and **subsasgn** is composed using **substruct('()', {k})**. The **type** field is of course '()' and the array index values are represented here by the **subs** field value **{k}**. The type field value, '()', is self-explanatory, but the meaning of **{k}** needs a little more investigation.

Examples are usually better than a long-winded explanation, and Table 4.2 provides some illustrative examples of how MATLAB packages **substruct** indices for both array-reference and cell-reference operators. In lines 1–5, one-dimensional indices are packaged in a cell array with only one cell. In lines 2–3, index range syntax is expanded to include all values in the range, and the size of the array is used to expand a range that includes the keyword **end**. In line 4, a colon range causes a string to be written into the cell. In the remaining lines, multidimensional indices are packaged in a cell array with multiple cells. Each cell contains the numerical indices for one dimension. Each dimension is expanded following the same rules used for one-dimensional expansion. Line 8 demonstrates expansion with the keyword **end**. Line 9 demonstrates ':'. Line 11 demonstrates the result of an expansion of a nonconsecutive range.

TABLE 4.2
Array-Reference and Cell-Reference Index Conversion Examples

Line	Array-Operator Syntax	subsref/subsasgn index.subs
1	(1)	{[1]}
2	(1:5)	{[1 2 3 4 5]}
3	(1:end) where size(a)==[1 6]	{[1 2 3 4 5 6]}
4	(:)	{':'}
5	([])	{[]}
6	(1, 2, 3)	{[1] [2] [3]}
7	(1:3, 3:4, 5)	{[1 2 3] [3 4] [5]}
8	(1:3, 2:end, 5) where size(a)==[3 4 5]	{[1 2 3] [2 3 4] [5]}
9	(1, :, 3)	{[1] ':' [3]}
10	(1, [], 3)	{1, [], 3}
11	([1 3], [3:4 6], 5)	{[1 3] [3 4 6] [5]}

Indexing over multiple dimensions, each with the possibility for empty, numeric, and `':'` ranges, would require a lot of code. Fortunately, we rarely need to look at the contents of **index.subs** because we can coerce MATLAB to perform most of the indexing.

4.1.2.10 subsref Array-Reference

Code for the initial version of the **subsref** array-reference case is shown in Code Listing 22. We get into this case when **subsref** is called with **index(1).type** equal to `'()'`. While there are not too many lines of code, there is still a lot going on.

```
Code Listing 22, Initial Version of subref's Array-Reference Case
1    case '()'
2      this_subset = this(index(1).subs{:});
3      if length(index) == 1
4        varargout = {this_subset};
5      else
6        % trick subsref into returning more than 1 ans
7        varargout = cell(size(this_subset));
8        [varargout{:}] = subsref(this_subset, index(2:end));
9      end
```

In line 2, as promised, we are throwing **index(1).subs{:}** over the fence and asking MATLAB to return a properly indexed subset. We don't need to worry about multiple dimensions, index expansion, or whether a `':'` might be lurking in one of the **subs{:}** cells. The simple syntax in line 2 gives objects the ability to become arrays of objects. Of course this ability also means that every member function must treat **this** as if were an array, but the trade off isn't bad considering what we get in return.

The syntax in line 2 certainly appears rather ordinary, but think about what must be going on behind the scenes. First, MATLAB converts operator syntax into a call to **subsref**. The functional form would look something like

this_subset = subsref(this, substruct('()', {index(1).subs});

Next, MATLAB applies search rules to find the appropriate version of **subsref**. The argument **this** has a type of **cShape**. Normally, MATLAB would call **/@cShape/subsref.m** and the result would be an endless recursive loop. So how do we get away with this? Why doesn't MATLAB recursively call the tailored version of **subsref**? For that matter, why didn't we have the same problem in the dot-reference case accessing **this.mSize**?

The short answer is that **subsref** and **subsasgn** have some special rules. When access operator syntax is used inside a member function, the syntax is converted into a call to the built-in version of **subsref** or **subsasgn** rather than the tailored version. Consider the alternative. Every time code in a member function wanted to access a private variable, it would have to use **builtin**, the function name, and a **substruct** index. Class developers would never stand for it. The resulting class code would be difficult to write and even harder to maintain.

Instead, it appears that MATLAB's designers bent the rules to allow access-operator syntax to call the built-in versions of **subsref** or **subsasgn**, but only from within the confines of a member function. Thus, from inside a member function, access-operator syntax treats the object's structure as if the object-ness has been stripped away. This behavior does not violate encapsulation because member functions are allowed access to the object's private structure. Thus, if we need the value of a public variable, we cannot get it using the dot-reference operator because the private structure does contain an element with the public name. To access or mutate a public variable from within a member function, we have to use the functional form of **subsref** or **subsasgn**.

For a length-one index, line 4 assigns the subset into **varargout{1}**. Lines 7–8 fill **varargout** in the case of deeper indexing. Line 7 preallocates **varargout** based on the size of the subset. If we trusted the value of **nargout**, its value would be used instead. Line 8 calls **subsref** using the functional form. This allows the tailored version to recursively call itself to handle, for example, an array-reference operator followed by a dot-reference operator. Inside the recursive call, **nargout** is correctly set to the length of the preallocated **varargout**. The multiple values returned by the call will be assigned into the corresponding indices of **varargout**. After assignment, there is a possibility of a mismatch between **nargout** and the length of **varargout**. The **nargout**-anomaly code developed for the dot-reference case will work here too.

4.1.2.11   subsasgn Array-Reference

Code for the initial version of the **subsasgn** array-reference case is shown in Code Listing 23. We get into this case when **subsasgn** is called with **index(1).type** equal to `'()'`. The **subsasgn** code looks simple, but again, there is a lot going on.

Code Listing 23, Initial Version of subasgn's Array-Reference Case

```
1    case '()'
2      if isempty(this)
3        this = cShape;
4      end
5      if length(index) == 1
6        this = builtin('subsasgn', this, index, varargin{end:-
         1:1});
7      else
8        this_subset = this(index(1).subs{:});   % get the subset
9        this_subset = subsasgn(this_subset, index(2:end),
         varargin{:});
11       this(index(1).subs{:}) = this_subset; % put subset back
12     end
```

If **this** is passed in as an empty object, lines 2–4 create a default object and assign the default into **this**. Subsequent assignment relies on the assumption that this is not empty, and line 3 enforces the assumption. For a length-one index, line 6 calls the built-in version of **subsasgn**. The assignment call will fail if the input values in **varargin** are not objects of the class. The indices for **varargin** go in reverse order because operator conversion reversed the arguments when it assigned them into the cell array. The built-in version expects the arguments to be in the correct order. Using the built-in version also gives us the benefit of automatic array expansion. If an object is assigned into an array element that does not yet exist, MATLAB will automatically expand the array by filling the missing elements with a default version of the object. This is one reason why a default, no-argument constructor is required.

Another benefit gained by using the built-in version in line 6 is the ability to assign **[]** to an index and free memory. In fact, this is one way to create an empty object. For example, consider the following set of commands. Line 1 creates an object array with one element. Line 2 deletes the element, freeing memory, but it does not completely delete the variable **shape**. Line 3 shows us that **shape** still exists and still has the type **cShape**. Passing **shape** as a function argument will correctly locate **cShape** member functions. Line 6 shows us that one of the **size** dimensions is indeed zero, and line 9 correctly tells us that **shape** is empty. There are several ways to create an empty object, and member functions must be written so they are capable of correctly dealing with them.

```
1    >> shape    = cShape;
2    >> shape(1) = [];
3    >> class(shape)
4    ans =
5    cShape
6    >> size(shape)
7    ans =
8      1       0
9    >> isempty(shape)
10   ans =
11     1
```

Back to Code Listing 23, lines 8–10 take over in the case of deeper indexing. Compared to **subsref**, the procedure in **subsasgn** is a little more complicated because the assignment must ripple through different levels before it can be correctly assigned into the object. The strategy is to first obtain a subset, second perform **subsasgn** on the subset, and third assign the modified subset back into the correctly indexed locations of the object's array. Line 8 uses standard operator notation to retrieve the subset. In line 9, the subset assignment calls **subsasgn**, resulting in a recursive call. Here it is important to pass **varargin** in the same order received. The dot-reference recursive call will then properly reverse the order when it assigns values to deeper-indexed elements. Finally, line 10 uses operator notation to assign the mutated subset back into the original locations.

As with **subsref**, **subsasgn** can also get confused when operator conversion incorrectly sets **nargout**. There is no decent work-around, and thus clients are prohibited from using otherwise legal syntax. One example of the prohibited syntax is

```
[shape(2:3).Size] = deal(10, 20);
```

MATLAB examines the left-hand side and (incorrectly) determines that **deal** should produce only one output. MATLAB passes **nargout=1** to **deal**, and from that point forward the number of arguments actually needed by the left-hand side and the number of values returned by the right-hand side are hopelessly mismatched. This behavior applies not only to **deal** but also to any function that returns more than one value. Due to a related quirk, the following syntax is okay:

```
[shape.Size] = deal(10, 20, 30);
```

In this case, MATLAB can correctly determine the number of values required by the left-hand side and it passes the correct **nargout** value into **deal**. It is important to realize that even though **[shape.Size]** works, **[shape(:).Size]** will not. This is significant because many clients prefer the latter syntax. Perhaps some of these anomalies will be cleared up in future versions. For now, a certain amount of client training will be necessary.

4.1.2.12 Cell-Reference Indexing

The cell-reference operator looks something like the following:

```
b = a{k};
```

```
a{k} = b;
```

Unlike the other two reference operators, cell-reference operators are not always converted into the syntax needed to execute a tailored version of **subsref** or **subsasgn**. Taking advantage of this behavior allows MATLAB to manage cell arrays of objects without our help. We can choose to add cell array–handling code to **subsref** and **subsasgn**, but such code is seldom required. Under most circumstances, the tailored versions of **subsref** and **subsasgn** should generate an error in the cell-reference case. By throwing an error, the tailored versions of **subsref** and

subsasgn encourage the syntax that allows MATLAB to manage the cells. Under these conditions, cell-reference code is easy. All we need to do is return an error. This behavior is also consistent with the way MATLAB treats cell arrays of structures.

Objects can still be inserted into cell arrays, and indeed, cell arrays are very important for object-oriented programming. The syntax for creating cell arrays of objects is nothing special. For example, consider the following two commands:

```
a = cShape;
```

```
b{1} = cShape;
```

Both commands create an object. The first command assigns the object into the variable **a**. The second command assigns the object into cell array **b**. In the first command, **a**'s type is **cShape**, but in the second, **b**'s type is **cell**. The type of **b{1}** is of course **cShape**. The differences in type can be seen when we try to index each variable with a cell-reference operator. For **a{1}**, since **a** is an object, MATLAB is forced to call **/@cShape/subsref**. For **b{1}**, since **b** is a cell, MATLAB indexes the cell array using the built-in version.

4.1.3 INITIAL SOLUTION FOR SUBSREF.M

Putting all three indexing sections together leads to the **subsref** function shown in Code Listing 24. The preceding sections detailed individual functional blocks. Lines 5–22 implement the code used to convert between public and private member variables. Lines 24–31 take care of deeper indexing levels when the dot-reference operator is the initial index. Lines 33–41 implement the code for array-reference. Lines 43–44 generate an error in response to a cell-reference. Finally, lines 50–60 repackage the output when we don't trust the value of **nargout**. Later we will make more improvements to the code in this function. These later improvements will still preserve the basic functional flow of **subsref**.

Code Listing 24, Initial Solution for subsref

```
1    function varargout = subsref(this, index)
2
3    switch index(1).type
4
5      case '.'
6        switch index(1).subs
7          case 'Size'
8            if isempty(this)
9              varargout = {};
10           else
11             varargout = {this.mSize};
12           end
13         case 'ColorRgb'
14           if isempty(this)
15             varargout = {};
16           else
17             rgb = hsv2rgb([this.mColorHsv]')';
18             varargout = mat2cell(rgb, 3, ones(1, size(rgb,2)));
19           end
20         otherwise
```

```
21          error(['??? Reference to non-existent field ' index(1).
               subs '.']);
22      end
23
24      if length(index) > 1
25        if length(this(:)) == 1
26          varargout = {subsref([varargout{:}], index(2:end))};
27        else
28          [err_id, err_msg] = array_reference_error(index(2).
               type);
29          error(err_id, err_msg);
30        end
31      end
32
33      case '()'
34          this_subset = this(index(1).subs{:});
35          if length(index) == 1
36              varargout = {this_subset};
37          else
38              % trick subsref into returning more than 1 ans
39              varargout = cell(size(this_subset));
40              [varargout{:}] = subsref(this_subset, index
                  (2:end));
41          end
42
43      case '{}'
44        error('??? cShape object, not a cell array');
45
46      otherwise
47          error(['??? Unexpected index.type of ' index(1).
               type]);
48  end
49
50  if length(varargout) > 1 & nargout <= 1
51    if iscellstr(varargout) || any([cellfun('isempty',
       varargout)])
52      varargout = {varargout};
53    else
54      try
55        varargout = {[varargout{:}]};
56      catch
57        varargout = {varargout};
58      end
59    end
60  end
```

4.1.4 INITIAL SOLUTION FOR SUBSASGN.M

Putting all three indexing sections together leads to the **subsasgn** function shown in Code Listing 25. The preceding sections detailed individual functional blocks. Lines 5–37 represent the functional block used to convert between public and private member variables. Lines 39–49 represent the functional block used for array-reference mutation. Lines 51–52 generate an error in response to cell-reference mutation. Later, when we make more improvements, this basic functional flow for **subsasgn** will remain intact.

Code Listing 25, Initial Solution for subsasgn

```
1    function this = subsasgn(this, index, varargin)
2
3    switch index(1).type
4
5      case '.'
6        switch index(1).subs
7        case 'Size'
8          if length(index) > 1
9            this.mSize = ...
10             subsasgn(this.mSize, index(2:end), varargin{end:-
               1:1});
11             this.mScale = subsasgn(this.mScale, index(2:end),
               1);
12         else
13           new_size = zeros(2, length(varargin));
14           for k = 1:size(new_size, 2)
15             try
16               new_size(:, k) = varargin{k}(:);
17             catch
18               error('Size must be a scalar or length == 2');
19             end
20           end
21           new_size = num2cell(new_size, 1);
22           [this.mSize] = deal(new_size{end:-1:1});
23           [this.mScale] = deal(ones(2,1));
24         end
25      case 'ColorRgb'
26          if length(index) > 1
27            rgb = hsv2rgb([this.mColorHsv]')';
28            rgb = subsasgn(rgb, index(2:end), varargin{end:-
              1:1});
29            this.mColorHsv = rgb2hsv(rgb')';
30          else
31            hsv = rgb2hsv([varargin{end:-1:1}]')';
32            hsv = num2cell(hsv, 1);
33            [this.mColorHsv] = deal(hsv{:});
34          end
```

```
35    otherwise
36      error(['??? Reference to non-existent field ' index(1).
        subs '.']);
37    end
38
39  case '()'
40    if isempty(this)
41      this = cShape;
42    end
43    if length(index) == 1
44      this = builtin('subsasgn', this, index, varargin{end:-
        1:1});
45    else
46      this_subset = this(index(1).subs{:});   % get the subset
47      this_subset = ...
48          subsasgn(this_subset, index(2:end), varargin{end:-
            1:1});
49      this(index(1).subs{:}) = this_subset; % put subset back
50    end
51
52    case '{}'
53      error('??? cShape object, not a cell array');
54
55    otherwise
56      error(['??? Unexpected index.type of ' index(1).type]);
57  end
```

4.1.5 OPERATOR OVERLOAD, MTIMES

While **subsref** and **subsasgn** represent one type of operator overload, **mtimes** represents the more typical overload situation. The operator associated with **mtimes** is *****. When MATLAB interprets *****, it passes the values on the left- and right-hand sides of the operator into **mtimes**, and users expect a return value that represents the product between the left- and right-hand arguments. The constructor for **cShape** increased superiority over **double**, meaning that the object might occupy either the left-hand or the right-hand argument. We don't know in advance which argument holds the argument, so we need to perform a test.

The implementation for the tailored version of **mtimes** is shown in Code Listing 26. Line 4 checks whether the left-hand argument's type is **cShape**. The **isa** function is very convenient for this type of test because it returns a logical **true** or **false**. If the left-hand argument's type is not **cShape**, then the right-hand argument must be. In either case, the object is assigned into **this** and the scale factor is assigned into **scale**. Lines 12–19 ensure that **scale**'s format is correctly configured. A scalar **scale** value is expanded into a 2×1 column. Similarly, a 1×2 row is converted into a 2×1 column. Any other input **scale** format generates an error. Lines 21–22 perform the scaling multiplication by multiplying both **mSize** and **mScale** by **scale**. The results of each multiplication are stored back into their respective private variables. This code has not been vectorized to support nonscalar objects, and at least for now it hardly seems worth the trouble to do so.

Code Listing 26, Tailored Version of cShape's mtimes

```
1    function this = mtimes(lhs, rhs)
2
3    % one input must be cShape type, which one
4    if isa(lhs, 'cShape')
5      this = lhs;
6      scale = rhs;
7    else
8      this = rhs;
9      scale = lhs;
10   end
11
12   switch length(scale(:))
13     case 1
14       scale = [scale; scale];
15     case 2
16       scale = scale(:);
17     otherwise
18       error('??? Error using ==> mtimes');
19   end
20
21   this.mSize = this.mSize .* scale;
22   this.mScale = this.mScale .* scale;
```

4.2 THE TEST DRIVE

Whew — developing a compact, robust, general implementation for **subsref** and **subsasgn** took us into many dusty corners of MATLAB. It also required some advanced MATLAB coding techniques. Pat yourself on the back for a job done well. If you decide to use the **cShape** model to build your own class, it should be easy to modify variable names and add new member functions.

Before we move on to the example commands in the test drive, let's summarize exactly what we have done and what we have not done. We have written a pair of member functions that create a convenient interface. The interface is convenient because it mimics the way MATLAB structures can be indexed. We have not exposed any private variables. The interface functions **subsref** and **subsasgn** still stand between a client and our private member variables. In fact, we were careful to choose different names for public and private variables. A client might think that the object contains public member variables, but appearances can be deceiving.

The development of **subsref** and **subsasgn** covered a lot of ground. Consequently, the test drive will also cover a lot of ground. To maintain some semblance of order, the test drive examples are split into two sections, one for **subsasgn** and one for **subsref**. The test drive for **subsasgn** is first because it populates the objects that serve as a source for the **subsref** examples. Otherwise, we wouldn't have anything interesting to access.

4.2.1 SUBSASGN TEST DRIVE

The command-line entries shown in Code Listing 27 provide a small sample of **cShape**'s newly developed **subsasgn** capability. Except for a couple of commands, the interface does indeed make the **shape** object look like a structure.

```
Code Listing 27, Chapter 4 Test Drive Command Listing for subsasgn
1    >> cd 'C:/oop_guide/chapter_4'
2    >> clear classes; fclose all; close all force; diary off; clc;
3    >> shape = cShape;
4    >> shape(2) = shape(1);
5    >> shape(2:3) = [shape(1) shape(2)];
6    >> shape(2).Size = [2;3];
7    >> shape(2).Size(1) = 20;
8    >> [shape(2:3).Size] = deal([20;21], [30;31]);
9    ??? Too many outputs requested.  Most likely cause is missing
     [] around
10   left hand side that has a comma separated list expansion.
11
12   >> [shape.Size] = deal([10;11], [20], [30 31]);
13   >> temp = shape(3);
14   >> shape(3) = [];
15   >> shape = [shape temp];
16   >>
17   >> shape(2).ColorRgb = [0 1 0]';
18   >> shape(3).ColorRgb = [0 0.5 0.5]';
19   >> shape(3).ColorRgb(3) = 1.0;
```

Line 1 changes to the correct directory. Line 2 contains a set of clear commands that clean up many things. In addition to clearing workspace variables, **clear classes** also resets MATLAB's understanding of class structures. Next, **fclose all** closes any open files. After that, **close all force** closes any open plot windows, even if their handles are not visible. If diary capture is on, **diary off** closes the diary. Finally, **clc** clears the command window so we can begin with a fresh screen. You don't always need all these clear commands, but usually there is no harm done in using them. Additional detail concerning any of these commands can be found using the help facility.

After the clear commands, line 3 uses the constructor to create a **cShape** object. The next few lines exercise the syntax and exercise both **subsref** and **subsasgn**. Line 4 copies the object at index 1 into element 2. Element 2 did not previously exist so **subsasgn** opened some space before adding the copy. Line 5 concatenates two objects and assigns the result into elements 2:3. Not bad for about 100 lines of code, and we aren't done yet. Line 6 demonstrates a length-one, dot-reference assignment; and line 7 demonstrates deeper indexing. Line 8 tries to assign two indexed public variables but results in an error. With a structure, the syntax would be valid. With objects, the **nargout** anomaly confounds our ability to support this syntax. At least MATLAB throws an error rather than assigning to the wrong location. Line 12 is almost the same as line 8 except there is no array-reference operator and MATLAB can resolve all of the sizes. Also, notice the use of three different array formats inside **deal**. Code in **subsasgn** will convert each array into a column vector before assigning them into the object. Line 13 saves a temporary copy of the third element, and line 14 deletes element 3 and reduces the matrix length to 2. Line 15 uses operator syntax for **horzcat** to add the element back to the end. Lines 17–19 demonstrate the capability to assign different elements of **ColorRgb**. Remember, **ColorRgb** looks like a structure element but the value is actually being converted and stored as an HSV 3-tuple in **mColorHsv**. The conversion is not apparent from the interface.

4.2.2 SUBSREF TEST DRIVE

Now that we have some **cShape** objects with known values, we can exercise **subsref**. We can also confirm the operation of **subsasgn** because we know what values to expect from each access. The command-line entries shown in Code Listing 28 provide a sample of **cShape's** newly developed **subsref** capability.

Code Listing 28, Chapter 4 Test Drive Command Listing for subsref

```
1   >> set(0, 'FormatSpacing', 'compact');
2   >> ShapeCopy = shape;
3   >> OneShape = shape(2);
4   >> ShapeSubSet = shape(2:3);
5   >> ShapeSize = shape(2).Size
6   ShapeSize =
7      20
8      20
9   >> ShapeSize = [shape.Size]
10  ShapeSize =
11     10     20     30
12     11     20     31
13  >> ShapeSize = {shape.Size}
14  ShapeSize =
15     [2x1 double]    [2x1 double]    [2x1 double]
16  >> ShapeSize = [shape(:).Size]
17  ShapeSize =
18     10     20     30
19     11     20     31
20  >> ShapeSize = {shape(:).Size}
21  ShapeSize =
22     [2x3 double]
23  >> ShapeHorizSize = shape(2).Size(1)
24  ShapeHorizSize =
25     20
26  >> [shape.ColorRgb]
27  ans =
28          0          0          0
29          0     1.0000     0.5000
30     1.0000          0     1.0000
31  >> shape(1) = 1.5 * shape(1) * [2; 3];
32  >> shape(1).Size
33  ans =
34     3.0000e+001
35     4.9500e+001
36  >> shape(1) = reset(shape(1));
37  >> shape(1).Size
38  ans =
39     10
```

```
40        11
41   >> display(shape)
42   shape =
43        cShape object: 1-by-3
44   >> display(shape(1))
45        cShape object: 1-by-1
```

The **set** command in line 1 is optional. It reduces the number of blank lines displayed after each result. The two **FormatSpacing** options are **loose** and **compact**. If you prefer a display with blank lines, substitute **loose** for **compact** and reissue the command. You can set many different environment variables. If you are curious, the command **set(0)** will list them all. In addition, type **get(0)** and look at the difference between the two listings. Maybe our classes would benefit from a similar display.

Lines 2–4 demonstrate assignment. The syntax in these commands looks perfectly normal.* Lines 5–8 exercise **subsref** and display the result. The values shown in 7–8 confirm the assignment used in the **subsasgn** test drive. The **Size** member variable was assigned using a scalar value of 20, and the displayed result confirms that the scalar value was correctly converted into a pair of width and height values. The commands in lines 9, 13, 16, and 20 demonstrate the **nargout** anomaly.

There is nothing unusual about the outputs from the commands on line 9 and 14. We know that **shape** has 3 elements and the **[]** and **{}** operators collect the element values into arrays with the correct dimension. Like lines 10–12, outputs for the command in line 16 are correct. This is simply due to good luck. In line 16, the **(:)** index on **shape** causes **subsref** to receive an inconsistent value for **nargout**. When **subsref** detects this inconsistency, it formats the output as a normal array and returns the result. Since the syntax on line 16 asked for a normal array, everything is copasetic. On line 20, when the syntax requests a cell array, the wheels fall off. When **subsref** detects an inconsistent value for **nargout**, it again formats the output as a regular array. This time the conversion assumption is wrong, and the result on lines 21–22 has an unexpected form.

Line 23 demonstrates the use of three indexing levels. The first level is **shape(2)**, the second level is **shape(2).Size,** and the third is **shape(2).Size(1)**. The value displayed on lines 24–25 agrees with the previously assigned value. Line 26 displays RGB color values. The object does not store RGB values so the values displayed on lines 27–30 represent calculated values. These calculations were done inside **subsref**, where stored HSV color values are converted into RGB equivalent values. The opposite conversion occurs inside **subsasgn**. The **subsasgn** and **subsref** combination is consistent because the values on lines 27–30 are the same values assigned earlier.

Commands on lines 31 and 32 demonstrate the overloaded **mtimes** operator. A shape's size can be scaled by pre- or postmultiplying by a scalar or a length-2 vector. Overloading **mtimes** seems much more convenient compared to **setScale**. Lines 36 and 37 reset the scaled size back to original values and display the result.

Finally, **display** commands in lines 31 and 34 give some information about the object, but the information is not particularly useful. It would be much better if the public member variables and their values were displayed. Ideally, we should also be able to type the variable name with no trailing semicolon and receive a cogent display. Overloading **display** is very similar to overloading any operator. The difference with the display operator is that its absence triggers the function call. In the next chapter, we will develop an implementation for **display**, the fourth member of the group of eight.

---

* Some object-oriented languages allow you to overload the assignment operator; MATLAB does not.

4.3 SUMMARY

The descriptions and implementations of **subsref** and **subsasgn** are the most involved topics in this book. They are also among the most important. It turns out that the implementations are difficult precisely because they are so important. Each **case** in the dot-access **switch** statement corresponds to a public member variable. Thus, **subsref** and **subsasgn** represent much of the interface and their contents implement the conversions between public and private member variables. The tailored versions must also be able to handle object arrays and vector syntax. Getting all of this right for every class we develop isn't easy. One thing we learned in this chapter is to involve MATLAB built-in functions whenever possible. The built-in functions provide functionality that is documented, tested, and fast. Another thing we have learned from experience is the process of managing complexity by breaking it down into smaller units that are more manageable. Later we will investigate a convenient way to do this.

It took us several attempts, but in the end we achieved the goal of building a class interface that mimicked the structure interface. Overloading **subsref** and **subsasgn** also allowed us to introduce the concept of public member variables and define the relationship between public and private members. At first, it appeared that supporting dot-reference, array-reference, and cell-reference operators would degrade encapsulation. By the time we finished with the implementations, these operators actually enhanced its benefits. The real power of the interface resulted from the ability to hide, combine, and manipulate private member variables on their way to and from the public interface.

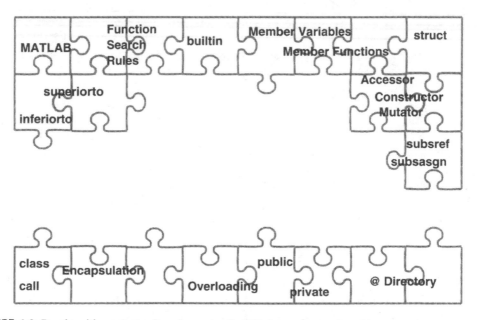

FIGURE 4.2 Puzzle with **subsref, subsasgn, builtin**, and **overloading**.

The implementations of **subsref** and **subsasgn** required a discussion of **substruct** and forced the issue of general operator overloading and the **builtin** command. We learned that almost every operator has an associated function call. In most cases, operator syntax and the associated functional form are identical. We pointed out a couple of instances where the two diverge and included work-around code. We also discussed **superiorto** and **inferiorto** relative to argument lists and the function search path. With all these new pieces in place, the object-oriented puzzle looks like Figure 4.2.

4.4 INDEPENDENT INVESTIGATIONS

1. Add code to perform additional input error checking, in particular the indices for the index-length-greater-than-one assignment of **Size**.
2. The code for **subsasgn**'s **Size** dot-reference case is getting long. Collect the code into a subfunction and call it.
3. Create a **/@cShape/private** directory and move the subfunction from exercise 2 into the directory. Does **subsasgn** still find this function? What is the difference?
4. One of the public member variables is **Size**. If **size.m** is overloaded instead, would this result in a similar interface? Is this new use for **size** potentially confusing? Is it okay to change the behavior of a familiar function? What about a less familiar function? Would **size** also be used as a mutator? Overload **size** and see how you like it.

5 Displaying an Object's State

Being able to view the state of an object is vitally important to class development, client use, and code maintenance. Being forced to index and display individual values is too tedious and far too time-consuming. MATLAB provides a decent display mechanism for scalars, arrays, and structures. Our classes deserve no less. As we have seen, MATLAB does not provide a good built-in display for objects, but now we know how to tailor functions to do whatever we want. All we need to know is the name of the built-in function.

5.1 DISPLAYING OBJECTS

MATLAB's two primary display functions are **display.m** and **disp.m**. The biggest difference between them is a connection between **display** and the semicolon operator. When a semicolon terminates a command, MATLAB does not call display. The opposite statement is also true. If a command does not end in a semicolon, MATLAB calls **display**. This behavior is very convenient and makes **display** a good overload candidate. Otherwise, all we will continue to see is the following cryptic message:

```
>> shape = cShape

shape =

  cShape object: 1-by-1
```

Of course, we could also overload **disp**, **sprintf**, **num2str**, and **evalc**; however, these functions pale in convenience and importance to **display**. Developing a general solution for the other display functions does not add much value.

The function **display** is overloaded the same way any other function is overloaded. A customized member function named **display.m** is added to the class directory. After that, whenever **display** needs to operate on an object, the tailored version of **display.m** will be found. This is true when called directly as in **display(shape)**, or indirectly by leaving off the semicolon.

5.1.1 WHAT SHOULD BE DISPLAYED?

The question of what to display might sound like a trick question, but it is not a trick. It isn't easy to answer either. Unlike structures, objects have both public and private variables. Also different from structures, a public variable might be read-only, write-only, or read-write. There are also at least two audiences for the displayed information, clients and developers. The number of options makes it difficult to settle on a universal implementation for **display**.

In **cShape**, for example, developers might find it convenient to display stored HSV color values along with calculated RGB values. Developers and clients alike might like to see the value of **mScale** from time to time. Violating encapsulation by allowing client code to depend on private variables is a bad idea, but is it really a violation to allow a client to display internal states during client code debug and development? For some data and some developers, it might be okay. Once we nail down the kind of information to display, the implementation becomes easier.

When deciding what should be displayed, there are at least three information categories or user-related topics to consider:

- value information for public member variables
- class membership lists and permissions
- class development and debug-related data

The first category represents a view that should look similar, if not identical, to a structure's display. This helps extend the illusion of a class as a structure. Instead of structure elements, the display includes public member variables. We will call this the standard view. The second category represents a view that provides a brief summary of the interface, a summary that can often be used in lieu of **help**. The display for the second category should include a list of public member variables along with their type. A list of valid assignment values is also useful. The environment commands **set(0)** and **get(0)** can serve as a model for the display. The third category is intended primarily for class developers engaged in code development or maintenance. This view is impossible to specify rigorously but should probably include all public member variables and often includes a large selection of private member variables. We will call this view *developer view*.

For the first two views, MATLAB provides some guidance in the form of displays that exist elsewhere. For developer view, there really is no precedence. Developer view's format is also more difficult to pin down because it is largely a matter of taste. Some developers prefer a standard structure-like display, some prefer a **whos**-like format, and some prefer a format that provides even more detail. In fact, different formats can be useful during different stages of development. Developer view demands flexibility, and indeed, we can organize class variables and **display** to support flexibility.

Adding flexibility isn't completely related to **display**. Part of the motivation is to reveal more ways that objects are fundamentally different from structures and develop some insight into how those differences might be exploited. Providing a design for **display** that allows almost unlimited flexibility serves many purposes.

If we want to model the second-view category after **get(0)** and **set(0)**, we need to develop tailored versions of these two functions. Once developed, **get(cShape)** and **set(cShape)** would display the appropriate lists. Like **display, get** and **set** are also members of the group of eight. The chapters in this section take on the group of eight one at a time. This chapter is devoted to **display**. Chapter 8 is devoted to **get** and **set**.

In any display, variables come in only four flavors:

- public member variables
- read-only public member variables
- write-only public member variables
- private member variables

There is almost universal agreement that standard view should include public member variables. After all, public variables are public for a reason and one of the best ways to advertise their availability is via **display**. Most also agree that the standard display should not include private variables. In some classes, it might make sense to include selected private variables, but generally, private variables are private for a reason. Omitting them from the standard view helps keep them private.

It is harder to reach a consensus on read-only and write-only variables. Part of the reason why it is difficult to decide is the observation that MATLAB's structure display has no provision for such "oddly behaved" elements. We don't have a firm foundation on which to base our opinions because read-only and write-only do not exist for structures. Perhaps the interface design can shed some light on these variables.

In most situations, read-only and write-only permissions flow naturally from the class design and its interface definition. In a well-designed class with an intuitive interface, the idea of writing a value into a read-only variable should never occur. Even if the interface is not perfect, a client can display a read-only value even if it isn't included in the standard **display** view. This alone justifies including read-only variables in the standard view. Write-only variables are much less common. When the interface definition designates a variable as write-only, we should probably respect the designation. For this reason, we will not include write-only variables in the standard view. Modifications to standard display policy can always be addressed on a case-by-case basis.

5.1.2 STANDARD STRUCTURE DISPLAY

MATLAB's built-in **display** outputs for a scalar structure and a structure array are shown in Code Listing 29. These outputs serve as the bogie for an object's standard display. MATLAB can already display a structure, and an object is based on a structure. Maybe the tailored version of **display** can take advantage of MATLAB's built-in capability. The trick comes in organizing the right set of commands.

Code Listing 29, The Normal Display for a Structure

```
1   >> set(0, 'FormatSpacing', 'compact');
2   >> shape = struct('Size', [1;1], 'Scale', [1;1], 'ColorRgb',
    [0;0;1]);
3   >> shape
4   shape =
5          Size: [2x1 double]
6         Scale: [2x1 double]
7      ColorRgb: [3x1 double]
8   >> shape = [shape shape];
9   >> shape
10  shape =
11  1x2 struct array with fields:
12      Size
13      Scale
14      ColorRgb
```

Sometimes when we are inside a member function MATLAB allows us to treat **this** as a structure. For example, we can access and mutate elements using dot-reference and array-reference operators. It is very tempting to write a one-line display function that uses one of the following commands:

```
1 this % note: no semicolon

2 display(this);

3 builtin('display', this);

4 display(struct(this));
```

Try to figure out what will happen in each case before reading further.

Commands 1 and 2 are functionally equivalent and produce the same bad result. The result is an infinite recursive loop. In the best case, you will receive a maximum-recursion error message; and in the worst case, a crash. Inside the tailored version of **display.m**, **this** is still an object. MATLAB path rules always find the tailored version of **display** before they find the built-in version. The only two functions allowed to break this rule are **subsref** and **subsasgn**, and they only get to break the rules when operator syntax is used.

Command 3 is not recursive but the output is the same familiar cryptic display. Inside a member function, **this** is still an object and the built-in **display** function has only one format for displaying an object. The command did not crash, but the output is too cryptic.

Command 4 uses **struct** to change the object into a structure and then displays the structure. The built-in **struct** command strips away the object's identity, and that allows the built-in version of **display** to output the structure. The output from a tailored version of **display** that uses command number 4 is shown in Code Listing 30. Unfortunately, this output includes all of the object's private variables and we are trying to display the public elements.

Code Listing 30, Displaying the Object's Private Structure

```
1    >> shape = cShape;
2    >> shape
3            mSize: [2x1 double]
4           mScale: [2x1 double]
5        mColorHsv: [3x1 double]
```

At this point, some of you might be thinking, "Why don't we just write a type-specific version of **struct** that returns a structure constructed from the public member variables?" I like the way you think. Like **display**, **struct** is another member of the group of eight. In Chapter 7, we will develop a tailored-version of **struct** that will do exactly that. In fact, some of the code developed in this chapter will be moved into **struct**. By the time we get to Chapter 9, the syntax in command number 4 will work because a tailored version of **struct** will exist. All of that must wait because we need a cogent display capability right now.

5.1.3 PUBLIC MEMBER VARIABLE DISPLAY

For a scalar **cShape object**, **display**'s output should look like the output shown in Code Listing 31. On line 3, the name of the variable is repeated along with an equal sign. Lines 4 and 5 display the public member variables. There are no "m" prefixes on the names, and the shapes' use of RGB color values is obvious.

Code Listing 31, Desired Format for the cShape Display Output

```
1    >s> shape = cShape;
2    >> shape
3    shape =
4            Size: [2x1 double]
5         ColorRgb: [3x1 double]
```

5.1.3.1 Implementing display.m, Attempt 1

The first version of **display** used to produce the output in Code Listing 31 is shown in Code Listing 32. The source can be found in the class directory under subdirectory **chapter_5/display-first-attempt/@cShape**. Change into the first attempt directory if you want to experiment.

Lines 3–4 construct a temporary structure from the public variables. Line 3 simply copies a private value into the appropriate public field. Line 4 uses **subsref** to access the public **ColorRgb** value because, privately, color is stored in HSV format. An in-line conversion is needed,

---

Code Listing 32, First Attempt at an Implementation for cShape's Tailored display.m

```
1    function display(this)
2    % assign values to a temporary struct
3    public_struct.Size = this.mSize;
4    public_struct.ColorRgb = subsref(this, substruct('.',
     'ColorRgb'));
5    % use disp and inputname for the display header
6    disp([inputname(1) ' =']);
7    % use disp and the temporary structure
8    disp(public_struct);
```

---

and code to perform the conversion already exists inside **subsref**. Calling **subsref** is better than repeating code even though **subsref**'s function syntax is a little awkward.

At first blush, it is tempting to access **ColorRgb** using operator syntax, for example, **this.ColorRgb**. Ordinarily, operator syntax and the equivalent functional form produce the same result. However, remember that reference operators inside a member function break the rules. From inside a member function, the only way we can get **subsref** to return a public variable is by using the functional form.

In line 6, **inputname** retrieves the name of the variable. The **inputname** function retrieves a name the client will recognize. We don't want to display **this** or **public_struct** because the client has no idea that these variables exist. The name along with an equals sign are displayed using **disp**. Finally, in line 8, the fields of the temporary structure are displayed. Using **disp** allows MATLAB to do most of the output formatting.

5.1.3.2 Implementing display.m, Attempt 2

Our first attempt is a good beginning. Before it is ready for prime time, we need to consider a couple of details.

1. What do we display if **inputname(1)** returns **[]**?
2. How do we format the output when **this** is an array?
3. How should the spacing change in response to

```
set(0, 'FormatSpacing', 'loose') and
set(0, 'FormatSpacing', 'compact')?
```

These details are not difficult to manage and can be resolved in several different ways. The code shown in Code Listing 33 addresses these three questions. This source can be found in the directory **chapter_5/display-improved/@cShape/display.m**. Change into the display-improved directory if you want to experiment.

To address question 1, lines 4–7 set **display_name** to **'ans'** whenever **inputname(1)** returns **[]**.

To address question 2, a temporary structure is only created for a scalar **this**. The code in lines 12–19 is very similar to the commands in Code Listing 32. Substituting **display** for **disp** in line 19 guarantees compatibility with all environment settings, including the state of **'FormatSpacing'**.

The display code for a nonscalar **this** does not need to create a temporary structure because no values are displayed. Instead, line 22 uses **eval** to assign the object to a variable with the correct display name. Line 24 uses **eval** along with **builtin** and **'display'** to write the

---

Code Listing 33, Second Attempt at an Implementation for cShape's Tailored display.m

```
1    function display(this)
2
3    % handle empty inputname
4    display_name = inputname(1);
5    if isempty(display_name)
6        display_name = 'ans';
7    end
8
9    % handle scalar vs. vector this
10   % note: [] this jumps to else
11   if length(this) == 1  % scalar case
12       % assign values to a temporary struct
13       public_struct.Size = this.mSize;
14       public_struct.ColorRgb = ...
15           subsref(this, substruct('.', 'ColorRgb'));
16       % use eval to assign temp struct into display_name
          variable
17       eval([display_name ' = public_struct;']);
18       % use eval to call display on the display_name structure
19       eval(['display(' display_name ');']);
20   else  % array case
21       % use eval to assign this into display_name variable
22       eval([display_name ' = this;']);
23       % use eval to call builtin display for size info
24       eval(['builtin(''display'', ' display_name ');']);
25       % still need to display variable names explicitly
26       disp('     with public member variables:');
27       disp('          Size');
28       disp('          ColorRgb');
29       if strcmp(get(0, 'FormatSpacing'), 'loose')
30           disp(' ');
31       end
32   end
```

---

cryptic default-formatted object information. This information serves as a very nice header because it identifies the variable as an object.

Next, we need a list of fieldnames, or in this case a list of public member variable names. Lines 26–28 display the list of public variable names in a way that is consistent with the display format for nonscalar structure arrays. Finally, lines 29–31 check the state of **'FormatSpacing'** and add an extra line if the state is **'loose'**. Together this code takes care of all three questions.

Example outputs are shown in Code Listing 34. When **shape** is a scalar, the **display** output looks identical to the equivalent structure display. This is expected because the output was created by displaying a structure. When **shape** is nonscalar, the **display** output is similar, but not identical, to the structure display. The differences are that we identify the variable as an object and we identify element names as public member variables. This display output is exactly what we want. Now we will add flexibility.

Code Listing 34, Example Display Output for the Tailored Version of display.m

```
1    >> shape = cShape
2    shape =
3            Size: [2x1 double]
4         ColorRgb: [3x1 double]
5    >> shape = [shape shape]
6    shape =
7         cShape object: 1-by-2
8         with public member variables:
9            Size
10            ColorRgb
```

5.2 DEVELOPER VIEW

An object's standard **display** view mimics MATLAB's structure display. This gives objects the benefit of presenting a common look and feel; however, it also gives objects the same limitations. Lines 3–4 in Code Listing 34 illustrate the primary limitation. Values stored in the public variables are arranged in columns, and MATLAB displays size information instead of values. If the data were arranged in rows, the output would include values. This behavior is lame, particularly when you realize a simple transpose will allow values to be displayed. For a more informative display, the interface definition could have specified row vectors; however, a row orientation makes it more difficult to concatenate values from object arrays. A desire for maximum compatibility saddles the standard view.

This is part of the motivation behind the additional flexibility. Giving developers a way to swap in a better display makes object-oriented development proceed at a faster pace. Since each developer's tastes are unique and since certain views aid different phases of development, we need a flexible implementation. One way to address code flexibility is to specify a standard function interface and use a function handle to store the currently desired function.

A function handle is a standard MATLAB type. A function handle allows a variable to hold a function reference. Very simplistically, a function handle is equivalent to the function's name. A function handle can reference almost any function using a value that can be changed dynamically. If you want to execute a new function, you don't need to change source code; you simply change the value of a variable. A display implementation based on a function handle gives us a convenient way to change the view quickly and easily. This is particularly true if we store the function handle in a private member variable. After that, all we need are some standard functions, a way to set the handle, and some code that will use it.

Use **mDisplayFunc** for the name of the private variable. An updated version of the constructor code with developer view enabled is included in Code Listing 37. Ordinarily, the constructor will assign **[]** and **display** will default to the standard view. For now, anyway, a developer can temporarily modify the constructor so that it assigns a function handle, or a developer can temporarily add a **setDisplayFunc** member function to the class directory. Code that uses the function handle will assume the following function definition.

```
function display_function(this, display_name)
```

In the definition, **this** is a length-one object and **display_name** is a string that contains the object variable's name. Since we want to be able to swap out display functions, all custom display functions must conform to this definition.

5.2.1 IMPLEMENTING DISPLAY.M WITH DEVELOPER VIEW OPTIONS

Code Listing 33 presented a very good implementation of **display** for the standard view. Here we simply modify that implementation so that a nonempty **mDisplayFunc** value will trigger a call to the special-purpose display function. The new version of **display.m** is shown in Code Listing 35.

Code Listing 35, Improved Display Implementation with Developer View Options

```
1     function display(this, display_name)
2
3     if nargin < 2
4        % assign 'ans' if inputname(1) empty
5        display_name = inputname(1);
6        if isempty(display_name)
7           display_name = 'ans';
8        end
9     end
10
11    % check whether mDisplayFunc has a value
12    % if it has a value feval the value to get the display
13    use_standard_view = cellfun('isempty',
       {this(:).mDisplayFunc});
14    if all(use_standard_view)
15       standard_view(this, display_name);
16    else
17       for k = 1:length(this(:))
18           if use_standard_view(k)
19               standard_view(this(k), display_name);
20           else
21               indexed_display_name = sprintf('%s(%d)',
                   display_name, k);
22      feval(this(k).mDisplayFunc, this(k),
       indexed_display_name);
23           end
24       end
25    end
26
27    % --------------------------
28    function standard_view(this, display_name)
29    if ~isempty( ...
30           [strfind(display_name, '.') ...
31           strfind(display_name, '(') ...
32           strfind(display_name, '{')])
33       display_name = 'ans';
34    end
35    % handle scalar vs. non-scalar this
36    % note: if isempty(this), jumps to else
```

```
37    if length(this) == 1  % scalar case
38        % assign values to a temporary struct
39        public_struct.Size = this.mSize;
40        public_struct.ColorRgb = ...
41            subsref(this, substruct('.', 'ColorRgb'));
42        % use eval to assign temp struct into display_name
           variable
43        eval([display_name ' = public_struct;']);
44        % use eval to call display on the display_name structure
45        eval(['display(' display_name ');']);
46    else  % array case
47        % use eval to assign this into display_name variable
48        eval([display_name ' = this;']);
49        % use eval to call builtin display for size info
50        eval(['builtin(''display'', ' display_name ');']);
51        % still need to display variable names explicitly
52        disp('    with public member variables:');
53        disp('        Size');
54        disp('        ColorRgb');
55        if strcmp(get(0, 'FormatSpacing'), 'loose')
56            disp(' ');
57        end
58    end
59
60    % ------------------------------
61    function developer_view(this, display_name)
62    disp('----- Public Member Variables -----');
63    standard_view(this, display_name);
64    disp('..... Private Member Variables .....');
65    full_display(this, display_name, true);
```

The implementation code is organized into two subfunctions. The subfunction **standard_view** is nearly identical to the previous **display** code in Code Listing 33. The subfunction **developer_view** can be used as the function stored in **mDisplayFunc**. The main display function checks requested display options and calls the appropriate function.

Lines 3–9 came directly from Code Listing 33 with one small tweak. The function now accepts two input arguments. The second argument is a string representing the desired display name. When only one input is passed in, **display_name** is assigned a value exactly as before. The additional input gives us more flexibility to configure the output format.

Line 13 builds a logical array used to steer execution to the requested display option for every object in the object array. For scalar objects, there is only one function handle, but for object arrays, every index might use a different handle. A handle for every object provides a lot of fine control over the display. It also makes it easier to concatenate objects or form subsets. Working from the inside out, **{this(:).mDisplayFunc}** creates a cell array of function handles. Each cell index corresponds to the same object-array index. The next level uses **cellfun** to "map" a function onto each cell in a cell array. Prior to version 7.1, the list of "map-able" functions was somewhat limited. In this case, **'isempty'** is the one we need and it is fully supported. The return from

cellfun is an array of logical values the same length as the input cell array. If a value is **true**, it means that the object's **mDisplayFunc** field is empty and the standard view should be used.

If no object in the array specifies developer view, the test in line 14 is **true** and line 14 passes the whole object into **standard_view**. In that case, the output is the same as before, in Code Listing 34. The reason the output is the same is because the contents of **standard_view** in lines 28–58 were copied from the implementation in Code Listing 33.

If any object specifies developer view, the test in line 14 is **false**, the new code executes, and the output format is different. For nonscalar object arrays, each object is separately displayed. Line 17 loops over every object in the array and calls the display option specified by each. Line 19 calls **standard_view.** Lines 21–22 update the display name and use **feval** to call the function handle stored in **this(k).mDisplayFunc**. The value in **this(k).mDisplayFunc** can be either a function handle or the string name of a function. The **feval** call is more run-time efficient with a function handle, but in **display** the difference in efficiency doesn't matter. For convenience, a simple-minded but very informative developer view function is included as a subfunction.

In lines 61–66, the function **developer_view** displays both public and private member variables. Line 63 displays the public variables by calling **standard_view**. Private variables are displayed by calling a utility function named **full_display**. The third argument allows **full_display** to use **builtin** to turn the object into a structure prior to its display. Passing **true** specifies **builtin** and keeps the tailored version of **struct** from getting in the way. This is one of those rare times when **builtin** with **'struct'** is acceptable. The function **full_display** is found in the **/oop_guide/utils/wizard_gui** directory and provides a more cogent output compared to **display**. Any variable type can be passed into **full_display**.

5.3 THE TEST DRIVE

The command-line entries shown in Code Listing 36 provide a sample of **cShape's** newly developed **display** capability. Under the **/chapter_5/display-standard-view** directory, the constructor sets **mDisplayFunc** to empty and the listing demonstrates the normal view. In these three cases, the output looks nearly identical to the output that we would expect if **shape** was a structure or structure array.

Code Listing 36, Chapter 5 Test Drive Command Listing for Display

```
1    >> cd 'C:/oop_guide/chapter_5/display-standard-view'
2    >> clear classes; fclose all; close all force; diary off; clc;
3    >> shape = cShape
4    shape =
5           Size: [2x1 double]
6        ColorRgb: [3x1 double]
7    >> shape = [shape shape]
8    shape =
9        cShape object: 1-by-2
10       with public member variables:
11          Size
12          ColorRgb
13   >> shape(2)
14   ans =
15          Size: [2x1 double]
16       ColorRgb: [3x1 double]
```

We also know there is a developer view option lurking inside **display**. Soon we will add some control options, but for now at least, we need to modify the constructor to demonstrate it. The modified constructor is shown in Code Listing 37. The only addition occurs in line 6. Since the default value of **mDisplayFunc** is now **'developer_view'**, developer view will be active for all objects instantiated by this constructor. To deactivate developer view and activate the standard view, change the assignment in line 6 back to **[]**. The constructor located under the directory **chapter_5/display-developer-view** includes the **'developer_view'** assignment.

Code Listing 37, cShape Constructor with Developer View Enabled by Default

```
1    function this = cShape
2    this = struct( ...
3      'mSize', ones(2,1),   ... % scaled [width height]' of
         bounding box
4      'mScale', ones(2,1), ... % [width height]' scale factor
5      'mColorHsv', rgb2hsv([0 0 1])', ... % [H S V]' of border,
         default, blue
6      'mDisplayFunc', 'developer_view' ... % function format
         fun(this, name)
7      );
8    this = class(this, 'cShape');
9    superiorto('double')
```

With developer view enabled, the same commands from Code Listing 36 result in the display of a lot more data. This can be seen in the output provided in Code Listing 38. The output under the title **Public Member Variables** is formatted similar to standard view, but there is now another section titled **Private Member Variables** The private outputs are formatted differently because **full_display** rather than the built-in version of **display** is used for the private structure. The function **full_display** is found in the **/oop_guide/utils/wizard_gui** directory and as you can see in, for example, lines 8–11, it provides superior detail. The output format from **full_display** allows lines to be cut and pasted into the command window or into an m-file. The output format also shows every indexing level. This is a real benefit for deeply nested data structures.

Code Listing 38, Chapter 5 Test Drive Command Listing Using the Alternate Display

```
1    >> clear classes; fclose all; close all force; diary off;
2    >> cd 'C:/oop_guide/chapter_5/display-developer-view'
3    >> shape = cShape
4    ----- Public Member Variables -----
5    ans =
6            Size: [2x1 double]
7       ColorRgb: [3x1 double]
8    ..... Private Member Variables .....
9    shape(1).mSize = [1    1]';
10   shape(1).mScale = [1    1]';
11   shape(1).mColorHsv = [0.66667              1              1]';
12   shape(1).mDisplayFunc = 'developer_view';
```

```
13
14  >> shape = [shape shape]
15  ----- Public Member Variables -----
16  ans =
17         Size: [2x1 double]
18     ColorRgb: [3x1 double]
19  ..... Private Member Variables .....
20  shape(1).mSize = [1   1]';
21  shape(1).mScale = [1   1]';
22  shape(1).mColorHsv = [0.66667            1            1]';
23  shape(1).mDisplayFunc = 'developer_view';
24  ----- Public Member Variables -----
25  ans =
26         Size: [2x1 double]
27     ColorRgb: [3x1 double]
28  ..... Private Member Variables .....
29  shape(2).mSize = [1   1]';
30  shape(2).mScale = [1   1]';
31  shape(2).mColorHsv = [0.66667            1            1]';
32  shape(2).mDisplayFunc = 'developer_view';
```

5.4 SUMMARY

The process of developing of **display.m** demonstrates some of the power behind object-oriented programming and encapsulation. Unbeknownst to our clients, we added a private member variable and made enormous changes to the internal workings of the tailored **display** function. Such change is only possible because we are committed to keeping private areas of our objects private. The development of **display** helps us keep that commitment.

We have also provided developers with a very convenient development aid. By temporarily changing the constructor, a developer can change an object's behavior to display all object data. One version of this code lurks in the **display** function, but the design has a lot more flexibility. It takes some design work to create this kind of abstraction and it takes some advanced MATLAB techniques to make it work, but the end result is definitely worth the effort. There are plenty of applications where the use of function handles can greatly enhance the extendibility and maintainability of code. This chapter opened the door to a range of possibilities.

Display and function handle pieces have been added to the puzzle. These pieces give objects the look and feel of built-in variable types and add developer flexibility. That is quite a lot of benefit from three simple pieces. With a few more pieces, the puzzle in Figure 5.1 will have a complete frame.

5.5 INDEPENDENT INVESTIGATIONS

1. Pass a complicated structure with arrays and cell arrays into **full_display** and see what happens.
2. The developer view output for public variables does not show as much information as the private variables. Modify the code so that public variables are displayed using

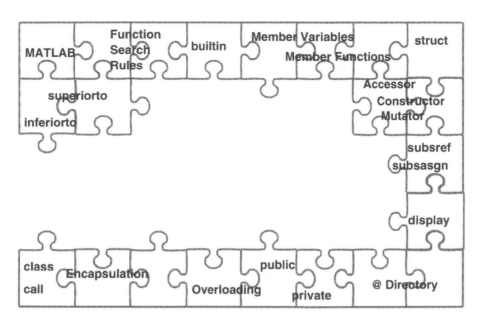

FIGURE 5.1 Puzzle with display and function handles.

      full_display format. (Hint: build a public structure and call **full_display**.)
Soon we will make this a lot easier.

3. Try to redefine MATLAB's builtin **display** function to use **full_display** instead.
   Make this work for built-in types as well as for user-defined types.

6 fieldnames.m

With the basic implementation behind us, we need to step up to the next level. We want to improve the implementations by making our classes more capable. With **subsref** and **subsasgn**, we set up **public** as a new category of member variables. In the tailored **display** function, we struggled to generate the structure-like output because a separate list of public variables is not available. In this chapter, we tailor **fieldnames** as a way to provide that list. The **fieldnames** function also plugs a leak in encapsulation. The built-in version of **fieldnames** returns a list of private names, a behavior we cannot tolerate.

Tailoring **fieldnames** also improves the modularity in the group-of-eight implementation. For example, in **display** we were forced to add public names to the implementation. Other functions in the group of eight also need access to the names. By including a member function that returns the public list, we can reduce the number of places where public names are repeated. Based on its role with structures, a tailored version of **fieldnames** is the logical place for the list to exist.

6.1 FIELDNAMES

While we could easily write a specific get function for this task (e.g., **getPublicNames**), MATLAB already defines a suitable function. For structures, the built-in version of **fieldnames** will return a **cellstr** filled with element names. The built-in version will also operate on objects. If you examine **help fieldnames**, you will notice that built-in version claims to return a list of an object's "public data fields." Unfortunately, help's use of "public" is confusing.

First, we are well aware that every field in the object's structure is private. We also know that our definition of public member variable comes about through the implementation of **subsref** and **subsasgn**. How is it possible for the built-in version of **fieldnames** to discover the names of the public variables? It isn't. There must be a mismatch between help's idea of public and ours.

We can test the built-in version. What we find is that the built-in version actually returns the field names of the object's underlying structure, that is, the names of the private member variables. This is not good. If we don't correct this situation, we have another potential window into the private structure. We have already discussed why revealing the private part of an object is a bad idea, and the same arguments apply to **fieldnames**. This is simply another function that seems to be at odds with encapsulation goals.

Of course, by now the solution path is clear. If we don't like what we get from the built-in version, we simply supply a tailored version that suits our purposes. In this case, we will tailor **fieldnames** so that it properly returns a list of public member variables. This will allow clients to interface with objects using **getfield**, **setfield**, or dynamic fieldname syntax.

6.2 CODE DEVELOPMENT

The built-in version of **fieldnames** accepts a structure as the input and returns a **cellstr** populated with the element names. The tailored version should work the same way for an object. Also, when used with objects, there is a more obscure syntax. A second string input with the value **'-full'** can be passed into **fieldnames**. The **'-full'** option tells **fieldnames** to add information about each field's type, attributes, and inheritance. This option appears to be an extension for Java. For native MATLAB objects, type in particular does not make a lot of sense.

The implementation will include code to process the `'-full'` option, but its purpose and output format are not well specified with respect to native MATLAB objects.

In the same way `'-full'` appears to be a Java-related option, we will add an option related to the group-of-eight interface. Recall the discussion of the commands **get(0)** and **set(0)**. If possible, we should give objects a similar interface, that is, an interface where commands like **get(cShape)** and **set(cShape)** will return a brief summary of the public variables. Java objects have this ability, and it is very convenient.

Most of the information displayed by these commands is information related to the public variable names, and not all of it the current value. This makes **fieldnames** a very logical place to store the additional data. The `'-full'` option does not include everything we need. We need to invent a new string value that will be used primarily from inside other group-of-eight member functions. In the case of **set(cShape)**, the output needs to include a list of the allowed values for each element. The list describes the possible element values, and following from this, the new string value will be `'-possible'`.

When `'-possible'` is the second argument to **fieldnames**, a special output format will be produced. The output will be a single cell array where odd-numbered elements contain the public member variable names and even-numbered elements contain a cell array filled with the allowed values for the preceding odd index name. If the set of allowed values is indeterminate, the cell array will be empty.

The tailored version of **fieldnames** is shown in Code Listing 39. Like the other examples, this version is tailored for **cShape**. Other classes would follow the syntax in this example but encode different names, types, and allowable values.

Code Listing 39, Initial Design for fieldnames.m

```
1   function names = fieldnames(this, varargin)
2   % returns the list of public member variable names
3   if nargin == 1
4      names = {'Size' 'ColorRgb'}'; % note: return as a column
5   else
6      switch varargin{1}
7      case '-full'
8         names = {'Size % double array' ...
9                  'ColorRgb % double array'}';
10     case '-possible'
11        names = {'Size' {{'double array (2x1)'}} ...
12                 'ColorRgb' {{'double array  (3x1)'}}}';
13     otherwise
14        error('Unsupported call to fieldnames');
15     end
16  end
```

In the one-argument case, line 4 returns a **cellstr** with a list of public variable names. The names are hard-coded into the function. These names need to match the public cases in **subsref** or problems might arise later. Class developers are responsible for keeping the files synchronized. The **switch** on line 6 is evaluated when more than one argument is passed. Lines 8–9 assemble the **cellstr** return when the caller requests the `'-full'` option. Lines 11–12 assemble the return when the caller requests `'-possible'`. This is our option, so we are free to define any syntax. The syntax in lines 11–12 allows each private variable to specify an allowed-value **cellstr** in addition to the name. This syntax makes it easier to separate and display the list of possible values.

6.3 THE TEST DRIVE

The test drive for **fieldnames** is easy because there are only three possible options. The results are shown in Code Listing 40. Line 3 builds an object and line 4 gets the public name list by calling **fieldnames** with only one argument. By leaving off the semicolon, the display shows that the list is consistent with the public interface. Line 8 invokes the **'-full'** option and the returned list includes names and some type information. Line 12 invokes the **'-possible'** option. The return value for this option has a format that lends itself to direct conversion into a structure. Line 13 demonstrates the conversion and displays the structure result.

```
Code Listing 40, Chapter 6 Test Drive Command Listing for fieldnames.m
1    >> cd /oop_guide/chapter_6
2    >> clear classes; clc
3    >> shape = cShape;
4    >> fieldnames(shape)
5    ans =
6        'Size'
7        'ColorRgb'
8    >> fieldnames(shape, '-full')
9    ans =
10       'Size % double array'
11       'ColorRgb % double array'
12   >> possible = fieldnames(shape, '-possible');
13   >> struct(possible{:})
14   ans =
15           Size: {'double array (2x1)'}
16       ColorRgb: {'double array  (3x1)'}
```

6.4 SUMMARY

The **fieldnames** function, while simple, is important because it prevents the built-in version of **fieldnames** from advertising private areas of our objects. The function also supports code modularity by consolidating the names of the public member variables in one location. In Chapter 5, prior to the existence of **fieldnames**, the list of public names was twice hard-coded inside **display.m**. Now that **fieldnames** exists, **display** code can be refactored to eliminate the hard-coded list. The refactored version of display is presented in §9.3. The tailored version of **fieldnames** also supports a new option that will be used to display a convenient public member summary. As we continue to develop the group of eight, the importance of **fieldnames** will become more and more evident.

6.5 INDEPENDENT INVESTIGATIONS

1. In the '-full' case, use **class** to inspect and assign the field's type. What are you going to do for object arrays?
2. Modify **display.m** to take advantage of **fieldnames**.

7 struct.m

In the previous chapter, we patched a hole in MATLAB's default encapsulation by tailoring **fieldnames**. In this chapter, we patch another hole by tailoring **struct**. As we have already seen, the built-in version of **struct** returns the names and values of private member variables. In fact, **struct**'s default behavior represents a risky situation because clients can use it to gain access to private data. We need to eliminate this possibility by developing a type-specific version of **struct.m**.

As a bonus, a standard function that returns an object's public structure is broadly useful. For example, look back at the scalar case of the tailored version of **display**. The strategy of allowing MATLAB to perform most of the formatting requires a structure of public variables. At that time, public structure generation was coded directly in line and we could not easily make use of it in developer view. Further proliferation of in-line structure-generation code makes class extensions very tedious and error prone. Consolidating structure generation into one function makes a lot of sense. We can even take advantage of the tailored version of **fieldnames** so that even public names are not directly coded into **struct**.

7.1 STRUCT

While we could easily write a specific get function for this task (e.g., **getPublicStructure**), MATLAB already defines a suitable function. The built-in version of **struct** already returns a structure associated with the object. The built-in version will also operate on objects. Unlike the help for **fieldnames**, **help struct** does not promise to return a structure of "public data fields."

The help files for **struct** describe a function that converts an object into its equivalent structure. Here our idea of "equivalent structure" and MATLAB's idea are definitely not the same. In our world, the structure should contain public member variables; however, the built-in version of **struct** returns a structure made up of the private variables. The **fieldnames** function was bad enough, but the **struct** function is even more despicable. It returns both the names and the values of the private variables!

While it is still true that MATLAB prevents changes to the private data, that does not prevent clients from using the values and even passing around the structures created from the object. Here is yet another place where MATLAB seems very lax about preventing client access to private data. We need to reinforce this area because the potential result of such permissiveness can be devastating. If left unchecked, clients will use this back door to destroy most of the benefits of encapsulation. Once a client ties code to the private structure returned by the default version of **struct**, later attempts to reorganize or improve the class will result in broken code and angry clients. While it might indeed be their fault, it becomes our problem. I have personally witnessed such chaos and can tell you it is no easy chore to clean it up. Preventing it from happening in the first place is a much better plan.

Like always, if we don't like what the built-in version gives us, we simply tailor the function to suit our purposes. In this particular case, tailoring is not perfect because we can't prevent clever or devious clients from using **builtin** to tie their code to an object's private data. A client can bypass all our carefully crafted member functions by using, for example,

```
shape_struct = builtin('struct', shape)
```

When a client uses **builtin** in this way, **shape_struct** is not an object, but rather a structure. With a structure, the client loses the ability to call member functions, but in return gains the ability to read and write any field in the structure. Mutation does not carry into the object, but once a client has a structure, the object is usually forgotten. Unfortunately, there is no way to prevent a client from using **builtin**.

For this very reason, clients should be told about **builtin** and strongly cautioned against its use. There is no conceivable reason for a client to circumvent the behavior of any type-specific member function by using a call to **builtin**. This decision belongs to a class developer and not a client. Class developers can and often do use **builtin** to coerce MATLAB into doing work for them; however, if class developers are doing their job properly, it is extremely rare for a client to have the same need. This is particularly true with **struct**.

7.2 CODE DEVELOPMENT

The first time we noticed a need for a function like **struct** was during the implementation of **display**. We didn't yet have such a function, so we resorted to building the structure in line. The code used in **display** built a structure for a scalar object, and it will serve as a decent starting point for the tailored, nonscalar version of **struct**. All we have to do is adapt and generalize. The important lines of code from **display** are repeated below.

```
1    public_struct.Size = this.mSize;
2    public_struct.ColorRgb = ...
3           subsref(this, substruct('.', 'ColorRgb'));
```

This code has three problems:

1. the use of public names
2. in-line conversions from private variables to public
3. only works on scalar objects

The first problem is easily solved by calling our newly tailored version of **fieldnames**. We never need to hard-code the public names because we can easily get them in the form of a **cellstr**. The second problem is solved by realizing that **subsref** already includes the necessary conversions. In fact, lines 2–3 above already use **subsref**. Code in the generalized version of **display** must always use **subsref** to obtain public member values. Using both **fieldnames** and **subsref** allows for a non-class-specific implementation. The third problem isn't hard to solve, but it does require a **for** loop. The initial implementation is shown in Code Listing 41.

```
Code Listing 41, Initial Implementation for struct.m

1    function public_struct = struct(this)
2    names = fieldnames(this);  % tailored version returns public
     names
3    values = cell(length(names), length(this(:)));  % preallocate
4    for k = 1:length(names)
5        [values{k, :}] = subsref(this(:), substruct('.', names
         {k}));
6    end
7    public_struct = reshape(cell2struct(values, names, 1),
     size(this));
```

As the solution to problem 1, line 3 calls **fieldnames** to get a **cellstr** of public member variable names. Now that we have the names, we need values. Line 3 preallocates an empty cell array where the values will be stored. The size of the cell array is **length(names)** × **length(this)** or, equivalently, the number of public variables × the number of objects in the array. Line 4 loops over the names, and line 5 assigns public values. We avoid a double loop because the whole object array is passed into **subsref** and **subsref** returns **length(this)** answers. The magic of list expansion allows the assignment of multiple cell array elements. Finally, line 7 uses **cell2struct** to generate the structure as a row vector, and reshape converts the row into the same shape as **this**.

The function **cell2struct** is very powerful but somewhat obscure. The structure values and names are passed into **cell2struct** as cell arrays. The third argument tells **cell2struct** how to assign values in the **values** cell array to fieldnames in the **names** cell array. In the case of line 7, a 1 breaks up **values** into columns. Each value in the column is associated index for index with a name in **names**. After **cell2struct**, the resulting structure array will be 1 × **size(values,2)**.

7.3 THE TEST DRIVE

The test drive for **struct** is easy because there aren't many options. The results are shown in Code Listing 42. Line 3 builds an object, and lines 4–5 set some values. Line 6 returns the public structure. Because the returned value is a structure, we can use the **full_display** utility function if we want more detail. Lines 10–12 show the details, and the values match those assigned in lines 4–5. Line 13 uses a **horzcat** operator to create an object array. Line 14 obtains the structure array, and lines 19–23 display the details. Again, the detailed values match the values expected.

```
Code Listing 42, Chapter 7 Test Drive Command Listing for struct.m

1    >> cd /oop_guide/chapter_7
2    >> clear classes; clc
3    >> shape = cShape;
4    >> shape.Size = 2;
5    >> shape.ColorRgb = [1;1;1];
6    >> struct(shape)
7    ans =
8            Size: [2x1 double]
9        ColorHsv: [3x1 double]
10   >> full_display(ans)
11   ans.Size = [2    2]';
12   ans.ColorRgb = [1    1    1]';
13   >> shape = [cShape shape];
14   >> struct(shape)
15   ans =
16   1x2 struct array with fields:
17      Size
18      ColorRgb
19   >> full_display(ans)
20   ans(1, 1).Size = [1    1]';
21   ans(1, 1).ColorRgb = [0    0    1]';
22   ans(1, 2).Size = [2    2]';
23   ans(1, 2).ColorRgb = [1    1    1]';
```

7.4 SUMMARY

This function, while simple, is important because it closes a huge hole in the object's encapsulation. Now clients are presented with a uniform public front because **display**, **fieldnames**, and **struct** all advertise the same variables. The tailored version of **struct** takes advantage of code modularity relying on **fieldnames** and **subsref** to return public information. Notice that no class-dependent data are contained inside the implementation of **struct**. The tailored version also supports modularity by allowing other functions to obtain the public structure without having to resort to in-line code. Member functions can now take advantage of this support, and eventually we will modify some of the code in **display** to use both **struct** and **fieldnames**.

7.5 INDEPENDENT INVESTIGATIONS

1. Try to overload **builtin** and see what happens.
2. Modify **display.m** to take advantage of **struct**.
3. Modify **developer_view** (a subfunction inside **display.m**) to take advantage of **fieldnames**.

8 get.m, set.m

One of the exercises back in Chapter 3 asked you to examine the possible benefits of developing one **get** and one **set** instead of a **get** and **set** pair for every public variable. That was before the implementations of **subsref** and **subsasgn**. Since **subsref** and **subsasgn** provide such an elegant, natural interface, perhaps there is no longer a need for **get** or **set**. There are still benefits, but it seems the most compelling reasons were stolen away by **subsref** and **subsasgn**. In this chapter, we will examine some of the benefits and define implementations for **get** and **set** that add quite a lot of flexibility. The functions **get** and **set** complete the membership roles for the group of eight.

8.1 ARGUMENTS FOR THE MEMBER FUNCTIONS GET AND SET

A general **get** and **set** pair is still useful to both developers and clients. A **get** and **set** pair helps simplify syntax and increases code modularity. In special circumstances, **get** and **set** can be used to "conceal" object data. So-called concealed data are variables that shouldn't be part of the typical interface but still might be needed from time to time. A **get** and **set** pair can provide abbreviated information about the class in the same way that **get(0)** and **set(0)** provide information about the command environment. Finally, defining a **get** and **set** pair allows tab completion to work with objects. Without a **get** and **set** pair, tab completion displays a list of private variables. By closing another gap in MATLAB's default encapsulation, the deal for developing **get.m** and **set.m** is sealed.

8.1.1 FOR DEVELOPERS

Switch statements inside **subsref** and **subsasgn** convert between private data and the public interface. Often, the conversion code is simple and can be included directly in each case. In these cases, private-public conversion can only be accomplished using **subsref** or **subsasgn**. For clients, operator-syntax conversion automatically formats the arguments. From inside the class, **subsref** or **subsasgn** syntax is cumbersome. Using **substruct** to pack the index helps, but dot-reference access to public variables should be easier. For example, the current implementation of display uses the command

```
[values{k, :}] = subsref(this(:), substruct('.', names{k}));
```

Using **get** makes the command easier to read. In that case, the command uses the modified syntax

```
[values{k, :}] = get(this(:), names{k});
```

While this change might seem insignificant, it has a big impact on maintainability because the **get** syntax is easier to read at a glance.

Instead of "inventing" new function names like **get** and **set**, we could have tailored **getfield** and **setfield**. There are several reasons why **get** and **set** are better. First, in version 7.0, **getfield** and **setfield** are deprecated functions, i.e., they may not exist in future versions. We certainly don't want to develop new classes based on obsolete functions. Second, the argument syntax for **getfield** and **setfield** is too complicated. By using **get** and **set**, we don't need to support a complicated predefined syntax. Third, if we don't overload **getfield** and **setfield**, MATLAB automatically converts them into **subsref** and **subsasgn** calls. Finally, we are not really inventing the names **get** and **set**. These functions are already used to manipulate the command environment and for graphics handles. Indeed, the environment and graphics handles look a lot like objects. Even more important, tab completion uses **get** and **set** to obtain the completion list.

Clients primarily use access-operator syntax. This opens the possibility of concealing special functionality inside **get** or **set**. For example, even when

```
shape.mDisplayFunc = `developer_view';
```

throws a "field not found" error, mutation can be accomplished by calling **set** directly. The equivalent direct-call syntax looks like the following:

```
shape = set(shape, `mDisplayFunc', `developer_view');
```

To make this happen, both **subsasgn** and **set** must be properly implemented. This kind of concealed functionality might be used to support development, test, or quality assurance. Developers, testers, and inspectors usually demand more access to internal states compared to normal clients. It is also an easy way to include developer-level capability without advertising it as public. Concealed functionality still has public visibility because there are no formal checks that can be used to limit access to these so-called special-access variables. This makes it difficult to decide when to promote the visibility of a private variable to concealed.

Consider **mDisplayFunc** as an example. How do we decide whether to keep **mDisplay-Func** private or promote its visibility to concealed or even public? If we leave it as private, developers must modify the constructor or add a member function to assign a value. If we promote it to public visibility, then we need to document its behavior along with that of all the other public variables. An interface description that includes many obscure or special-use functions can make a simple class appear overwhelming. True public visibility also requires more diligence by developers to trap error conditions and protect class integrity. Concealed visibility is a gray area. There is more latitude in the documentation as well as with safety. The answer usually comes down to purpose and complexity. In general, it is unwise to add too much concealed functionality. You want clients to respect the boundaries imposed by the interface, and adding a lot of concealed functionality promotes bad habits.

8.1.2 For Clients

We generally discourage clients from using **get** and **set** in their source code; however, during development, **get** and **set** can provide a quick summary of the public variables. Using **get** and **set** with graphic handles provides a good example. The command window is another example. Open MATLAB and enter the commands **get(0)** and **set(0)** in the command window. For reference, the first few lines of each command are shown in Code Listing 43. With **get(0)**, you get a display that includes all the "get-able" variables along with their current values. The output is very similar to a structure display. With **set(0)**, you get a display that includes all the "set-able" variables along with a list of possible assignment values. Many times this is the only reminder you need. The displays from graphics handles are similar. Adding this capability to every class makes the use of objects more agreeable. With the added benefits, clients might actually prefer objects to structures.

The outputs in Code Listing 43 are also interesting for another reason. The list of "get-able" variables is different from the list of "set-able" variables. Just like the public variables in our objects, certain variables are read-write while others are read-only. Now that we are comfortable with encapsulation, we recognize this as the rule rather than the exception. Both the command window settings and graphics handles seem much more like objects than like structures.

Code Listing 43, Output Example for Built-In get and set

```
1    >> get(0)
2        CallbackObject = []
3        CommandWindowSize = [134 26]
4        CurrentFigure = []
5        Diary = off
6        DiaryFile = diary
7        Echo = off
8        FixedWidthFontName = Courier
9        FormatSpacing = loose
10
11   >> set(0)
12       CurrentFigure
13       Diary: [ on | off ]
14       DiaryFile
15       Echo: [ on | off ]
16       FixedWidthFontName
17       FormatSpacing: [ loose | compact ]
```

8.1.3 TAB COMPLETION

A very convenient command-line option is "tab completion." With tab completion, you type the first few characters of a command or variable name and hit the Tab key. At that point, MATLAB will either fill in the rest of the command or display a list of items that begin with the characters typed. This helps speed development and reduces the burden of remembering complete command or variable names.

Tab completion calls on **get** and **set** to populate the name list. If we don't implement **get** and **set**, the name list isn't empty. Instead, it contains the names of the class' private variables. An empty list would be better because the list of private names represents another breach of encapsulation. In this case, the list of private names is also worthless. If we accept a name from the list, we will be presented with an error message telling us that it is illegal to access an object's private variables. There is really no choice: we must tailor **get** and **set** for every class.

8.2 CODE DEVELOPMENT

Inside **get** and **set**, a switch statement will be used to steer the execution into the correct public case. In fact, the switch statements needed by **get** and **set** already exist inside the dot-reference sections of **subsref** and **subsasgn**, respectively. The function calls are a little different, but if we grab the dot-reference switch code and wrap it in a new interface the implementation is quick and easy. During the implementation for **get** and **set**, you will notice a lot of code duplication between **get** and **subsref** and between **set** and **subsasgn**. In fact, the dot-reference switches can be replaced by calls to **get** or **set**. In this chapter, the focus centers on the implementations of **get** and **set**. In the next chapter, we will clean up code in several group-of-eight functions by replacing in-line code with calls to **fieldnames**, **struct**, **get**, and **set**.

8.2.1 IMPLEMENTING GET AND SET

The implementations for **get** and **set** need to do three things: access and mutate public variables, access and mutate concealed variables, and display summary information. To access and mutate public variables, we will copy the switch cases from **subsref** and **subsasgn** into **get** and **set**. To implement concealed variables, **get** and **set** need code to allow them to figure out from where they were called. The easiest way to figure this out is to examine the format of the input arguments. The input arguments also steer the execution to display summary information. Too few input arguments will trigger **get** and **set** to display a summary.

Because the arguments are used to steer the execution, we need to examine them more closely. The function definitions listing all arguments are given by the following:

```
1    function varargout = get(this, index)
2    function varargout = set(this, index, varargin)
```

The functions are member functions, and consequently the object occupies the first argument position. In addition, in both functions the **index** variable occupies the second position. The format of **index** will be used to grant or deny access to the concealed variables. When **index** is a simple string, **get** and **set** will allow access to concealed variables. In this case, **switch** statements can use the value without modification because it already names the desired variable. When **index** is not a string, **get** and **set** will deny access to concealed variables. In this case, **get** and **set** assume a **substruct** format for **index**. The element at **index (1)** will specify dot-reference so that **substruct, index (1).type** will be equal to '**.**' and **index (1).subs** is the string value used for the switch.

At first, allowing two formats for **index** might seem odd, but it turns out to be very convenient. A typical call to **get** might look something like the following:

```
shape_size = get(shape, 'Size');
```

Here, passing the public name as the **index** simplifies the syntax. The simple arguments also match the typical syntax for **getfield**. We don't specify a dot-reference operator because **get** is specifically tailored to return public variables. The dot-reference operator is inherent in its operation.

On the other hand, when a public variable is accessed using operator syntax, for example,

```
shape_size = shape.Size;
```

MATLAB automatically packages the indices into a **substruct**. The **substruct index** is passed into **subsref** or **subsasgn**, and the dot-referenced public variable name is contained in **index(1).subs**. Under these conditions, **subsref** and **get** should behave the same way. The same is true for **subsasgn** and **set**. Because they share the same behavior, it is smart to let them share the code that implements the behavior. One way to do this is to allow **get** and **set** to perform the actual dot-reference indexing and let **subsref** call **get** and **subsasgn** call **set**. We can even use the **substruct index** passed into **subsref** or **subsasgn** as a cue to disallow access to concealed variables. In this chapter, we won't make changes to **subsref** or **subsasgn**, but we will implement **get** and **set** so that the changes are easier to make when we get to §10.1.1.3 and §10.1.1.4.

The number of input arguments is used to select between access/mutate or summary display. Calling **get** or **set** with only one argument, for example,

```
get(shape)       % shape is an object of type cShape

set(cShape)      % constructor creates a temporary object
```

results in a summary display of all "get-able" or "set-able" public variables. Calling **set** with two arguments, for example,

```
set(cShape, 'Size')
```

results in a summary display of the indexed variable only.

When **this** is a scalar object, **get** returns one value and **set** assigns one value. When **this** is nonscalar, **get** returns a cell array composed of one value from each object in the object array. In addition, when **this** is nonscalar, **set** potentially needs more than one assignment value. In the calling syntax, the values appear as a comma-separated list. MATLAB packages the comma-separated arguments into individual cells of **varargin**.

Execution based on both the number and type of the input arguments leads to an implementation with several logical paths. Supporting public and concealed variables adds a few more. The implementations will be easier to follow if we first construct a high-level block diagram.

We are now in a position to draw a high-level block diagram for these functions. The block diagrams are shown in Figure 8.1 and Figure 8.2. The logical flow is similar for both because in many ways they both do the same sort of things. They have to check the number of input arguments, search the public names, determine whether concealed access is allowed, throw an error for unknown names, and convert between public and private data. The diagram for **set** is a little more complicated because of its support for both full and subset summary displays. Similarities allow the implementations to share the same general structure. The initial implementations of **get** and **set** are shown in Code Listing 44 and Code Listing 45.

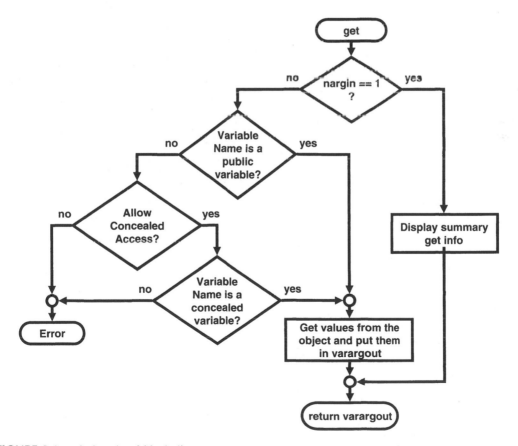

FIGURE 8.1 get's functional block diagram.

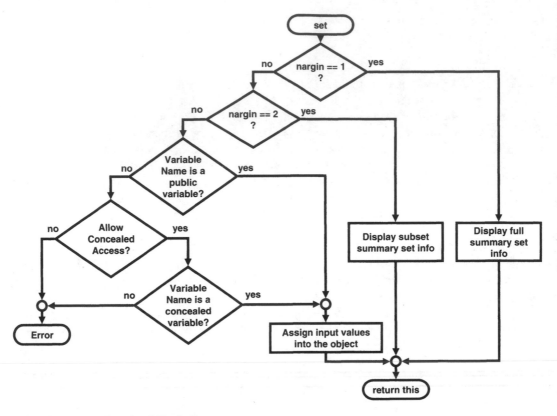

FIGURE 8.2 set's functional block diagram.

8.2.2 INITIAL GET.M

The implementation in Code Listing 44 follows the block diagram in Figure 8.1, and much of the code should look at least vaguely familiar. The public variable cases in lines 23–41 came directly from the implementation of **subsref** in Chapter 4.

Code Listing 44, Initial Implementation for get.m

```
1    function varargout = get(this, index)
2    % one argument, display info and return
3    if nargin == 1
4       if nargout == 0
5          disp(struct(this(1)));
6       else
7          varargout = cell(1,max([1, nargout]));
8          varargout{1} = struct(this(1));
9       end
10      return;
11   end
12
13   % if index is a string, we will allow special access
14   called_by_name = ischar(index);
15
```

```
16   % the set switch below needs a substruct
17   if called_by_name
18       index = substruct('.', index);
19   end
20
21   % public-member-variable section
22   found = true;   % otherwise-case will flip to false
23   switch index(1).subs
24       case 'Size'
25           if isempty(this)
26               varargout = {};
27           else
28               varargout = {this.mSize};
29           end
30       case 'ColorRgb'
31           if isempty(this)
32               varargout = {};
33           else
34               rgb = hsv2rgb([this.mColorHsv]')';
35               varargout = mat2cell(rgb, 3, ones(1, size(rgb,2)));
36           end
37       otherwise
38           found = false;   % didn't find it in the public section
39   end
40
41   % concealed member variables, not strictly public
42   if ~found && called_by_name
43       found = true;
44       switch index(1).subs
45           case 'mDisplayFunc'
46               if isempty(this)
47                   varargout = {};
48               else
49                   varargout = {this.mDisplayFunc};
50               end
51           otherwise
52               found = false;   % didn't find it in the special
                    section
53       end
54   end
55
56   if ~found
57     error(['??? Reference to non-existent field ' index(1).subs
       '.']);
58   end
59
60   if length(varargout) > 1 & nargout <= 1
```

```
61        if iscellstr(varargout) || any([cellfun('isempty',
          varargout)]))
62            varargout = {varargout};
63        else
64            try
65                varargout = {[varargout{:}]};
66            catch
67                varargout = {varargout};
68            end
69        end
70  end
```

Lines 3–11 implement the true branch of the block diagram's first decision block. On line 3, if only one input was passed, **nargin** will equal 1. In the case of no requested output, line 5 uses the tailored version of **struct** to obtain the public structure and then passes that structure to **disp**. The net result is a display of the public elements. If outputs are requested, line 7 builds a **varargout** cell array with the correct number of cells and line 8 assigns the public structure into the first cell. Tab completion uses this behavior to obtain the public variable completion list.

If both an object and an **index** were passed, execution skips to line 14. Line 14 uses an **ischar** test to determine whether the **index** is a simple name string or something else. The value **called_by_name** governs concealed variable access. If **index** is a string, **called_by_name** is **true** and concealed access is permitted.

Lines 17–19 give **index** a uniform format. There are two choices for converting **index**: convert a **substruct** into a string or convert a string into a **substruct**. Lines 17–19 convert a string into a **substruct**. Later, when we encounter complicated examples of private to public conversion, the use of a **substruct** simplifies the implementation.

The remaining lines are organized into four functional blocks: public access (lines 22–39), concealed access (lines 42–54), error processing (lines 56–58), and **varargout** conversion (lines 60–70). The variable **found** is used to control entry into each of these blocks. In the public variable block, line 22 sets **found** to **true** before attempting to match the indexed name with the public variable cases. If one of the public variable cases matches the indexed name, the case assigns public values into **varargout** and **found** remains **true**. Otherwise, line 38 sets **found** to **false**. The commands contained in each case were described line by line in Chapter 4.

Line 42 guards the concealed variable block. The guard allows entry only when the calling syntax allows access to concealed variables and the value has not yet been found. The variable **called_by_name** is true if concealed access is permitted. Once entered, the concealed variable block operates the same as the public variable block. Of course, the cases contain concealed variable names rather than public variable names. Line 43 sets **found** to **true** before attempting to match the indexed name with a case. If one of the concealed variable cases matches the indexed name, the case assigns concealed values into **varargout** and **found** remains **true**. Otherwise, line 52 sets **found** to **false**. Notice that on line 45, **mDisplayFunc** is a concealed variable. Populating **varargout** with concealed values is the same as populating **varargout** with public values.

Line 56 guards the field not found error. If the indexed field didn't match an available case, **found** will be **false** and line 57 throws an error. The syntax mimics the error message generated when a structure is dot-referenced with a name that does not match one of its elements. If the indexed field did match a case, **found** will be **true** and **varargout** will contain the indexed values.

Finally, the size of **varargout** must to be repackaged to conform to the value of **nargout**. Repackaging is only necessary when **nargout** is zero or one and the length of **varargout** is larger than one. Values in **varargout** are concatenated according to the same rules developed for **subsref**, and lines 60–70 were copied directly from Chapter 4's implementation of **subsref**.

8.2.3 INITIAL SET.M

The implementation in Code Listing 45 follows the block diagram in Figure 8.2. Like **get**, much of the **set** code will look familiar because a lot of it came directly from the implementation of **subsasgn** in Chapter 4.

Code Listing 45, Initial Design for set.m

```
1    function varargout = set(this, index, varargin)
2    % one argument or two arguments, display info and return
3    if nargin < 3
4        possible = fieldnames(this, '-possible');
5        possible_struct = struct(possible{:});
6        if nargout == 0
7            if nargin == 1
8                disp(possible_struct);
9            else
10               try
11                   temp_struct.(index) = possible_struct.(index);
12                   disp(temp_struct);
13               catch
14                   warning(['??? Reference to non-existent field
                     ' ...
15                   index '.']);
16               end
17           end
18       else
19           varargout = cell(1,max([1, nargout]));
20           varargout{1} = possible_struct;
21       end
22       return;
23   end
24
25   called_by_name = ischar(index);
26
27   % the set switch below needs a substruct
28   if called_by_name
29       index = substruct('.', index);
30   end
31
32   % public-member-variable section
33   found = true;  % otherwise-case will flip to false
34   switch index(1).subs
35       case 'Size'
36           if length(index) > 1
```

```
37          this.mSize = subsasgn(this.mSize, index(2:end),
            varargin{:});
38          this.mScale = subsasgn(this.mScale, index(2:end), 1);
39        else
40          new_size = zeros(2, length(varargin));
41          for k = 1:size(new_size, 2)
42            try
43              new_size(:, k) = varargin{k}(:);
44            catch
45              error('Size must be a scalar or length == 2');
46            end
47          end
48          new_size = num2cell(new_size, 1);
49          [this.mSize] = deal(new_size{:});
50          [this.mScale] = deal(ones(2,1));
51        end
52      case 'ColorRgb'
53        if length(index) > 1
54          rgb = hsv2rgb(this.mColorHsv')';
55          rgb = subsasgn(rgb, index(2:end), varargin{:});
56          this.mColorHsv = rgb2hsv(rgb')';
57        else
58          hsv = rgb2hsv([varargin{:}]')';
59          hsv = mat2cell(hsv, 3, ones(1, size(hsv,2)));
60          [this.mColorHsv] = deal(hsv{:});
61        end
62    otherwise
63      found = false;
64  end
65
66  % concealed member variables, not strictly public
67  if ~found && called_by_name
68      found = true;
69      switch index(1).subs
70          case 'mDisplayFunc'
71              if length(index) > 1
72                  this.mDisplayFunc = ...
73                      subsasgn(this.mDisplayFunc, ...
74                          index(2:end), varargin{:});
75              else
76                  [this.mDisplayFunc] = deal(varargin{:});
77              end
78      otherwise
79          found = false;  % didn't find it in the special section
80      end
81  end
82
```

```
83   if ~found
84       error(['??? Reference to non-existent field '
         index(1).subs '.']);
85   end
86
87   varargout{1} = this;
```

Lines 3–23 implement the first two true branches found in **set**'s block diagram and govern the behavior of the summary display. Line 4 uses the **'-possible'** option added to the tailored version of **fieldnames** to obtain a cell array containing public names and their possible values. The cell array format allows the **struct** command in line 5 to create a structure with public names as fields and possible value strings as values. When there is no requested output, lines 7–17 format and display summary information. If only the object was passed, line 8 displays the entire structure of public names and possible values. If both object and **index** were passed, line 11 uses the **index** to create a temporary structure that contains only the indexed element. Line 11 can assume that **index** is a string because **subsasgn** always passes at least three arguments. Line 12 then displays the temporary structure. If lines 11–12 cause an error, the warning on lines 14–15 is displayed. The error might not actually be the result of a nonexistent field, but it is certainly the most likely error.

Tab completion will request an output, and lines 19–20 handle the request. Line 19 allocates **varargout** with the correct number of elements, and line 20 assigns the structure of possible values into the first element. With this structure, tab completion can populate the selection list.

If three or more arguments were passed, execution skips to line 25. Concealed access rights and index conversion commands are identical to the code in **get**. Line 25 uses an **ischar** test to determine whether the **index** is a simple name string or something else. The value **called_by_name** governs concealed variable mutation. If **index** is a string, **called_by_name** is **true** and concealed mutation is permitted. Lines 28–30 give **index** a uniform format by converting a string **index** into a **substruct**.

Again as in **get**, the remaining lines are organized into three functional blocks: public access (lines 33–64), concealed access (lines 67–81), and error processing (lines 83–85). The variable **found** is used to control entry into each of these blocks. In the public variable block, line 22 sets **found** to **true** before attempting to match the indexed name with the public variable cases. If one of the public variable cases matches the indexed name, the case assigns input values into the indexed variable of **this** and **found** remains **true**. Otherwise, line 38 sets **found** to **false**. The commands contained in each case were described line by line in Chapter 4. Different from the Chapter 4 description is how the input values are indexed. In **subsasgn**, access-operator conversion reverses the order of the input values. With **set**, there is no operator conversion and the input values are correctly ordered.

Line 67 guards the concealed variable block. The guard allows entry only when the calling syntax supports concealed variables mutation and the indexed name has not yet been found. The variable **called_by_name** is true if concealed mutation is permitted. Once entered, the concealed variable block operates the same as the public variable block. Of course, the cases contain concealed variable names rather than public variable names. Line 68 sets **found** to **true** before attempting to match the indexed name with a case. If one of the concealed variable cases matches the indexed name, the case assigns input values into the indexed variable of **this** and **found** remains **true**. Otherwise, line 79 sets **found** to **false**. Notice that on line 70, **mDisplayFunc** is a writeable concealed variable. The only difference between this case and the case described in Chapter 4 is the index order of the input values.

Line 83 guards the field not found error. If the indexed field didn't match an available case, **found** will be **false** and line 84 throws an error. The syntax mimics the error message generated when a structure is dot-referenced with a name that does not match one of its elements. If the indexed field matches a case, **found** will be **true** and **this** will contain mutated values. Line 87 returns **this** as the first and only element of **varargout** even when **nargout==0**.

8.3   THE TEST DRIVE

In the test drive, we will test both the typical string-name syntax and the **substruct** syntax. In the next chapter, the **substruct** syntax option will be used to support **subsref** and **subsasgn**, and we need to make sure **get** and **set** are ready. We will use the values from the test drive in Chapter 4. Instead of dot-reference operators, we will use calls to **get** and **set**. We can also use **mDisplayFunc** to experiment with concealed variables. Some commands and outputs for **get** and **set** are shown in Code Listing 46 and Code Listing 47.

```
Code Listing 46, Chapter 8 Test Drive Command Listing for set.m
1    >> cd 'C:/oop_guide/chapter_8'
2    >> clear classes; fclose all; close all force; diary off; clc;
3    >> shape(1) = cShape;
4    >> shape(2) = shape(1);
5    >> shape(2:3) = [shape(1) shape(2)];
6    >> shape(2) = set(shape(2), 'Size', [2;3]);
7    >> shape(2) = set(shape(2), substruct('.', 'Size'), [2;3]);
8    >> shape = set(shape, 'Size', [10;11], [20;21], [30;31]);
9    >> shape(2) = set(shape(2), 'ColorRgb', [0 1 0]');
10   >> shape(3) = set(shape(3), 'ColorRgb', [0 0.5 0.5]');
11   >> set(shape)
12           Size: {'double array (2x1)'}
13        ColorRgb: {'double array   (3x1)'}
14   >> set(shape, 'Size')
15           Size: {'double array (2x1)'}
16   >> shape = set(shape, 'mDisplayFunc', 'developer_view');
17   >> shape(1)
18   ----- Public Member Variables -----
19   ans =
20           Size: [2x1 double]
21        ColorRgb: [3x1 double]
22   ..... Private Member Variables .....
23   ans(1).mSize = [10   11]';
24   ans(1).mScale = [1   1]';
25   ans(1).mColorHsv = [0.66667              1              1]';
26   ans(1).mDisplayFunc = 'developer_view';
27   >> shape(1) = set(shape(1), substruct('.', 'mDisplayFunc'),
     []);
28   ??? Error using ==> cShape.set
29   ??? Reference to non-existent field mDisplayFunc.
```

Line 1 changes to this chapter's directory, and line 2 clears the workspace. Lines 3–5 construct an object array. Line 6 sets **shape(2)**'s **'Size'** public variable using name-string syntax, and line 7 repeats the command using **substruct** syntax. Lines 8–10 assign values we will check when we get to display public variables. Line 11 demonstrates the one-input summary display. Lines 12–13 display the public variable names along with the allowed value syntax. Line 14 demonstrates the output of an indexed summary display. The output on line 15 matches the first line of the one-input summary display. Line 16 sets the concealed variable **'mDisplayFunc'**, and lines 17–26 demonstrate the resulting expanded output. Notice that line 16 mutated all three objects in the array even though only one input value was provided. For reference, line 8 supplied three input values. Line 27 attempts to set **'mDisplayFunc'** using **substruct** syntax. Lines 28–29 correctly complain that **'mDisplayFunc'** is not a field. This is correct because **substruct** syntax can't be used to mutate concealed variables.

Code Listing 47, Chapter 8 Test Drive Command Listing for get.m

```
1    >> get(shape, 'Size')
2    ans =
3         10    20    30
4         11    21    31
5    >> get(shape(2), 'ColorRgb')
6    ans =
7         0
8         1
9         0
10   >> get(shape(3), 'ColorRgb')
11   ans =
12                0
13       5.0000e-001
14       5.0000e-001
15     >> get(shape)
16          Size: [2x1 double]
17       ColorRgb: [3x1 double]
```

Lines 1–4 confirm that **set** does not need to reverse the input values. The values are correct, but the line 1 outputs are concatenated because **nargout** is zero. Lines 5–14 confirm that RGB values written into the object are the same values accessed. Finally, lines 15–17 demonstrate the use of **get**'s summary display.

8.4 SUMMARY

In this chapter, we closed all the remaining holes in MATLAB's default encapsulation. Defining **get** and **set** enables effective tab completion, provides a handy summary of the public member variables, introduces concealed variable visibility, and gives class developers a friendly syntax for accessing public variables. The implementations for **get** and **set** borrow heavily from Chapter 4, but the code is better organized. The organization will immediately allow simplifications to **subsref** and **subsasgn**. Later the organization will easily support inheritance.

The previous few chapters added many pieces to the implementation, but we have neglected to add those pieces to our puzzle. With recent additions of **fieldnames**, **struct**, **get**, and **set**, every group-of-eight function has an initial implementation. We can and we will improve

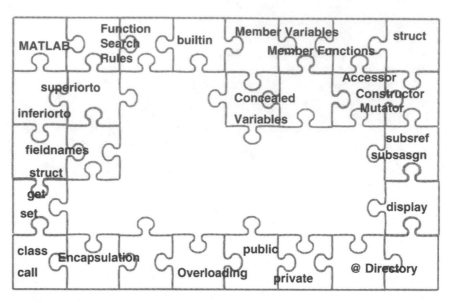

FIGURE 8.3 All the pieces of the frame are in place.

them, but now that all have an implementation, the frame of the puzzle is complete. A picture of our progress is shown in Figure 8.3. The rest of the development focuses on improving what we have already developed and on extending the scope of the framework.

8.5 INDEPENDENT INVESTIGATIONS

1. Give **get** the ability to accept a **cellstr** with multiple public member variable names. How should return values be organized? Is it a lot easier to support scalar objects compared to general object arrays?
2. Give **set** the ability to accept a **cellstr** with multiple public member variable names and a cell array of input values. How does object array support complicate the code?

9 Simplify Using get, set, fieldnames, and struct

Throughout this section, we have developed the implementations for a small but very important collection of member functions. In their order of development, the functions belonging to this so-called group-of-eight are as follows:

1. default constructor (e.g., **cShape**)
2. **subsref**
3. **subsasgn**
4. **display**
5. **fieldnames**
6. **struct**
7. **get**
8. **set**

For the current implementations, we considered the following two goals:

1. Make the class interface mimic the built-in structure interface.
2. Coerce MATLAB to do as much of the work as possible.

For the most part, the group of eight successfully reproduces a structure-like interface. It takes all eight to produce a robust reproduction. The reproduction is so good that in many cases, clients will not even be aware they are using objects. The group of eight also takes maximum advantage of function-search rules to allow MATLAB to find and use built-in functions. Learning how to use an obscure built-in function is always preferable to developing a new function.

Before we start using the group-of-eight functions, we need to add another constraint and revisit our earlier implementations. This second pass will create a collection of bulletproof functions that can be used to create a safe alternative to structures. The additional constraint is to

- collect class-specific code into the smallest possible set of functions.

Certainly low-level functions like **fieldnames**, **get**, and **set** need to include class-specific code, but **subsref**, **subsasgn**, and **display** may not.

In their current states, implementations for **subsref**, **subsasgn**, and **display** contain class-specific code simply because they were developed first. In this chapter, we revisit these functions and make them class independent. By the end of this chapter, half the functions in the group of eight can be copied from class to class with no additional class-specific tailoring. This situation represents reuse at its best. The four functions are **struct**, **subsref**, **subsasgn**, and **display**. We spent a lot of time and effort designing and developing the implementations, and it is comforting to realize that a lot of that work will never be repeated.

9.1 IMPROVING SUBSREF.M

The improved implementation for **subsref** is included in Code Listing 48. The primary difference between this version and the version in §4.1.3 occurs in the dot-reference case. Lines 5–9 are different, and only those lines are described below. A detailed description of the other lines can be found in §4.1.3. Rather than including a case for each public variable name, public values are accessed using **get**. By eliminating the public-name cases, **subsref** no longer contains class-specific code.

Code Listing 48, Improved Implementation for subsref.m

```
1    function varargout = subsref(this, index)
2
3    switch index(1).type
4      case '.'
5        if isempty(this)
6          varargout = cell(0);
7        else
8          varargout = cell(1, max(length(this(:)), nargout));
9        end
10       try
11         [varargout{:}] = get(this, index);
12       catch
13         rethrow(lasterror);
14       end
15
16       if length(index) > 1
17         if length(this) == 1
18           varargout = {subsref([varargout{:}], index(2:end))};
19         else
20           [err_id, err_msg] = array_reference_error(index(2).
             type);
21           error(err_id, err_msg);
22         end
23       end
24
25     case '()'
26         this_subset = this(index(1).subs{:});
27         if length(index) == 1
28             varargout = {this_subset};
29         else
30             % trick subsref into returning more than 1 ans
31             varargout = cell(size(this_subset));
32             [varargout{:}] = subsref(this_subset, index
               (2:end));
33         end
34
35     case '{}'
```

```
36           error(['??? ' class(this) ' object, is not a cell
             array']);
37
38      otherwise
39         error(['??? Unexpected index.type of ' index(1).type]);
40   end
41
42   if length(varargout) > 1 & nargout <= 1
43     if iscellstr(varargout) || any([cellfun('isempty',
       varargout)])
44       varargout = {varargout};
45     else
46       try
47         varargout = {[varargout{:}]};
48       catch
49         varargout = {varargout};
50       end
51     end
52   end
```

Lines 5–9 preallocate the output cell array. When **get** is called in line 11, the length of **varargout** will determine **get**'s value of **nargout**. Preallocation is important because it tricks MATLAB into passing the proper **nargout** value. If the object is empty, line 6 preallocates an empty **varargout**. Otherwise, line 8 preallocates using the maximum of the number of objects in the array or **subsref**'s **nargout** value.

The call to **get** in line 11 is surrounded by a **try-catch** statement. If a "field not found" error occurs during the call to **get**, line 13 catches and rethrows the error. The **rethrow** allows the execution to halt inside **subsref** rather than deep within some unknown member function.

9.2 IMPROVING SUBSASGN.M

The improved implementation for **subsasgn** is included in Code Listing 49. The primary difference between this version and the version in §4.1.4 occurs in the dot-reference case, but the array-reference case also includes some changes. Only the changes are described below. A detailed description of the other lines can be found in §4.1.4. Rather than including a case for each public variable name, public values are mutated using **set**. By eliminating the public name cases, **subsasgn** no longer contains class-specific code. We are also careful to keep the array reference changes non-class-specific.

Code Listing 49, Improved Implementation for subsasgn.m

```
1    function this = subsasgn(this, index, varargin)
2
3    switch index(1).type
4      case '.'
5        try
6          this = set(this, index, varargin{end:-1:1});
7        catch
```

```
8            rethrow(lasterror);
9        end
10
11   case '()'
12     if isempty(this)
13       % due to superiorto, need to look at this and varargin
14       if isa(this, mfilename('class'))
15         this = eval(class(this));
16       else
17         this = eval(class(varargin{1}));
18       end
19     end
20     if length(index) == 1
21       this = builtin('subsasgn', this, index, varargin{:});
22     else
23       this_subset = this(index(1).subs{:});   % get the subset
24       this_subset = subsasgn(this_subset, index(2:end),
         varargin{:});
25       this(index(1).subs{:}) = this_subset; % put subset back
26     end
27
28   case '{}'
29       error(['??? ' class(this) ' object, is not a cell
         array']);
30
31   otherwise
32     error(['??? Unexpected index.type of ' index(1).type]);
33 end
```

Replacing the public member cases is the call to **set** on line 6. Notice the index reversal on the input values contained in **varargin**. Field not found errors are caught and rethrown by line 8. The **rethrow** allows the execution to halt inside **subsasgn** rather than deep within some unknown member function.

Lines 12–19 correct a potential error that might occur when array-access mutation is used on an empty object. The variable is still identified as an object even though one or more of its dimensions is zero. Under the empty object condition, line 15 gets the class name with **class(this)** and uses **eval** to invoke the constructor. Lines 12–19 also correct a potential error condition where **this** is completely empty (i.e., **[]**) and **subsasgn** was selected based on **varargin**'s type rather than **this**. The use of either **superiorto** or **inferiorto** can lead to this condition. In this situation, line 17 gets the class name with **class(varargin{1})** and uses **eval** to invoke the constructor. The **isa** check in line 14 allows **this** to be properly assigned with a default value regardless of which argument directed the call.

9.3 IMPROVING DISPLAY.M

The improved implementation for **display** is included in Code Listing 50. The modified **display** replaces the use of public variable names with calls to **struct** and **fieldnames**. These changes show up in the **standard_view** subfunction. The format for **developer_view** also changes slightly.

Code Listing 50, Improved Implementation for display.m

```
1    function display(this, display_name)
2
3    if nargin < 2
4        % assign 'ans' if inputname(1) empty
5        display_name = inputname(1);
6        if isempty(display_name)
7            display_name = 'ans';
8        end
9    end
10
11   % check whether mDisplayFunc has a value
12   % if it has a value feval the value to get the display
13   DisplayFunc = cell(size(this));
14   [DisplayFunc{:}] = get(this, 'mDisplayFunc');
15   use_standard_view = cellfun('isempty', DisplayFunc(:));
16   if all(use_standard_view)
17     standard_view(this, display_name);
18   else
19     for k = 1:length(this(:))
20       if use_standard_view(k)
21         standard_view(this(k), display_name);
22       else
23         indexed_display_name = sprintf('%s(%d)', display_name,
         k);
24         feval(get(this(k), 'mDisplayFunc'), this(k), indexed_
         display_name);
25       end
26     end
27   end
28
29   % -------------------------
30   function standard_view(this, display_name)
31   if ~isempty( ...
32           [strfind(display_name, '.') ...
33           strfind(display_name, '(') ...
34           strfind(display_name, '{')])
35       display_name = 'ans';
36   end
37   % handle scalar vs. non-scalar this
38   % note: if isempty(this), jumps to else
39   if length(this) == 1  % scalar case
40       % use eval to assign public struct into display_name
         variable
41       eval([display_name ' = struct(this);']);
42       % use eval to call display on the display_name structure
```

```
43        eval(['display(' display_name ');']);
44  else  % array case
45        % use eval to assign this into display_name variable
46        eval([display_name ' = this;']);
47        % use eval to call builtin display for size info
48        eval(['builtin(''display'', ' display_name ');']);
49        % still need to display variable names explicitly
50        disp('     with public member variables:');
51        % get list of public names with fieldname
52        names = fieldnames(this);
53        % loop over the name list and display
54        for name = names'
55            disp(['          ' name{1}]);
56        end
57        % display extra line if loose
58        if strcmp(get(0, 'FormatSpacing'), 'loose')
59            disp(' ');
60        end
61  end
62
63  % --------------------------
64  function developer_view(this, display_name)
65  disp('----- Public Member Variables -----');
66  full_display(struct(this), display_name);
67  disp('..... Private Member Variables .....');
68  full_display(builtin('struct', this), display_name, true);
```

Lines 13–14 and 24 substitute a **get** call for **mDisplayFunc** for the previous dot-reference access. Using **get** helps decouple **display** from the object's structure. In line 41, a call to the tailored version of **struct** replaces previous calls to **subsref** and **get**. The use of **struct** eliminates the need to build the structure inside **standard_view**. For nonscalar object arrays, line 52 gets a list of variable names using the tailored version of **fieldnames** and lines 54–56 loop over the list writing each name in the command window. The use of **fieldnames** eliminates the need to code the public variable names into **standard_view**.

Inside **developer_view**, line 66 uses **full_display** to format and display the public structure. Often this results in a longer display with more data. With this change, the public display format matches the private display format and the result is easier to read. Commands in the test drive demonstrate **developer_view**'s new output.

9.4 TEST DRIVE

An important part of encapsulation is the ability to improve the private implementation without upsetting client code. In this chapter, we made significant changes to three core interface functions. If encapsulation works, we should be able to repeat the commands from Chapter 4 and get the same results from **subsref** and **subsasgn**. The commands in Code Listing 51 are indeed the same commands used in Chapter 4. Except for the output of the **display** commands, the results are identical. In Chapter 4, the tailored version of **display** did not yet exist, so we got a cryptic output from the built-in version. Now that we have a tailored version, the outputs on lines 62–66 and 68–70 display the same information we would get from a structure.

Code Listing 51, Chapter 9 Test Drive Command Listing: A Repeat of the Commands from Chapter 4

```
1    >> cd 'C:/oop_guide/chapter_9'
2    >> clear classes; fclose all; close all force; diary off;
3    >> set(0, 'FormatSpacing', 'compact')
4    >> shape = cShape;
5    >> shape(2) = shape(1);
6    >> shape(2:3) = [shape(1) shape(2)];
7    >> shape(2).Size = [2;3];
8    >> shape(2).Size(1) = 20;
9    >> [shape(2:3).Size] = deal([20], [30 31]);
10   ??? Too many outputs requested.  Most likely cause is missing
     [] around
11   left hand side that has a comma separated list expansion.
12
13   >> [shape.Size] = deal([10;11], [20], [30 31]);
14   >> temp = shape(3);
15   >> shape(3) = [];
16   >> shape = [shape temp];
17
18   >> shape(2).ColorRgb = [0 1 0]';
19   >> shape(3).ColorRgb = [0 0.5 0.5]';
20   >> shape(3).ColorRgb(3) = 1.0;
21   >>
22   >> ShapeCopy = shape;
23   >> OneShape = shape(2);
24   >> ShapeSubSet = shape(2:3);
25   >> ShapeSize = shape(2).Size
26   ShapeSize =
27       20
28       20
29   >> ShapeSize = [shape(:).Size]
30   ShapeSize =
31       10    20    30
32       11    20    31
33   >> ShapeSize = [shape.Size]
34   ShapeSize =
35       10    20    30
36       11    20    31
37   >> ShapeSize = {shape(:).Size}
38   ShapeSize =
39       [2x3 double]
40   >> ShapeSize = {shape.Size}
41   ShapeSize =
42       [2x1 double]    [2x1 double]    [2x1 double]
43   >> ShapeHorizSize = shape(2).Size(1)
```

```
44   ShapeHorizSize =
45      20
46   >> [shape.ColorRgb]
47   ans =
48            0            0            0
49            0       1.0000       0.5000
50       1.0000            0       1.0000
51   >> shape(1) = 1.5 * shape(1) * [2; 3];
52   >> shape(1).Size
53   ans =
54      3.0000e+001
55      4.9500e+001
56   >> shape(1) = reset(shape(1));
57   >> shape(1).Size
58   ans =
59      10
60      11
61   >> display(shape)
62   shape =
63      cShape object: 1-by-3
64      with public member variables:
65         Size
66         ColorRgb
67   >> display(shape(1))
68   ans =
69            Size: [2x1 double]
70         ColorRgb: [3x1 double]
```

The display outputs on lines 62–66 and 68–70 above represent a vast improvement over the outputs from the built-in version. With **developer_view**, the output will display values. This is true even for object arrays and oddly shaped variables. The output from **developer_view** is shown in Code Listing 52. Line 1 uses **set** to assign a display-format function. We can't use a dot-reference operator because **'mDisplayFunc'** is a concealed variable. Line 2 displays the entire object array. There are three objects in the array, and **developer_view** shows the contents of all three. The output can be seen in lines 3–26. Unlike the normal **display** format, this output is formatted to look like a normal MATLAB command. Display lines can be cut from public member variable sections and pasted into a command line or into client code. The output also displays the names and values for both public and private variables. The display is a violation of encapsulation, but it is easy to see how this output format can be useful during debugging, testing, and quality assurance. Line 28 displays only the first array element. The output format in lines 29–36 uses the same format but limits the number of elements.

Code Listing 52, Chapter 9 Additional Test-Drive Commands

```
1   >> shape = set(shape, 'mDisplayFunc', 'developer_view');
2   >> display(shape)
3   -----   Public Member Variables   -----
4   shape(1).Size = [10   11]';
```

```
 5    shape(1).ColorRgb = [0    0    1]';
 6    .....   Private Member Variables   .....
 7    shape(1).mSize = [10    11]';
 8    shape(1).mScale = [1    1]';
 9    shape(1).mColorHsv = [0.66667              1              1]';
10    shape(1).mDisplayFunc = 'developer_view';
11    -----   Public Member Variables   -----
12    shape(2).Size = [20    20]';
13    shape(2).ColorRgb = [0    1    0]';
14    .....   Private Member Variables   .....
15    shape(2).mSize = [20    20]';
16    shape(2).mScale = [1    1]';
17    shape(2).mColorHsv = [0.33333              1              1]';
18    shape(2).mDisplayFunc = 'developer_view';
19    -----   Public Member Variables   -----
20    shape(3).Size = [30    31]';
21    shape(3).ColorRgb = [0              0.5              1]';
22    .....   Private Member Variables   .....
23    shape(3).mSize = [30    31]';
24    shape(3).mScale = [1    1]';
25    shape(3).mColorHsv = [0.58333              1              1]';
26    shape(3).mDisplayFunc = 'developer_view';
27    >>
28    >> display(shape(1))
29    -----   Public Member Variables   -----
30    ans(1).Size = [10    11]';
31    ans(1).ColorRgb = [0    0    1]';
32    .....   Private Member Variables   .....
33    ans(1).mSize = [10    11]';
34    ans(1).mScale = [1    1]';
35    ans(1).mColorHsv = [0.66667              1              1]';
36    ans(1).mDisplayFunc = 'developer_view';
```

9.5 SUMMARY

In this chapter, we didn't add any new functionality to group-of-eight functions; however, we significantly improved the overall organization. Half of the group is now completely class independent. This is important because **subsref**, **subsasgn**, **struct**, and **display** will never suffer from errors due to class-to-class tailoring. It also improves our ability to maintain and evolve each class because changes affect fewer functions. As we move into the next section, we will continue to isolate class-specific code into specific files and then use those files to make member functions easier to maintain.

The chapters in this section have stressed the importance of encapsulation, and most of our work has centered on improving MATLAB's default encapsulation. All that work paid off. In this chapter, we were able to improve the private implementation without upsetting the format or output of earlier commands. Commands from Chapter 4 continue to work exactly as before.

9.6 INDEPENDENT INVESTIGATIONS

1. Create a new display function called **expanded_view** that uses **full_display** format to display an object's public variables only.
2. Build an object array and set some elements to use '**expanded_view**', set others to use '**develope_view**', and leave a few set with the default view. Now display the whole object array and observe the output. If you don't like the format, improve it.
3. Remove the **class** call from the constructor and try to create a **cShape** object. Do you get an object back from the constructor? What happens to the public variables? Is this behavior potentially useful?

10 Drawing a Shape

Before we leave this section, let's have some fun. For a shape, one of the first things you think about is "What does it look like?" Acting on that thought by drawing the shape object in a figure window exercises private member variables associated with the shape's size, scale, and color. The old cliché about a picture painting a thousand words means we can tell at a glance when the values are in the correct range. Drawing the shape also opens the door to many other class considerations. For example, we should update the drawing when the size, scale, or color changes. Encapsulation allows us to easily detect these changes and redraw the figure. Of course, we can't draw anything until we answer the question "What sort of shape do we draw?" Do we draw a square, a circle, or some random shape? Our current shape class doesn't include any sort of data to help answer that question. We need to add some member variables, and that forces us to think about generalizing a **draw** member function.

10.1 READY, SET, DRAW

We know the shape's size and its color, but we can't draw it because we don't know what it looks like. The possibilities are endless. There are lines, squares, circles, and even stars. There are open shapes, closed shapes, convex shapes, and concave shapes. You certainly have to wonder whether it's possible to generalize all shapes into a small number of member variables and a single **draw** function. Even if such a generalization were possible, the implementation would be very difficult. In this chapter, we are going to keep things simple. Here is the plan.

We will define a private member variable called **mPoints** and a public member function named **draw**. The variable will hold a $2 \times n$ array of x–y corner points, one corner per column. The **draw** function will create a figure window and plot the corner points using solid, straight-line segments. The first corner will be stored in **mPoints(:,1)**, and the last in **mPoints(:,end)**. If the shape is supposed to be closed, **mPoints(:,1)** must be equal to **mPoints(:,end)**. This plan will get us started, with the details worked out during the implementation.

10.1.1 IMPLEMENTATION

The plan calls for a new private member variable, **mPoints**. Anytime a private variable is added to a class, we need to consider how that change affects the four class-dependent members of the group of eight. The constructor will always change because the new private variable needs to be added to the private structure and initialized. Changes to the other three — **fieldnames**, **get**, and **set** — depend on the desired interface. In this case, a public variable named **Points** will be used to read and write the array of corner points. With both read and write permission, the new public variable imposes changes on all three.

A new member variable, public or private, also causes us to consider its effect on member functions outside the group of eight. Currently this includes two functions, **mtimes** and **reset**. Since both functions modify **mScale**, it is possible that both functions will need to modify **mPoints**.

Additional functionality can also impose changes to the interface, and adding draw capability represents a major upgrade in functionality. The definition for **draw** is simple but the implications arising from **draw** are not. From the client's perspective, the syntax is simple, given by

```
shape = draw(shape);
```

Not as simple is the behavior. There are a number of questions to consider. For example:

- If **draw** is called more than once for the same object, should **draw** open a new figure every time or reuse the existing figure?
- If the length of the object array is greater than 1, should each element get its own figure or should all objects in the array be drawn in the same figure?
- If **mSize**, **mScale**, **mColorHsv**, or **mPoints** changes, should the object automatically redraw itself?
- Should **reset** also close an object's figure?

There is no definitive right or wrong answer to any of these questions. It is also very interesting that we can even consider the idea of an object redrawing itself. With structures, this would not be an option. The selected answers and some of their implications are as follows:

- If **draw** is called more than once for the same object, the object should reuse its existing figure. Reusing a figure requires each object to save a handle to the appropriate figure window. The handle is saved in a private variable named **mFigureHandle**. If **mFig-ureHandle** is empty, the object should open a new figure.
- If the length of the object array is greater than 1, all objects in the array should be drawn in the same figure. Each element in the object array can stand on its own because each saves a copy of the figure handle. When array elements are pulled out of an array or when arrays are concatenated, mismatches in the handle values can occur. If a mismatch is detected during a draw, the object should close all mismatched figures and open a new figure window. We will live with the consequences of any other mismatched situation.
- If **mSize**, **mScale**, **mColorHsv**, or **mPoints** changes, the object should definitely redraw itself. To support redraw, a handle to each object's line plot will be saved in a private variable named **mPlotHandle**. With access to the plot handle, colors and even x–y values can be changed without having to redraw the entire figure. Initially, **mPlotHandle** will be empty.
- Calling **reset** on an object should close its figure window and assign empty into both **mFigureHandle** and **mPlotHandle**.

Adding all of this functionality requires changes to the constructor, **fieldnames**, **get**, **set**, **mtimes**, and **reset**. We will discuss each file's changes in that order. The implementation of **draw** will be discussed last. As always, after we make these changes and additions we will take the class out for a test drive.

10.1.1.1 Modify the Constructor

The modified constructor is shown in Code Listing 53. At first glance, it appears that a lot has changed. Primarily, this appearance is due to the structure being initialized element by element rather than passing all the names and initial values into a single **struct** call. There are two reasons for this change. First, when an initial value is a cell array, the syntax for element-by-element construction is a lot easier. Second, earlier versions of MATLAB had difficulty with name–value syntax when a constructor had to be called to obtain an initial value. Changing to element-by-element construction allows non-built-in types to be used as private variables. Element-by-element construction is a little less run-time efficient, and some of the functional changes in Code Listing 53 improve run-time performance.

Line 2 demonstrates a class-independent way to get the class name using **mfilename** with the **'class'** option. Any member function can use the **mfilename** technique, although it is particularly convenient in the constructor because there is no input object that can be queried using

---

Code Listing 53, Improving the Constructor Implementation

```
1    function this = cShape
2    class_name = mfilename('class');
3
4    persistent default_this
5    if isempty(default_this)
6       % piece-meal create to avoid object and cell problems
7       default_this = struct([]);   % initially empty structure
8       default_this(1).mSize = ones(2,1); % scaled [width height]'
9       default_this(1).mScale = ones(2,1); % [width height]' scale
         factor
10      default_this(1).mColorHsv = [2/3; 1; 1]; % [H S V]' default
         is blue
11      default_this(1).mPoints = ...
12      [imag(exp(j*(0:4:20)*pi/5)); real(exp(j*(0:4:20)*pi/5))];
13      default_this(1).mFigureHandle = []; % handle for shape's
         figure window
14      default_this(1).mPlotHandle = [];    % handle for shape's
         line plot
15      default_this(1).mDisplayFunc = []; % handle for non-default
         display
16      default_this = class(default_this, class_name);
17      superiorto('double');
18   end
19   this = default_this;
```

---

class. Line 4 declares **default_this** as persistent, lines 5–18 fill the persistent variable with values, and line 19 returns the persistent value in **this**. Holding a copy of the default-valued object can significantly improve run time. This is particularly true for complicated classes and run-time-intensive initialization.

New private variables are also included in the class, and lines 11–14 add the new variables and initialize their values. Lines 11–12 add the private variable **mPoints** and initialize it with a collection of corners. The corner points line on the unit circle separated by 144°. When the corners are plotted in order, a star is drawn. Lines 13–14 add the private variables **mFigureHandle** and **mPlotHandle** and initialize both to empty. Drawing the object assigns nonempty values into these variables.

10.1.1.2 Modify fieldnames

The modified version of **fieldnames** is shown in Code Listing 54. Lines 3, 9, and 13 now contain the new public variable **Points**. We don't expect much use of the **'-full'** option, but the **'-possible'** option is used to format the **set** summary display. Line 13 provides a convenient reminder that the size of the corner point array needs to be $2 \times n$.

10.1.1.3 Modify get

The modified version of **get** is shown in Code Listing 55. The changes found on lines 37–42 are very easy because they follow the same pattern used by the other public variables. In the case of

Code Listing 54, Improved Implementation of fieldnames.m

```
1   function names = fieldnames(this, varargin)
2   if nargin == 1
3       names = {'Size' 'ColorRgb' 'Points'}';
4   else
5       switch varargin{1}
6       case '-full'
7           names = {'Size % double array' ...
8                    'ColorRgb % double array' ...
9                    'Points % double array'}';
10      case '-possible'
11          names = {'Size' {{'double array (2x1)'}} ...
12                   'ColorRgb' {{'double array  (3x1)'}} ...
13                   'Points' {{'double array  (2xN)'}}}';
14      otherwise
15          error('Unsupported call to fieldnames');
16      end
17  end
```

Code Listing 55, Improved Implementation of get.m

```
1   function varargout = get(this, index)
2
3   if nargin == 1 % one argument, display info and return
4       if nargout == 0
5           disp(struct(this(1)));
6       else
7           varargout = cell(1,max([1, nargout]));
8           varargout{1} = struct(this(1));
9       end
10      return;
11  end
12
13  % if index is a string, we will allow special access
14  called_by_name = ischar(index);
15
16  % the set switch below needs a substruct
17  if called_by_name
18      index = substruct('.', index);
19  end
20
21  % public-member-variable section
22  found = true;  % otherwise-case will flip to false
23  switch index(1).subs
24      case 'Size'
25          if isempty(this)
```

```
26                    varargout = {};
27            else
28                    varargout = {this.mSize};
29            end
30        case 'ColorRgb'
31            if isempty(this)
32                    varargout = {};
33            else
34                    rgb = hsv2rgb([this.mColorHsv]')';
35                    varargout = mat2cell(rgb, 3, ones(1, size(rgb,2)));
36            end
37        case 'Points'
38            if isempty(this)
39                    varargout = {};
40            else
41                    varargout = {this.mPoints};
42            end
43        otherwise
44            found = false;  % didn't find it in the public section
45    end
46
47    % concealed member variables, not strictly public
48    if ~found && called_by_name
49        found = true;
50        switch index(1).subs
51            case 'mDisplayFunc'
52                if isempty(this)
53                        varargout = {};
54                else
55                        varargout = {this.mDisplayFunc};
56                end
57            otherwise
58                found = false;  % didn't find it in the special
                    section
59        end
60    end
61
62    if ~found
63        error(['??? Reference to non-existent field '
       index(1).subs '.']);
64    end
65
66    if length(varargout) > 1 & nargout <= 1
67            if iscellstr(varargout) || any([cellfun('isempty',
           varargout)])
68                varargout = {varargout};
69        else
```

```
70          try
71              varargout = {[varargout{:}]};
72          catch
73              varargout = {varargout};
74          end
75      end
76  end
```

an empty object, line 39 returns nothing. For a nonempty object, line 41 packs each object's **mPoints** array into a separate cell and returns them to the caller.

10.1.1.4 Modify set

The modified version of **set** is shown in Code Listing 56. The changes to **set** are more extensive compared to those for **get** because the figure window only changes when member variables are changed. The biggest change occurs in lines 75–93, where the new **Points** public variable is implemented. Line 77 throws an error when indexing deeper than the first dot-reference level is detected. This is different from what we have done in the past, and it incrementally moves the class interface away from the look and feel of a structure. Later, if we decide to support individual element mutation, that code would replace the error message. Lines 79–83 check the size of each input array. If the first dimension is not two, an error is thrown. If the input sizes are okay, line 84 deals the input arrays into **mPoints**. Finally, lines 86–93 update the figure. For all objects in the array, line 87 gets a copy of the corner points and lines 89–91 assign the x–y data into each object's plot handle. Notice that public **Points** are being used for the plot. Either public or private values could be used because they represent the same array. To avoid errors caused by invalid handles, the **set** command occurs inside a **try** statement. For example, if a client closes a figure by clicking the close box, **mPlotHandle** will contain an invalid handle. If the handle is empty, nothing happens and no error is thrown. After the client requests a draw, however, the figure is kept up-to-date when an object's **Points** change.

Code Listing 56, Improved Version of set.m

```
1   function varargout = set(this, index, varargin)
2
3   if nargin < 3  % one or two arguments, display info and return
4     possible = fieldnames(this, '-possible');
5     possible_struct = struct(possible{:});
6     if nargout == 0
7       if nargin == 1
8         disp(possible_struct);
9       else
10        try
11          temp_struct.(index) = possible_struct.(index);
12          disp(temp_struct);
13        catch
14          warning(['??? Reference to non-existent field ' ...
15          index '.']);
16        end
17      end
```

```
18      else
19        varargout = cell(1,max([1, nargout]));
20        varargout{1} = possible_struct;
21      end
22      return;
23    end
24
25    called_by_name = ischar(index);
26
27    % the set switch below needs a substruct
28    if called_by_name
29      index = substruct('.', index);
30    end
31
32    % public-member-variable section
33    found = true;   % otherwise-case will flip to false
34    switch index(1).subs
35      case 'Size'
36        if length(index) > 1
37          this.mSize = subsasgn(this.mSize, index(2:end),
             varargin{:});
38          this.mScale = subsasgn(this.mScale, index(2:end), 1);
39        else
40          new_size = zeros(2, length(varargin));
41          for k = 1:size(new_size, 2)
42            try
43              new_size(:, k) = varargin{k}(:);
44            catch
45              error('Size must be a scalar or length == 2');
46            end
47          end
48          new_size = num2cell(new_size, 1);
49          [this.mSize] = deal(new_size{:});
50          [this.mScale] = deal(ones(2,1));
51        end
52        for k = 1:length(this(:))
53          points = get(this(k), 'Points');
54          try
55            set(this(k).mPlotHandle, ...
56              'XData', this.mSize(1) * points(1,:), ...
57              'YData', this.mSize(2) * points(2,:));
58          end
59        end
60      case 'ColorRgb'
61        if length(index) > 1
62          rgb = hsv2rgb(this.mColorHsv')';
63          rgb = subsasgn(rgb, index(2:end), varargin{:});
```

```
64          this.mColorHsv = rgb2hsv(rgb')';
65        else
66          hsv = rgb2hsv([varargin{:}]')';
67          hsv = mat2cell(hsv, 3, ones(1, size(hsv,2)));
68          [this.mColorHsv] = deal(hsv{:});
69        end
70        for k = 1:length(this(:))
71          try
72            set(this(k).mPlotHandle, 'Color', get(this(k),
             'ColorRgb'));
73          end
74        end
75      case 'Points'
76        if length(index) > 1
77          error('The entire Points array must be assigned at one
             time');
78        else
79          for k = 1:length(varargin)
80            if size(varargin{k}, 1) ~= 2
81              error('Points must be size 2xN');
82            end
83          end
84          [this.mPoints] = deal(varargin{:});
85        end
86        for k = 1:length(this(:))
87          points = get(this(k), 'Points');
88          try
89            set(this(k).mPlotHandle, ...
90              'XData', this.mSize(1) * points(1,:), ...
91              'YData', this.mSize(2) * points(2,:));
92          end
93        end
94      otherwise
95        found = false;
96    end
97
98    % concealed member variables, not strictly public
99    if ~found && called_by_name
100     found = true;
101     switch index(1).subs
102       case 'mDisplayFunc'
103         if length(index) > 1
104           this.mDisplayFunc = ...
105             subsasgn(this.mDisplayFunc, ...
106               index(2:end), varargin{:});
107         else
108           [this.mDisplayFunc] = deal(varargin{:});
```

```
109           end
110       otherwise
111         found = false;   % didn't find it in the special section
112       end
113   end
114
115   if ~found
116     error(['??? Reference to non-existent field ' index(1).
        subs '.']);
117   end
118
119   varargout{1} = this;
```

Lines 52–59 and lines 70–74 also keep the object up-to-date when **Size** or **ColorRgb** changes. For **Size** changes, line 53 gets a copy of the corner points and lines 55–57 assign the x–y data into each object's plot handle. Again, to avoid errors caused by invalid handles, the **set** command occurs inside a **try** statement. For **ColorRgb**, the procedure in lines 70–74 is similar except that the `'Color'` attribute is set rather than `'XData'` and `'YData'`.

10.1.1.5   Modify mtimes

The modified version of **mtimes** is shown in Code Listing 57. In this version, redraw code has been added to the end of **mtimes**, lines 24–31. This is the same set of commands used in the `'Size'` and `'Points'` cases of **set**. In a rigorous development, these commands should be moved into a separate function. In this chapter, we will keep them in line. As before, line 25 gets the points and lines 27–29 set `'XData'` and `'YData'` attributes.

Code Listing 57, Improved Version of mtimes.m

```
1     function this = mtimes(lhs, rhs)
2
3     % one input must be cShape type, which one
4     if isa(lhs, 'cShape')
5       this = lhs;
6       scale = rhs;
7     else
8       this = rhs;
9       scale = lhs;
10    end
11
12    switch length(scale(:))
13      case 1
14        scale = [scale; scale];
15      case 2
16        scale = scale(:);
17      otherwise
18        error('??? Error using ==> mtimes');
19    end
```

```
20
21     this.mSize = this.mSize .* scale;
22     this.mScale = this.mScale .* scale;
23
24     for k = 1:length(this(:))
25       points = get(this(k), 'Points');
26       try
27         set(this(k).mPlotHandle, ...
28           'XData', this.mSize(1) * points(1,:), ...
29           'YData', this.mSize(2) * points(2,:));
30       end
31     end
```

10.1.1.6   Modify reset

The modified version of **reset** is shown in Code Listing 58. In this version, **mSize** and **mScale** are reset as before but nothing happens to the values in **mPoints**. When we implement **draw**, **plot** must use a scaled version of the values in **mPoints**. Otherwise, this particular implementation of **reset** will not be correct. Lines 5–9 manage the figure window and the associated private variables. Line 6 closes the figure window by calling **delete** on the figure's handle. To avoid problems with invalid-handle errors, the **delete** command is placed inside a **try** statement. There is no need to include a **catch** statement. After closing the figure, lines 8–9 clean up the now invalid handles by overwriting their values with empty.

Code Listing 58, Improved Version of reset.m

```
1    function this = reset(this)
2    for k = 1:length(this(:))
3      this(k).mSize = this(k).mSize ./ this(k).mScale; % divide
       by scale
4      this(k).mScale = ones(2,1);   % reset scale to 1:1
5      try
6        delete(this(k).mFigureHandle);
7      end
8      this(k).mFigureHandle = [];
9      this(k).mPlotHandle = [];
10   end
```

10.1.1.7   Adding Member Function draw

The implementation for **draw** is shown in Code Listing 59. Line 2 verifies that the caller is requesting a return, and line 3 throws a warning if no return value is requested. This is necessary because **draw** mutates the object. The function saves figure handles and plot handles in the object. Both handle variables are private, but that does not change the fact that **draw** changes the state of the object. Unless the object is passed back to the client, there is no way to update size, scale, color, or corner point changes. This is a function where call-by-reference rather than call-by-value would be enormously beneficial. MATLAB always uses call-by-value.

If the calling syntax is okay, lines 5–29 are evaluated. On line 5, if the object is empty nothing is drawn. Otherwise, lines 6–17 inspect and manage the object's figure handles. Line 6 collects a

---

Code Listing 59, Improved Implementation of draw.m

```
1   function this = draw(this)
2   if nargout ~= 1
3     warning('draw must be called using: obj = draw(obj)');
4   else
5     if ~isempty(this)
6       handle_array = unique([this(:).mFigureHandle]);
7       if length(handle_array) ~= 1 % no handle or mismatched
8         for k = 1:length(handle_array)
9           try
10            delete(handle_array(k));  % close figures
11          end
12        end
13        figure_handle = figure;  % create new figure
14        [this.mFigureHandle] = deal(figure_handle);  % save it
15      else
16        figure(handle_array);  % use the handle
17      end
18
19      clf;   % clear the figure
20      hold on;  % all shapes drawn in the same figure
21      for k = 1:length(this(:))
22        this(k).mPlotHandle = plot(...
23          this(k).mSize(1) * this(k).mPoints(1,:), ...
24          this(k).mSize(2) * this(k).mPoints(2,:), ...
25          'Color', get(this(k), 'ColorRgb'));
26      end
27      hold off;
28    end
29  end
```

---

copy of the unique handles in **handle_array**. If the length of **handle_array** is one, line 16 uses **figure** to activate the correct graphics window. A length other than one means there is a handle mismatch or the object has never been drawn. Lines 8–12 **delete** any mismatched figures. The **delete** command is in a **try** statement to avoid invalid-handle errors. Line 13 then creates a new figure window, and line 14 assigns the handle into the object. In either case, the correct figure window is now active and ready to accept the plots.

Line 19 clears the figure, and line 20 allows multiple objects to be plotted in the same figure. The objects are plotted using the plot command in lines 22–25. Notice that the corner points are scaled by **mSize** on their way to **plot**. After the loop, line 27 returns **hold** to the **off** state because all the objects have been plotted.

10.2 TEST DRIVE

In this test drive, the scenery gets better. Instead of studying text outputs, we get to look at a graphical representation of the shape. Changing into the Chapter 10 directory and executing,

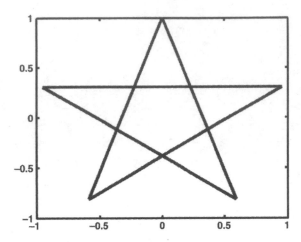

FIGURE 10.1 Default graphic for cShape object.

```
shape = cShape;

shape = draw(shape);
```

draws the figure shown in Figure 10.1. When the size and scale factors change, pay close attention to the axes. We are allowing MATLAB to scale the plot automatically. We could improve on that situation by designing in another set of scale-related member variables and functions. For this test drive, automatic scaling is okay.

Change the color to red using either

```
shape.ColorRgb = [1; 0; 0];
```

or

```
shape = set(shape, 'ColorRgb', [1; 0; 0]);
```

Clients should usually use dot-reference syntax vs. **set**, but the result from either is the same. The object will automatically redraw itself, and the new red star is shown in Figure 10.2.

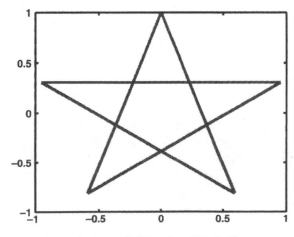

FIGURE 10.2 cShape graphic after assigning an RGB color of [1; 0; 0].

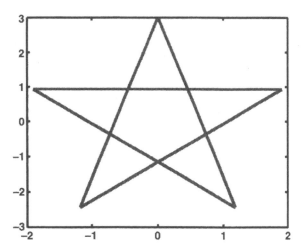

FIGURE 10.3 cShape graphic scaled using the size mutator.

The size can be changed in two ways, via the public member variable **Size** or by multiplying by a scaling constant. Changing the **Size** with

```
shape.Size = [2; 3];
```

results in the plot shown in Figure 10.3. The star takes up the same position in the plot; however, notice that the scales have changed.

The figure's size can also be changed by multiplying the shape by a constant. For example, the command

```
shape = 0.25 * shape;
```

results in the plot shown in Figure 10.4. Again, note the change in the scale. Multiplying is not quite the same as assigning the **Size** variable because multiplication also sets the private variable **mScale**. The only real implication of the difference occurs during **reset**.

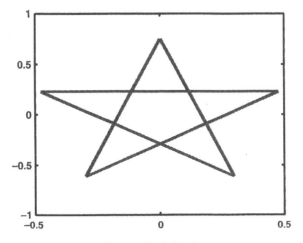

FIGURE 10.4 cShape graphic scaled using the overloaded mtimes.

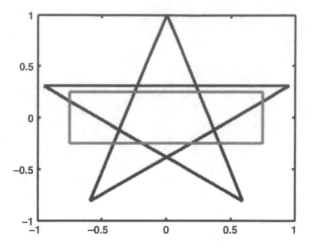

FIGURE 10.5 Graphic for an array of cShape objects.

The reset command

```
shape = reset(shape);
```

closes the figure window and resets private member variables back to undrawn values.

Arrays of **cShape** objects can also be drawn. For example, the set of commands

```
clear all;

shape = [cShape cShape];

shape(2).ColorRgb = [0; 1; 0];

shape(2).Points = [[-1; -1] [-1; 1] [1; 1] [1; -1] [-1; -1]];

shape(2) = [0.75; 0.25] * shape(2);

shape = draw(shape);
```

results in the figure shown in Figure 10.5. The commands build a length-2 array of **cShape** objects, and set the shape at index 2 so that it is first a green square. The x-direction is scaled by three fourths, and the y-direction is scaled by one fourth. Finally, when the shape array is drawn, both the default blue star and the mutated green rectangle are drawn in the same figure.

10.3 SUMMARY

This concludes the section on encapsulation. We have now uncovered most of the major issues involved in MATLAB object-oriented programming. The functions developed to support encapsulation can easily serve as a reference design for classes without inheritance. Group-of-eight functions should be included in every class you write. To do otherwise compromises encapsulation in some way. The group of eight functions are as follows:

- constructor
- **subsref.m**
- **subsasgn.m**
- **get.m**
- **set.m**
- **display.m**

- **fieldnames.m**
- **struct.m**

Four in this group can be reused with no class-dependent tailoring. It is possible to isolate these four into their own directory; however, it involves more complexity than it is worth. It is much easier to copy them into each new class directory. The remaining four — constructor, **get**, **set**, and **fieldnames** —are organized to make class-dependent tailoring as easy as possible. The organization includes private variables, public variables, and so-called concealed variables. Fortunately, some of the most difficult code in the class-dependent functions is not class dependent. Member names and the specific case code used to manage the conversion from public to private data are class dependent, but functionality like tab completion and multilevel indexing is identical from class to class.

Including all members in the group of eight gives our objects first-class status among MATLAB's built-in types. Object variables can be passed as arguments. Object variables can also be saved and loaded. They can be assigned into structure elements and even used as a private member variable for another class. Objects can be displayed, turned into structures, and, with additional member functions, converted into other types. In short, attention to detail makes objects appear as if they are an intrinsic part of the language. Indeed, that is exactly how it should be.

In the remaining sections, we will reexamine constructors, examine inheritance, and discuss many "gee-whiz" ideas. These topics are important but not nearly as important as encapsulation and the group of eight. As we will see, the organization included in the group of eight makes inheritance much easier to implement. Several standard functions will be added to the class, but these pale in importance next to the group of eight.

10.4 INDEPENDENT INVESTIGATIONS

1. Add member variables and functions that would allow clients to set the scale.
2. Like color, allow clients to specify the line style.
3. Instead of setting corner points, allow a client to pass in strings like **'Square'** and **'Triangle'**. Can you do this by modifying the code found in **case 'Points'** inside **set**? Do you need a string like **'Rectangle'**? Think about the public variable **Size**.
4. Add member variables and functions that allow clients to rotate the shape.

Part 2

Building a Hierarchy

This section focuses on building hierarchies because objects and hierarchies go hand in hand. For example, a hierarchy of shapes might include rectangles, stars, and circles. A hierarchical implementation allows one class to build on functions defined in another class. An object-oriented hierarchy can do this without a lot of rework. Throughout the first section, we simplified much of our code by coercing MATLAB into doing a lot of the work. In a small way, all classes are hierarchical because they build on the built-in types. MATLAB is always at the top of the hierarchy. A deeper hierarchy of classes follows the same philosophy. The lower-level class, sometimes called the *child*, tries to coerce a higher-level class, the *parent*, into doing as much as possible. This is the way of a hierarchy: always try to force the next higher level into doing all the work.

When a child class coerces a parent to perform an operation, the child is said to *inherit* that particular function from the parent. There are different flavors of inheritance. Differences depend on how control passes to the parent. A *parent–child* relationship is what we normally think of as inheritance, but anytime one class passes control to another, this is inheritance. When one class uses another class as a private member variable, this too is inheritance. Called *composition* or *aggregation*, using a class as a member variable often works better than parent–child inheritance and is just as powerful. In this section, we will examine both parent–child inheritance and composition.

Also in this section, we will find that efficient, bulletproof hierarchies can be coded in MATLAB. Hierarchies are built using both types of inheritance, parent–child and composition. The group-of-eight implementations from Section 1 are already organized to support inheritance. In this section, we will expand on the organization.

Recall from the first section how we tailored built-in MATLAB functions like **subsref**, **subsasgn**, **display**, and even **mtimes** to suit the needs of our classes. In a hierarchy, a child class can accomplish the same trick. This time, the child tailors a function already defined by the parent. The child simply includes a tailored version of the function in its own class directory. In the first section, even when a class redefined a function, we could still call MATLAB's built-in version using **builtin**. When a child redefines a parent function, a similar mechanism allows a child to call the parent's version. We can't use **builtin** because that will skip over the parent.

By the end of this section, you will be able to churn out bulletproof class implementations based on the reference designs. Soon the novelty will wear off and you will pine for a computer-aided way to create the group-of-eight scaffolding. The CD that accompanies this book includes a very complete MATLAB tool that will build the scaffolding and help you maintain and evolve each class. The last two chapters in this section document and demonstrate the Class Wizard tool.

Now in its third version, Class Wizard will rapidly generate core class functions based on lists of private and public variables and functions. These lists are entered using a graphical interface. Once entered, Class Wizard generates group-of-eight functions that include all the special functionality discussed throughout this book. Class Wizard is a versatile and extremely powerful tool. It is found on the disk in **/utils/wizard_gui**, and this directory must be added to the path. The dialog screens in Class Wizard require MATLAB version 7 or greater but will generate classes that work with version 6.5 or greater.

11 Constructor Redux

In the first part of this book, objects were constructed in the most basic way because no arguments were passed into the constructor. With a no-argument constructor, all objects are constructed using the same initial values. For the Part 1 **cShape** class, this basic approach worked because Part 1 focused primarily on encapsulation mechanics. Now that we understand encapsulation, we will turn our attention to inheritance and the development of class hierarchies. With the development of class hierarchies, we also need a richer set of construction options.

For example, if we want **cShape** to serve as a parent for **cStar** and **cSquare**, the constructors for **cStar** and **cSquare** need to initialize **mPoints** with different values. The best time to perform the initialization is during construction, and a constructor that accepts arguments is the best way to tailor the construction process. Instead of relying on hard-coded values, constructor arguments are used to initialize private variables. As with any function, we can pass any number of arguments into the constructor through **varargin**. The number of arguments along with their types can then be used to select the appropriate initialization commands. Different classes have different construction requirements. In this chapter, we develop an extendable organization we can use to implement general-purpose constructors.

11.1 SPECIFYING INITIAL VALUES

Two initial-value cases are so common that they have special names. The no-argument constructor is called the *default constructor*. We already know much about the default constructor because the default constructor was the constructor used in Part 1. For example, we know that MATLAB requires a default constructor for every class. The other common constructor is called the *copy constructor*. The copy constructor is a one-argument constructor and the lone argument has the same type as the name of the constructor. The copy constructor makes a copy of an existing object; however, in MATLAB, assignment also makes a copy. Assignment syntax is much easier and that diminishes the importance of a copy constructor. Perhaps the only difference between the two is the fact that we can tailor the copy constructor but we can't tailor assignment. The copy constructor is still important enough to be included in the standard implementation.

The standard object-oriented vocabulary gives these constructors different names because most object-oriented languages implement each constructor using a different function. Other languages can do this because their compiler or interpreter uses the number of arguments and the type of each to select an appropriate function. MATLAB works differently. In MATLAB, every class has only one constructor. To get multiple-constructor functionality, code inside the constructor steers the execution based on the value of **nargin**. Code for each **nargin** value can further inspect an argument's type and take appropriate action.

In addition to a default constructor and a copy constructor, a class can define constructors with any number of input arguments of any type.* Different classes have different construction needs, and that means every class' constructor is unique in terms of number of inputs and input types. The challenge in this chapter is to generalize all of these unique requirements into an implementation strategy that can be universally applied.

---

* The standard terminology is a little sloppy when we consider that MATLAB has only one constructor. When I talk about a specific type of constructor (e.g., copy or default), what I really mean is one of the unique execution paths through the constructor function. Each unique execution path is selected based on the number of input arguments and their types.

We already know how to construct a default object. In fact, our current default constructor optimizes run time by saving a copy of the default object as a persistent variable. Thus, it seems reasonable to begin the general construction process by first constructing a default object. Beginning with a default object is more than reasonable: it is essential for the development of a robust, maintainable set of constructors. For a particular type, MATLAB saves the object's structure during the very first call to **class**. Later, if the constructor calls **class** with a different structure, MATLAB throws an error. Beginning with a default object will eliminate structure-mismatch errors that might otherwise occur between different constructors.

Once we have a default object, a **switch** based on the value in **nargin** seems to be the best choice; however, a switch statement does not support a general-purpose implementation. A **switch** is not general because both the number of cases and the **nargin** value for each **case** change from class to class. A more general but much less obvious approach breaks out code associated with each supported **nargin** value into a separate m-file. Following a standard naming convention for each of these m-files allows the constructor to build the name on the fly and use **feval** to call it.

Following the more general **feval** approach is consistent with the group-of-eight design goal of building a robust implementation that will withstand the test of time. The constructor is robust because the same underlying code is always used. The constructor also tolerates change because private variables and **nargin** conditions can be added without upsetting functions that already exist. Using **feval** in this way can sometimes result in poor run-time performance. In those situations, the constructor can be tailored to use a **switch-case** approach. Individual cases can still call a separate m-file because the run-time improvement comes from eliminating the **feval** overhead.

At first, it seems that giving every supported **nargin** value its own function would add too many files to each class directory. Fortunately, function-search rules give us a way out of this dilemma. The so-called *helper functions* can be located in the class' private directory. As private member functions, they are not included in the public interface yet they are still available to the constructor. Private functions represent an important topic and before we get too involved with inheritance, we will take another brief side trip to examine the private class directory.

11.1.1 PRIVATE MEMBER FUNCTIONS

In the previous discussion of path-search priority, §3.2.3, the class directory was listed as third in priority. Both subfunctions and the private directory have higher priority. This priority system means that functions located in a class' private directory are callable from only two locations: the class directory and the private directory itself. The fact that the private directory is included represents a minor deviation from standard function-search rules. It means that functions in one private directory cannot call functions located in another private directory. For example, functions located in **/@cShape/private** cannot call a function located in **/@cShape/private/private**. In this way, both public and private member functions can call all other member functions, both public and private.

Functions located in a class' private directory are not part of the public interface because a client can't call them. Just like private member variables, the only functions able to access private member functions are other member functions. An m-file in the class directory is a public member function, and an m-file in the class' private directory is a private member function. It really is that easy.

The use of **/private** gives us an opportunity to modularize class functions and improve maintainability. Just like public member functions, a private member function can read and write private member variables and call other member functions. For the constructor, each **nargin**-specific function can be located in a class' private directory. This move helps simplify the constructor to the point where it can be made almost entirely class independent. Other functions in the group of eight can also benefit from private functions. For example, complicated **get** and **set** cases can be isolated in a private member function. Being second in priority also means that MATLAB can find private functions even if they do not use an object as an input argument. This makes the private directory a very convenient location for class-specific utility functions and encourages the development of modular code.

Under some conditions, a private member function can also improve run time. For example, a private function might allow member functions to get and set public variables without having to go through the overhead involved in **get** and **set**. This sets up more coupling than we usually prefer. Sometimes the run-time improvement is worth the trade. Member functions outside the group of eight can also use private member functions to share common code, increase modularity, and sometimes improve performance.

11.2 GENERALIZING THE CONSTRUCTOR

We can use a standard file-naming convention and private member functions to generalize the constructor. Except for calls to **superiorto** and **inferiorto**, the constructor file itself is class independent. The class-dependent sections from the previous version of the constructor can be found in the class' private directory. All the code used to build and initialize the default structure can be found in the private member function named **ctor_ini.m**. The abbreviation **ctor** is short for constructor, and the abbreviation **ini** is short for initialization. Code to convert the structure into an object, code to modify the superiority, and code to save the persistent copy will still be found in the main constructor function.

The **nargin**-dependent functions can also be found in the class' private directory. The function used for one input argument is named **ctor_1.m**; for two input arguments, **ctor_2.m**; and so on for any number of input arguments. There is no "numbered-**ctor**" function for the no-argument constructor because **ctor_ini** in conjunction with the main constructor function already produces a default object. We also don't include a numbered-**ctor** function for **nargin** conditions that we don't intend to support. This allows the main constructor to detect undefined-function errors and throw a different error with a more appropriate error message. Supporting a new **nargin** value simply means developing another numbered-**ctor** function and adding it to the private directory. Similarly, deleting a numbered-**ctor** function will remove support for the associated **nargin** value. This flexibility can be used to support development, testing, and quality assurance through construction methods not available to general clients.

The main constructor function is shown in Code Listing 60 and can be analyzed in two sections. The first section, lines 2–15, is the default, no-argument constructor; and the second section, lines 17–30, overwrites default values using any number of input arguments. As you examine the listing, note the complete absence of class-specific commands. Class-specific information is obtained in line 6 by calling **ctor_ini**.

Code Listing 60, Improved Constructor without Inheritance

```
1    function this = constructor(varargin)
2    class_name = mfilename('class');  % simply more general than
     'cShape'
3
4    persistent default_this
5    if isempty(default_this)
6      [default_this, superior, inferior] = ctor_ini;  % /private/
       ctor_ini.m
7      default_this = class(default_this, class_name);
8      if ~isempty(superior)
```

```
9        superiorto(superior{:});
10    end
11    if ~isempty(inferior)
12       inferiorto(inferior{:});
13    end
14  end
15  this = default_this;   % copies persistent to this
16
17  if nargin > 0   % if not default, pass varargin to helper
18    try
19      this = feval(sprintf('ctor_%d', nargin), this,
        varargin{:});
20    catch
21      err = lasterror;
22      switch err.identifier
23        case 'MATLAB:UndefinedFunction'
24          err.message = [['class ' class_name] ...
25                         [' cannot be constructed from '] ...
26                         [sprintf('%d', nargin) ' input
                           argument(s) ']];
27      end
28      rethrow(err);
29    end
30  end
```

The filename for this constructor is **cShape.m** but line 1 specifies **constructor** as the function's name. Due to a quirk of MATLAB, the function name inside an m-file does not need to match the filename. MATLAB finds and calls the function based on the filename, making the name in the function declaration irrelevant. This quirk allows the declaration on line 1 to be class independent. Of course, you can use the class name in the declaration if you prefer.

In keeping with the idea of class independence, line 2 gets the class name using **mfilename** with the **'class'** option. Instead of coding **'cShape'** into constructor commands, we can instead use the variable **class_name**. Again, if you prefer to make code in the constructor more explicit, you can instead choose to code the name into the constructor commands.

Line 4 declares **default_this** as a persistent variable, and the result of the initial default-valued instantiation is stored in **default_this**. Subsequent instantiations simply use the stored value. In complicated class hierarchies, this implementation detail can improve run-time performance. This strategy was introduced in §10.1.1.1. Lines 5–9 fill **default_this** with a default object, and line 15 copies the persistent object into **this**. The difference between then and now occurs on line 6. On line 6, a function call to **ctor_ini** initializes the private structure and gets class superiority information. This function is located in the class' private directory and is described in §11.2.1. Line 7 uses **class** to turn the structure into an object, and lines 8–13 modify the class' superiority. Line 9 uses list expansion on **superior**, and line 12 uses list expansion on **inferior**.

If **nargin** is zero, construction is complete and the constructor returns the default object. When the constructor call includes arguments, line 19 builds the name of a function and uses **feval** to call it. The function name is constructed using **'ctor_'** as a prefix and the value of **nargin** as a suffix. The default object and all constructor arguments are passed into the numbered-**ctor** private helper function. The private function uses input values to modify the object's private variables and passes the object back to the constructor. An example of a numbered-**ctor** function is described in §11.2.2. Functions triggered by other **nargin** values follow the format described in §11.2.2.

The **feval** call on line 19 is embedded in a **try-catch** statement. A **try-catch** statement is used so that we don't have to include every possible numbered-**ctor** function. An error during numbered-**ctor** initialization will force the execution into the **catch** block in lines 21–28. Line 21 gets the cause of the error from **lasterror** and line 22 selects the appropriate error-handling **case**. If the error resulted from an undefined function, lines 24–26 reformat the error message so the client will see a reasonable message. In this case, the message indicates an unsupported number of input arguments. Line 28 rethrows the error.

The constructor code does not need advance knowledge of the available numbered-**ctor** helpers. The constructor simply calls a function consistent with **nargin** and hopes for the best. The function also prepares for the worst by trapping and reporting errors. The constructor's laissez-faire attitude makes it easy to add cases and begin using them. All you need to do is add a numbered-**ctor** function to the private directory and start constructing objects with that number of arguments. The only caveat is to make sure there are no numbered-**ctor** functions on the general search path that might be found when the private function does not exist.

11.2.1 CONSTRUCTOR HELPER /PRIVATE/CTOR_INI.M

The class-specific portions of the class' default initialization code have been moved into **/private/ctor_ini.m**. When the design of the constructor relies on "**ctor**-helper" functions, **ctor_ini.m** joins the group of eight as a required function. The complete set of required functions will still be referred to as the group of eight because there are still only eight public functions. The **ctor_ini** function is shown in Code Listing 61. The default structure commands come directly from the constructor code discussed in §10.1.1.1. The helper returns a variable named **this**; however, the value has not yet been converted from a structure into an object.

Code Listing 61, Modular Code, Constructor Helper /private/ctor_ini.m

```
1    function [this, superior, inferior] = ctor_ini
2    % piece-meal create to avoid object and cell problems
3    this = struct([]);   % initially empty structure
4    this(1).mSize = ones(2,1); % scaled [width height]' of
     bounding box
5    this(1).mScale = ones(2,1); % [width height]' scale factor
6    this(1).mColorHsv = [2/3; 1; 1]; % [H S V]' of border,
     default is blue
7    this(1).mPoints = ...
8      [imag(exp(j*(0:4:20)*pi/5)); real(exp(j*(0:4:20)*pi/5))];
9    this(1).mFigureHandle = []; % handle for shape's figure window
10   this(1).mPlotHandle = [];   % handle for shape's line plot
11   this(1).mDisplayFunc = []; % function handle for non-default
     display
12
13   superior = {'double'};
14   inferior = {};
```

Lines 13 and 14 define and return arguments that the main constructor will pass into **superiorto** and **inferiorto**. By defining these in **ctor_ini**, the body of the constructor maintains class independence. The constructor uses simple list expansion on these variables, and that means their format is a **cellstr** of class names. In this case, **cShape** is superior to **double**.

11.2.2 Constructor Helper Example /private/ctor_1.m

To get a flavor for the implementation of a numbered-**ctor** function, let's build one. We will build **/private/ctor_1.m** because a one-argument **ctor**-helper includes support for the copy constructor. A one-argument **ctor**-helper also allows a **Points** array to be assigned during construction. Code inside **ctor_1** is responsible for figuring out which assignment is being requested. There is only one input because that is a condition for calling **ctor_1**. The type of the single argument or the value contained in the argument must be used to make that determination. Many other object-oriented languages perform this task for us. With MATLAB, we have to include selection code inside every numbered-**ctor** function that supports more than one construction method.

The implementation for **/private/ctor_1.m** is shown in Code Listing 62. Line 3 uses **isa** to check whether the lone input's type is **cShape**. If the **isa** check is true, line 4 uses assignment to return a copy of the input. Arranging the copy constructor as the first among all the type checks is typical in **ctor_1** implementations. The second check on line 5 looks for an empty input. If the input is empty, line 6 assigns a 2×0 array into **mPoints**. The value is still empty, but the 2×0 size prevents certain indexing errors. The third check on line 7 looks for a numeric input, and line 8 assigns the input to the public variable '**Points**'. Assigning the public variable here serves several purposes. First, it demonstrates that **this** is an object, and as such, code in **ctor_1** can elect to use the public interface. Second, it highlights the fact that clients will likely see constructor arguments from a public-interface point of view. Third, it offloads input error checking onto code that already exists in **set**. If input error checking becomes more restrictive, we will not need to modify **ctor_1**. Finally, if no previous check is appropriate for the input, lines 11–12 throw an error. Other numbered-**ctor** functions follow the same model, but the number of combinations is potentially larger due to the larger number of inputs.

Code Listing 62, Modular Code, Constructor Helper /private/ctor_1.m Example

```
1    function this = ctor_1(this, InitialPoints)
2
3    if isa(InitialPoints, 'cShape')  % copy constructor
4      this = InitialPoints;  % let MATLAB do the copy assignment
5    elseif isempty(InitialPoints)
6      this.mPoints = zeros(2,0); % empty, size 2x0
7    elseif isnumeric(InitialPoints)
8      this = set(this, 'Points', InitialPoints);  % copy in the
         data
9    else
10     % any other input produces an error
11     error(['Input is not appropriate for constructing a ' ...
12       class(this) ' object.']);
13   end
```

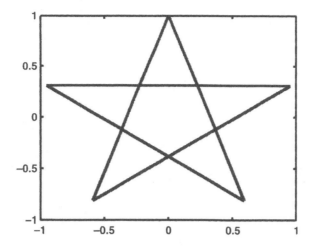

FIGURE 11.1 Default constructor graphic for a cShape object.

11.3 TEST DRIVE

From outside the class, very little has changed between the implementations in Chapter 10 and this chapter: encapsulation at work again. Internally, the organization of the constructor changed radically and we need to test those changes. The default constructor should work the same as in Chapter 10. We can confirm this with the following commands:

```
>> shape = cShape;
>> shape = draw(shape);
```

Indeed, the same result is shown in Figure 11.1.

We should also be able to construct a shape with corner points different from the default values. All we need to do is pass an array of points through the constructor and draw the shape. Here is one example:

```
>> shape(2) = cShape([-1 0 1 0 -1; 0 -1 0 1 0]);
>> shape(2).ColorRgb = [1; 0; 0];
>> shape = draw(shape);
```

What shape do you expect to see? The result is shown in Figure 11.2.

Now what about the other constructors? The copy constructor is easy. The following command will construct a copy:

```
>> shape_copy = cShape(shape(2));
```

To confirm that we really have a copy, we can draw the copy or look at the values contained in **shape_copy.Points**. Displaying the contents shows us the following:

```
>> shape_copy.Points

ans =

 -1  0  1  0 -1
  0 -1  0  1  0
```

Indeed, we have a copy of the original.

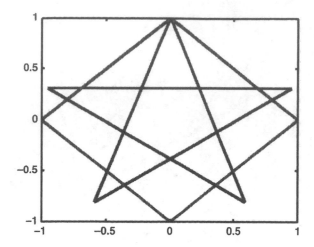

FIGURE 11.2 Example graphic of object constructed from a corner-point array.

During the copy, every field in **shape(2)** was copied into **shape_copy**. Usually an element-by-element copy is exactly the desired result. In this case, however, there is a small but important problem. Use **developer_view** to look at the public and private variables of both **shape(2)** and **shape_copy**. The commands and outputs are shown in Code Listing 63.

Code Listing 63, Chapter 11 Test-Drive Commands (Partial List)

```
1    >> shape = set(shape, 'mDisplayFunc', 'developer_view');
2    >> shape_copy = shape(2);
3    >> shape(2)
4    -----    Public Member Variables    -----
5    ans(1).Size = [1    1]';
6    ans(1).ColorRgb = [1    0    0]';
7    ans(1).Points(1, :) = [-1    0    1    0   -1];
8    ans(1).Points(2, :) = [0   -1    0    1    0];
9    .....    Private Member Variables    .....
10   ans(1).mSize = [1    1]';
11   ans(1).mScale = [1    1]';
12   ans(1).mColorHsv = [0    1    1]';
13   ans(1).mPoints(1, :) = [-1    0    1    0   -1];
14   ans(1).mPoints(2, :) = [0   -1    0    1    0];
15   ans(1).mFigureHandle = [1];
16   ans(1).mPlotHandle = [155.0139];
17   ans(1).mDisplayFunc = 'developer_view';
18   >> shape_copy
19   -----    Public Member Variables    -----
20   shape_copy(1).Size = [1    1]';
21   shape_copy(1).ColorRgb = [1    0    0]';
22   shape_copy(1).Points(1, :) = [-1    0    1    0   -1];
23   shape_copy(1).Points(2, :) = [0   -1    0    1    0];
24   .....    Private Member Variables    .....
25   shape_copy(1).mSize = [1    1]';
```

```
26   shape_copy(1).mScale = [1   1]';
27   shape_copy(1).mColorHsv = [0   1   1]';
28   shape_copy(1).mPoints(1, :) = [-1   0   1   0 -1];
29   shape_copy(1).mPoints(2, :) = [0 -1   0   1   0];
30   shape_copy(1).mFigureHandle = [1];
31   shape_copy(1).mPlotHandle = [155.0139];
32   shape_copy(1).mDisplayFunc = 'developer_view';
```

Look closely at the handle values on lines 15–16 and 30–31. Both objects contain the same figure handle value and the same plot handle value. This means that both the original object and its copy point to the same figure window and the same line plot. The problem with two objects pointing to the same figure can be demonstrated by resetting the copy. Entering the command

shape_copy = reset(shape_copy);

closes the figure associated with both the original and the copy.

Here's the problem. The copy contains valid handles even though the copy has never been drawn. We can fix this problem in **ctor_1** by adding lines that assign empty to both handles before returning the copy. Unfortunately, clients can also use assignment to create a copy. Unlike the copy constructor, with assignment, we have no ability to modify the copy before it is assigned. When the object contains a handle, an exact copy may or may not be the desired result. We are again at the mercy of MATLAB, and this is unfortunate because it represents another limitation with no viable work-around. For this reason, the implementation of **ctor_1** takes the path of least resistance by creating a copy constructor such that the following two commands result in the same private values for **shape_copy**.

>> shape_copy = cShape(shape);

>> shape_copy = shape;

Finally, look at the one-argument constructor that passes **[]** as an argument. The commands

shape = cShape([]);

shape = draw(shape)

result in the figure shown in Figure 11.3. The figure is empty because **mPoints** is empty.

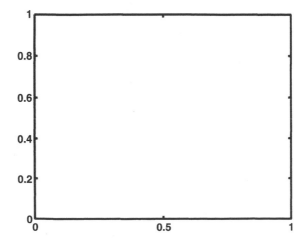

FIGURE 11.3 Example graphic for shape with no corner points.

11.4 SUMMARY

Viewed from outside the class, very little has changed between the implementations in Chapter 10 and this chapter. This is encapsulation at work again. Internally, the organization of the constructor changed radically. We now have a general design that will easily support growth in both the number and type of the class' constructors. To do this we isolated nearly all the application-specific code into separate functions located in the class' private directory. These functions do not pollute the public interface because they are callable only from within other member functions. We also added a one-argument constructor and discussed how the **ctor_1** helper strategy would extend to other numbered-**ctor** functions.

This chapter did not begin the process of designing and building a hierarchy, but you probably see where we are heading. For example, in this chapter, star and diamond represent two specific types of shapes. If we introduce **cStar** and **cDiamond** classes, they can reuse all the **cShape** code we have already developed. The brute-force way to reuse **cShape** would be to copy all of its code into **/@cStar** and **/@cDiamond**. The object-oriented way to reuse the code is to construct a **cShape** object and use it as an integral part of both **cStar** and **cDiamond**. Giving **cShape**'s constructor, the ability to construct an object with specified corner points makes object-oriented reuse a lot more convenient.

As the hierarchy extends, we might need a two-argument constructor that allows construction with both corner points and a color value. The numbered-**ctor** strategy implemented in this chapter makes this type of extension both easy and safe. It is easy because the main constructor function is already designed to use the new helper. As long as its name is **ctor_2.m** and it is placed in the class' private directory, the main constructor function will automatically use it when two arguments are passed into the constructor. It is safe because the new constructor is the only modified file. The main constructor function and all preexisting helpers work exactly as before because they did not change. Similarly, deleting a numbered-**ctor** function only affects construction with the associated number of arguments. This flexibility can be used to support development, testing, and quality assurance without upsetting the code being developed, tested, or inspected.

In the private member function discussion, we used numbered-**ctor** functions as an example of private member functions. It should be clear that we could also add private member functions to improve maintainability or extendibility for other members of the group of eight. In fact, we can add private member functions to improve the maintainability of any member function, public or private. Private member functions lead to the creation of modular code because function search rules were designed so that private functions do not pollute the public interface.

As we continue with our discussion of inheritance, **cShape** will continue to be used as an example. You might be surprised that such a simple class will be able to serve in this capacity. If you examine the details of **cShape**, what is surprising is the true complexity of the implementation. Unified Modeling Language (UML) uses a diagram called the *static-structure diagram* to help illustrate class details. The full UML static-structure diagram for the current version of **cShape** is shown in Figure 11.4. Organized into two sections, the upper section contains member variables and the lower section contains member functions. The + symbols designate public members; and the − symbols, private. There is indeed a lot going on in our "simple" **cShape** implementation. It is good that we now have a standard organizational framework to control the complexity.

The list of functions in the lower section reminds us of the slight mismatch between standard object-oriented terminology and MATLAB's object model. The first four functions in the list represent four different constructors. In order, they are the default constructor, the copy constructor, an empty-points constructor, and an array-of-points constructor. From this chapter we understand that all of these separately listed constructors are implemented using only one public function. The same holds true for other functions in the list with more than one entry. The UML diagram and object-oriented design in general focus on all of the different ways a member function can be called. It is up to the class developer to interpret the design and convert it into an implementation.

cShape
+Size : array = mSize +ColorRgb : array = hsv2rgb(mColorHsv) +Points : array = mPoints -mSize : array = [1;1] -mScale : array = [1;1] -mColorHsv : array = [0.67;1;1] -mPoints : array = [imag(exp(j*(0:4:20)*pi/5)); real(exp(j*(0:4:20)*pi/5))] -mFigureHandle : handle = [] -mPlotHandle : handle = [] -mDisplayFunc : function handle = []
+cShape() : cShape +cShape(in In : cShape) : cShape +cShape(in In : []) : cShape +cShape(in In : array) : cShape +display(in this : cShape) +fieldnames(in this : cShape) : cellstr +fieldnames(in this : cShape, in type : string = -full) : cellstr +fieldnames(in this : cShape, in type : string = -possible) : cellstr +struct(in this : cShape) : structure +subsref(in this : cShape, in index : substruct) : untyped +subsasgn(in this : cShape, in index : substruct, in set_val : untyped) : cShape +get(in this : cShape, in index : substruct) : untyped +get(in this : cShape, in index : string) : untyped +get(in this : cShape) : untyped +set(in this : cShape, in index : substruct, in set_val : untyped) : cShape +set(in this : cShape, in index : string, in set_val : untyped) : cShape +set(in this : cShape, in index : string) : cShape +set(in this : cShape) : cShape +draw(in this : cShape) +mtimes(in lhs : cShape, in rhs : array) : cShape +mtimes(in lhs : array, in rhs : cShape) : cShape +reset(in this : cShape) : cShape -ctor_ini() : cShape -ctor_1(in this : cShape, in In : cShape) : cShape -ctor_1(in this : cShape, in In : []) : cShape -ctor_1(in this : cShape, in In : array) : cShape

FIGURE 11.4 UML static structure diagram for cShape.

11.5 INDEPENDENT INVESTIGATIONS

1. Investigate the result of commands **class** and **size** when used for the variables created by the following commands:

```
a = zeros(0);

b = ones([3 4 0]);

c = struct('name', {}, 'value', {});

d = [1 2 3]';

d(:,true) = [];

x = [];

y = {};

z = '';
```

Are all empties the same? What happens if you ask for the element **c.name**? What about **[c.name]**?

2. Modify the copy constructor so that it sets the figure handles and plot handles to **[]** before passing the object back to the client.

3. Add another one-input constructor that initializes corner values based on a string input. We have already defined corner point values for a star, a square, and a diamond, so it should be relatively easy to write a constructor that will create the appropriate objects for the following:

```
star = cShape('star');

square = cShape('square');

diamond = cShape('diamond');
```

   A. If you also want a **'rectangle'** case, can you use the corner points for a square and then overwrite the default size or scale? Which one would you overwrite so that after **reset** you will still have a rectangle?

   B. Now implement a shape that does not use corners. For example, what changes do you need to make to **cShape** members to allow for circles? Would it be easier to create a new **cCircle** class?

4. Investigate the use of a different strategy for constructor arguments and the changes that would occur to the main constructor function and the private helpers. A popular syntax used for setting attributes in graphics objects uses an attribute string followed by the attribute value. What changes would be required to support similar constructor syntax? For example:

```
shape(1) = cShape;

shape(2) = cShape('Points', [-1 0 1 0 -1; 0 -1 0 1 0]);

shape(3) = cShape('ColorRgb', [1;0;0], ...

  'Points', [-1 0 1 0 -1; 0 -1 0 1 0]);
```

Can the result from one of the exercises in Chapter 8 be used to make this type of assignment easier? Would it be too much trouble to include support for both a numbered-**ctor** approach and this approach?

12 Constructing Simple Hierarchies with Inheritance

Using **cShape**, we have drawn shapes that look like a star, a rectangle, and a diamond.* Even though these three shapes have a lot in common, we still recognize them as three different shapes. The organization of this simple shape taxonomy looks like Figure 12.1. With inheritance, we can build a set of classes to recreate this taxonomy without copying a lot of code. Member functions common to all shapes are found only in **/@cShape**. Member functions with code tailored for each particular shape type are found in each particular directory. Inheritance is the glue that allows us to build the hierarchy and allows MATLAB to find the appropriate function.

Inheritance builds a hierarchy by allowing us to specify a relationship between a parent and child class. In the relationship, a child class is said to inherit attributes and behaviors from the parent.** Behaviors are synonymous with member functions, and in MATLAB, finding a member function involves the function path. For sure, MATLAB will search for a function in the child class' directory. With inheritance, if the function is not found in the child's directory, MATLAB will also search the parent's directory. If we are going to allow MATLAB to call one of the parent's functions, the object must contain all of the parent's member variables. The second part of inheritance relates to data. A child object contains all parent data but parent data are still encapsulated. The child is allowed entry to the parent's members-only club, but the child does not enjoy all of the same privileges.

The parent offers inheritance and the child gets to choose what to accept. In the simplest case, the child accepts everything the parent has to offer. The child redefines none of the parent's functions and adds no new member variables. The only difference probably occurs in the child's default construction values. Getting a little more complicated, a child might be happy with the parent's variables but needs to redefine the behavior of a member function. This important aspect of inheritance can be tricky because inheritance does not circumvent encapsulation. Encapsulation means that only parent member functions can access parent member variables. Private parent variables are not available from inside a child's new or redefined function. The parent-class-only restriction applies to both private variables and private functions. This is a situation where concealed variables can be useful. Finally, in the general case, a child can add new member variables, add new member functions, and redefine parent functions. Supporting the general case might seem difficult, but with a systematic approach, inheritance is actually easy.

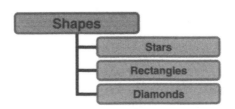

FIGURE 12.1 The simple shape taxonomy.

---

* In the opening paragraphs of Chapter 1, I promised to remind you before the information in §1.3 became important. If you accepted my invitation to skip directly to Chapter 2, now would be a very good time review §1.3.
** The terms superclass and subclass, respectively, are often used as an alternative to parent and child.

Inheritance supports code reuse in several ways. In the hierarchy, a child can rely on functions located in the parent-class directory. Many different child classes from the same parent can easily reuse the same function. In client code, a child can temporarily masquerade as a parent because the child's interface contains the same public members. Any client code that worked with a parent object will still work with a child.

Inheritance occurs without the parent even knowing that the child exists. This is important because coupling in the hierarchy only goes one way. Inheritance couples the child to the parent but not the other way around. Changes in the parent ripple down the hierarchy to all the children, but changes to children are not reflected in the parent. Achieving the promise of one-way-only coupling is one reason we spent so much time nailing shut every possible hole in encapsulation.

12.1 SIMPLE INHERITANCE

Since this is the first chapter on inheritance, we are going to walk before we run. We will use **cShape** as the parent class for **cStar** and **cDiamond**, but the only functional difference will occur in the constructor. A simplified diagram of the inheritance relationship is shown in Figure 12.2. We could further simplify inheritance by only supporting scalar objects. In the simple case with scalar objects, the implementation is too easy. That example would be almost worthless compared to an example that includes full array support. As with encapsulation, our goal with inheritance is to develop a robust example that can be used as a reference design for other classes. To get to that point we need to add a few improvements to the group of eight. These modifications are only necessary for child classes; however, there is no harm in adding inheritance support to every class. If the hierarchy needs to evolve, the basic scaffolding will already be in place.

12.1.1 CONSTRUCTOR

Every class needs a constructor; it is an object-oriented requirement. Without a constructor, the child class would never be able to declare its inheritance. As with any constructor, a child-class constructor must define a structure. The parent is part of that structure, but the parent isn't added the same way as private member variables. Parents are added to the class structure via the **class** command. This is the same **class** command we used in Part 1, but with inheritance there are more than two arguments. The additional arguments are parent-class objects. A child class can inherit from one parent or from multiple parents. Inheritance from more than one parent is called multiple inheritance. There is considerable debate in the object-oriented community about the usefulness of multiple inheritance. In the shape example, we will demonstrate inheritance from only one parent. The general-purpose code that supports inheritance will not be limited to single inheritance. The general-purpose code will support base classes with no inheritance as well as child classes with single or multiple inheritance.

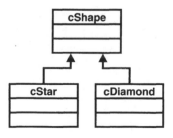

FIGURE 12.2 The inheritance structure of cStar and cDiamond.

Modifications to the existing set of files are easy. We will add a new helper function to keep track of parent names, but the main organization stays the same. There will still be a main constructor with a function name the same as the class name, a default **ctor_ini** helper, and any desired numbered-**ctor** functions. The **default_this** object returned by **class** will still be stored as a persistent variable, but with inheritance more arguments are passed into **class**. With inheritance, the **class** call must include more than two arguments. The first two arguments are the same as before, and the new arguments are objects of each parent class. We need to construct each parent and we can use the default parent constructor or can construct each parent using constructor arguments. We still save a copy of the default child object, but that does not limit us to calling only the default parent-class constructor.

The default child object can be based on a parent constructed using any available parent-class constructor. For example, in **cDiamond.m** we expect to see commands similar to the following:

```
parent_shape = cShape([-1 0 1 0 -1; 0 -1 0 1 0]);

default_this = class(default_struct, class_name, parent_shape);
```

The first line creates a **cShape** object with a specific set of corner points. These corner points draw a diamond. The second line creates an object using the child's default structure and the nondefault parent. To modify the general framework, we will isolate class-specific inheritance commands in a small number of files. This allows the group-of-eight files to keep their general-purpose design.

The first argument in the **class** call is a structure. We already said the parent would hold all the member variables, so we need an empty structure. This is not a problem because **ctor_ini.m** can easily return a structure without any elements. Indeed, the current version of **cShape**'s **ctor_ini** initially creates a no-element structure. Code Listing 64 lists the contents of a **ctor_ini** function that can be used to construct **cDiamond** objects. If you want to add private member variables to the child, you already know how to add them. Simply modify **ctor_ini** to add elements to **this_struct**. The general code in the main constructor will take care of the rest.

Code Listing 64, Modular Code, Simple ctor_ini with Inheritance

```
1   function [this_struct, superior, inferior, parents] =
    ctor_ini
2   this_struct = struct([]);
3   superior = {'double'};
4   inferior = {};
5   parents{1} = cShape([-1 0 1 0 -1; 0 -1 0 1 0]);
6   parent_list(parents{:})
```

With inheritance, the class call requires one or more parent objects. The return-argument list for **ctor_ini** has been expanded to include a cell array of parent objects. An empty cell array is passed back when there is no inheritance. When the cell array is not empty, all objects in the array are passed into **class** and used as parents. In this particular example, line 5 constructs a **cShape** object with a specific set of corner points and assigns the object into the first element of **parents**. Notice on line 5 that we are not merely accepting what the default **cShape** constructor has to offer. Instead, we are instantiating the **cShape** parent with arguments specifically tailored for the child. The same general technique can be used inside other constructor helper functions. The main constructor can now use the specific parent object when it creates the default version of the child. We will see how that works in Code Listing 66.

Line 6 passes the cell array of parents into a private helper function named **parent_list**. The helper function examines the array of parents and saves their names in a persistent variable. When a member function needs to know the names of its parents, it can call **parent_list** to get the persistent list. As we will soon see, the parent names are a very important part of inheritance.

The listing for **parent_list** is provided in Code Listing 65. This function has no class-specific code because the persistent variable is initialized based on the input. For the group-of-eight framework, every class must have a private **parent_list** helper function.

Code Listing 65, Modular Code, cStar's Private parent_list Function

```
1    function parents = parent_list(varargin)
2    persistent parent_cellstr
3
4    if nargin > 0
5      parent_cellstr = cell(nargin, 1);
6      for index = 1:nargin
7        parent_cellstr{index,1} = class(varargin{index});
8      end
9      if sscanf(version, '%g%x') < 7.0 && nargout == 1
10       % parent is stored in object using lower case in v.6.5
11       % if not being called from ctor, change parent_name to
          lower case
12       parent_cellstr = lower(parent_cellstr);
13     end
14   end
15   parents = parent_cellstr;
```

Line 2 declares the persistent variable **parent_cellstr**. The list of parent-class names is assigned into its elements. Lines 4–14 execute when **parent_list** is called with one or more arguments. Line 5 preallocates space for each input. Lines 6–8 loop over the input arguments. Line 7 uses **class** to assign the type of each input argument into an element of **parent_cellstr**.

After the loop, lines 9–13 implement a work-around for a problem that existed in MATLAB prior to version 7.0. Prior to version 7.0, MATLAB referred to parent classes using lowercase names. The commands in lines 9–13 detect the version and convert the class names to lowercase when necessary. If you are developing exclusively for versions 7.0 and above, your **parent_list** function doesn't need to include this code.

Finally, line 15 copies the persistent list of parent names into the **parents** return argument. The only place this helper should be called with inputs is from **ctor_ini**. After that, the helper can be called with no arguments whenever a list of parent-class types is needed.

With these modifications to the private helper functions in place, we can modify code in the main constructor to take advantage of them. A copy of the main constructor is shown in Code Listing 66. You have to look closely to find the changes. Line 6 now gets a cell array of parent objects from **ctor_ini**, and line 7 expands the parent-object list when it calls **class**. All other lines remain as they were.

The commands in Code Listing 66 represent the final version of the main constructor. The main constructor and the **parent_list** helper function can be reused in every class implementation. Both functions are appropriate for base classes with no inheritance as well as child classes with single and multiple inheritance. Code Listing 66 is the final reference design for the main constructor, replacing all previously developed versions.

Code Listing 66, Main Constructor with Support for Parent–Child Inheritance

```
1   function this = constructor(varargin)
2   class_name = mfilename('class');  % simply more general than
    'cShape'
3
4   persistent default_this
5   if isempty(default_this)
6     [default_struct, superior, inferior, parents] = ctor_ini;
7     default_this = class(default_struct, class_name,
      parents{:});
8     if ~isempty(superior)
9       superiorto(superior{:});
10    end
11    if ~isempty(inferior)
12      inferiorto(inferior{:});
13    end
14  end
15  this = default_this;  % copies persistent to this
16
17  if nargin > 0  % if not default, pass varargin to helper
18    try
19      this = feval(sprintf('ctor_%d', nargin), this,
        varargin{:});
20    catch
21      err = lasterror;
22      switch err.identifier
23        case 'MATLAB:UndefinedFunction'
24          err.message = [['class ' class_name] ...
25                         [' cannot be constructed from '] ...
26                         [sprintf('%d', nargin) ' input
                           argument(s) ']];
27      end
28      rethrow(err);
29    end
30  end
```

The private member functions that support Code Listing 66 — **ctor_ini**, **ctor_1**, and **parent_list** — are also complete. These files cannot be reused without class-specific tailoring because moving class-specific commands out of the main constructor and into these functions was one of our goals. Even so, these files can be used as a template for other class implementations because their contents are organized to make tailoring easy.

12.1.2 OTHER STANDARD MEMBER FUNCTIONS

At first, you might think, "Hey, that's all we need." If MATLAB worked like other object-oriented languages, we would indeed be finished. As we discovered throughout Part 1, however, MATLAB does not always behave the same as other object-oriented languages. Implementing inheritance also exposes differences, and because of that, the group of eight needs a little more work before our child classes can deal with arrays and vectorization. The differences also mean that we need to include a few more files in our child-class directories. Presently, the only files in **/@cStar** are **cStar.m**, **/private/ctor_ini.m**, and **private/parent_list.m**. MATLAB forwards all other function calls to the parent directory, **/@cShape**.

Our **cStar** class has a constructor, and we can indeed create an object. All we have to do is call the constructor, for example:

```
star = cStar;
```

We can also access public member variables. For example, accessing **Size** displays the following:

```
star.Size

ans =

   1

   1
```

The parent's version of **subsref** is being called, and it correctly returns the default value for **Size**. For scalar objects, everything seems to be working well. For nonscalar objects, however, the wheels fall off. Build an array of stars and try the same dot-reference command. Here is what happens*:

```
star = [cStar cStar];

star.Size

??? Dot name reference on non-scalar structure.
```

To find the cause of this error, we need to trace the call into the parent's version of **subsref** and examine some values. If you are following along, put a breakpoint at the beginning of **/@cShape/get.m**. When the execution gets to the breakpoint, step through the code (F11, or click the equivalent toolbar icon). You will eventually find that the error occurs inside **/@cShape/get.m** on the line

```
varargout = {this.mSize};
```

Now we know where, but don't know why.

To understand why, we need to dig deeper, but how? We can't display **this** because **cShape**'s **display** function relies on **get** and **get** is somehow the source of the problem. We can't use **struct(this)** either because **struct** also relies on **get**. Even **developer_view** lets us down.

To discover the cause of the error, we need to rely on functions that are not redefined by the parent. As a start, we can inspect the object's type. The functions **class** and **isa** are used for this purpose.

```
K>> class(this)

ans =

cStar
```

---

* Depending on your version of MATLAB, you might get the following error message instead:
??? Field reference for multiple structure elements that is followed by more reference blocks is an error.
Both messages refer to the same root cause.

```
K>> isa(this, 'cShape')

ans =

1
```

Using **class** informs us that **this** is an object of type **cStar**. We started with a **cStar** so this might seem reasonable. The problem is that we are inside a function in **cShape**'s directory. Shouldn't the object's type be reported as **cShape**? At least in the next command, when we use **isa** to check for the type **cShape**, the answer comes back **true**. There is still something troubling about the fact that the primary type of **this** is **cStar**. Perhaps the type will point us to the root cause of the error.

If you are familiar with how inheritance works in other languages, you might expect an object to display a type consistent with the function. When you are in a **/@cStar** function, you expect **cStar** as the object's type; and when you are in a **/@cShape** function, you expect the object to suppress its child-class additions to become an object of type **cShape**.

In other languages the term used for this behavior is *slicing*. Before passing a child object into a parent-class function, the compiler temporarily slices the child layer off the object. This exposes the data in the object's parent. When the parent function receives the sliced object, the object contains only parent-class members. The parent function can correctly operate on the object because it only seems to contain parent data. After its trip through the parent-class function, the compiler glues the sliced-off child layer back onto the object. The parent portion may have changed, and the original child portion is restored intact. We need to examine **this** to find out if MATLAB is doing anything to our object. Fortunately, from Part 1 we have a few tricks up our sleeve.

When we get into a real bind, we can use the built-in version of either **fieldnames** or **struct**. In general, **builtin** is dangerous, but sometimes we have to take the gloves off when we are debugging a tough problem. The result from the built-in version of **struct** is as follows:

```
K>> builtin('struct', this)

ans =

1x2 struct array with fields:

  cShape
```

This simple result gives us a lot of insight into how MATLAB stores parent objects. That insight allows us to understand the cause of our error.

The output from '**class**' tells us that this is an object of type **cStar**, and the output from '**struct**' tells us that **cStar** object's have one field in their private structure. The call to **ctor_ini** returned a no-element structure, so MATLAB must have added the field during the three-argument call to **class**. Indeed, the fieldname and parent's class match.* This is exactly how MATLAB stores the parent part of a child object. For more than one parent, more than one field will be added. As part of the structure, the parent object is simply another private variable. Inside a child's member function, the parent is referenced like any other private variable, for example, **this.cShape**. The structure of **this** is the root of our problem.

Inside **get** when MATLAB encounters **{this.mSize}**, it automatically converts operator syntax into a call to the built-in version of **subsref**. Operator conversion sorts out the fact we are asking for a parent variable, expands the index into **this(:).cShape.mSize**, and calls the built-in version of **subsref**. For scalar objects, the built-in **subsref** can index to any dot-reference level and the built-in **subsref** can correctly slice the object's structure. For nonscalar objects, the built-in **subsref** will only index into one level. If we want full support for both inheritance and nonscalar objects, we must add slicing code to some of the child's member functions.

---

* In versions prior to 7.0, the parent object's fieldname matches a lowercase version of the parent's type.

Related to both inheritance and slicing is a special type of function called a *virtual function*. In practical terms, a virtual function is a public function that exists in both the parent's directory and the child's. The child does not inherit the parent's function but rather chooses to redefine the function so that it does something different for child-class objects vs. parent-class objects. MATLAB decides which version to use based on the argument type. If one member function calls another member function, the argument type is used to decide where to find the called member function. Even when the calling member function is a parent function, the call will execute a child function. The object-oriented word used to describe this behavior is *polymorphism*. Getting the full power of polymorphism is tricky because we have to be careful about when we slice an object. If we slice it too soon, we lose the ability to run child-class functions.

It seems slicing code might be added in one of two places: parent-class member functions or child-class member functions. Inside the parent, slicing code would look something like the following:

```
parent = [this(:).cShape];

Size = [parent(:).Size];
```

There are at least three problems with this approach. First, we prefer an inheritance relationship where the parent never needs to know it is being used as a parent. Modifying parent-class functions violates that preference. Second, in a multiple-inheritance situation, the priority for choosing a parent lies with the child. Third, the parent-class structure element is not available from inside parent-class member functions. When the built-in **subsref** slices **this**, it removes the child portion and thus there is no longer a **cShape** field. The whole object is a **cShape**. The correct place to slice is inside the child. We just need to be a little careful when we allow a child class to redefine a parent-class function.

Let's examine the remaining group-of-eight functions. The two access-operator functions, **subsref** and **subsasgn**, each contain three cases. Dot-references are forwarded to **get** or **set**. No slicing on the part of **subsref** or **subsasgn** is required to forward this request. Any required slicing is done inside **get** and **set**. Array-reference code treats each index level separately, and thus no slicing code is required. Cell-references already throw an error, and thus they require no further slicing. Since inheritance introduces no changes to **subsref** and **subsasgn**, a child class can choose to include or omit them from its class directory.

Next in the list is **display**. Here there are two options, standard display and developer view. Standard display relies on the tailored version of **struct**, while developer view relies on **builtin** and **full_display**. As long as **struct** returns a full set of public variable names, **display** can get the values without slicing. Similarly, neither the built-in version of **struct** nor **full_display** needs any additional slicing code. Any required slicing occurs when **struct** is called. Even though **struct** has to travel up the inheritance hierarchy, **struct** needs no additional slicing code. Instead, **struct** relies on slicing code inside **fieldnames** and **get**. This means that **display** and **struct** are also optional for child classes.

To support combined inheritance and object arrays, the remaining three group-of-eight functions — **fieldnames**, **get**, and **set** — need to slice their objects. All three can generalize their slicing code by using **parent_list** to obtain a list of parent-class names. Coding **fieldnames**, **get**, and **set** to handle an empty list allows for a general solution. Of course, the name list inside fieldnames and the cases inside **get** and **set** will still need class-specific tailoring; however, slicing code can be reused as is. Generalizing on **parent_list** has other positive implications, the primary advantage being that the **parent_list** order can be used to establish parent-class priority.

The Part 1 organization of **fieldnames**, **get**, and **set** makes it relatively easy to add slicing code. For **fieldnames**, public names from parent-class **fieldnames** calls are concatenated with any additional child-class names. In the case of **get** and **set**, they are already organized into functional blocks that represent public member variables, concealed variables, and error processing. To support slicing and inheritance, we need to add another functional block just before error processing. This way, the dot-reference request can be forwarded to each parent prior to throwing an error. In effect, we are setting up a standard precedence for indexing member variables that is quite similar to the overarching function-search rules.

12.1.2.1 Child Class fieldnames

The child classes in this chapter don't add public member variables, but that is not typical. Ordinarily a child class adds variables and functions. Private variables are added through the constructor, public variables are added using cases in **get** and **set**, and functions are added to the class directory. Private variables and public functions take care of themselves, but public variable names need to be available from **fieldnames**.

Calling the parent's version of **fieldnames** returns a list of the parent's public variables. Calling the child's version of **fieldnames** returns a list of the child's public variables. Due to inheritance, the child's list needs to include the names from every parent plus those names added by the child. The easiest way to assemble the list is to call **parent_list**, slice the object into each parent listed, concatenate the variable names from the parents, and finally add the child's names. Code to implement this process is shown in Code Listing 67.

Code Listing 67, Implementing Parent Slicing in cStar's fieldnames.m

```
1   function names = fieldnames(this, varargin)
2
3   names = {};
4
5   % first fill up names with parent public names
6   parent_name = parent_list;  % get the parent name cellstr
7   for parent_name = parent_list'
8     parent = [this.(parent_name{1})];
9     names = [names; fieldnames(parent, varargin{:})];
10  end
11
12  % then add additional names for child
13  % note: return names as a column
14  if nargin == 1
15    % no extra fields for this child class
16  else
17     switch varargin{1}
18     case '-full'
19      % no extra fields for this child class
20     case '-possible'
21      % no extra fields for this child class
22     otherwise
23      error('Unsupported call to fieldnames');
24     end
25  end
```

Line 6 calls the parent list, and lines 7–10 loop over all the parent names returned. Line 8 slices the object using dynamic fieldname syntax, and line 9 calls each parent's **fieldnames**. The result from each call is concatenated into **names**. After assembling the parent-class names **cellstr**, lines 14–25 add the names for public variables added by the child. In this particular case, there are no additional names and lines 14–25 don't add anything. These lines were included in the listing to remind us what needs to be done whenever the child adds public variables.

12.1.2.2 Child Class get

Inside **get,** parent-forwarding code slices out the parent object and forwards the sliced object along with index arguments to each parent's version of **get**. The parent's version of **get** looks for the dot-reference name among its public variables and either returns a value or forwards the request to the parent's parent. This way it doesn't matter how deeply a child is rooted in the hierarchy because the call traverses the hierarchy one level at a time. If the call makes it all the way to the highest level yet still does not find a reference to the dot-reference name, the error block will throw an error. With single inheritance, it really doesn't matter which version of **get** throws the error. With multiple inheritance, these errors need to be caught and handled by the child. Before throwing an error, the child needs to wait until all parent objects have been given an opportunity to respond.

Code to implement **get** for both **cStar** and **cDiamond** is shown in Code Listing 68. This listing contains the same functional blocks as before, and it contains a new parent-forwarding section. The public and concealed variable blocks don't include any cases because currently the child classes do not contain additional variables. Even requests for the concealed variable **mDisplayFunc** will be forwarded to the parent. The empty **switch** statements are here to remind us of the other sections and give us a head start if we want to add child-class variables. The error-processing block is included, and the error has been upgraded so that it assigns an identifier as well as a message. An error with an identifier is much easier to catch compared to one without. After error processing, the value of **nargout** is used to condition the output.

```
Code Listing 68, Implementing Parent Forwarding in cStar's get.m
1    function varargout = get(this, index, varargin)
2
3    % one argument, display info and return
4    if nargin == 1
5      if nargout == 0
6        disp(struct(this(1)));
7      else
8        varargout = cell(1,max([1, nargout]));
9        varargout{1} = struct(this(1));
10     end
11     return;
12   end
13
14   % if index is a string, we will allow special access
15   called_by_name = ischar(index);
16
17   % the set switch below needs a substruct
18   if called_by_name
```

```matlab
19     index = substruct('.', index);
20   end
21
22   found = false;
23
24   % public-member-variable section
25   found = true;   % otherwise-case will flip to false
26   switch index(1).subs
27     % No additional public variables
28     otherwise
29       found = false;   % didn't find it in the public section
30   end
31
32   % concealed member variables, not strictly public
33   if ~found && called_by_name
34     found = true;
35     switch index(1).subs
36       % No additional concealed variables
37       % mDisplayFunc exists in the parent
38       otherwise
39         found = false;   % didn't find it in the public section
40       end
41   end
42
43   % parent forwarding block
44   if ~found
45
46     if called_by_name
47       forward_index = index(1).subs;
48     else
49       forward_index = index;
50     end
51
52     if nargout == 0
53       varargout = cell(size(this));
54     else
55       varargout = cell(1, nargout);
56     end
57
58     for parent_name = parent_list'  % loop over parent cellstr
59       try
60         parent = [this.(parent_name{1})];
61         [varargout{:}] = get(parent, forward_index,
            varargin{:});
62         found = true;   % catch will assign false if not found
63         break;   % can only get here if field is found
64       catch
```

```
65        found = false;
66        err = lasterror;
67        switch err.identifier
68          case 'MATLAB:nonExistentField'
69            % NOP
70          otherwise
71            rethrow(err);
72        end
73      end
74    end
75  end
76
77  % error block
78  if ~found
79    error('MATLAB:nonExistentField', ...
80      'Reference to non-existent field identifier %s', ...
81      index(1).subs);
82  end
83
84  % nargout adjustment
85  if length(varargout) > 1 & nargout <= 1
86    if iscellstr(varargout) || any([cellfun('isempty',
      varargout)])
87      varargout = {varargout};
88    else
89      try
90        varargout = {[varargout{:}]};
91      catch
92        varargout = {varargout};
93      end
94    end
95  end
```

The parent-forwarding section can be found in lines 43–76. As with the other functional blocks, entrance to parent forwarding is guarded on line 44 by **if ~found**. We don't need to ask the parent for a value if we have already found it in the child. Lines 46–50 change the input index back into its original form. This change allows the parent to determine whether to allow access to concealed variables.

Lines 52–56 initialize **varargout** to the right size so that **nargout** inside of the parent's **get** will return the correct number of values. We have used this trick before. Preallocating **varargout** allows the parent's **get** to return the correct number of arguments. Line 58 loops over the names returned by the call to **parent_list**. Line 60 slices the object using dynamic fieldname syntax. In **cStar**, for example, the equivalent nondynamic syntax would be written as **this.cShape**. Parent objects are stored in the child object as private structure elements with element names identical to the parent's type. The variable **parent** is now a parent-class object. Once **parent** is passed out of the child-class function, all associations with the child are severed. MATLAB treats **parent** as a parent-class object because the child has been sliced away.

Line 61 and normal object-oriented function selection forward the **get** request to the parent. If line 61 successfully returns a value, line 62 sets **found** to **true**. Line 63 then breaks out of the **parent_name** loop. Once the loop receives a value from one parent, there is no reason to ask another. If line 61 is not successful, the parent at the top of the hierarchy will throw a **'MATLAB:nonExistentField'** error. Lines 62–63 are skipped, and the error is caught by line 64. Line 65 makes sure **found** is set to **false**, line 66 loads the error into **err**, and line 67 selects a **case** based on the error identifier. If the identifier is **'MATLAB:nonExistentField'**, program control jumps back to the beginning of the **parent_name** loop. Maybe the value will be found in the next parent. Any other error is a lot more serious and is rethrown by line 71. If the **parent_name** loop completes without finding a value, **found** will be **false** and standard error processing will occur.

The parent-forwarding section in lines 43–76 is general and can be included in every class' **get**. This is even true for parentless base classes because **parent_list** returns an empty **cellstr**. The standard implementation of **get** will always include a parent-forwarding block.

12.1.2.3 Child Class set

After inserting a parent-forwarding section inside **get**, we are in an excellent position to insert the same functionality into **set**. The basic idea is the same but the direction is different. With **set**, we are trying to assign, not access, parent values. Assignment is a little harder because we need to slice the object, forward the request, *and* glue the child portion back to the parent. Code to implement **get** for both **cStar** and **cDiamond** is shown in Code Listing 69. The parent-forwarding block in this listing is general and can be added to every version of **set**.

```
Code Listing 69, Implementing Parent Forwarding in cStar's set.m

1    function varargout = set(this, index, varargin)
2
3    % one/two arguments, display info and return
4    if nargin < 3
5      possible = fieldnames(this, '-possible');
6      possible_struct = struct(possible{:});
7      if nargout == 0
8        if nargin == 1
9          disp(struct(this(1)));
10       else
11         try
12           temp_struct.(index) = possible_struct.(index);
13           disp(temp_struct);
14         catch
15           warning(['??? Reference to non-existent field ' ...
16           index '.']);
17         end
18       end
19     else
20       varargout = cell(1,max([1, nargout]));
21       varargout{1} = struct(this(1));
22     end
23     return;
```

```matlab
24  end
25
26  % if index is a string, we will allow special access
27  called_by_name = ischar(index);
28
29  % the set switch below needs a substruct
30  if called_by_name
31    index = substruct('.', index);
32  end
33
34  % public-member-variable section
35  found = true;   % otherwise-case will flip to false
36  switch index(1).subs
37    % No additional public variables
38    otherwise
39      found = false;   % didn't find it in the public section
40  end
41
42  % concealed member variables, not strictly public
43  if ~found && called_by_name
44    found = true;
45    switch index(1).subs
46      % No additional concealed variables
47      % mDisplayFunc exists in the parent
48      otherwise
49        found = false;   % didn't find it in the public section
50    end
51  end
52
53  % parent forwarding block
54  if ~found
55
56    if called_by_name
57      forward_index = index(1).subs;
58    else
59      forward_index = index;
60    end
61
62    for parent_name = parent_list'   % loop over parent cellstr
63      try
64        parent = [this.(parent_name{1})];
65        parent = set(parent, forward_index, varargin{:});
66        parent = num2cell(parent);
67        [this.(parent_name{1})] = deal(parent{:});
68        found = true;   % catch will assign false if not found
69        break;   % can only get here if field is found
70      catch
```

```
71        found = false;
72        err = lasterror;
73        switch err.identifier
74          case 'MATLAB:nonExistentField'
75            % NOP
76          otherwise
77            rethrow(err);
78          end
79        end
80      end
81  end
82
83  % error block
84  if ~found
85    error('MATLAB:nonExistentField', ...
86      'Reference to non-existent field identifier %s', ...
87      index(1).subs);
88  end
89
90  varargout{1} = this;
```

Here the parent-forwarding block is found in lines 53–80. The only differences from **get**'s parent-forwarding block occur in lines 65–67. Like **get**, line 64 performs the slice so that **parent** contains a parent-class object. In line 65, the **parent** is used as an input to **set**. Passing the parent-class object allows MATLAB to find and use the parent's member function. Line 66 converts **parent** into a cell array so that line 67 can easily deal the elements back into their proper location. Line 67 is the place where the parent and child are glued back together. Line 64 performed the slice, and line 67 reassembles the pieces. The **catch** statement that begins on line 70 handles assignment errors.

12.1.3 PARENT SLICING IN NONSTANDARD MEMBER FUNCTIONS

Quite often, a member function outside the group of eight needs to call a parent member function. To do this, slicing code must be added; however, slice-and-forward code inside nonstandard member functions usually targets a specific parent. For standard group-of-eight functions, slice-and-forward code can successfully loop over every parent because every parent contains all the standard functions. This is not the case for nonstandard functions.

Currently **cShape** has three nonstandard functions, **draw**, **mtimes**, and **reset**. For each, **cStar** and **cDiamond** can choose to redefine these functions or allow MATLAB to run the parent version directly. For scalar objects, MATLAB can directly run the parent version whenever no additional child-class variable is involved in the function. This is very convenient because it means most member functions are not tailored by the child. For nonscalar objects, a tailored version with slice-and-forward code must be included anytime the parent version uses private member variables. This is unfortunate because it usually forces the child to overload every nonstandard member function. When a child inherits from more than one parent, all nonstandard functions from every parent must be tailored or at least considered for tailoring.

One of the biggest benefits of inheritance is an ability to reuse parent-class functions without child-class tailoring. MATLAB does not currently have intrinsic support for the combination of inheritance and nonscalar objects. There are also issues with deeper levels of inheritance Lack of intrinsic support forces difficult decisions. We can choose to allow only scalar objects. We still get the benefit of object-oriented reuse, but we lose one of the most powerful reasons for using MATLAB: vectorization. If we choose to support nonscalar objects, we diminish some of the typical reasons for using an object-oriented approach: reuse and polymorphism. We still get some reuse because child-class functions only need to include slice-and-forward code. The bulk of the functionality still resides in the parent. We lose polymorphism because after the child-class function slices the object, only parent-class functions can be called. For MATLAB, the lesser-of-two-evils choice is to support vectorization at the expense of reuse and polymorphism.

12.1.3.1   draw.m

Supporting nonscalar objects with **draw** means that each child class needs to define a function named **draw.m**. In this example, the child version must include slice-and-forward code but can rely on the parent's version to do all the drawing. Like **set**, **draw** is a mutator and the child's version of **draw** will follow **set**'s example. The implementation is shown in Code Listing 70. Some of the lines in the **else** block could be combined, but this example breaks each operation into a separate line.

Code Listing 70, Parent Slice and Forward inside Child-Class draw.m

```
1  function this = draw(this, varargin)
2  if nargout ~= 1
3    warning('draw must be called using: obj = draw(obj)');
4  else
5    parent = [this.cShape];
6    parent = draw(parent, varargin{:});
7    parent = num2cell(parent(:));
8    [this.cShape] = deal(parent{:});
9  end
```

Notice in line 1 that this version of **draw** will accept more than one argument. Including **varargin** as an input and forwarding the values to the parent helps insulate the child's slice-and-forward function from future changes that might occur in the parent. Like the parent's version, lines 2–3 enforce the use of **draw** as a mutator. If the client doesn't ask for a return value, it's an error. Line 5 slices the object into an array of **cShape** parents. This is different from the parent-forwarding loop used inside **get** and **set**. Unlike the general situation that exists in **get** and **set**, inside **draw** we already know which parent contains **draw**. Line 6 calls **draw** using the parent as both an input and output argument. Calling draw on the parent will potentially change the parent. Lines 7–8 assign the mutated parent back into the child-object array. We can follow a similar approach with all class-specific member functions.

12.1.3.2   mtimes.m

Overloading **mtimes** for the child follows the same strategy as **draw**. The child's version needs to slice the object, forward to the parent, and reassemble the object. Before the object can be sliced, it needs to be identified. The implementation is shown in Code Listing 71.

Line 2 identifies which input variable is the object and which is the scale factor. Inheritance allows **isa** to use the name **'cShape'**. Lines 3 and 7 assign the appropriate input to **this**. Lines 4 and 8 slice, forward, and distribute the mutated parent array into cells. Lines 5 and 9 deal the mutated parent objects back into the child objects.

Code Listing 71, Parent Slice and Forward in Child-Class mtimes.m

```
1    function this = mtimes(lhs, rhs)
2    if isa(lhs, 'cShape')
3      this = lhs;
4      parent = num2cell(mtimes([this.cShape], rhs));
5      [this.cShape] = deal(parent{:});
6    else
8      parent = num2cell(mtimes(lhs, [this.cShape]));
9      [this.cShape] = deal(parent{:});
10   end
```

12.1.3.3   reset.m

Tailoring **reset** is even easier because there is only a single input. Again, the child's version needs to slice the object, forward to the parent, and reassemble the object. The implementation is shown in Code Listing 72. Lines 1 and 2 isolate the child-class function from parent-class changes by including **vararg in**. Line 2 slices, forwards, and collects the reset parent objects in cells of **parent**. Line 3 deals the cells back into the child objects.

Code Listing 72, Parent Slice and Forward in Child-Class reset.m

```
1    function this = reset(this, varargin)
2    parent = num2cell(reset([this.cShape], varargin{:}));
3    [this.cShape] = deal(parent{:});
```

12.2   TEST DRIVE

If we correctly understand what simple inheritance means and if we implemented it correctly, we should be able to substitute a child object for a parent object almost anywhere. In this particular example, simple inheritance implies that **cDiamond** and **cStar** objects can be used anywhere we previously used a **cShape** object. A complete copy of the parent's interface is passed down the inheritance hierarchy to the child. The interface copy comes primarily through inheritance and not by duplicating code. Let's create some objects and see what happens. The commands using **cStar** are shown in Code Listing 73.

Code Listing 73, Chapter 12 Test Drive Command Listing: Exercising the Interface for a cStar Object

```
1    >> cd '/oop_guide/chapter_12'
2    >> set(0, 'FormatSpacing', 'compact')
3    >> clear classes; fclose all; close all force;
4    >> star = cStar;
5    >> star2 = cStar(star);
6    >> whos
7     Name             Size           Bytes   Class
8
9     ans              1x1               8    double array
```

```
10    star                  1x1              1020   cStar object
11    star2                 1x1              1020   cStar object
12
13  Grand total is 53 elements using 2048 bytes
14
15  >> disp(star.Size')
16     1        1
17  >> disp(star.ColorRgb')
18     0        0        1
19  >> disp(star.Points)
20    0  5.8779e-01 -9.5106e-01  9.5106e-01 -5.8779e-01 -4.8986e-16
21  1.0000e+00 -8.0902e-01  3.0902e-01  3.0902e-01 -8.0902e-01
    1.0000e+00
22  >> star.Size = [2;3];
23  >> disp(star.Size')
24     2        3
25  >> star
26  star =
27         Size: [2x1 double]
28     ColorRgb: [3x1 double]
29       Points: [2x6 double]
30  >> fieldnames(star)
31  ans =
32     'Size'
33     'ColorRgb'
34     'Points'
35  >> fieldnames(star, '-full')
36  ans =
37     'Size % double array'
38     'ColorRgb % double array'
39     'Points % double array'
40  >> fieldnames(star, '-possible')
41  ans =
42     'Size'
43     {1x1 cell}
44     'ColorRgb'
45     {1x1 cell}
46     'Points'
47     {1x1 cell}
48  >> struct(star)
49  ans =
50         Size: [2x1 double]
51     ColorRgb: [3x1 double]
52       Points: [2x6 double]
53  >> star = draw(star);
54  >> star = 2 * star * 2;
55  >> star = reset(star);
```

```
56  >> star = [cStar cStar; cStar cStar];
57  >> size(star)
58  ans =
59     2     2
60  >> [star.Size]
61  ans =
62     1        1        1        1
63     1        1        1        1
64  >> {star.Size}
65  ans =
66     [2x1 double]    [2x1 double]    [2x1 double]    [2x1 double]
67  >>
68  >> disp(class(star))
69  cStar
70  >> disp(isa(star, 'cShape'))
71     1
72  >> disp(isa(star, 'cDiamond'))
73     0
```

The number of commands in Code Listing 73 displays a lot of capability given the fact that beyond the implementation of **cShape**, very little work was required. We could repeat the same set of commands for **cDiamond**. All of these commands were used extensively throughout Part 1. Here they are briefly summarized. A more thorough discussion can be found in Part 1.

The first **cStar** object is created in line 4. Here, MATLAB finds the constructor named **/@cStar/cStar.m**. The constructor is a copy of the standard group-of-eight constructor. The constructor was designed to be generic because it relies on **/@cStar/private/ctor_ini.m** for all class-specific details. There are no input arguments, so the constructor returns a default **cStar** object. In line 5, one argument is passed into the constructor. In this case, the constructor relies on **/@cStar/private/ctor_1.m** to construct a copy of the input object.

Let's take a short diversion and examine the details involved in child-class construction. The fact of a hierarchy complicates object construction because the process is now distributed. Multiple functions are involved, and these functions are spread across several directories. Ordinarily, such (dis)organization would lead to maintenance problems. With inheritance, however, a hierarchy with enforced encapsulation allows the organization to work smoothly. Even so, the organization is important and we must always keep in mind what is going on behind the scenes during child construction.

Figure 12.3 displays a diagram of the calling tree along with each function's path. Even with one level of inheritance, there are many functions to call. The depth of the calling tree and the ease

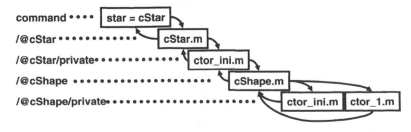

FIGURE 12.3 Call tree for cStar's default constructor.

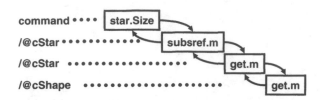

FIGURE 12.4 Call tree for cStar's dot-reference accessor.

with which such depth is created are exactly why object-oriented programming received low grades for performance in the early years. Since then, we have learned some tricks on managing performance so that object-oriented programming can sometimes achieve higher efficiency compared to other techniques. During the construction of default objects, a persistent copy of the default object lets us short-circuit this calling tree and improve performance. MATLAB return a copy of the persistent object much faster than executing the nested constructor functions. The persistent copy is even more valuable when the hierarchy is deep or parent construction is complicated.

Back to the commands: the next few commands, lines 15–22, confirm that we have access to public member variables. Access to **Size**, **ColorRgb**, and **Points** is demonstrated. Remember that the private variables associated with these public variables do not belong to **cStar** but rather to the parent **cShape**. Slice-and-forward code inside **cStar**'s **set** and **get** appears to be working correctly. Let's briefly look at the calling tree for these operations.

MATLAB converts the dot-reference operator into a tailored call to **subsref.m**. The child class can choose to include or omit **subsref** because polymorphism allows the parent's version to work as a substitute. The calling tree in Figure 12.4 assumes the child includes all group-of-eight functions. Some of the file locations would be different if the child omits some of the standard functions. Inside **subsref**, there is an object-oriented call to **get.m** and MATLAB finds **get** in **/@cStar**. Slice-and-forward code inside the child's version of **get** forwards the index to the parent. This process would be repeated for any number of parents, and in this case, the public variables are found and values are passed back to the command window. The order is a little easier because we never need to call the parent's version of **subsref**. Assignment works the same way except that **subsasgn** and **set** are used instead of **subsref** and **get**.

Line 25 has no trailing semicolon, and that triggers a call to **display**. Other standard functions like **fieldnames** and **struct** are demonstrated on lines 30–52. In these standard functions, slice-and-forward code assembles the desired result. All of this appears to be working because the outputs are the same as those at the end of Part 1.

Parent–child inheritance also provides **cStar** with a graphics interface. The result of **draw** in line 53 is shown in Figure 12.5. The scale is not 1:1 because we set the **Size** to **[2; 3]** back in the command on line 22. Figure 12.5 shows the result after pre- and postmultiplying by two in line 54. The reset in line 55 closes the graphics window.

Lines 56–59 demonstrate that we are able to create arrays of **cStar** objects, and lines 60–66 demonstrate that we can access the object array even with the use of inheritance. Finally, lines 68–73 investigate the object's type. Here we note that the primary type returned by **class** is **cStar**. In line 70 when we explicitly ask whether **star** is a **cShape** object, the answer is yes. That means the variable **star** is of course a **cStar** object, and inheritance allows **star** to masquerade as a **cShape** object too. Line 72 correctly tells us that **star** is not a **cDiamond** object.

So far, the test drive commands have pointed out similarities between inheritance and the shape classes developed at the end of Part 1. In Chapter 10, stars and diamond shapes both used **cShape** as their type. In this chapter, star and diamond shapes each have their own type and both **cStar** and **cDiamond** classes inherit from **cShape**. The command on line 72 points out that star shapes are not the same as diamond shapes and that difference casts a big shadow on the design. We are back to a place where we need to wrestle with a choice between scalar and vectorized objects. We will move that fight into the next chapter.

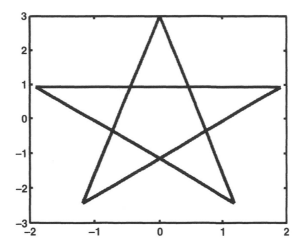

FIGURE 12.5 cStar graphic (simple inheritance) after setting the size to [2; 3].

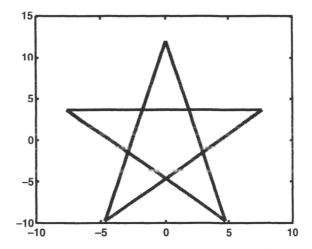

FIGURE 12.6 cStar graphic (simple inheritance) after scaling via multiplication, 2 * star * 2.

12.3 SUMMARY

If you thought that inheritance was going to be hard, hopefully this short chapter has dispelled that belief. The mechanics of inheritance are easy because we spent a lot of effort in the first section. First, bulletproof encapsulation always makes inheritance easier. Second, the code organization from Part 1 made it easy to add generic slice-and-forward code to the core group-of-eight functions. We also showed how to add slice-and-forward code to other child member functions so that both inheritance and object arrays can work in harmony.

Four functions in the standard group of eight received inheritance-related additions. The constructor, **get**, **set**, and **fieldnames** now include slice-and-forward code as part of their general implementation. The slice-and-forward code is based on the output of the private **parent_list** helper function. In classes without inheritance, **parent_list** returns an empty **cellstr**. An empty list bypasses slice-and-forward code sections. In classes with inheritance, **parent_list** returns a list of parent-class names and these names are used to slice out each parent and recall the original function, this time using the parent as an argument.

12.4   INDEPENDENT INVESTIGATIONS

1. Try your hand at adding a couple of other shape-specific classes. You might try adding a square or a triangle. For some real fun, try creating the corner points using **rand**. Think about how you might add a shape with no corners, like a circle.
2. Define a child of **cStar** called **cGreenStar**, and construct it so that when drawn the star is green rather than blue.

13 Object Arrays with Inheritance

With the introduction of **cStar** and **cDiamond**, the same class no longer represents both stars and diamonds. Even though both are derived from **cShape** and even though neither adds new features, **cStar** and **cDiamond** objects are different. These differences cast a big shadow on design because they force difficult choices between inheritance and vectorization. Here we discuss the differences and add some implementation details to our classes.

13.1 WHEN IS A CSHAPE NOT A CSHAPE?

One of the nice things about inheritance, virtual functions, polymorphism, and arrays of objects is the promise that MATLAB will always find and execute the right function based on the object's type. Following this to its conclusion, you might get the idea that a **cShape** array should be able to hold objects in any combination of **cShape**, **cStar**, and **cDiamond**. In reality, the vectorized implementation inside **cShape**'s group of eight cannot deal with a mixture of types. Vectorized operations rely on every object having exactly the same private structure, and exactly the same type. Therefore, even though **cStar** objects can masquerade as **cShape** objects, with respect to building object arrays, there is definitely a difference.

Unfortunately, MATLAB currently permits some questionable syntax. For example, using the code from Chapter 12, the commands in Code Listing 74 execute without causing an immediate error. The command in line 1 concatenates objects of different types. Line 2 is a variation on line 1. To make matters worse, the class reported for **my_shapes(2)** from both forms of concatenation is **cStar**. Concatenation does not cause an immediate error because the underlying structures are the same. This loophole must be closed. To close it, we need to add some code to **subsasgn** and we need to tailor **cat**, **horzcat**, and **vertcat**. The commands on line 7 are particularly bad because they eventually result in an internal memory error.

Code Listing 74, Questionable Inheritance Syntax

```
1   >> my_shapes = [cStar cDiamond];
2   >> my_shapes = cStar; my_shapes(2) = cDiamond;
3   >> class(my_shapes(2));
4   ans =
5   cStar
6   >>
7   >> shape = cShape; shape(2) = cStar;
```

These changes eliminate the possibility of a single object array being populated with different types, but they do not eliminate the promise of inheritance, virtual functions, polymorphism, and arrays of objects. A cell array populated with different object types can still be used. The syntax is not quite as convenient as a regular array, but short of developing specialized container classes, a cell array is a good compromise. These issues will be discussed in the test drive.

13.1.1 CHANGES TO SUBSASGN

Rather than repeating the entire listing for **subsasgn**, only the modified **case '()'** section is shown in Code Listing 75. In this listing, the modifications occur as additions in lines 11–17. These additions check the values in **varargin** to make sure they all match the type of the class. If they don't match, an error is thrown.

```
Code Listing 75, Changes to subsasgn That Trap Mismatched Array Types
1    case '()'
2      if isempty(this)
3      % due to superiorto, need to look at this and varargin
4      if isa(this, mfilename('class'))
5        this = eval(class(this));
6      else
7        this = eval(class(varargin{1}));
8      end
9    end
10   if length(index) == 1
11     if length(varargin) > 1
12       error('OOP:UnexpectedInputSize', ...
13         ['Only one input is allowed for () assignment.']);
14     end
15     if isempty(varargin{1}) || ...
16         strcmp(class(varargin{1}), mfilename('class'))
17       this = builtin('subsasgn', this, index, varargin{end:-
         1:1});
18     else
19       error('OOP:UnexpectedType', ...
20         ['Conversion to ' mfilename('class') ' from ' ...
21         class(mismatched{1}) ' is not possible.']);
22     end
23   else
24     this_subset = this(index(1).subs{:});   % get the subset
25     this_subset = subsasgn(this_subset, index(2:end),
       varargin{:});
26     this(index(1).subs{:}) = this_subset; % put subset back
27   end
```

Lines 11–14 generate an error when **varargin** contains more than one assignment value. Since the array-reference operator is assigning array elements, the input must be an array and there should be only one. If there is more than one, lines 12–13 throw an error. Lines 15–22 check the input type. The input can be empty or can be an array of objects of the current class. Recall from Chapter 9 that **mfilename('class')** is a general way to obtain the name of the current class. If the checks on lines 15–16 are okay, line 17 uses the built-in version of **subsasgn** to index and assign elements. If the checks are not okay, lines 19–21 throw an error.

13.1.2 VERTCAT AND HORZCAT

When objects are concatenated, the current built-in versions of **cat**, **vertcat**, and **horzcat** do not carefully inspect the types. If the underlying structures are the same, the built-in versions will concatenate objects of different types, usually resulting in an internal memory error when the combined variable is used. To avoid this situation, our classes will perform some additional checking. Performing the additional checks means adding **vertcat.m**, **horzcat.m**, and **cat.m** as member functions to every class. These standard member functions are not in the same league as the group-of-eight functions because they don't do anything to the object. Ideally, the built-in functions would already include this kind of check. For example, **cell2mat** does not require tailoring because the built-in version correctly checks element types prior to concatenation.

The **vertcat** function is shown in Code Listing 76. For **horzcat**, even though the function name is different, the body is identical to Code Listing 76. The **cat** function is very similar and is shown in Code Listing 77.

Code Listing 76, Implementing Input Type Checking for vertcat.m

```
1    function this = vertcat(varargin)
2    mismatched = varargin( ...
3      ~cellfun('isclass', varargin, mfilename('class')));
4    if ~isempty(mismatched)
5      error('MATLAB:UnableToConvert', ...
6        ['Conversion to ' mfilename('class') ' from ' ...
7        class(mismatched{1}) ' is not possible.']);
8    end
9
10   this = builtin(mfilename, varargin{:});
```

Code Listing 77, Implementing Input Type Checking for cat.m

```
1    function this = cat(varargin)
2    mismatched = varargin( ...
3      [false ~cellfun('isclass', varargin(2:end), mfilename
         ('class'))]);
4    if ~isempty(mismatched)
5      error('MATLAB:UnableToConvert', ...
6        ['Conversion to ' mfilename('class') ' from ' ...
7        class(mismatched{1}) ' is not possible.']);
8    end
9
10   this = builtin(mfilename, varargin{:});
```

In both functions, lines 2–3 create a cell array of mismatched inputs. The **cellfun** command applies an **isclass** check to the cells of **varargin**. For **vertcat** and **horzcat**, every cell is checked. For **cat**, the cell at **{1}** is not checked because it specifies the concatenation direction. The output of **cellfun** is a logical array. The element values are **true** where the input class matches **mfilename('class')**. If all elements match, the inputs are okay and **mismatched** will be empty. If **mismatched** is not empty, lines 5–7 throw an error. The error identifies the first mismatched type using **class(mismatched{1})** and the type from **mfilename('class')**. If **mismatched** is empty, line 10 uses **builtin** to forward the arguments to the built-in version of the function.

13.1.3 TEST DRIVE

Using a cell array to hold objects of different types is a good compromise because the variable types in a cell array's elements do not control the cell array's type. This allows a cell array to hold any combination of types. When each cell is indexed, the contents are used to select the appropriate functions. This is where the trade-off between performance and inheritance creeps in. Holding different object types in cell arrays leads to code that is difficult or inconvenient to vectorize. The **cellfun** command in MATLAB version 7.1 helps to some degree, but there are still important differences. What follows is a discussion of some examples.

Class code is designed so that an object can actually be an array of objects. All objects in the array must be of the same type. For example,

```
>> star = [cStar; cStar];
>> star(2).ColorRgb = [1; 0; 0];
>> star(1) = 1.5 * star(1);
>> star = draw(star);
>> diamond = [cDiamond; cDiamond];
>> diamond(1).ColorRgb = [0; 1; 0];
>> diamond(2).Size = [0.75; 1.25];
>> diamond = draw(diamond);
```

results in the figures shown in Figure 13.1 and Figure 13.2.

This chapter's additions to **subsasgn** and to the set of member functions prohibit assignment or concatenation of mismatched types, for example,

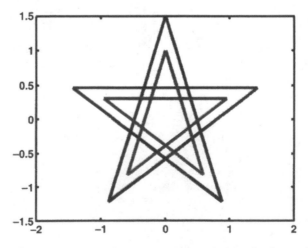

FIGURE 13.1 cStar graphic (simple inheritance plus an array of objects) after scaling via multiplication, 1.5* star(1).

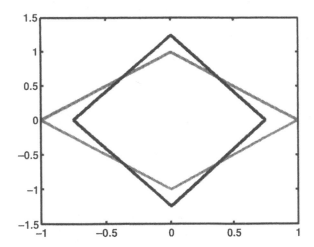

FIGURE 13.2 cDiamond graphic (simple inheritance plus an array of objects) after setting the size of (2) to [0.75; 1.25].

```
>> shape = [star diamond];
??? Error using ==> cStar.horzcat
Conversion to cStar from cDiamond is not possible.
```

Trying to concatenate a **cStar** object and a **cDiamond** object throws conversion error from **horzcat**. If we want to comingle different object types in a single array, we have to use a cell array, for example,

```
>> shape = {star diamond}
shape =
    [1x2 cStar]    [2x1 cDiamond]
```

The problem with a cell array is that we have to index each cell before calling member functions. Trying to call a member function on the entire cell array results in an error, for example,

```
>> shape_size = shape.Size;
??? Attempt to reference field of non-structure array.
```

Naturally, we can't use a dot-reference operator on **shape** because **shape** is a cell array. We have to use a loop instead. For example,

```
>> shap_size = [];
>> for k = 1:length(shape)
shape_size = [shape_size shape{k}.Size];
end
>> disp(shape_size)
  1.5000e+000  1.0000e+000  1.0000e+000  7.5000e-001
  1.5000e+000  1.0000e+000  1.0000e+000  1.2500e+000
```

builds the **shape_size** array using individual calls to **subsref**. Drawing the shapes works the same way. A loop is used, and the resulting figures are identical to Figure 13.1 and Figure 13.2.*

The process of looping over object arrays is common in other object-oriented languages, and it isn't too objectionable in MATLAB. It would be convenient if the loops could be vectorized, but for objects of different types, vectorization is not possible. One consequence is that we can't currently draw **cStar** objects and **cDiamond** objects in the same figure window.

Drawing multiple objects in the same figure is now a design issue. If we want to be able to draw all the shapes held in the same cell array in the same figure window, we need to alter the design of the interface. In this particular case, we simply need to modify **draw** to accept a figure handle as an optional argument. The modified **/@cShape/draw** is shown in Code Listing 78. This function was first developed in Chapter 10. Only the changes are discussed below.

Code Listing 78, Modified Implementation of draw That Will Accept an Input Figure Handle

```
1    function this = draw(this, figure_handle)
2    if nargin < 2
3      figure_handle = [];
4    end
5
6    if nargout ~= 1
7      warning('draw must be called using: obj = draw(obj)');
8    else
9      if ~isempty(this)
10       handle_array = unique([figure_handle
           this(:).mFigureHandle]);
11       if length(handle_array) ~= 1 % no handle or mismatched
12         for k = fliplr(find([handle_array ~= figure_handle]))
13           try
14             delete(handle_array(k));   % close figures
15           end
16           handle_array(k) = [];
17         end
18       end
19       if isempty(handle_array)
20         figure_handle = figure;   % create new figure
21       else
22         figure_handle = handle_array(1); % use existing
23       end
24       [this.mFigureHandle] = deal(figure_handle);   % save the
           handle
25     figure(handle_array);   % use the handle
26
27     if nargin < 2
28       clf;   % clear the figure
```

---

* In version 7.1, it is also possible to use **cellfun** instead of a loop. The syntax is certainly a lot less familiar:
shape = cellfun(@draw, shape, 'UniformOutput', false);.

```
29    end
30
31    hold on;   % all shapes drawn in the same figure
32    for k = 1:length(this(:))
33      this(k).mPlotHandle = plot(...
34        this(k).mSize(1)  * this(k).mPoints(1,:), ...
35        this(k).mSize(2)  * this(k).mPoints(2,:), ...
36        'Color', get(this(k), 'ColorRgb'));
37      end
38        hold off;
39      end
40  end
```

When a **figure_handle** isn't passed in, lines 2–4 initialize **figure_handle** with empty. Line 10 concatenates **figure_handle** with the object's figure handles before calling **unique**. When no **figure_handle** was passed in, concatenation with empty has no effect. The loop in lines 12–17 now loops over indices of **handle_array** that are not equal to the value of the passed-in handle value. The command **fliplr** is used to reverse the loop order because elements are removed during the loop. Line 14 closes each figure, and line 16 removes the handle from **handle_array**. On line 19, if **handle_array** is empty, line 20 creates a new figure; otherwise, the first element of **handle_array** will be reused. Line 24 assigns the handle into the objects, and line 25 activates the figure. Lines 27–29 clear the figure only when a handle was not passed into the function. When a handle is passed in, the caller is responsible for clearing the figure.

Now that we can pass in a figure handle to draw, we can create a loop that will draw all the shapes on one figure window. The following commands will draw the figure shown in Figure 13.3. It is a little crowded, but all have been drawn together.

```
>> fig_handle = figure;
>> for k = 1:length(shape)
shape{k} = draw(shape{k}, fig_handle);
end
```

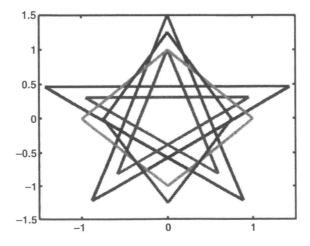

FIGURE 13.3 Combined graphics for cStar and cDiamond.

13.2 SUMMARY

In this chapter, we tied up some loose ends related to inheritance and arrays of objects. MATLAB's built-in functions allow the assignment of child objects into array elements of the parent, and they allow the assignment of different types as long as their private structures match. A simple modification to **subsasgn** and the addition of **cat**, **horzcat**, and **vertcat** member functions effectively eliminate assignment errors. These functions do not rise to the level of the group-of-eight functions because they don't really interact with the object. They simply error-check the input and pass that input along to the built-in version.

We also investigated how to manage arrays of objects with different types but the same set of member functions. A cell array must be used and cell arrays force us to abandon vectorized code, at least for some operations. The use of cell arrays also influences the interface design. The interface must always consider the possibility of holding objects in a cell array rather than in a regular array. In our shape example, the impact was small.

13.3 INDEPENDENT INVESTIGATIONS

1. With the shape cell array populated with **cStar** and **cDiamond**, experiment with changing the color or size of individual shapes.
2. Can you change all shapes to the same color with one assignment? Do you have to use a loop or **cellfun**?

14 Child-Class Members

An important facet of parent–child inheritance is the child's ability to tailor any function that would otherwise be conveyed from the parent. In Chapters 12 and 13, the child-class functions didn't do anything other than slice and forward. They couldn't do much more than that because the child classes inherited all of their data from the parent. Closely related to member function tailoring is the child's ability to go beyond inheritance by adding private member variables, public member variables, and member functions.

Adding new m-files is straightforward. Adding new public member variables is a little more difficult because additional variable names need to be incorporated in the group-of-eight functions. Supporting these additions is exactly the reason behind the organization of **get.m** and **set.m**. In Chapters 12 and 13, these functions contained slice-and-forward sections only. There was no reason to include sections for public or concealed variables because **cStar** and **cDiamond** had none. In this chapter, we will add a public variable to **cStar** and examine the effects on both the implementation and inheritance.

14.1 FUNCTION REDEFINITION

A class can tailor the behavior of almost any built-in function. The group-of-eight functions are a good example of tailoring. We also used the fact that a tailored function can call the built-in version to coerce MATLAB into doing most of the heavy lifting. In Chapters 12 and 13, we examined parent–child inheritance and noted that a child class can tailor the behavior of many parent-class functions. Using a slice-and-forward strategy, a tailored child's function can coerce the parent into doing most of the heavy lifting. The limiting factors in slice and forward are the parent's public interface and the visibility of variables. A child-class function is not limited to include only slice-and-forward code. A child-class function doesn't have to call the parent function at all, but when it does, the child can add behavior either before or after the call to the parent. Such redefinition allows the hierarchy to extend beyond its original intent without changing the original code. We get the maximum amount of reuse with the smallest number of side effects.

Adding a title string to figures that contain a star is a nice addition that fits nicely into the shape hierarchy. We could hold the title string at the parent level and give every shape the same capability. Since we already know how to add things at the parent level, we will instead give only **cStar** objects a title. We will create the public variable **Title** and store the string in the private variable **mTitle**. The constructor will set a default value of **'A Star is born'**, and a client can change the string at any time.

Since we are adding a new member variable to **cStar**, the following four group-of-eight functions will need to be modified:

/@cStar/private/ctor_ini.m

/@cStar/fieldnames.m

/@cStar/get.m

/@cStar/set.m

The constructor will add and initialize the new private variable, **fieldnames** will add the new public variable to its name list, and **get and set** will add accessor and mutator code for the title. Outside the group of eight, **/@cStar/draw.m** needs to add the title to the figure window. We will take on the changes to each function in turn.

14.1.1 /@cStar/private/ctor_ini.m with Private Member Variables

The modification to **/@cStar/public/ctor_ini.m** is quite pedestrian. Instead of returning an empty structure, the structure contains one element, **mTitle**. The code for the function is shown in Code Listing 79. Line 2 creates an empty structure, and line 3 adds **mTitle** and initializes its value. All other private variables for **cStar** are encapsulated within the parent.

Code Listing 79, Adding a Private Variable to a Child-Class Constructor

```
1   function [this, superior, inferior, parents] = ctor_ini
2   this = struct([]);
3   this(1).mTitle = 'A Star is born';
4   superior = {'double'};
5   inferior = {};
6   parents{1} = ...
7     cShape([imag(exp(j*(0:4:20)*pi/5)); real(exp(j*(0:4:20)*
      pi/5))]);
8   parent_list(parents{:});
```

After a **clear classes** command, the constructor change allows the creation of new-style **cStar** objects. The new private variable is part of the structure, but its presence cannot be observed until new capabilities are added to the interface. Until then, new-style **cStar** objects will appear to be the same as before.

14.1.2 /@cStar/fieldnames.m with Additional Public Members

In Chapter 12, **fieldnames** only needed to include a slice-and-forward operation. Since we intend to add a public variable, **fieldnames** needs to add a name to the list. The new name could be added anywhere in the list, but the beginning or the end is the most convenient. As a standard convention, the child class will add its variables to the end of the parent's **fieldnames** list. This convention also means that the fields of **struct** will be arranged in the same order. The child's version of **fieldnames** first slices the object and forwards it to the parent function. It then concatenates new names to the end of the parent's list. The code for **/@cStar/fieldnames** is shown in Code Listing 80.

Code Listing 80, Adding a Public Variable to a Child-Class fieldnames.m

```
1   function names = fieldnames(this, varargin)
2   names = {};
3
4   % First fill up names with parent's public names
5   for parent_name = parent_list'
6     names = [names; fieldnames([this.(parent_name{1})],
      varargin{:})];
7   end
8
```

```
9    % then add additional names for child
10   if nargin == 1
11     names = [names; {'Title'}']; % note: return as a column
12   else
13     switch varargin{1}
14     case '-full'
15       names = [names; {'Title % string'}'];
16     case '-possible'
17       names = [names; {'Title' {{'string'}}}'];
18     otherwise
19       error('Unsupported call to fieldnames');
20     end
21   end
```

Line 2 initializes **names** with empty so that subsequent names can always be concatenated onto the end. Lines 5–7 represent the standard **fieldnames** slice-and-forward operation. With multiple inheritance, the loop adds each parent's public names in order. Except for the names added, lines 9–21 look exactly like the lines developed for **cShape**. Line 11 assembles the typical return by simply adding child names to the end of the list. Lines 15 and 16 assemble special-purpose lists. Each class adds its public names to the list and relies on slice-and-forward code to include parent names.

14.1.3 /@cSTAR/GET.M WITH ADDITIONAL PUBLIC MEMBERS

The accessor function **get.m** is already organized into different sections. Adding read access for **Title** is a simple matter of adding a case and code to the public variable section. The case code looks identical to the public variable case code from Part 1. This is reasonable because, now as then, the code is simply converting from a private value to a public one. The modified public variable section for **/@cStar/get** is shown in Code Listing 81. The syntax of the case code was discussed in §8.2. Other sections of **/@cStar/get** are the same as those developed in Chapter 12. The child's public variable section does not include cases for the parent's public variables because the slice-and-forward section automatically takes care of that operation.

Code Listing 81, Child-Class Public Member Variables in get.m

```
1    % public-member-variable section
2    found = true;  % otherwise-case will flip to false
3    switch index(1).subs
4      case 'Title'
5        if isempty(this)
6          varargout = {};
7        else
8          varargout = {this.mTitle};
9        end
10     otherwise
11       found = false;  % didn't find it in the public section
12   end
```

14.1.4 /@cStar/set.m with Additional Public Members

Similar to **get**, the mutator function **set** is also organized into different sections. Adding write access for **Title** is again a simple matter of adding a case and code to the public variable section. The case code can be modeled after the public variable case code from Part 1. Again, this is a reasonable approach because, now as then, the code converts from a public value to a private one.

Whenever the title is modified, the figure needs to be redrawn. This is a problem because the only command available, **this = draw(this)**, introduces an error. This error occurs if the shape's figure does not yet exist. In this case, **draw** will pop open a figure window even though the client has not yet requested one. The parent class needs an interface change or this particular drawing error cannot be avoided.

There are several options: make the value in private variable **cShape.mFigureHandle** observable, create a **/@cShape/redraw** function that behaves differently compared to **/@cShape/draw**, or pass an argument into **/@cShape/draw** that modifies its behavior. Here we will take the first approach and make **mFigureHandle** a read-only concealed variable. This approach is flexible, but flexibility comes at a cost. The figure handle will now be available to any client that understands how to use concealed variables. The concealed variable section in **/@cShape/get** now has another case besides **mDisplayFunc**. An additional concealed variable case is included in the example code for Chapter 14 and beyond, but is not listed or described.

The modified public variable section for **/@cStar/set** is shown in Code Listing 82. The syntax of the case code was discussed in §8.2, and other sections of **/@cStar/set** are the same as those developed in Chapter 12. The child's public variable section does not include cases for the parent's public variables because the slice-and-forward section automatically takes care of that operation.

Code Listing 82, Child-Class Public Member Variables in set.m

```
1    % public-member-variable section
2    found = true;   % otherwise-case will flip to false
3    switch index(1).subs
4      case 'Title'
5        if length(index) > 1
6          this.mTitle = ...
7            subsasgn(this.mTitle, index(2:end), varargin{:});
8        else
9          [this.mTitle] = deal(varargin{:});
10       end
11       for k = 1:length(this)
12         figure(get(this(k), 'mFigureHandle'));
13         title(this(k).mTitle);
14       end
15     otherwise
16       found = false;
17   end
```

The addition to **cShape**'s concealed variables allows lines 11–14 to modify the title for figure handles associated with star objects. The figure might also include other shapes, but it will also include a star. If the shape has not yet been drawn, the figure handle will be empty. The figure command in line 12 will not activate a figure, and the title command on line 13 will do nothing.

14.1.5 /@cStar/draw.m with a Title

The modifications to **ctor_ini**, **get**, and **set** have given **cStar** both private and public variables associated with a title. Next, we add the code to **/@cStar/draw** that completes the job of displaying a title on the figure. After Chapter 12's slice-and-forward code creates each figure, additional code activates each window and uses the title command to set the title. This is the same procedure used in **/@cStar/set**. The new implementation of **/@cStar/draw** is shown in Code Listing 83.

```
Code Listing 83, Child-Class draw.m Using Additional Child-Class Members

1    function this = draw(this, varargin)
2    if nargout ~= 1
3      warning('draw must be called using: obj = draw(obj)');
4    else
5      parent = num2cell(draw([this.cShape], varargin{:}));
6      [this.cShape] = deal(parent{:});
7    end
8
9    for k = 1:length(this)
10     figure(get(this(k), 'mFigureHandle'));
11     title(this(k).mTitle);
12   end
```

Lines 1–7 are a repeat of the **draw** function from Chapter 12, and lines 9–12 were borrowed from **/@cStar/set**. Line 10 activates each figure, and line 11 uses the **title** command to set the figure's title.

14.2 TEST DRIVE

For this test drive, we need to confirm that we indeed get a title for **cStar** objects and we need to investigate what happens when stars and diamonds are drawn on the same figure. A few of the many possible commands are shown in Code Listing 84. Commands 2–10 repeat some of the test drive commands from Chapter 13. The graphical results shown in Figure 14.1 and Figure 14.2 are almost the same as before, in Figure 13.1 and Figure 13.2. The difference can be seen at the top of Figure 14.1. The star figure now has a title.

```
Code Listing 84, Chapter 14 Test Drive Command Listing for Child-Class Member
Variables

1    >> cd '/oop_guide/chapter_14'
2    >> clear classes; fclose all; close all force; diary off;
3    >> star = [cStar   cStar];
4    >> star(2).ColorRgb = [1; 0; 0];
5    >> star(1) = 1.5 * star(1);
6    >> star = draw(star);
7    >> diamond = [cDiamond; cDiamond];
8    >> diamond(1).ColorRgb = [0; 1; 0];
9    >> diamond(2).Size = [0.75; 1.25];
```

```
10  >> diamond = draw(diamond);
11  >>
12  >> shape = {star diamond};
13  >> fig_handle = figure;
14  >> for k = 1:length(shape)
15  shape{k} = draw(shape{k}, fig_handle);
16  end
17  >> star = draw(star);
18  >> star(1).Title = 'Shooting Star';
```

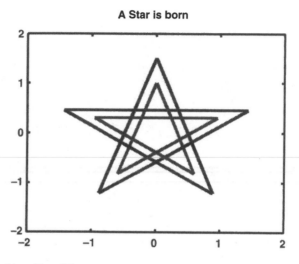

FIGURE 14.1 cStar graphic with a title.

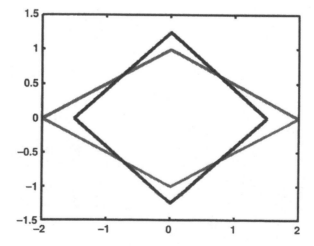

FIGURE 14.2 cDiamond graphic, no title.

Commands 12–16 draw the star and diamond arrays on the same figure. The figure is shown in Figure 14.3. The figure now has a title because the figure includes a star. Finally, the command in line 18 demonstrates what happens when the title of one of the stars is modified. The graphic

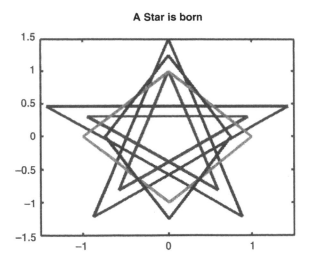

FIGURE 14.3 Combined cStar and cDiamond graphics, now with a title.

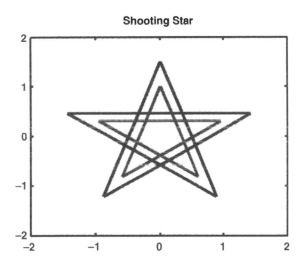

FIGURE 14.4 cStar graphic, now with a new title.

result is shown in Figure 14.4. The figure is titled using the title string from the last object drawn. Drawing the entire array would return the title back to the default because **star(2)** still contains the default value.

14.3 SUMMARY

This short chapter reinforced many things we have already learned about objects. Adding new variables to child classes involves encapsulation, slicing, and forwarding. The addition also takes advantage of the previous group-of-eight organization. The organization makes adding a new child variable the same as adding a variable to any class, inherited or not. Private variables are added and initialized in **ctor_ini**. Public variables require modifications to **fieldnames**, **get**, and **set**. The use of the **parent_list** helper function allows code generalization and thus makes the code relatively immune to child-class evolution. Typically, member functions outside the group of eight will also need modifications to support the new variables. In the **cStar** example, **draw** was the only nonstandard function that changed.

14.4 INDEPENDENT INVESTIGATIONS

1. Create a **cStar** object, a **cDiamond** object, and a **cShape** object. Use the **whos** command to look at the number of bytes occupied by each object. Why are the byte sizes different?
2. Modify **draw** so that the title consists of a concatenation of the titles from all objects in the figure.
3. Add a title to the **cDiamond** class and repeat investigation 2.

15 Constructing Simple Hierarchies with Composition

There is another common form of inheritance, very different from parent–child inheritance, called composition.* Using an object in composition is easy. All you have to do is assign an object as the value for a private member variable. For example, if **double** represents a class, we could say that **this.mSize** is one element of the composition. This means that even simple classes use a composition of built-in types. Complex classes add structures and objects to the composition. Unlike parent–child inheritance where the parent's interface is public, the interface of every object in the composition remains private.

In composition, there are always two objects involved. We need to define some terminology so we can keep these two objects straight. The first object is composed from a collection of private member variables of various types. Let's call this object the primary object. In our example code, **cShape**, **cStar**, and **cDiamond** are all primary objects. Every private member variable held by the primary object can be an object. Let's call these objects secondary objects. In our example code, **mSize** and **mPoints** represent two secondary objects.

In MATLAB, there is overlap between parent–child inheritance and composition. Parent–child inheritance is a special case of composition. The child is a primary object and the parent is a secondary object. This might seem backward but it is consistent with the way primary and secondary were defined. The parent is a secondary object because the parent object is stored as an element in the child's private structure. In Chapters 12 through 14, the element **this.cShape** was automatically added to child objects.

The difference between parent–child inheritance and composition is the object's visibility. In parent–child inheritance, *all* public features of the parent are automatically included in the child's public interface. In parent–child inheritance, the child has limited control over the public interface conveyed from the parent. In composition, *no* public feature of the secondary object is automatically included in the primary object's public interface. In composition, the primary object always has total control over its public interface. The primary object can choose to expose all, part, or nothing from the secondary object's public interface. This exposure can be further limited to, for example, read-only privilege.

15.1 COMPOSITION

To demonstrate composition we are first going to create a class that makes it a little bit easier to manage a shape's plot handle and its line style. Out of the large set of possible line attributes, **cLineStyle** encapsulates the conversion between RGB and CSV and demonstrates how to encapsulate controls for line width. Other attributes would follow the same strategy. There are too many to list but some of the more common attributes include color, line width, line style, markers, and marker color. All of these and more are available through the shape's plot handle and the handle-graphics **get** and **set** functions. In fact, storing the plot handle as a private member variable already represents composition. Although not implemented in the same way as a class, a graphics handle is very similar to an object.

---

* MATLAB help files and documents use the term *aggregation* instead of *composition*. The Unified Modeling Language (UML) community and most object-oriented references use composition.

15.1.1 THE cLineStyle CLASS

The first step creates a class implementation for **cLineStyle**. The implementation takes full advantage of group-of-eight development by reusing standard code for the constructor, **display**, **struct**, **subsref**, **subsasgn**, **private/ctor_1**, and **private/parent_list**. All class-dependent modifications are isolated to **private/ctor_ini**, **fieldnames**, **get**, and **set**. The modifications are also easy to make because they follow the standard prescription. It is also worth noting that once the **cLineStyle** class has been implemented, it can be tested independently. It does not have to be included in a composition to work properly. This independence is important because it helps partition the complexity and generally improves software quality.

The process of creating the **cLineStyle** class is identical to the process of creating any new class that uses the standard group-of-eight approach. The process is enumerated below, and the subsections that follow describe the details involved in each change.

1. Create a new class directory and class private directory with the appropriate location and name. For this example, the new class directory is

   /oop_guide/chapter_15/@cLineStyle

   and the new private directory is

   /oop_guide/chapter_15/@cLineStyle/private

2. Copy the set of standard files from any convenient class directory into the new directory. For this example, the source location is
   /oop_guide/chapter_15/@cShape
   The standard set of files includes the group of eight plus a few helpers. The list of files includes

```
>> copyfile 'cShape.m' '../@cLineStyle/cLineStyle.m'

>> copyfile 'subsref.m' '../@cLineStyle'

>> copyfile 'subsasgn.m' '../@cLineStyle'

>> copyfile 'struct.m' '../@cLineStyle'

>> copyfile 'display.m' '../@cLineStyle'

>> copyfile 'fieldnames.m' '../@cLineStyle'

>> copyfile 'get.m' '../@cLineStyle'

>> copyfile 'set.m' '../@cLineStyle'

>>

>> copyfile 'private/parent_list.m' '../@cLineStyle/private'

>> copyfile 'private/ctor_ini.m' '../@cLineStyle/private'

>> copyfile 'private/ctor_1.m' '../@cLineStyle/private'
```

3. Modify **ctor_ini.m** to reflect the correct list of private member variables and initial values. All base classes must include **mDisplayFunc** as a private variable because **display** depends on it.
4. Modify **fieldnames.m** to reflect the correct list of public member variables.

5. Modify **get.m** with cases for each public member variable. Include concealed variable cases if they are appropriate to the class design.
6. Modify **set.m** with cases for each public member variable. Include concealed variable cases if they are appropriate to the class design.

Out of the many possible line attributes, two were selected for encapsulation inside **cLineStyle**. Color is one obvious choice because **cShape** already includes a lot of code to manage the conversion between RGB and CSV values. Moving lines of code out of **cShape** and into **cLineStyle** allows other classes to include the same functionality without having to repeat lines of code. Moving the code also makes **cShape** easier to maintain, evolve, and test. The other attribute is line width. Currently, **cShape** objects cannot change the line width, but the addition of a public member variable will allow it. To complete the composition, we will set the following requirements for the **cLineStyle**'s interface:

- Get and set the line's RGB color through a **Color** public variable.
- Change the plot's line color whenever the object's line color changes.
- Get and set the line width as a positive integer through a **LineWidth** public variable.
- Change the plot's line width whenever the object's line width changes.
- Get and set the line's graphic's handle through a **LineHandle** public variable.

The public names **Color** and **LineWidth** are the same names used by the line's handle-graphics attributes.

15.1.1.1 cLineStyle's private/ctor_ini

The **ctor_ini** private helper function builds the object's private structure and assigns default values. For this class we need four private variables. These variables are as follows:

mDisplayFunc: The standard group-of-eight **display** function requires this variable. The only exception occurs in parent–child inheritance. The child class does not need to add **mDisplayFunc** to its structure because it should already exist in the parent. The default value is **[]**.

mColorHsv: The code to manage line color will be moved from **cShape** into **cLineStyle**. That code already relies on **mColorHsv** as a private variable. The default value is blue: **[0; 0; 1]**.

mLineWidth: This private variable holds the width of the line as an integer value. The integer value can be directly used in the **plot** function and in the handle-graphics **set** function. The default value is 1.

mLineHandle: This private variable holds the value of the line's plot handle. The value in **mLineHandle** can be used to change the figure color and width when the values change. The default value is **[]**.

The code to implement this collection of private variables and default values is shown in Code Listing 85. The mapping between the description above and the code is straightforward.

Code Listing 85, Modular Code, cLineStyle's /private/ctor_ini.m

```
1    function [this, superior, inferior, parents] = ctor_ini
2    this = struct([]); % initially empty structure
3    this(1).mDisplayFunc = []; % function handle for non-default
     display
```

```
4    this(1).mColorHsv = [2/3; 1; 1]; % [H S V]' of border,
     default is blue
5    this(1).mLineWidth = 1; % line weight: 'normal' == 1 'bold'
     == 3
6    this(1).mLineHandle = []; % handle for shape's line plot
7    superior = {};
8    inferior = {};
9    parents = {};
10   parent_list(parents{:});
```

15.1.1.2   cLineStyle's fieldnames

Whereas **ctor_ini** defines the collection of private variables, **fieldnames** defines the collection of public variables. In this case, there are only three: **Color**, **LineWeight**, and **LineHandle**. The public variables and the values they hold come directly from the requirements. The code to implement fieldnames for these public variables is shown in Code Listing 86.

```
Code Listing 86, Modular Code, cLineStyle's fieldnames.m

1    function names = fieldnames(this, varargin)
2    names = {};
3
4    % first fill up names with parent public names
5    parent_name = parent_list;  % get the parent name cellstr
6    for parent_name = parent_list'
7      names = [names; fieldnames([this.(parent_name{1})],
       varargin{:})];
8    end
9
10   % returns the list of public member variable names
11   if nargin == 1
12     names = {'Color' 'LineWidth' 'LineHandle'}';
13   else
14     switch varargin{1}
15     case '-full'
16       names = {'Color % double array' ...
17                'LineWidth' % positive integer' ...
18                'LineHandle % plot handle'}';
19     case '-possible'
20       names = {'Color' {{'double array  (3x1)'}} ...
21                'LineWidth' {{'positive integer'}} ...
22                'LineHandle' {{'plot handle'}}}';
23     Otherwise
24       error('Unsupported call to fieldnames');
25     end
26   end
```

The parent-forwarding code in lines 4–8 is not necessary because **parent_list** returns an empty **cellstr**. It is included because it is part of the standard template. When **fieldnames** is called with one input argument, line 12 returns a **cellstr** populated with the three public variable names. Lines 16–18 and 20–22 return additional information that depend respectively on **'-full'** and **'-possible'** flag values. In line 21, note the possible values for **LineWeight** are **'normal'** or **'bold'**.

15.1.1.3 cLineStyle's get

The public variable section for **cLineStyle**'s **get** is shown in Code Listing 87. By now, the code in this listing should look familiar. The value of **found** on line 2 is used to control entry into subsequent concealed variable, parent-forwarding, and error code blocks. Inside the **switch** beginning on line 3, there is a **case** for each public member variable. Lines 4–10 came directly from the public member variable section of **cShape**'s previous implementation. The remaining cases simply map one private variable into one public variable. This public variable section is just about as easy as it gets. The remaining sections of **cLineStyle**'s **get** function use code from the standard group-of-eight template.

Code Listing 87, Public Variable Implementation in cLineStyle's get.m

```
1    % public-member-variable section
2    found = true;   % otherwise-case will flip to false
3    switch index(1).subs
4      case 'Color'
5        if isempty(this)
6          varargout = {};
7        else
8          rgb = hsv2rgb([this.mColorHsv]')';
9          varargout = mat2cell(rgb, 3, ones(1, size(rgb,2)));
10       end
11     case 'LineWidth'
12       if isempty(this)
13         varargout = {};
14       else
15         varargout = {this.mLineWidth};
16       end
17     case 'LineHandle'
18       if isempty(this)
19         varargout = {};
20       else
21         varargout = {this.mLineHandle};
22       end
23     otherwise
24         found = false;   % didn't find it in the public section
25   end
```

15.1.1.4   cLineStyle's set

The public variable section for **cLineStyle**'s **set** is shown in Code Listing 88. Compared to the same cases in **get**, the code in this listing is a little more involved but that is primarily due to input-value checking. The listing should still be familiar, particularly after you find all of the common landmarks. The value of **found** on line 2 is used to control entry into subsequent concealed variable, parent-forwarding, and error code blocks. Inside the **switch** beginning on line 3, there is a **case** for each public member variable.

```
Code Listing 88, Public Variable Implementation in cLineStyle's set.m
1    % public-member-variable section
2    found = true;   % otherwise-case will flip to false
3    switch index(1).subs
4
5      case 'Color'
6        if length(index) > 1
7          rgb = hsv2rgb(this.mColorHsv')';
8          rgb = subsasgn(rgb, index(2:end), varargin{:});
9          this.mColorHsv = rgb2hsv(rgb')';
10       else
11         hsv = rgb2hsv([varargin{:}]')';
12         hsv = mat2cell(hsv, 3, ones(1, size(hsv,2)));
13         [this.mColorHsv] = deal(hsv{:});
14       end
15       for k = 1:length(this(:))
16         try
17           set(this(k).mLineHandle, 'Color', get(this(k),
               'Color'));
18         End
19       End
20
21      case 'LineWidth'
22        if length(index) > 1
23          error([index(1).subs ' does not support indexing']);
24        end
25        if any([varargin{:}] < 1)
26          error([index(1).subs ' input values must be >= 1']);
27        end
28        if length(varargin) ~= 1 && length(varargin) ~=
            length(this(:))
29        error([index(1).subs ' input length is not correct']);
30        end
31        [this.mLineWidth] = deal(varargin{:});
32        for k = 1:length(this(:))
33          Try
34            set(this(k).mLineHandle, ...
35              'LineWidth', get(this(k), 'LineWidth'));
```

```
36            End
37          end
38
39     case 'LineHandle'
40        if length(index) > 1
41           error([index(1).subs ' does not support indexing']);
42        end
43        if length(varargin) ~= 1 && length(varargin) ~=
          length(this(:))
44           error([index(1).subs ' input length is not correct']);
45        end
46        [this.mLineHandle] = deal(varargin{:});
47
48     otherwise
49        found = false;    % didn't find it in the public section
50     end
```

Lines 5–14 came directly from the public member variable section of **cShape**'s previous implementation. Lines 15–19 loop over the objects in **this** and **set** the handle graphic's **'Color'** attribute to the newly assigned value. The new RGB value is accessed by calling **get** on each **cLineStyle** object.

Lines 21–37 deal with **LineWidth**. Lines 22–30 check the inputs for several conditions. First, no additional indexing beyond the initial dot-reference name is allowed. Second, all of the width values must be greater than or equal to one. Third, the length of the input must be one or equal to the size of the object array. If the input values pass these checks, line 31 deals the new line-width values into **this.mLineWidth**. Lines 32–37 then loop over the objects in this and set the handle graphic's **LineWidth** value. The new value is accessed by calling **get** on each **cLineStyle** object.

Lines 39–46 deal with **LineHandle**. Lines 40–45 check the inputs for several conditions. First, no additional indexing beyond the initial dot-reference name is allowed. Second, the length of the input must be 1 or equal to the size of the object array. If the input values pass these checks, line 46 deals the new line-width values into **this.mLineHandle**. The remaining sections of **cLineStyle**'s **set** function use code from the standard group-of-eight template.

15.1.1.5 cLineStyle's private/ctor_2

With **cLineStyle**, we have an opportunity to create a constructor helper function that takes two input arguments: color and width. The standard constructor is designed to call the helper as long as it has the correct name. In this case, the name is **/private/ctor_2.m**. The implementation is shown in Code Listing 89.

Code Listing 89, Modular Code, cLineStyle Constructor, private/ctor_2.m

```
1   function this = ctor_2(this, color, width)
2   this = set(this, 'Color', color);
3   this = set(this, 'LineWidth', width);
```

The function definition on line 1 defines three inputs because **this** is passed along with the two inputs originally passed into the constructor. Lines 2 and 3 use **set** to assign the RGB color value and the line weight. Using **set** works correctly here because the main constructor converted **this** into an object before it called the helper. By using this two-input constructor, **cShape**'s constructor can specify both the color and line width for default **cShape** objects.

15.1.2 USING A PRIMARY cSHAPE AND A SECONDARY cLINESTYLE

To create the composition we simply add a **cLineStyle** object to **cShape**'s collection of private member variables. This addition occurs inside **@cShape/private/ctor_ini.m**. Since the object's structure has been modified, don't forget to **clear   classes** before using the new **cShape** class. With the addition of a **cLineStyle** object, we can also eliminate **mColorHsv** and **mPlotHandle**. Of course, we also have to change any member function that relies on **mColorHsv** and **mPlotHandle** as private variables. Group-of-eight functions subject to change include **ctor_ini.m**, **get.m**, and **set.m**. Member functions outside the group of eight that require work include **draw.m**, **mtimes.m**, and **reset.m** because they currently use **mPlotHandle**. Changes to private variables affect **cShape**'s internal implementation. They do not affect **cShape**'s public interface.

Even though **cLineStyle** includes a public variable for **LineWidth**, **LineWidth** does not automatically become part of **cShape**'s public interface. Due to composition, **cShape**'s **cLineStyle** object is private and so is its interface. As it stands, clients will not be able to change the shape's line width. If we want to permit clients to change the width, we need to include this ability by adding to **cShape**'s public interface. There are several ways to implement the addition; however, they all boil down to a choice between two alternatives. One alternative exposes the entire secondary object, while the other only exposes part of the secondary object. No single choice is always right or always wrong. Part of the design effort involves deciding between the two.

Exposing the secondary object is easy: treat the object like any other private variable by including cases in **get** and **set** to access and mutate the object as a whole. This approach can be convenient because it automatically allows the primary class to evolve along with the secondary object. Of course, this approach also introduces a high level of coupling between the primary and secondary implementations. This approach can also be problematic because complete exposure typically introduces a read-modify-write approach to mutation. Since multiple levels of dot-reference indexing on arrays are not allowed,* clients have to copy the object to a local variable, modify the copy, and write the modified copy back into the primary object. This process is convenient for the primary-object developer but tedious for primary-object clients. Rather than exposing the whole secondary object, it is usually better to use parent–child inheritance.

Exposing only part of the secondary object is also easy but it generally requires more work. In this case, the secondary object and its public members remain hidden behind the primary object's interface. If a client needs a value from the secondary object, a primary-object member function always operates as an intermediary. The client asks the primary object for a value and in turn, the primary object's function asks the secondary object for a value. When the secondary object returns a value, the primary object's function forwards the value to the client. Here, the primary object always maintains control over the interface. The primary-object interface chooses which elements to expose and which to leave hidden. This interface also chooses how to expose secondary object elements. The primary object's interface can rename elements and modify their formats. The example code in this chapter demonstrates this important capability.

To add line-width capability to **cShape** we are not going to expose the entire secondary object, but rather we are going to define a public member variable named **LineWeight**. Clients can set **LineWeight** to one of only two values: **'normal'** or **'bold'**. The **LineWeight case** inside **set** will convert these strings into **LineWidth** integers, and the **LineWeight case**

---

* This statement applies to built-in functions. In the tailored versions of **subsref** and **subsasgn**, a limit was implemented to match built-in behavior. It is possible to relax the limit at the risk of introducing nonstandard syntax.

inside **get** will convert **LineWidth** integers back into strings. Clients see the width as only '**normal**' or '**bold**', but inside **cShape**'s member functions, integer values are available from the secondary object. Implementing this behavior will demonstrate how the primary object's interface can easily buffer the interaction between client and secondary object.

15.1.2.1 Composition Changes to cShape's ctor_ini.m

The **cLineStyle** object needs a private variable, and two existing private variables need to be removed. The **cLineStyle** object will be stored in the private variable **mLineStyle**. With this change, **mColorHsv** and **mPlotHandle** are no longer needed because the secondary object manages their values. The modified constructor helper is shown in Code Listing 90. In line 9, a call to **cLineStyle**'s constructor initializes the **mLineStyle** object. The first argument is an RGB color, and the second is the default line width. Since two arguments are passed, **cLineStyle**'s constructor will use **/@cLineStyle/ctor_2** to complete the assignment.

```
Code Listing 90, Modular Code, Modified Implementation of cShape's ctor_ini.m

1    function [this, superior, inferior] = ctor_ini
2    this = struct([]);   % initially empty structure
3    this(1).mDisplayFunc = [];  % function handle for non-default
     display
4    this(1).mSize = ones(2,1); % scaled [width height]' of
     bounding box
5    this(1).mScale = ones(2,1); % [width height]' scale factor
6    this(1).mPoints = ...
7      [imag(exp(j*(0:4:20)*pi/5)); real(exp(j*(0:4:20)*pi/5))];
8    this(1).mFigureHandle = []; % handle to the figure's window
9    this(1).mLineStyle = cLineStyle([0;0;1], 1); % color blue,
     width 1
10   superior = {'double'};
11   inferior = {};
12   parents = {};
13   parent_list(parents{:});
```

15.1.2.2 Adding LineWeight to cShape's fieldnames.m

Adding a new public variable always adds a new name to the **cellstr** lists returned by **fieldnames**. The modified code is shown in Code Listing 91. Additions to the previous version occur in lines 12, 19, and 24. Note in line 24, the possible values for **LineWeight** are listed as '**normal**' or '**bold**'. These possible values are displayed in response to **set(cShape)**.

```
Code Listing 91, Adding LineWeight to cShape's fieldnames.m

1    function names = fieldnames(this, varargin)
2    names = {};
3
4    % first fill up names with parent public names
5    parent_name = parent_list;  % get the parent name cellstr
6    for parent_name = parent_list'
```

```
7     names = [names; fieldnames([this.(parent_name{1})],
        varargin{:})];
8   end
9
10  % returns the list of public member variable names
11  if nargin == 1
12    names = {'Size' 'ColorRgb' 'Points' 'LineWeight'}';
13  else
14    switch varargin{1}
15    case '-full'
16      names = {'Size % double array' ...
17               'ColorRgb % double array' ...
18               'Points % double array' ...
19               'LineWeight % string'}';
20    case '-possible'
21      names = {'Size' {{'double array (2x1)'}} ...
22               'ColorRgb' {{'double array  (3x1)'}} ...
23               'Points' {{'double array  (2xN)'}} ...
24               'LineWeight' {{'normal' 'bold'}}}';
25    otherwise
26      error('Unsupported call to fieldnames');
27    end
28  end
```

15.1.2.3 Composition Changes to cShape's get.m

A change to the way **ColorRgb** is stored and a new public member variable trigger changes to **cShape**'s **get.m**. These changes are isolated to two public member variable **case** statements. The **case** blocks for `'ColorRgb'` and `'LineWeight'` are shown in Code Listing 92.

Code Listing 92, Adding ColorRgb and LineWeight Cases to cShape's get.m

```
1    case 'ColorRgb'
2      if isempty(this)
3        varargout = {};
4      else
5        line_style = [this.mLineStyle];
6        varargout = {line_style.Color};
7      end
8    case 'LineWeight'
9      if isempty(this)
10       varargout = {};
11     else
12       line_style = [this.mLineStyle];
13       line_width = [line_style.LineWidth];
14       varargout = cell(1,length(this(:)));
15       varargout(line_width == 1) = {'normal'};
```

```
16      varargout(line_width == 3) = {'bold'};
17   end
```

The new case code for **'ColorRgb'** is shorter because the conversion from HSV to RGB now occurs inside the secondary object. Line 5 creates an array of **cLineStyle** objects, and line 6 uses dot-reference syntax to access **Color** values. Line 5 is necessary because **{this.mLineStyle.Color}** throws an error if **this** is a nonscalar array. Line 6 is composition in action. The dot-reference syntax is converted into a function call that looks like

```
varargout = {subsref(line_style, substruct('.', 'Color'))};
```

and MATLAB uses path rules to find the appropriate version of **subsref**. Since **line_style** is a **cLineStyle** object, MATLAB finds and executes **@cLineStyle/subsref.m**.

The **case** code for **'LineWeight'** was added in lines 8–17. Line 12 creates an array of **cLineStyle** objects, and line 13 uses dot-reference syntax to access **LineWidth** values. Line 14 preallocates **varargout**, and lines 15–16 fill **varargout** with strings. Line 15–16 use a logical array to select the indices that receive **'normal'** or **'bold'**. Elements where the **==** test is **true** are assigned, and elements where the **==** test is **false** are not assigned. Line 15 tests with 1 and assigns **'normal'**. Line 16 tests with 3 and assigns **'bold'**. Clients never see values of 1 or 3 but rather only values of **'normal'** or **'bold'**.

15.1.2.4 Composition Changes to cShape's set.m

A change to the way **ColorRgb** is stored and a new public member variable also trigger changes to **cShape**'s **set.m**. These changes are also isolated to the same two public member variable **case** statements. The **case** blocks for **'ColorRgb'** and **'LineWeight'** are shown in Code Listing 93. This listing appears more complicated than the previous version. In reality, the increase in code length is primarily due to rigorous input value testing.

Code Listing 93, Adding ColorRgb and LineWeight Cases to cShape's set.m

```
1    case 'ColorRgb'
2      index(1).subs = 'Color';
3      line_style = set([this.mLineStyle], index, varargin{:});
4      line_style = num2cell(line_style);
5      [this.mLineStyle] = deal(line_style{:});
6
7    case 'LineWeight'
8      if length(index) > 1
9        error([index(1).subs ' does not support indexing']);
10     end
11     if length(varargin) ~= 1 && length(varargin) ~=
         length(this(:))
12       error([index(1).subs ' incorrect input size']);
13     end
14     normal_sieve = strcmp(varargin, 'normal');
15     bold_sieve   = strcmp(varargin, 'bold');
16     if ~all(normal_sieve | bold_sieve)
17       error([index(1).subs ' input values not ''normal'' or
         ''bold''']);
```

```
18    end
19    varargin(normal_sieve) = {1};
20    varargin(bold_sieve)    = {3};
21    index(1).subs = 'LineWidth';
22    line_style = set([this.mLineStyle], index, varargin{:});
23    line_style = num2cell(line_style);
24    [this.mLineStyle] = deal(line_style{:});
```

The new case code for `ColorRgb` is shorter because the conversion from RGB to HSV now occurs inside the secondary object. Line 3 is about to forward the **set** arguments to the secondary object, and line 2 prepares for this forward by modifying **index**. Line 2 changes the dot-reference name to `Color` because that is the name used in the secondary object's interface. There is no reason to check the length of **index** because line 3 puts that ball in **cLineStyle**'s court. Line 3 concatenates the **cLineStyle** objects and calls **set**. MATLAB finds and executes **@cLineStyle/set.m** and assigns the modified object into **line_style**. This is again composition in action. Line 4 changes **line_style** into a cell array, and line 5 deals the modified objects back into their original locations.

The **case** code for `LineWeight` was added in lines 7–24. Lines 8–18 perform various input value checks. First, lines 8–10 disallow indexing deeper than the first dot-reference level. Next, lines 11–13 make sure the number of arguments in **varargin** is compatible with the length of the object array. One input argument is okay because it will be assigned to every object in the array. With more than one argument, the number must equal the length of the object array. Lines 14–18 check the string values in **varargin**. Elements of **normal_sieve** will be **true** only at indices where the input string is identically equal to `normal`. Similarly, elements of **bold_sieve** will be **true** only at indices where the input string is identically equal to `bold`. If **normal_sieve** and **bold_sieve** are both **false** at the same index value, something is wrong with the input. On line 16, **normal_sieve** or **bold_sieve** is used to determine when something is wrong.

If the input values pass all the tests, line 19 overwrites `normal` with 1 and line 20 overwrites `bold` with 3. Line 22 is about to toss everything into **cLineStyle**'s court, and line 21 prepares for this by changing the dot-reference name from **LineWeight** to **LineWidth**. Now the **set** in line 22 will correctly return a modified version of the object. This is another example of composition. Line 23 converts the **line_style** array into a cell array, and line 24 deals the modified objects back into their original locations.

15.1.2.5 Composition Changes to cShape's draw.m

When a shape object is drawn, saving its plot handle makes it easy to change the shape's line attributes. Previously, the plot handle was saved in a private variable. With composition, the plot handle is saved in **mLineStyle.LineHandle**. The modified **plot** command in **/@cStar/draw** is shown in Code Listing 94. In line 1, the handle is stored in the secondary object; and in line 5, the **LineWidth** value stored in the secondary object is added as an argument. In line 1, MATLAB uses **/@cLineStyle/subsasgn**, and in lines 4 and 5, **/@cLineStyle/subsref**.

15.1.2.6 Composition Changes to cShape's Other Member Functions

In **mtimes.m**, the plot handle is used to set the shape's new corner points. In **reset.m**, the plot handle is assigned an empty value. In both functions, **this(k).mPlotHandle** has been changed to **this(k).mLineStyle.LineHandle**. In the case of **mtimes**, MATLAB uses **/@cLin-**

Code Listing 94, Modified Implementation of cShape's draw.m

```
1  this(k).mLineStyle.LineHandle = plot( ...
2    this(k).mSize(1) * this(k).mPoints(1,:), ...
3    this(k).mSize(2) * this(k).mPoints(2,:), ...
4    'Color', this(k).mLineStyle.Color, ...
5    'LineWidth', this(k).mLineStyle.LineWidth ...
6  );
```

---

eStyle/subsref to access the graphics handle. In the case of **reset**, MATLAB mutates the graphics handle using **/@cLineStyle/subsasgn**. Both represent composition.

15.2 TEST DRIVE

Using a **cLineStyle** object in composition involved some significant changes to **cShape**'s implementation. A private variable for the secondary object was added, and several private variables were deleted. The first few commands in the test drive need to confirm that these structural changes did not change **cShape**'s public interface or alter its behavior. Repeating the commands from Code Listing 84 and comparing the outputs will serve this purpose. For easy reference, these commands are included as the first eighteen lines in Code Listing 95. Executing lines 1–18 results in the same figures previously shown in Figures 14.1 through Figure 14.4. You can also experiment with other elements included in the public interface.

Code Listing 95, Chapter 15 Test Drive Command Listing for Composition

```
1   >> cd '/oop_guide/chapter_15'
2   >> clear classes; fclose all; close all force; diary off;
3   >> star = [cStar   cStar];
4   >> star(2).ColorRgb = [1; 0; 0];
5   >> star(1) = 1.5 * star(1);
6   >> star = draw(star);
7   >> diamond = [cDiamond; cDiamond];
8   >> diamond(1).ColorRgb = [0; 1; 0];
9   >> diamond(2).Size = [0.75; 1.25];
10  >> diamond = draw(diamond);
11  >>
12  >> shape = {star diamond};
13  >> fig_handle = figure;
14  >> for k = 1:length(shape)
15  shape{k} = draw(shape{k}, fig_handle);
16  end
17  >> star = draw(star);
18  >> star(1).Title = 'Shooting Star';
19  >>
20  >> shape{1}(1).LineWeight = 'bold';
21  >> shape{1}(1)
22  ans =
23           Size: [2x1 double]
```

```
24         ColorRgb:  [3x1 double]
25           Points:  [2x6 double]
26       LineWeight:  'bold'
27            Title:  'A Star is born'
```

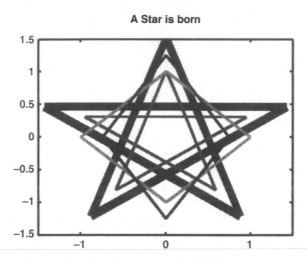

FIGURE 15.1 Combined graphic, now with shape {1}(1) changed to 'bold'.

We can also demonstrate the line-width addition to the collection of public variables. The command in line 20 results in the shapes shown in Figure 15.1. The largest star is now bold. The outputs on lines 22–27 confirm that the **LineWeight** public variable is indeed **'bold'**.

15.3 SUMMARY

In many ways, **cLineStyle** represents a different interface to the values associated with each shape's graphics handle, but developing a replacement interface was never a goal. The real goal is to demonstrate the various aspects of object-oriented programming by creating a series of classes that are meaningful in the context of the original **cShape** class. By coincidence, the example evolved in a direction where **cLineStyle** makes sense as a secondary-object class. Even so, it is interesting to point out some of the differences between the handle-graphics interface and the simple object-oriented interface.

The first difference is syntax. Using a graphics handle always requires a call to **set**, for example, **set(handle, 'Color', [1 0 0])**. By comparison, the interface for **cLineStyle** uses dot-reference syntax to perform the same operation, for example, **line.Color = 3**. The second difference is control. With handle-graphics commands, you can't control the collection of available attributes and you can't redefine the format. By comparison, a class interface makes it easy to limit the available attributes and define an alternate format. A class interface also allows the creation of new attributes. Assigning **'normal'** or **'bold'** to control the line width is one example. The third difference is persistence. Attribute data held in an object do not vanish when the figure window is closed. The final difference is stability. The handle-graphics commands are built in and tested. It would take much time and effort to test a class interface to the same degree.

Drawing a **cStar** object exercises member functions belonging to the child, the parent, and a secondary object. Even in this simple example, there are many layers and many function calls. The simplified UML static structure diagram in Figure 15.2 provides a good map of the layers.

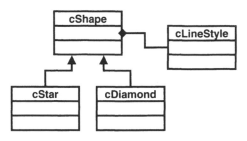

FIGURE 15.2 Simplified UML static structure diagram with inheritance and composition.

The arrows indicate parent–child inheritance, and the diamond indicates composition. This diagram helps reveal the path each function takes during execution. For example, drawing a scalar **cStar** object uses the set of member functions shown in Table 15.1.

In particular, **subsref, subsasgn, get**, and **set** receive quite a workout, and most of the calls to these functions are a direct consequence of slice and forward. A few of these calls in Table 15.1 can be eliminated, but in general, traversing each level in the hierarchy introduces a certain amount of overhead that cannot be avoided. This is unfortunate because even without objects, run-time performance is MATLAB's primary weakness. With objects, there is always a fine line to walk between efficiency and coupling. The additional overhead means that you have to be very judicious in your choice of syntax, in the design of each class, and in the design of the hierarchy.

Performance optimization is a very involved discipline. The biggest gains usually come from vectorization. The fact that the group-of-eight implementation fully supports vectorization can provide a huge performance benefit compared to a scalar-only implementation. This means that developers need to consider vectorization when designing the software architecture. The fact that most other object-oriented languages don't support vectorization makes a MATLAB design unique. Other performance tweaks can be added, but typically the gains are small. For example, calls to **subsref, subsasgn, get**, and **set** can sometimes be reduced by accessing and mutating several private variables through one public variable name. Another way to increase performance

TABLE 15.1
Member Functions Used to Draw a Scalar cShape Object

Number of Calls	Function
1	**@cStar/draw**
1	**@cStar/get**
1	**@cStar/private/parent_list**
1	**@cShape/draw**
1	**@cShape/subsref**
1	**@cShape/get**
2	**@cShape/horzcat**
2	**@cLineStyle/subsref**
2	**@cLineStyle/get**
1	**@cLineStyle/subsasgn**
1	**@cLineStyle/set**

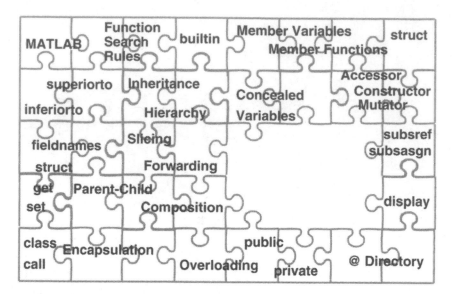

FIGURE 15.3 Puzzle, now with the inheritance pieces.

involves the use of variable-specific **get and set** member functions. Except for vectorization, these techniques usually degrade other aspects of software quality.

Parent–child inheritance and composition have different levels of visibility. Parent–child inheritance is sometimes called public inheritance because the parent's public interface remains public. Similarly, composition is also called private inheritance because the secondary object's public interface is hidden behind the primary object's interface. During design, these visibility differences help us decide how to use a secondary object. If the entire interface of the secondary object needs to be exposed, parent–child inheritance is usually the best choice. In this case, the primary object *is-a* specialized version of the secondary. If only a small percentage of the secondary object needs to be exposed, choose composition. In this case, the primary object *has-a* secondary object.

The last time we added puzzle pieces was at the end of Chapter 8. Since then, we have uncovered a large number of pieces related to inheritance. We can add pieces for hierarchies, slicing, forwarding, parent–child inheritance, and composition. After adding these pieces, the object-oriented picture in Figure 15.3 is coming together. Only a few more pieces and the puzzle will be complete.

15.4 INDEPENDENT INVESTIGATIONS

1. Add the capability to change the style of the line. The addition to **cLineStyle** should store the handle-graphics **LineStyle** characters, but **cShape**'s interface can use the same characters or use descriptions like **'solid'** or **'dotted'**.
2. In §15.1.2 we discussed read-write-modify syntax when a secondary object is made available through a single public variable name. This exercise investigates that syntax further.
   a. Add a public variable named **LineStyle** that allows direct access and mutation for the private secondary object **mLineStyle**. Changes to **/@cShape/fieldnames**, **/@cShape/get**, and **/@cShape/set** will be required.
   b. Create an object with the command **star = cStar** and confirm that you can read and write **LineStyle**, for example, **style = star.LineStyle**.
   c. Did you include an **isa** check in **set**'s **LineStyle** case? Is it usually a good idea to include this type of checking? Why or why not?

d. Try to access **ColorRgb** through **LineStyle** but don't make a copy of the secondary object. The command to do this would be **star.LineStyle.ColorRgb**.

e. Draw the **star** using the command **star = draw(star)**. Mutate **ColorRgb** via **LineStyle**, for example, **star.LineStyle.ColorRgb = [1;0;0];**. Did the color change?

f. Modify the **LineStyle** cases in **get** and **set** so that **length(index) == 1** throws an error and repeat investigation 0. This should have generated an error. Can this approach be used as an alternative to get-modify-set syntax?

g. Create an array of **cStar** objects with the command **star = [star star];** and repeat investigations 0. and 0. What is the difference? What can you do to make this work?

16 General Assignment and Mutator Helper Functions

In our constant quest for software quality, consistent interfaces and modular code are very important. In light of this, we need to turn our attention on **get** and **set**. If you examine the current implementations of **get** or **set**, the logic in almost every case statement is different. These differences are currently necessary because the interface for each public variable is unique. It is preferable to keep the group-of-eight functions as uniform as possible and that means trying to move interface differences out of **get** and **set**. There isn't a lot we can do about individual cases, but we can simplify the code contained in each. To do this we will develop a helper-function technique that pushes most of the differences out of **get** and **set** and into the helper. This technique will improve code modularity and improvements in modularity directly relate to improvements in code quality.

As always, the driving force is code quality. As the public interface grows in complexity, it would be bad if the complexity of **get** and **set** grew faster than the interface. If we include all the code directly in these functions, that is exactly what will happen. We will get a riot of cases, and every case is essentially unique. If we don't develop a good strategy for the **case** code, an interface definition can easily overwhelm our ability to grow and maintain the code. A good strategy will allow us to use a common approach and can lead to the efficient use of automated generation tools for the group of eight.

16.1 HELPER FUNCTION STRATEGY

The designs for **get** and **set** already partition the code into sections associated with public variables, concealed variables, parent forwarding, and error checking. The public variable and concealed variable sections are further partitioned into separate cases for each variable. This organization naturally separates each case into a self-contained code block, independent from the other cases. It is also important to observe that case code in **get** generally uses the same variables and follows a similar pattern as the case code in **set**. It makes sense that this would be true because **get** and **set** cases represent inverse operations on the same variable. With such close coupling, there is a strong argument for organizing the input and output conversion code into the same function.

In a class with many public variables, the public variable switch blocks can quickly become a development bottleneck. We can modularize the switch statement by taking advantage of the fact that each case is self-contained. Here it makes a lot of sense to move the code for each variable into its own private helper function.

Based on these two observations, we now have a reasonable way to organize code into smaller, more manageable pieces. We could easily create a helper function for every public variable, but first we need to draw a fine line between run-time performance and code organization. Using a separate helper function means adding yet another function call in the evaluation of **subsref** and **subsasgn**. If the operation inside the helper function is simple, the overhead of the additional function call can eat up more run time than the operation itself. On the other hand, member functions might be able to improve their run time by calling the helper thus eliminating the overhead in **get** and **set**.

There isn't a single approach that will always guarantee the best run time, but it is reasonable to ask whether every public member variable should be matched with a private helper function. The best locations for simple functions might be **get** and **set**. Public member variables with a direct link to a single private member variable certainly fit the simple-function category. The case code for these so-called *direct-link* public member variables is fast and simple and it is difficult to justify a separate helper function. For other public variables, the picture isn't as clear. As a general approach, it is very easy to separate public variables into direct link and non-direct link. We will proceed along this path with the understanding that run-time optimization will sometimes force us to include code for simple, non-direct-link variables in **get** and **set**.

16.1.1 DIRECT-LINK PUBLIC VARIABLES

For scalar objects, directly returning or mutating a private variable through a public variable is trivial. Access involves returning the value of the associated private variable, and mutation involves storing an assignment value into it. Supporting multiple index levels is also easy. We have already discussed these situations and have developed the case code to handle them. Before we discuss the more difficult case of non-direct-link access and mutation, we will review the direct-link code. Values returned by the helper functions need to conform to the code already developed. Otherwise, we will need to modify the code found in the current group of eight.

16.1.1.1 get and subsref

The standard, direct-link **case** code for **get** is shown in Code Listing 96. Here we assume a public variable name of `'VarName'` and a private variable name of `'mVarName'`. Matching the public and private names in this way is not required, but it does seem to improve code maintenance. Line 1 begins the **case** for the `'VarName'` public variable. Line 2 checks the length of the object and returns nothing when the object is empty. When the object is not empty, line 5 uses standard dot-reference list expansion to collect private variable values from every index. These values are saved in **varargout**.

Code Listing 96, Standard Direct-Link-Variable Access Case for get.m

```
1   case 'VarName'
2     if isempty(this)
3       varargout = {};
4     else
5       varargout = {this.mVarName};
6     end
```

Near the end of **get**, the code shown in Code Listing 97 compares the size of **varargout** with the value of **nargout** and adjusts the output format. As previously discussed, this code is required because the value of **nargout** is not always consistent with the size of the object. The comparison code in line 2 only needs to compare with one because that is the only value where the confusion occurs. Line 4 looks for strings and empty cells and, if they exist, packages the output so that concatenation will not destroy the cellular structure. Otherwise, line 7 tries to concatenate the outputs in an array. If the concatenation fails, line 9 packages the return so that it retains its cellular structure.

Finally, if **get** was called from **subsref**, indices deeper than the first dot-reference level might exist. After **subsref** calls **get**, Code Listing 98 forwards additional indices to **subsref**. Following standard dot-reference syntax means that this forward is only allowed for scalar objects.

Code Listing 97, Varargout Size-Conversion Code

```
1    % varargout conversion
2    if length(varargout) > 1 & nargout <= 1
3      if iscellstr(varargout) || any([cellfun('isempty',
       varargout)])
4        varargout = {varargout};
5      else
6        try
7          varargout = {[varargout{:}]};
8        catch
9          varargout = {varargout};
10       end
11     end
12   end
```

Code Listing 98, Handling Additional Indexing Levels in subsref.m

```
1    if length(index) > 1
2      if length(this(:)) == 1
3        varargout = {subsref([varargout{:}], index(2:end))};
4      else
5        [err_id, err_msg] = array_reference_error(index(2).type);
6        error(err_id, err_msg);
7      end
8    end
```

The test in line 2 determines whether to allow the forward or throw an error. The forward is on line 3, and the errors are thrown in lines 5–6.

16.1.1.2 set and subsasgn

The standard, direct-link **case** code for **set** is shown in Code Listing 99. Here we also assume a public variable name of **'VarName'** and a private variable name of **'mVarName'**. Line 1 begins the **case** for the **'VarName'** public variable. Line 2 checks the length of the index. When there is more than one index level, line 3 makes sure the object is scalar, and if so, line 4 forwards the private variable, the remaining indices, and the assignment values to **subsasgn**. If the object is nonscalar, lines 6–7 throw the appropriate error. Throwing a meaningful error message is an improvement over previous implementations of **set**. When there is only one index, line 10 deals values into the private variable. Each **case** is self-contained. There is no additional dot-reference support code inside **set** or **subsasgn**.

Code Listing 99, Standard Direct-Link-Variable Access Case for set.m

```
1    case 'VarName'
2      if length(index) > 1
3        if length(this(:)) == 1
```

```
4          this.mVarName = subsasgn(this.mVarName, index(2:end),
             varargin{:});
5      else
6          [err_id, err_msg] = array_reference_error(index(2)
             .type);
7          error(err_id, err_msg);
8      end
9    else
10     [this.mVarName] = deal(varargin{:});
11   end
```

16.1.2 GET AND SET HELPER FUNCTIONS

Unlike direct-link variables, the code for every non-direct-link variable is unique to the behavior of each public variable. Using a helper function with a standard interface is preferable to sprinkling **get** and **set** with nonstandard blocks of code. Using a helper function also enables automatic code generation. To reduce the number of helper functions, to improve maintenance, and to support advanced syntax, accessor and mutator functionality are combined into each public variable's helper. Combining both functions in one file makes the interface a little more difficult, but the benefits outweigh this concern. In addition, once we define the interface and develop the helper's structure we can reuse them for all that follow.

Helper functions are located in the class' private directory. Helper functions for the constructor include the string **`ctor_`** in their name. Helper functions for **get** and **set** include the name of the public variable and the string **`_helper`**. We will use **/@cLineStyle/Color** as an example for discussing the helper-function interface and implementation. The standard name for this helper becomes **Color_helper.**

16.1.2.1 Helper functions, get, and set

Once we develop the code for **Color_helper**, we can reuse it to implement helper functions for other public variables. Since **get** and **set** both call the helper, the function's input must include a way to specify access versus mutate. The input must also include the same input originally passed into **get** or **set**. Different values can be passed depending on access or mutate; however, it is easier to define the input as the union of arguments required for both access and mutation. This collection of input arguments includes the following:

which: A variable that specifies whether an access or a mutate operation is desired. The string **`get`** will designate access; and **`set`**, mutation.
this: The object array is passed into the helper via **this**.
index: Being inside a particular helper function means that **get** or **set** already processed the first dot-reference name. The **index** value is formatted as a **substruct** and includes elements **2:end** from **get**'s or **set**'s original **index** value.
varargin: The assignment values for mutation are passed into the helper as cells in **varargin**. These are the same **varargin** values passed into **set**.

Similarly, it is also easier to return both the object and **varargout** rather than define one output variable and force it to share duty. In addition, two logical values help create a more powerful interface. The collection of helper-function output arguments includes the following:

do_sub_indexing: This logical value allows the helper, rather than **get** or **subsref**, to perform all indexing beyond the initial dot-reference. The helper function returns a value of **true** when it wants **get** or **subsref** to take care of deeper indexing. When code inside the helper performs all of the indexing, the return value is set to **false**. Typically, the helper will not index deeper than the first dot-reference level and thus typically returns **true**.

do_assignin: This logical value supports some special mutator syntax that we will discuss in Part 3. At least for now, the helper will return **false**.

this: The object array passed into the helper and possibly modified is passed back out using **this**.

varargout: The accessed values are contained in the **varargout** cell array. The format for **varargout** from an accessor is the same format used for direct-link variables, one value per cell. The **varargout** return from a mutator is always empty.

16.1.2.2 Final template for get.m

The implementation of **get**'s case code follows easily from the above input–output description. The entire **get** function is shown in Code Listing 100 because there are several important changes that need to be discussed.

Code Listing 100, Final Version of get.m Implemented for cLineStyle

```
1    function varargout = get(this, index, varargin)
2
3    do_sub_indexing = true;  % helper might do all sub indexing
4    do_assignin = false; % special variable, see book section 3
5
6    % one argument, display info and return
7    if nargin == 1
8      if nargout == 0
9        disp(struct(this(1)));
10     else
11       varargout = cell(1,max([1, nargout]));
12       varargout{1} = struct(this(1));
13     end
14     return;
15   end
16
17   % if index is a string, we will allow special access
18   called_by_name = ischar(index);
19
20   % the set switch below needs a substruct
21   if called_by_name
22     index = substruct('.', index);
23   end
24
25   % public-member-variable section
26   found = true;  % otherwise-case will flip to false
27   switch index(1).subs
```

```
28     case 'Color'
29       if isempty(this)
30         varargout = {};
31       else
32         varargout = cell(size(this)); % trick next function's
            nargout
33         % either index(2:end) or varargin{1} should be empty
34         [do_sub_indexing, do_assignin, this, varargout{:}] =
            ...
35           Color_helper('get', this, [index(2:end)
              varargin{:}]);
36       end
37     case 'LineWidth'
38       if isempty(this)
39         varargout = {};
40       else
41         varargout = {this.mLineWidth};
42       end
43     case 'LineHandle'
44       if isempty(this)
45         varargout = {};
46       else
47         varargout = {this.mLineHandle};
48       end
49     otherwise
50       found = false;  % didn't find it in the public section
51   end
52
53   % concealed member variables, not strictly public
54   if ~found && called_by_name
55     found = true;
56     switch index(1).subs
57       case 'mDisplayFunc' % class-wizard reserved field
58         if isempty(this)
59           varargout = {};
60         else
61           varargout = {this.mDisplayFunc};
62         end
63       otherwise
64         found = false; % didn't find it in the concealed section
65     end
66   end
67
68   % parent forwarding block
69   if ~found
70     if called_by_name
71       forward_index = index(1).subs;
```

```
72      else
73        forward_index = index;
74      end
75
76      if nargout == 0
77        varargout = cell(size(this));
78      else
79        varargout = cell(1, nargout);
80      end
81
82      for parent_name = parent_list'  % loop over parent cellstr
83        try
84          parent = [this.(parent_name{1})];
85          [varargout{:}] = get(parent, forward_index,
             varargin{:});
86          found = true;  % catch will assign false if not found
87          do_sub_indexing = false;  % assume parent did all sub-
             indexing
88          break;  % can only get here if field is found
89        catch
90          found = false;
91          err = lasterror;
92          switch err.identifier
93            case 'MATLAB:nonExistentField'
94              % NOP
95            otherwise
96              rethrow(err);
97          end
98        end
99      end
100     if do_assignin
101       parent = num2cell(parent);
102       [this.(parent_name{1})] = deal(parent{:});
103     end
104   end
105
106   % error checking
107   if ~found
108     error('MATLAB:nonExistentField', ...
109       'Reference to non-existent field identifier %s', ...
110       index(1).subs);
111   end
112
113   % nargout adjustment
114   if length(varargout) > 1 & nargout <= 1
115     if iscellstr(varargout) || any([cellfun('isempty',
         varargout)])
```

```
116      varargout = {varargout};
117    else
118      try
119        varargout = {[varargout{:}]};
120      catch
121        varargout = {varargout};
122      end
123    end
124  end
125
126  % special syntax block, see book section 3
127  if do_assignin
128    var_name = inputname(1);
129    if isempty(var_name)
130      warning('get with assignment is only for non-indexed
           objects');
131    else
132      assignin('caller', var_name, this);
133      caller = evalin('caller', 'mfilename');
134      if ~isempty(strmatch(caller, {'subsref' 'subsasgn' 'get'
           'set'}))
135        assignin('caller', 'do_assignin', true);
136      end
137    end
138  end
139
140  % deep indexing block
141  if do_sub_indexing
142    index = [index(2:end) varargin{:}];
143    if length(index) > 0
144      if length(this) == 1
145        varargout = {subsref([varargout{:}], index)};
146
147      else
148        [err_id, er_msg] =
           array_reference_error(index(1).type);
149      end
150    end
151  end
```

The first changes occur in lines 3 and 4. The local variables **do_sub_indexing** and **do_assignin** guard code blocks near the end of this now standard version of **get**. Helper functions return values for these two variables, but we never know in advance whether a direct-link public variable or a non-direct-link variable is being accessed. Lines 3 and 4 assign initial values compatible with direct-link access. During non-direct-link access, the helper function assigns values to these variables.

The next change brings us into the public member variable section. The **case** for **'Color'**, lines 28–36, uses a helper function. As before, line 28 identifies the **'Color' case**, and when the object is empty, line 30 returns an empty **varargout**. When the object is not empty, line 32 prepares for the helper call by preallocating **varargout**. Lines 34–35 call the helper. There are three input arguments and three plus **length(varargout)** outputs.

The first input, **'get'**, tells the helper to perform an access operation. The second input, **this**, is the source of the access. The third input is a concatenation of **index(2:end)** and **varargin{:}**. The values in **index** and **varargin** depend on the path leading up to the helper call. If the path began with dot-reference syntax, **index(2:end)** will contain additional indices converted from operator notation and **varargin** will be empty. If the path began with a call to **get**, **index(2:end)** will be empty but **varargin** might include an additional **substruct** index. The concatenation assembles the entire **index** and passes it into the helper.

One important thing to notice is the fact that there is no limit imposed on the length of the index passed into the helper. Ordinarily MATLAB places limits on indexing into nonscalar variables. In most situations, the group-of-eight implementation also places limits on indexing. The length of the **index** passed into the helper is an exception because the helper is responsible for these decisions. When the helper accepts this responsibility it returns a value of **false** in **do_sub_indexing**.

The helper returns values for **do_sub_indexing, do_assignin, this**, and **varargout**. Allowing the helper to index into the dot-referenced value and return a **do_sub_indexing** value of **false** means that values returned from the helper might be fully indexed. This has implications for **subsref** because, currently, **subsref** will incorrectly reindex the values. To fix this problem, indexing code is moved out of **subsref** and into lines 140–151. The code previously shown in Code Listing 98 will no longer exist in the standard version of **subsref**. Instead, all standard versions of **get** will include the ability to perform deeper indexing. It should come as no surprise that the **do_sub_indexing** flag guards this ability.

The helper also returns a value for **do_assignin. Do_assignin** is used as a guard value for lines 127–138. These lines implement some special syntax that will be described in Part 3. Until we take up that discussion, the value returned by the helper will always be **false**. That way, until we discuss the pros and cons of returning a **true** value, we will skip over 127–138. You might also notice other **do_assignin**-related additions. These additions are also discussed in Part 3.

The final addition occurs on line 87 inside the parent-forwarding section. When the **get** forward in line 85 executes without error, line 86 sets **found** equal to **true** and line 87 sets **do_sub_indexing** to **false**. Now that we have moved the indexing code into **get**, the parent's version will have already performed any necessary indexing and we don't want to reindex the values. Of course, this also means that all of our classes need to be updated with the new group-of-eight functions described in this chapter.

16.1.2.3 Final Template for set.m

Case code for **set** is shown in Code Listing 101.

Code Listing 101, Final Version of set.m Implemented for cLineStyle

```
1      function varargout = set(this, index, varargin)
2
3      do_assignin = false;  % special variable, see book section 3
4
5      if nargin < 3  % one or two arguments, display info and return
```

```
6      possible = fieldnames(this, '-possible');
7      possible_struct = struct(possible{:});
8      if nargout == 0
9        if nargin == 1
10         disp(possible_struct);
11       else
12         try
13           temp_struct.(index) = possible_struct.(index);
14           disp(temp_struct);
15         catch
16           warning(['??? Reference to non-existent field ' ...
17           index '.']);
18         end
19       end
20     else
21       varargout = cell(1,max([1, nargout]));
22       varargout{1} = possible_struct;
23     end
24     return;
25   end
26
27   called_by_name = ischar(index);
28
29   % the set switch below needs a substruct
30   if called_by_name
31       index = substruct('.', index);
32   end
33
34   % public-member-variable section
35   found = true;  % otherwise-case will flip to false
36   switch index(1).subs
37     case 'Color'
38       [do_sub_indexing, do_assignin, this] = ...
39         Color_helper('set', this, index(2:end), varargin{:});
40     case 'LineWidth'
41       [do_sub_indexing, do_assignin, this] = ...
42         LineWidth_helper('set', this, index(2:end),
43           varargin{:});
44     case 'LineHandle'
45       if length(index) > 1
46         if length(this) == 1
47           this.mLineHandle = ...
48             subsasgn(this.mLineHandle,
49             index(2:end), varargin{:});
50         else
51           [err_id, err_msg] = array_reference_error(index(1)
52             .type);
```

```
51          error(err_id, err_msg);
52        end
53      else
54        [this.mLineHandle] = deal(varargin{:});
55      end
56    otherwise
57      found = false;
58  end
59
60  % concealed member variables, not strictly public
61  if ~found && called_by_name
62    found = true;
63    switch index(1).subs
64      case 'mDisplayFunc'
65        if length(index) > 1
66          this.mDisplayFunc = ...
67            subsasgn(this.mDisplayFunc, ...
68              index(2:end), varargin{:});
69        else
70          [this.mDisplayFunc] = deal(varargin{:});
71        end
72      otherwise
73        found = false;  % didn't find it in the special section
74      end
75  end
76
77  % parent forwarding block
78  if ~found
79    if called_by_name
80      forward_index = index(1).subs;
81    else
82      forward_index = index;
83    end
84
85    for parent_name = parent_list' % loop over parent cellstr
86      try
87        parent = set([this.(parent_name{1})], forward_index,
           varargin{:});
88        parent = num2cell(parent);
89        [this.(parent_name{1})] = deal(parent{:});
90        found = true;  % catch will assign false if not found
91        break;   % can only get here if field is found
92      catch
93        found = false;
94        err = lasterror;
95        switch err.identifier
96          case 'MATLAB:nonExistentField'
```

```
97                  % NOP
98              otherwise
99                  rethrow(err);
100         end
101       end
102     end
103   end
104
105   if ~found
106     error('MATLAB:nonExistentField', ...
107       '??? Reference to non-existent field ', ...
108       index(1).subs);
109   end
110
111   if do_assignin % set used in special way, see book section 3
112     var_name = inputname(1);
113         if isempty(var_name)
114             warning('MATLAB:invalidInputname', ...
115             'No assignment: set with assignment needs a non-
                indexed object');
116         else
117             assignin('caller', var_name, this);
118             caller = evalin('caller', 'mfilename');
119             if ~isempty(strmatch(caller, {'subsref' 'subsasgn'
                'get' 'set'}))
120                assignin('caller', 'do_assignin', true);
121             end
122         end
123   end
124
125   varargout{1} = this;
```

The first change to **set** occurs in line 3. The logical variable **do_assignin** guards entry into the block of code added in lines 110–122. Behavior related to **do_assignin** will be described in Part 3. Until then, **do_assignin** should be **false** and line 3 assigns **false** as the initial value.

The next change brings us into the public member variable section. The **case** for 'Color', lines 37–39, uses a helper function. Line 37 identifies the 'Color' case, and lines 38–39 call the helper. This time the first argument is 'set' because we want to execute the mutator. The remaining three arguments are the object, the additional indices, and the assignment values. The helper returns values for **do_sub_indexing**, **do_assignin**, and the mutated object. In this case, **do_sub_indexing** is a dummy variable because it is never used by **set**.

The case for 'LineWidth' is interesting because **get** uses direct-link code but **set** uses a helper. This is typical because the standard organization moves input-value-checking code into the helper. The mutator needs to check the input values, but the accessor does not. Thus, the mutator uses a helper but the accessor does not. Finally, the case for **LineHandle** uses the standard direct-link syntax.

16.1.2.4   Color Helper Function

Code for one combined accessor–mutator helper function is shown in Code Listing 102. This particular helper is used for the public member variable color. Code in the listing should look familiar because most of the lines came directly from member functions in Chapter 15. Of course, the organization is different and there is a lot going on in this function.

Code Listing 102, Final Version of cLineStyle's Color_helper.m

```
1    function [do_sub_indexing, do_assignin, this, varargout] =
     ...
2      Color_helper(which, this, index, varargin)
3
4    switch which
5
6      case 'get'   % ACCESSOR
7        do_sub_indexing = true;  % true and get will index deeper
8        do_assignin = false; % typically false, see book section 3
9        rgb = hsv2rgb([this.mColorHsv]')';  % convert color format
10       varargout = num2cell(rgb, 1);   % num2cell instead of
         mat2cell
11
12     case 'set'   % MUTATOR
13       do_sub_indexing = false;  % mutator must do deeper indexing
14       do_assignin = false; % typically false, see book section 3
15       varargout = {};      % mutator doesn't use varargout
16       if isempty(index)   % only an initial dot-reference value
17         rgb = [varargin{:}];   % input values are rgb
18       else   % deeper indexing
19         if length(this) == 1
20           rgb = subsasgn(get(this, 'Color'), index,
             varargin{:});
21         else
22           [err_id, err_msg] = array_reference_error(index(1).
             type);
23           error(err_id, err_msg);
24         end
25       end
26       hsv = num2cell(rgb2hsv(rgb')', 1);  % convert rgb to hsv
27       [this.mColorHsv] = deal(hsv{:});  % assign new hsv values
28
29       for k = 1:length(this(:))
30         try
31           set(this(k).mLineHandle, 'Color', get(this(k),
             'Color'));
32         end
33       end
34
```

```
35     otherwise
36       error('OOP:unsupportedOption', ['Unknown helper option: '
         which]);
37   end
```

First notice the file is separated into two sections: accessor (lines 3–10) and mutator (lines 12–37). This is not necessarily required, but it is a convenient organization. Both sections assign values to **do_sub_indexing**, **do_assignin**, and **varargout**. The accessor code can allow **get** to finish deeper indexing by setting **do_sub_indexing** equal to **true**. That is what this helper does on line 7. The accessor code can also elect to perform deeper indexing by setting **do_sub_indexing** equal to **false**. The mutator code must always perform deeper indexing and will always set **do_sub_indexing** equal to **false**.

The accessor code then converts private HSV values into RGB values on line 9. To populate the **varargout** cell array, line 10 converts the RGB array values into a cell array. The mutator code doesn't return values via **varargout**, so it sets **varargout** to empty in line 15.

Instead of using **varargout**, mutator code performs the mutation in place and returns the mutated object. When the variable name is the only index, line 17 copies input RGB values into a temporary variable. When there are additional indices, line 19 checks the size of the object array. If the array is scalar, line 20 uses **subsasgn** to assign the subset. If the array is nonscalar, lines 22–23 throw an error by calling **array_reference_error**.

After populating the **rgb** temporary variable, line 26 converts the RGB values into HSV values and stores the HSV values in a cell array. Line 27 then deals the cell values into the correct locations. Finally, lines 29–33 loop over all the objects in the array and set their line colors to the newly assigned values. Just like before, using the handle-graphics **set** silently does nothing when the handle is empty.

16.1.2.5 The Other Classes and Member Functions

Before **cLineStyle** can be used in our current collection of classes, we need to code **LineWidth_helper**. The implementation follows the same strategy used for **Color_helper**. The code is included in the Chapter 16 **@cLineStyle/private** directory. The mutator section includes index checking, value checking, and input size checking identical to Chapter 15's **set** case.

While not technically required, we should also be able to convert member functions for **cShape**, **cStar**, and **cDiamond** into this chapter's newly established, group-of-eight format. The old class organization will work with the new version of **cLineStyle** because its public interface didn't change. The problem with keeping the old class organization is one of consistency. A collection of classes is much easier to maintain if they all consistently conform to the same internal strategy. Affected group-of-eight member functions are **get**, **set**, **subsref**, and **subsasgn**.

The new organization also uses helper functions for non-direct-link public variables. The previous implementations for **cShape**, **cStar**, and **cDiamond** were also reorganized to use helpers. Implementations of the various helper functions follow the same strategy laid out in this chapter. The newly organized class files can be found in the **chapter_16** directory. You should look at these files and pay close attention to the helper functions in the private directories.

16.2 TEST DRIVE

The code in this chapter represents reorganization with no new functionality. All of the commands from previous chapters should still work the same as they did before. We need to rerun some of our test commands to make sure our classes still behave the same. Some of the Chapter 15

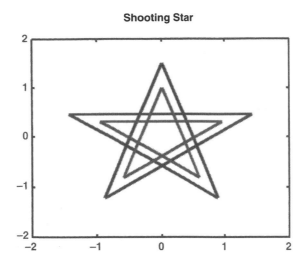

FIGURE 16.1 cStar graphic after implementing helper-function syntax.

commands for **cStar** objects are repeated in Code Listing 103. The commands confirm that the helper-function interface is working correctly across our parent–child and primary-secondary hierarchies. The figure that results from the command in line 6 is shown in Figure 16.1.

```
Code Listing 103, Chapter 16 Test Drive Command Listing: The cStar Interface
1    >> cd '/oop_guide/chapter_16'
2    >> clear classes; fclose all; close all force; diary off;
3    >> star = [cStar cStar];
4    >> star(2).ColorRgb = [1;0;0];
5    >> star(1) = 1.5 * star(1);
6    >> star = draw(star);
7    >> star(1).Title = 'Shooting Star';
8    >> star(1).LineWeight = 'bold';
9    >> star(1)
10   ans =
11           Size: [2x1 double]
12       ColorRgb: [3x1 double]
13         Points: [2x6 double]
14     LineWeight: 'bold'
15          Title: 'Shooting Star'
```

16.3 SUMMARY

The focus of this chapter was the organization of **get** and **set**. By changing the organization, we improved the modularity of the standard group of eight. To do this we considered two situations: direct-link variables and variables that use a helper function. Direct-link variables are easy to access and mutate because there is no data conversion or input checking. The code to access and mutate these variables is short and essentially the same every time. Public variables that use a helper include those that convert data from one representation to another and those that perform any sort if input check during mutation.

Moving accessor and mutator code outside of **get** and **set** also has another benefit. It allows computer-aided-software-engineering (CASE) tools to manage the addition and removal of private, public, and concealed variables. Without helper functions and their standard interface, every time a class changes, a lot of hand tailoring is required. The next chapter introduces a very capable CASE tool that exploits all of the group of eight's organizational elements.

16.4 INDEPENDENT INVESTIGATIONS

1. Repeat the same commands using a **cDiamond** object instead of a **cStar** object.
2. Experiment with the implementation by accessing and mutating elements using multiple indexing levels.

17 Class Wizard

With sixteen chapters under your belt, you can now create sophisticated, robust MATLAB classes on your own. During the first few implementations, it is easy to stay motivated because there are many new twists and turns. After the first few, however, the repetitive syntax can quickly become monotonous and time-consuming. At some point, you need to shift back into a product focus but the implementation mechanics are too tedious to allow your attention to waver. Once you shift from "How do I implement objects?" back to "How do I use objects to implement products?" you are likely to find yourself wishing for some sort of class-generation tool. Standard, repetitive tasks like building the group-of-eight functions are ideally suited for automation. Of course, this did not happen by accident. Modularity along with a constant drive to isolate class-dependent code into a small subset of functions makes automation possible.

This chapter introduces an automated code-generation tool that simplifies group-of-eight development for MATLAB classes. Using the tool, you can define a collection of public and private member variables along with an associated collection of public and private member functions. The tool will use these to generate fully functional class code that follows the guidelines developed in the previous sixteen chapters. All of the various bells and whistles are included. The tool will even give you a head start on class tailoring by generating a function template for public functions and helpers. The template includes the function definition along with reasonably complete header comments. This is convenient because it gives variable names and comment headers a consistent form with shared comments across all members of the class.

The automation tool is called **class_wizard.m**. The Class Wizard tool uses a graphical interface entirely developed using MATLAB's standard development tools. Dialog screens and callback functions were developed using Guide* and MATLAB 7.0. In addition, all of the code in **class_wizard.m** is native MATLAB. The main Class Wizard function along with other required functions can be found on the source disk in **/oop_guide/utility/wizard_gui**. I recommend that you add this directory to the MATLAB path or copy all the files to a directory already on the path. If you don't want to put the wizard on your path, you can **cd** into its directory to run it.

The first time you run Class Wizard, you will immediately recognize its organization. Data-entry areas on the main dialog correspond to specific areas in the group of eight. There are entry areas for parent classes, private variables, concealed variables, public variables, and constructors. The **more...** button opens another dialog where details for public functions and some other advanced elements can be entered. We will discuss these advanced elements in Part 3.

In this chapter, you will find a concise introduction to Class Wizard. The introduction describes the various data-entry screens, field formats, file operations, and class generation. The descriptions assume that you are already familiar with the organization and implementation strategy behind the group of eight and their helpers. For example, descriptions in this chapter assume that you are familiar with private, concealed, and public variables and understand how they relate to one another. This chapter describes data entry for the code-generation tool, but in reality, the full documentation for Class Wizard is the topic of this book.

---

* Guide is a standard MATLAB utility that can be used to efficiently create cross-platform graphical user interfaces. MATLAB version 7.0 added button groups to the standard set of graphical components, and Class Wizard uses button groups. For this reason Class Wizard will not run properly under versions of MATLAB below 7.0. There were also some changes to the object model; however, Class Wizard produces class code that is backward compatible with MATLAB version 6.5.

The collection of member functions and their internal syntax mirrors the code examples already discussed. We can easily enter data that will result in a collection of shape classes that behave the same as the previous examples. In fact, that is the goal of the next chapter. Between this chapter and the next, you will discover that implementing class code is quick and easy. This is exactly how it should be because you need to reserve most of your time and effort for the most difficult part of object-oriented development, design.

17.1   FILE DEPENDENCIES

The prime motive for developing both the group-of-eight idiom and a code-generation tool is coupling. Here the coupling isn't exactly between modules of code but rather between the class definition and the associated m-file implementation. Early on, we organized group-of-eight functions to eliminate as much module-to-module coupling as possible. Now, Class Wizard will help control the coupling between the class definition and its implementation. The coupling can't be eliminated, only managed.

Let's first examine what is meant by definition-to-module coupling. The most basic class definition specifies a class name along with a small collection of public and private member variables. These names are distributed into group-of-eight code according to the diagram in Figure 17.1. Arrows connect the names used in the class definition to the modules where these names need to appear in code. The lines represent connections to class-independent modules. The dependencies in this figure are modest because dependency reduction was one of the main focal points for group-of-eight development. Even so, the arrows are still tangled and that creates a development headache. Class evolution requires that we keep several files in synch. Trying to implement several changes at once is a recipe for disaster. Making the situation even worse is the fact that an omission in one file can go undetected until the class is in use. For example, suppose you add a public member variable to **get** and **set** but forget to update **fieldnames**. This type of error doesn't usually cause a crash, but the lack of consistency can be very annoying to clients.

The lines and arrows on the dependency graph become even more entwined when parent–child inheritance is considered. This graph is shown in Figure 17.2. Here, **parent_list** joins with **get**, **set**, and **fieldnames** to form a Maginot line that prevents the coupling from extending deeply into the group of eight. Unless we make concessions to functionality, the arrows can't be untangled. This is where Class Wizard comes to the rescue. Using a single definition, Class Wizard keeps the standard member functions in synch. Changes to the class definition automatically migrate into every affected function. Organizing the code into the group of eight plus associated helper functions allows Class Wizard to manage the coupling. Allowing Class Wizard to manage this complexity aids development, evolution, and maintenance. The result is quality.

17.2   DATA-ENTRY DIALOG BOXES

The main class-generation file is **class_wizard.m** and can be found in the **/oop_guide/utility/wizard_gui** directory. This is the third version of the tool but the first version to use a graphical user interface (GUI) for definition entry. The GUI was developed

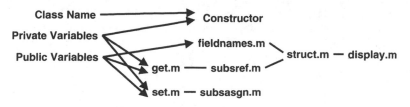

FIGURE 17.1 Dependency diagram for a simple class.

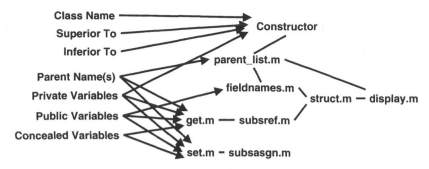

FIGURE 17.2 Dependency diagram with inheritance.

using Guide and MATLAB 7.0. The main screen uses dialog elements that are not available in MATLAB 6.5. Because of these elements, MATLAB 7.0 or higher is required to enter class definitions and generate files. All of the generated code is backward compatible with MATLAB 6.5 and higher.

The GUI is organized around a main screen containing buttons and menus. Each button or menu selection opens a secondary dialog dedicated to data entry for one small subset of the definition. There are separate dialog boxes for parent classes, public and private member variables, and public and private member functions. Most of these will be immediately familiar because they follow directly from the group-of-eight organization. Navigating into the dialogs and entering data requires additional explanation. That is the purpose of this chapter.

The most important content of a source file is the code; however, the total cost of development is lower when certain conventions are established and followed. Common code idioms generally improve the overall code quality. In addition, tightly integrating a class into the help system makes the class easier to use and evokes quality. The primary output from Class Wizard is code; however, the output includes features that make it easier to include the code in a larger project. A significant amount of Class Wizard's functionality centers on managing and formatting this sort of data. For example, class definitions can include comments for both functions and variables. All files generated for the class will include these comments in their headers. These headers can be displayed by MATLAB's help system, and they yield big payoffs in productivity. As long as you fill the definition with content, Class Wizard will manage it by writing it out to the appropriate files.

17.2.1 MAIN CLASS WIZARD DIALOG

The main Class Wizard dialog gives you direct access to all class elements shown on the left-hand side of Figure 17.2. These include class name, parent classes, superiority, inferiority, member variables, and member functions. The red arrows indicate how these elements flow into the various class files. The primary access functions **get.m** and **set.m** see the largest amount of customization, with **ctor_ini.m** running a close third.

The main dialog with a small amount of entered data is shown in Figure 17.3. The main screen includes items that represent the basic elements that are important for nearly every class. There are three direct-entry text fields, and an assortment of radio buttons, check boxes, buttons, and menus. The main screen displays a lot of summary information, but the details and the ability to change data require a button click or a menu selection. A few definition items are accessible on the main dialog, primarily **Class Name**, **Superior To**, and **Inferior To**.

The string entered into the **Class Name** field is used as the name of the constructor. The same name should also be used in the directory name, but the directory name is specified separately during file save operations. The suggested naming convention for classes includes a lowercase "**c**" as the first character. To help remind you of this convention, the field for **Class Name** initially

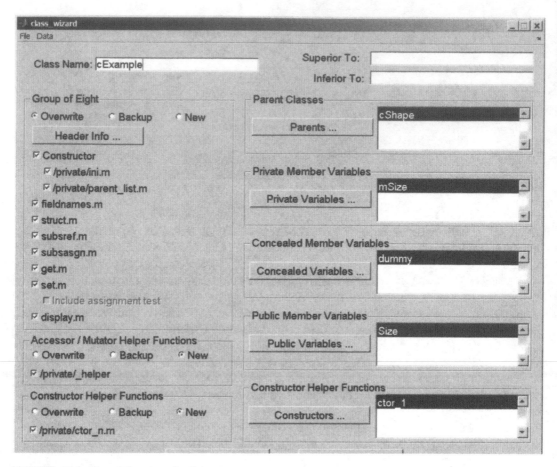

FIGURE 17.3 Class Wizard, main dialog.

contains a lowercase **c**. The lowercase **c** is not required, and you can enter any legal class name in the field.

Comma-separated names in the **Superior To** and **Inferior To** fields are used to set the function-selection hierarchy. Comma-separated lists are transcribed as written into the input arguments for calls to **superiorto** or **inferiorto**, respectively. These function calls must be made during the construction process. If the fields are populated, **superiorto** and **inferiorto** commands will be written into the constructor.

Along the left-hand side of the dialog, check boxes and radio buttons are grouped according to the files they control: group-of-eight files, accessor or mutator helper files, and constructor helper files. Check boxes and radio buttons exert generation control over individual group-of-eight files, and they exert control over all files in each group of helper functions. The radio buttons are more important than the check boxes because they control what happens to files that already exist. There are three choices:

Overwrite: When the file already exists, the original file is deleted and the new file is written in its place. When this happens, there is no way to recover the contents of the original file. Do not choose this option for files with tailored changes because the changes will be lost when the file is regenerated. Code in the group of eight should not normally require tailoring. Thus, the normal radio selection for the group-of-eight files is

Overwrite. Helper functions always require tailoring. Thus, the normal radio selection for both groups of helpers is **New**.

Backup: When the file already exists, the original file is renamed before the new file is written. The backup name includes the original filename along with a condensed version of the current date and time. Multiple backup copies for a particular file can coexist in a directory because the date and time for each will be different. This option is not usually selected unless new calling arguments or header information needs to be generated for a tailored function. After the new function template is generated, tailored code from the backup copy must be manually cut and inserted in the new file.

New: When this radio button is selected, only new files will be created. If a file already exists, Class Wizard does not regenerate the file but rather leaves the existing file alone. Under normal conditions, this is the best option to choose for files outside the group of eight.

By default, **Overwrite** is the selected action for group-of-eight functions and **New** is selected for all other files. These default values are the best selections for most situations. Group-of-eight functions are organized so that hand tailoring is almost never required. Allowing Class Wizard to overwrite these files keeps the interface in synch with the data enters through the GUI. All other files are usually a target for extensive tailoring. Selecting **New** for these files prevents them from being overwritten.

When a check box is checked, Class Wizard will attempt to create the file. Whether the file is saved to disk depends on the radio state. When a check box is unchecked, Class Wizard will skip file creation. Each group-of-eight file has its own check box, and by default, each box is checked. For normal operation, leave the box checked. Accessor and mutator helper functions and constructor helper functions also have check boxes. The default value is checked. Presently, there is no way to control the creation of individual helpers except through the radio buttons. For normal operation, leave the boxes checked.

Additional data-entry screens are accessed through various buttons or through menu selections. Buttons are arranged with a summary view of the data they control. There are buttons for additional header information **Header Info** ..., parent-class definition **Parents** ..., private member variables **Private Variables** ..., concealed member variables **Concealed Variables** ..., public member variables **Public Variables** ..., and constructor helper functions **Constructors** .... The **More** ... button displays another dialog with even more class fields. The **Build Class Files** button runs the class-generation code. Descriptions of the data-entry dialogs associated with these buttons are included in the following sections.

17.2.1.1 Header Information Dialog

Clicking the **Header Info** ... button on the main screen opens the header-input dialog box shown in Figure 17.4. The header-info dialog contains fields that are written into the header of every automatically generated member function. Input fields left blank are ignored and do not create a blank line in the header. For a new class, the first time you open the header-info dialog, all the fields will be empty. After entering data in individual fields, the values can be saved to a separate file. A menu selection allows you to recall the standard values for the next class. This way, you can avoid repeatedly typing the same information.

The menu item **DefaultHeaderInfo** has two options: **Load** **<ctrl-L>** and **Save** **<ctrl-S>**. Selecting **DefaultHeaderInfo::Save** will save the field contents in the file **default_header.mat**. This file is always located in the same directory where Class Wizard is stored. There is not a filename option and there are no overwrite warnings. Selecting **Default-HeaderInfo::Load** will read the previously saved values.

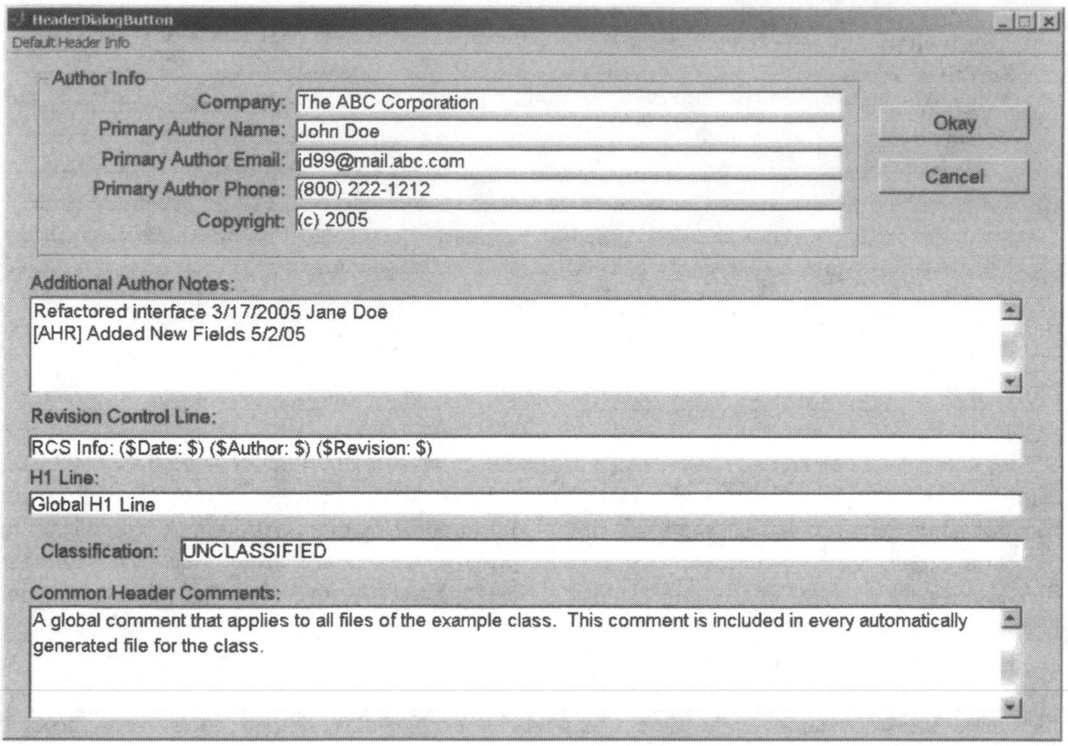

FIGURE 17.4 Class Wizard, **Header Info** ... dialog.

For the most part, these fields are self-explanatory. If you enter values shown in Figure 17.4 and generate class files, all file headers will contain the values. For example, the header from **subsref.m** is shown in Code Listing 104. In line 1, we find the generated function call. The arguments are always consistent with data in class definition. Line 2 includes the class name, function name, and text entered into the **HeaderInfo::H1 Line** textbox. The class name and function name are still included in the header even if **HeaderInfo::H1 Line** is blank. Line 3 includes the string from the **Classification** field. The **Classification** string is also appended as the last line in each file. Line 5 repeats the function declaration as comment. When help displays the header information, the function declaration is an important part of that display. MATLAB does not automatically include the declaration, so Class Wizard writes it in as a comment. Lines 7–8 contain the comment specified in the **Common Header Comments** field. As this comment says, it is repeated in the header of every file. Lines 10–12 are unique to **subsref**. Other files will contain different comments tailored for their contents. Since **subsref** deals with public variables, a listing of the public member variables is included. Lines 14–21 include the **Author Info** data, including the contents of the **author notes**. Line 22 comes from the **Revision Control Line** field. Finally, line 23 reminds you of the amount of tedious work saved by using Class Wizard. Sometimes, it is nice to know the tool version and the generation date.

Code Listing 104, Header Comments Generated by Class Wizard

```
1    function varargout = subsref(this, index)
2    %SUBSREF for class cExample, Global H1 Line
3    %  UNCLASSIFIED
4    %
```

```
5    % function varargout = subsref(this, index)
6    %
7    % A global comment that applies to all files of the example
     class.  This
8    % comment is included in every automatically generated file
     for the class.
9    %
10   % Public Member Variables
11   % Size: double (2x1): The horiz (1,1) and vert (2,1) size
     of the
12   %    shape's bounding box
13   %
14   % Author Info
15   % The ABC Corporation
16   % John Doe
17   % jd99@mail.abc.com
18   % (800) 222-1212
19   % Refactored interface 3/17/2005 Jane Doe
20   % [AHR] Added new fields 5/2/05
21   % (c) 2005
22   % RCS Info: ($Date:   $)  ($Author:   $)  ($Revision: $)
23   % A Class Wizard v.3 assembled file generated: 20-Dec-2005
     13:23:23
```

17.2.1.2 Parents ... Dialog

Clicking the **Parents** ... button brings up the dialog shown in Figure 17.5. The dialog shown in the figure contains entries for one parent class. For a new class, the fields in this dialog would be empty except for a leading **c** in the **Parent Class Name** field. Like most of the tool's dialogs, the parent dialog is organized into three sections: input fields, action buttons, and a display. In the top of the dialog, data are entered in the various text fields. In the middle, buttons are used to save data, delete a line, or go back to the previous dialog. At the bottom, input data are displayed using the same format written into the member functions.

For the parent dialog box, two data-entry fields are described by the following:

Parent Class Name: holds the name of a class that will serve as a parent. The dialog accepts more than one parent name, but each **name-varargin** pair is added separately.
varargin: holds a comma separated list of input arguments. Enter the comma-separated list exactly as it should appear in a call to the constructor. The values in the input list can be values, variable names, or function calls. A somewhat complicated example is shown in Figure 17.5. This is the same constructor value previously used to initialize corner points for **cStar** objects.

Clicking the **Save Change** button will commit the changes and display a function call to the parent-class constructor. The display shows the constructor call made during default construction of the child. The parent-constructor call doesn't make its way into generated code exactly as displayed, but functionally the result is the same. During file generation, data from these fields are written into the **parent_list** function. Parent-class names are formatted as a **cellstr** and

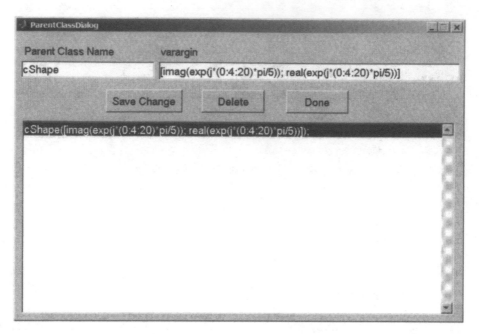

FIGURE 17.5 Class Wizard, **Parents** ... dialog.

their corresponding input arguments are formatted into a cell array. The format of the resulting code is identical to a hand-coded **parent_list**.

The **Save Change** button and two additional buttons located between the data-entry fields and the display list box cooperate to allow you to manage parent data. If parent lines already exist in the display list box, you can click on a line and it will become active. The line is highlighted and data from the line are copied into the data-entry fields. At this point, field values can be changed; however, those changes are not automatically reflected in the definition. The change must be committed by clicking the **Save Change** button. If you click anything other than **Save Change**, all changes to the line will be lost. This includes clicking another line or another button. You can also delete a parent by selecting the parent in the lower display and clicking the **Delete** button.

Establish a new parent-class dependency by selecting the first blank line in the lower display. If the list box is empty, point and click where the first line would normally appear. When you select an empty line, the **parent name** field will contain a **c** to remind you of the suggested convention. When you are finished entering data for the new parent, clicking **Save Change** will commit the new data and insert another blank line.

When you finish modifying the object's parent data, click the **Done** button. This will save your changes and return you to the main dialog. Parent-class names are shown in the list box adjacent to the **Parents** ... button. The names provide a quick summary. In the main dialog view, they are not active. You have to open the parent-class dialog to make any changes or see more detail.

17.2.1.3   Private Variable ... Dialog

Clicking the **Private Variables** ... button brings up the dialog shown in Figure 17.6. The dialog shown in the figure contains an entry for one variable. Like most of the tool's dialogs, the private-variable dialog is organized into three sections: input fields, action buttons, and a display. In Figure 17.6, the input fields contain values because a variable name in the display is selected. Selecting a blank line will insert an **m** in **Private Variable Name**, and the other fields will be blank. A leading **m** is the suggested convention for naming private member variables. The naming

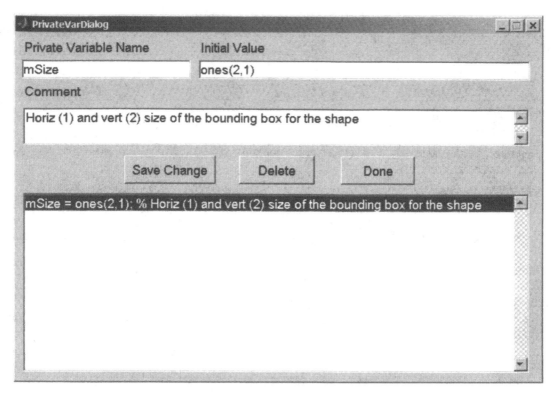

FIGURE 17.6 Class Wizard, **Private Variables** ... dialog.

convention is optional, and any legal variable name except **mDisplayFunc** can be entered in the field. The variable name **mDisplayFunc** is reserved for Class Wizard's use, and Class Wizard will include it in class code when necessary.

The three data-entry fields in the private variable dialog are described by the following:

Private Variable Name: holds the name of a private member variable. Private variables are added one at a time.

Initial Value: holds the default value that will be assigned to the variable by the constructor. The field value is entered using the exact syntax required in the assignment. The display list box formats the input exactly as it will be written into **ctor_ini.m.** What you see in the display list box is exactly what you get in **ctor_ini.m** Virtually any legal syntax can be used.

Comment: holds a text description of the variable. The text description is important because it will show up in the header of **ctor_ini.m**, where it will serve as a future reference for developers.

The three buttons, **Save Change, Delete**, and **Done**, are the same three buttons used in the parent-class dialog. Refer to §17.2.1.2 for a description of their behavior. When you finish modifying the object's parent data, click the **Done** button. This will save your changes and return you to the main dialog. Private member variable names are shown in the list box adjacent to the **Private Variables** ... button. The names provide a quick summary, and in the main dialog view they are not active. You have to open the private variable dialog to make changes or see more detail.

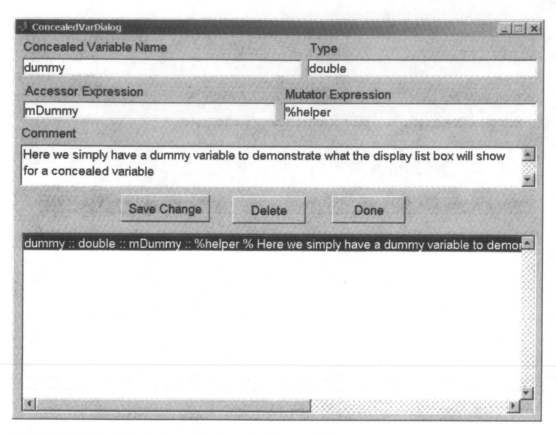

FIGURE 17.7 Class Wizard, **Concealed Variables** ... dialog.

17.2.1.4 Concealed Variables ... Dialog

Clicking the **Concealed Variables** ... button brings up the dialog shown in Figure 17.7. The dialog shown in the figure contains an entry for one variable. Like most of the tool's dialogs, the concealed variable dialog is organized into three sections: input fields, action buttons, and a display. In Figure 17.7, the input fields contain values because a variable name in the display is selected. Selecting a blank line will empty all values in the input fields. Even the name field will be empty because there is no suggested naming convention. Any legal variable name except **mDisplayFunc** can be entered in the field. The variable name **mDisplayFunc** is reserved for Class Wizard's use, and Class Wizard will include it in class code when necessary.

The five data-entry fields in the concealed variable dialog are described by the following:

Concealed Variable Name: holds the name of a concealed member variable. Concealed variables are added one at a time.

Type: holds a string that describes the variable's type. In response to **get(obj)** or **set(obj)**, concealed variables are not displayed; however, the type string is included in the header comments of several files, **get** and **set** for example.

Accessor Expression: holds the expression used for accessing the variable. The contents of this field are limited to two special cases: the exact name of a private member variable or the keyword **%helper**. When the name of a private member variable is used, direct-link accessor code is included in **get.m**. This option also allows clients to specify additional indices beyond the first dot-reference. The **%helper** keyword causes helper-function syntax (non-direct-link) to be used inside **get.m**. The **%helper** keyword also triggers the generation of a helper-function stub. The stub contains a complete header along with some initial code and comments. Accessing a concealed variable with a default helper will not cause an error, but the return value will be empty until the helper is customized.

Mutator Expression: holds the expression used for assigning values into the variable. Like the accessor, the contents of this field are limited to two special cases: the exact name of a private member variable or the keyword **%helper**. When the name of a private member variable is used, direct-link mutator code is included in **set.m**. This option also allows clients to specify additional indices beyond the first dot-reference. The **%helper** keyword causes helper-function syntax to be used inside **set.m**. The **%helper** keyword also triggers the generation of a helper-function stub. The stub contains a complete header along with some initial code and comments. Mutating a concealed variable with a default helper will not cause an error, but values in the object will not be modified until the helper is customized.

Comment: holds a text description of the variable. The text description is important because it will show up along with the variable name and variable type in various header comments, where it will serve as a reference to other developers.

In this case, the display list box does not provide a what-you-see-is-what-you-get (WYSIWYG) format. WYSIWYG is not possible because each name links to multiple files in the group-of-eight and each file uses the name differently. Instead of WYSIWYG, the display box shows individual fields separated by double colons. This achieves the goal of providing a good one-line overview without the complications involved in writing the exact syntax.

The three buttons, **Save Change**, **Delete**, and **Done**, are the same three buttons used in the parent-class dialog. Refer to §17.2.1.2 for a description of their behavior. When you finish modifying the object's concealed data, click the **Done** button. This will save your changes and return you to the main dialog. Concealed-variable names are shown in the list box adjacent to the **Concealed Variables** ... button. The names provide a quick summary, and in the main dialog view they are not active. You have to open the concealed variable dialog to make changes or see more detail.

17.2.1.5 Public Variables ... Dialog

Clicking the **Public Variables** ... button brings up the dialog shown in Figure 17.8. The dialog shown in the figure contains an entry for one variable. Like most of the tool's dialogs, the public variable dialog is organized into three sections: input fields, action buttons, and a display. In Figure 17.8, the input fields contain values because a variable name in the display is selected. Selecting a blank line will empty all values in the input fields. Even the name field will be empty because there is no suggested naming convention. Any legal variable name can be entered in the name field.

The fields in this dialog are identical to those for concealed variables because in reality the only difference is the simplified syntax used to access public variables. Public variables can be accessed or mutated using the dot-reference operator via **subsref** and **subsasgn**, while access to concealed-variables is limited to **get** and **set**. In the code, public variables are written into the public section of **get** and **set** while concealed variables are written into the concealed section. Beyond that, there is little difference between public and concealed. The five data-entry fields in the public variable dialog are as follows:

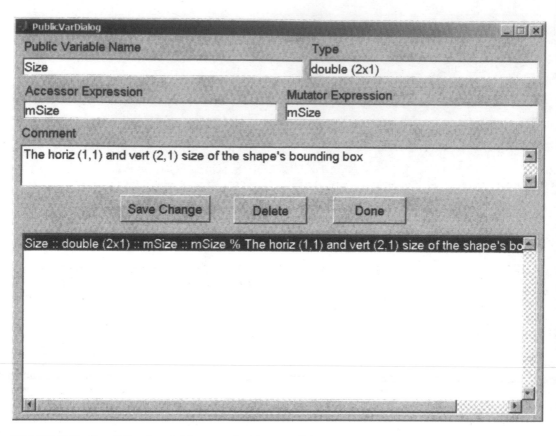

FIGURE 17.8 Class Wizard, **Public Variables** ... dialog.

Public Variable Name: holds the name of a public member variable. Public variables are added one at a time.

Type: holds a string that describes the variable's type. This string is displayed along with the variable name when **get(obj)** or **set(obj)** is used to display member variable hints. The type string also shows up in the header comments of various files, **get** and **set** for example.

Accessor Expression: holds the expression used for accessing the variable. The contents of this field are limited to two special cases: the exact name of a private member variable or the keyword **%helper**. When the name of a private member variable is used, direct-link accessor code is used inside **get.m**. This option also allows clients to specify additional indices beyond the first dot-reference. The **%helper** keyword causes helper-function syntax (non-direct-link) to be used inside **get.m**. The **%helper** keyword also triggers the generation of a helper-function stub. The stub contains a complete header along with some initial code and comments. Accessing a public variable with a default helper will not cause an error, but the return value will be empty until the helper is customized.

Mutator Expression: holds the expression used for assigning values into the variable. Like the accessor, the contents of this field are limited to two special cases: the exact name of a private member variable or the keyword **%helper**. When the name of a private member variable is used, direct-link mutator code is used inside **set.m**. This option also allows clients to specify additional indices beyond the first dot-reference. The **%helper** keyword causes helper-function syntax to be used inside **set.m**. The **%helper** keyword also triggers the generation of a helper-function stub. The stub contains a complete header along with some initial code and comments. Mutating a public variable with a default helper will not cause an error, but values in the object will not be modified until the helper is customized.

Comment: holds a text description of the variable. The text description is important because it will show up along with the variable name and variable type in various header comments, where it will serve as a reference to other developers.

In this case, the display list box does not provide a what-you-see-is-what-you-get (WYSIWYG) format. WYSIWYG is not possible because each name links to multiple files in the group of eight and each file uses the name differently. Instead of WYSIWYG, the display box shows individual fields separated by double colons. This achieves the goal of providing a good one-line overview without the complications involved in writing the exact syntax.

The three buttons, **Save Change**, **Delete**, and **Done**, are the same three buttons used in the parent-class dialog. Refer to §17.2.1.2 for a description of their behavior. When you finish modifying the object's public data, click the **Done** button. This will save your changes and return you to the main dialog. Public variable names are shown in the list box adjacent to the **Public Variables** ... button. The names provide a quick summary, and in the main dialog view they are not active. You have to open the public variable dialog to make changes or see more detail.

17.2.1.6 Constructors ... Dialog

Clicking the **Constructors** ... button brings up the dialog shown in Figure 17.9. The dialog shown in the figure contains an entry for one constructor in addition to the default. Like most of the tool's dialogs, the constructor dialog is organized into three sections: input fields, action buttons, and a display. In Figure 17.9, the lone input field contains a value because a constructor name in the display is selected. Selecting a blank line will empty this field.

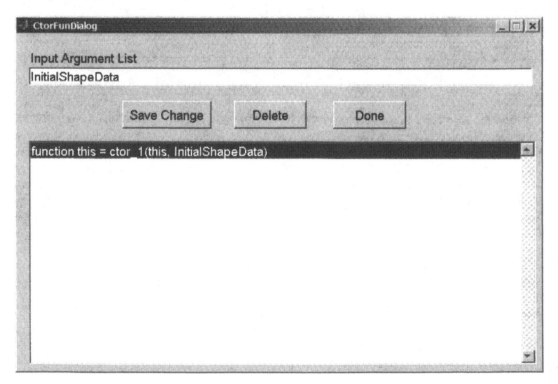

FIGURE 17.9 Class Wizard, **Constructors** ... dialog.

In the selected case, the constructor-helper function will be named **ctor_1** because there is one input argument. This is consistent with the constructor-helper naming convention previously discussed. Inputs are specified using the comma-separated list, and Class Wizard generates a stub for the helper.

The single data-entry field in the constructor dialog is described by the following:

Input Argument List: holds a comma-separated list of input arguments for each constructor-helper function. The variable name **this** should never be included in the input argument list. When files are generated, helper-function names are set according to the number of variables in each comma-separated list. The function prototype for each helper includes **this** along with the names in the comma-separated list. Functional stubs for each constructor helper are written into the class' private directory. The default stub does not know how to use the input arguments, so you must tailor each helper according to the specific application. Variables from each comma-separated list are added to the data dictionary. Comments can be associated with each dictionary name using the main dialog's **Data** menu item.

The display list box provides a WYSIWYG format for the function definition of each helper. In this case displayed in Figure 17.9, the function name is **ctor_1** because the constructor is meant for the case when an object is constructed from one input. The function prototype for **ctor_1** actually contains two inputs: **this** and the variable from the **Input Argument List** field. The object itself is passed in and out of the constructor because the whole purpose is to populate the object with values other than default. The constructor helper can modify the value's existing private variables but cannot add new fields. This helps protect the integrity of the objects.

The three buttons, **Save Change**, **Delete**, and **Done**, are the same three buttons used in the parent-class dialog. Refer to §17.2.1.2 for a description of their behavior. When you finish modifying the object's public data, click the **Done** button. This will save your changes and return you to the main dialog. Helper names are shown in the list box adjacent to the **Constructors** ... button. The names provide a quick summary, and in the main dialog view they are not active. You have to open the constructor dialog to make changes or see more detail.

17.2.1.7   More ... Dialog

Clicking the **More** ... button brings up the dialog shown in Figure 17.10. This dialog provides access to a group of data-entry dialogs for additional class features. Most of these features involve Part 3 topics; however, **Private Functions** ... and **Public Functions** ... are immediately useful. With these buttons, you can enter data for class-specific public and private functions. Dialogs are activated by respectively clicking the buttons **Public Functions** ... and **Private Functions** .... Unlike functions in the group of eight, Class Wizard does not know how to configure code for general public and private functions. Instead, Class Wizard resorts to the same strategy used for helper functions and generates a function stub. The function stub will contain a consistently formatted function call and a header that includes detailed function comments. These comments draw from the data dictionary to include information for input–output variables. As a result, the generated member functions usually have more detailed comments compared to those that are not automatically generated. The stub also includes enough code to allow the function to execute, albeit at a greatly reduced level of function.

The other buttons in the dialog represent class features that are less common but no less useful under the right circumstances. At first, the number of buttons is daunting; however, the layouts of the underlying dialogs are very similar if not identical to those we have already discussed. Entering data follows the same procedure. The data end up in slightly different locations. You already know the most important locations, and the next section discusses a few more elements.

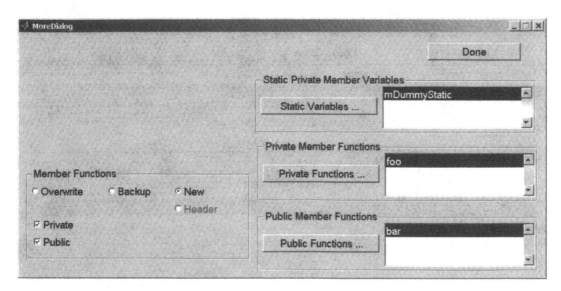

FIGURE 17.10 Class Wizard, **More** ... dialog.

17.2.1.8 Static Variables ... Dialog

Clicking the **Static Variables** ... button brings up the dialog shown in Figure 17.11. The dialog shown in the figure contains an entry for one variable. Like most of the tool's dialogs, the static variable dialog is organized into three sections: input fields, action buttons, and a display. In Figure 17.11 the input fields contain values because a variable name in the display is selected. Selecting a blank line will insert an **m** in **Static Variable Name**, and the other fields will be blank. A leading **m** shows up by default because a static variable is a special kind of private variable. The difference between static and private is scope. With a private variable, every object gets its own copy; but with a static variable, every object of the class shares one copy. If one object sets the value, that value shows up in all objects of the class.

When static variables are defined, the private helper function **static.m** is used to manage them. The interface to **static.m** is very similar to the interface defined for accessor–mutator helpers. The details are described in Chapter 20.

The three data-entry fields in the static variable dialog are described by the following:

Static Variable Name: holds the name of a static member variable. Static variables are added one at a time.

Initial Value: holds the default value that will be assigned to the variable by the constructor. The field value is entered using the exact syntax required in the assignment. The display list box formats the input exactly as it will be written into **ctor_ini.m.** What you see in the display list box is exactly what you get in **ctor_ini.m**. Virtually any legal syntax can be used.

Comment: holds a text description of the variable. The text description is important because it will show up in the header of **ctor_ini.m**, where it will serve as a future reference for developers.

The three buttons, **Save Change**, **Delete**, and **Done**, are the same three buttons used in the parent-class dialog. Refer to §17.2.1.2 for a description of their behavior. When you finish modifying the object's parent data, click the **Done** button. This will save your changes and return you to the more dialog. Static member variable names are shown in the list box adjacent to the **Static Variables** ... button. The names provide a quick summary, and in the more dialog

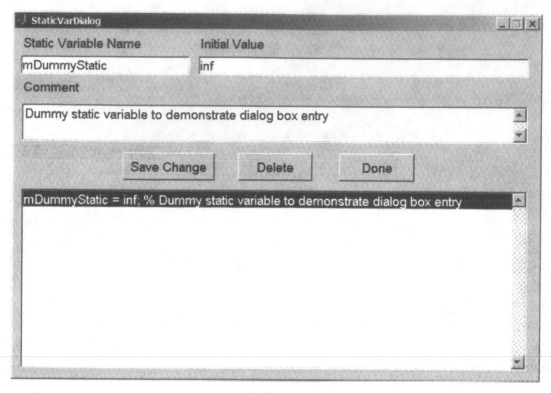

FIGURE 17.11 Class Wizard, **Static Variables** ... dialog.

view they are not active. You have to open the static variable dialog to make changes or see more detail.

17.2.1.9 Private Functions ... Dialog

Clicking the **Private Functions** ... button brings up the dialog shown in Figure 17.12. The dialog shown in the figure contains an entry for one function. Like most of the tool's dialogs, the private-function dialog is organized into three sections: input fields, action buttons, and a display. In Figure 17.12, the input fields contain values because a function name in the display is selected. Selecting a blank line will empty all values in the input fields. Even the name field will be empty because there is no suggested naming convention. Any legal function name can be entered in the name field.

In reality, constructor helpers, accessor–mutator helpers, and **parent_list.m** are private functions; however, these are part of the group-of-eight interface and are managed separately from class-specific private functions. Only class-specific private functions show up in this list.

Private functions, like most functions, can be described by a function name, a list of input arguments, a list of output arguments, and a comment. The data-entry fields for these four function elements are described by the following:

Function Name: holds the desired name for the function. Any valid function name can be used.

Input Argument List: holds a comma-separated list of input arguments for the function. If a copy of the object must be passed, **this** must be included in the argument list. By convention, when it exists, **this** should usually be the first argument in the list. In addition, notice there is no way to enter comments for individual arguments. Instead, variable names are added to the data dictionary using the **Data** menu on the main screen.

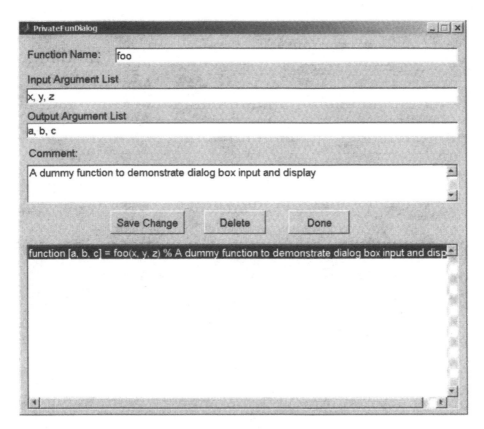

FIGURE 17.12 Class Wizard, **Private Function** ... dialog.

> **Output Argument List**: holds a comma-separated list of output arguments for the function. If a copy of the object is passed, **this** must be included in the argument list. By convention, when it exists, **this** should usually be the first argument in the argument list. As with variables in the input argument list, output variable names are added to the data dictionary.
>
> **Comment**: holds a text description of the function. The text description will be added to the header comments when the function is generated.

Clicking the **Save Change** button commits the changes and displays the function prototype in WYSIWYG format. During file generation, Class Wizard writes the same function prototype into the private function and follows the prototype with header comments. Of course, Class Wizard doesn't know how to write the real function body, but it can write a body that runs without error. The body of the private function must be manually modified to include the desired class-specific functionality.

The three buttons, **Save Change**, **Delete**, and **Done**, are the same three buttons used in the parent-class dialog. Refer to §17.2.1.2 for a description of their behavior. When you finish modifying the object's private-function data, click the **Done** button. This will save your changes and return you to the more dialog. Private-function names are shown in the list box adjacent to the **Private Functions** ... button. The names provide a quick summary, and in the more dialog view they are not active. You have to open the private-function dialog to make changes or see more detail.

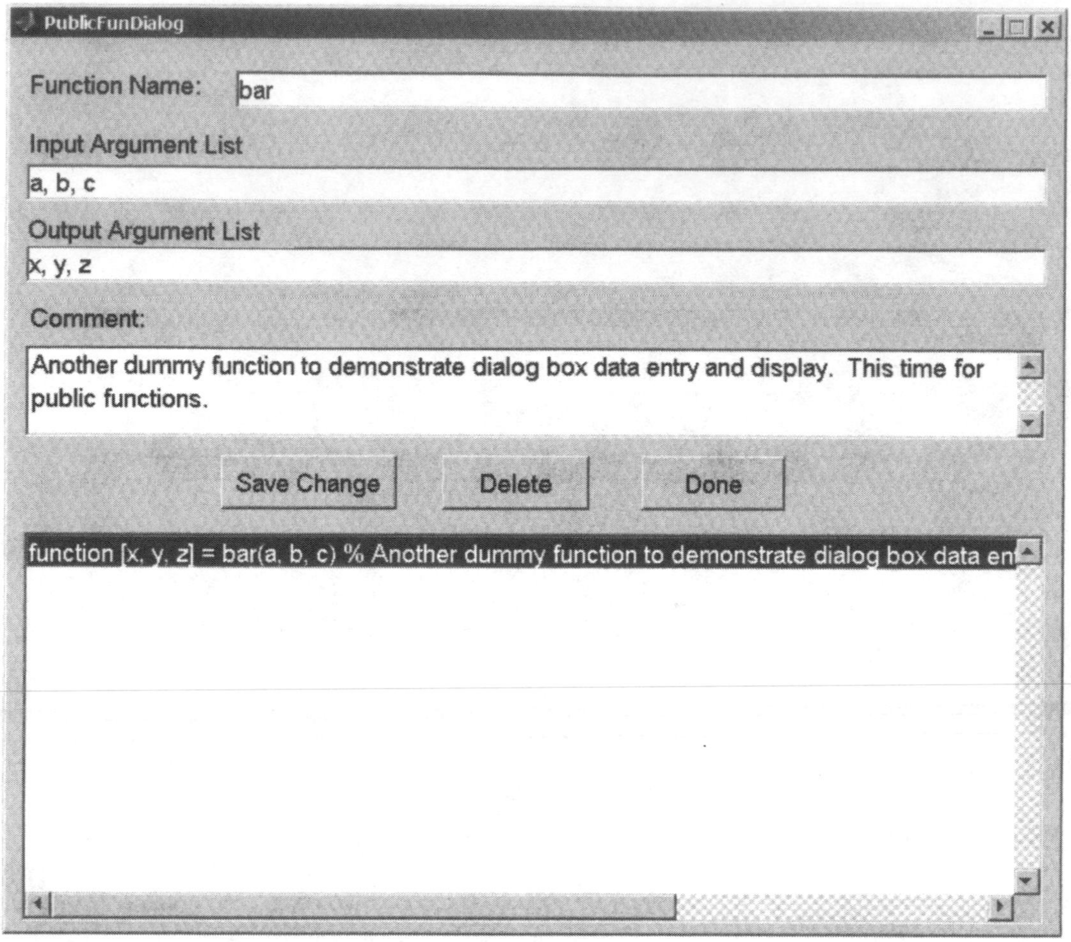

FIGURE 17.13 Class Wizard, **Public Function** ... dialog.

17.2.1.10 Public Functions ... Dialog

Clicking the **Public Functions** ... button brings up the dialog shown in Figure 17.13. The dialog shown in the figure contains an entry for one function. Like most of the tool's dialogs, the public-function dialog is organized into three sections: input fields, action buttons, and a display. In Figure 17.13, the input fields contain values because a function name in the display is selected. Selecting a blank line will empty all values in the input fields. Even the name field will be empty because there is no suggested naming convention. Any legal function name can be entered in the name field.

In reality, standard group-of-eight functions are public functions; however, group-of-eight functions are managed separately from class-specific public functions. Only class-specific public functions show up in this list.

Public functions, like most functions, can be described by a function name, a list of input arguments, a list of output arguments, and a comment. The data-entry fields for these four function elements are described by the following:

Function Name: holds the desired name for the function. Any valid function name can be used.

Input Argument List: holds a comma-separated list of input arguments for the function. If a copy of the object must be passed, **this** must be included in the argument list. By convention, when it exists, **this** should usually be the first argument in the list. In addition, notice there is no way to enter comments for individual arguments. Instead, variable names are added to the data dictionary using the **Data** menu on the main screen.

Output Argument List: holds a comma-separated list of output arguments for the function. If a copy of the object is passed, **this** must be included in the argument list. By convention, when it exists, **this** should usually be the first argument in the argument list. As with variables in the input argument list, output variable names are added to the data dictionary.

Comment: holds a text description of the function. The text description will be added to the header comments when the function is generated.

Clicking the **Save Change** button commits the changes and displays the function prototype in WYSIWYG format. During file generation, Class Wizard writes the same function prototype into the private function and follows the prototype with header comments. Of course, Class Wizard doesn't know how to write the real function body, but it can write a body that runs without error. The body of the private function must be manually modified to include the desired class-specific functionality.

The three buttons, **Save Change**, **Delete**, and **Done**, are the same three buttons used in the parent-class dialog. Refer to §17.2.1.2 for a description of their behavior. When you finish modifying the object's public-function data, click the **Done** button. This will save your changes and return you to the more dialog. Public-function names are shown in the list box adjacent to the **Public Functions** ... button. The names provide a quick summary, and in the more dialog view they are not active. You have to open the public-function dialog to make changes or see more detail.

17.2.1.11 File Menu

The main Class Wizard dialog has two menu items: **File** and **Data**. The **File** menu allows you to create a **New** class definition, **Open** ... an existing definition, **Save** the current definition, or **Save as** ... to save the current definition using a different file name. These menu items behave the same as any application that opens and saves files. Their behaviors are described as follows:

File::New: Select this item to begin a new class definition. The hot-key sequence is **ctrl-N**. All fields are reset to default initial values, usually empty. Currently, using **File::New** does not check for changes to the currently loaded values before loading a new file. You will not be warned to save your changes.

File::Open ...: Selecting this item allows you to open an existing file using the standard file-open dialog box. The hot-key combination is **ctrl-O**. This familiar dialog is shown in Figure 17.14. The file format for definition files is **.mat**. This format is convenient because it allows you to load the definition file directly in MATLAB and tweak the data in ways not available through Class Wizard.

File::Save: Selecting this item saves the current class definition file to the current file name. The hot-key sequence is **ctrl-S**. If there is no current filename, you will be prompted to enter one.

File::Save As ...: Selecting this item opens a standard dialog box for specifying the file name during a save. The hot-key sequence is **ctrl-A**. The familiar dialog is shown in Figure 17.15. The definition file can be stored anywhere; however, the best location is in the class directory. When class functions are generated, the definition file is automatically saved in the same directory as the functions.

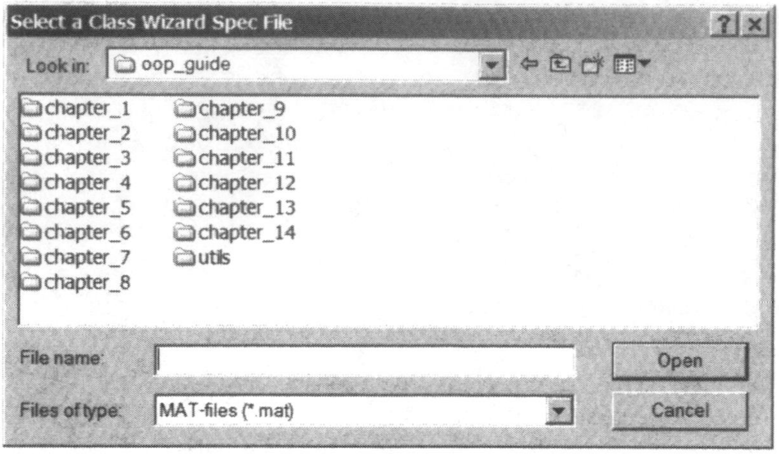

FIGURE 17.14 Class Wizard, standard File::Open ... dialog.

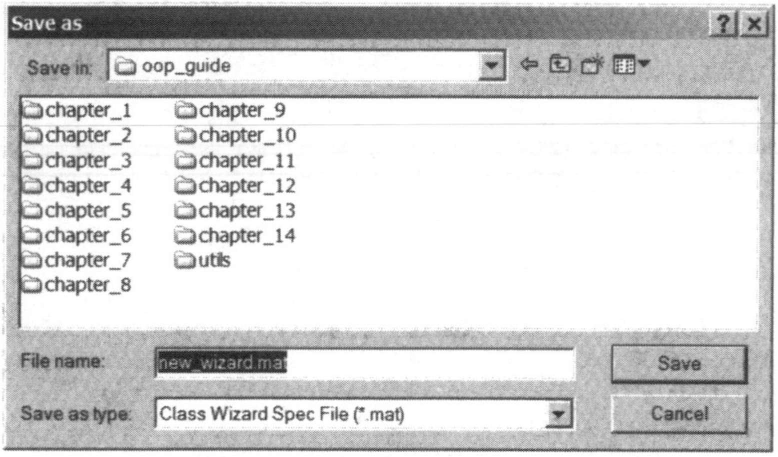

FIGURE 17.15 Class Wizard, standard File::Save As ... dialog.

17.2.1.12   Data Menu

In most class definitions, the same variable names are used in several functions. Rather than commenting these variables in several places, a data dictionary approach collects the variables into a central location. That way, comments only need to be entered once; and from there, Class Wizard can perform the tedious task of repeating the comments into each header. The **Data** menu is used to enter type and comment information for the function arguments defined for constructor helper functions, public functions, and private functions. The information entered through **Data::Dictionary ...** are written into header comments when the file is generated. The **Data::Dictionary ...** dialog is shown in Figure 17.16.

Like most of the tool's dialogs, the data dictionary dialog is organized into three sections: input fields, action buttons, and a display. In Figure 17.16, the input fields contain values because a variable name in the display is selected. The **Variable Name** field is grayed out because the name of the variable cannot be changed. This also means that new names can't be added to the definition via the dictionary. Names can only be added by defining a new name in a function call. Data in the other fields can be modified to reflect the appropriate descriptions. The three data fields in the data dictionary variable dialog are described by the following:

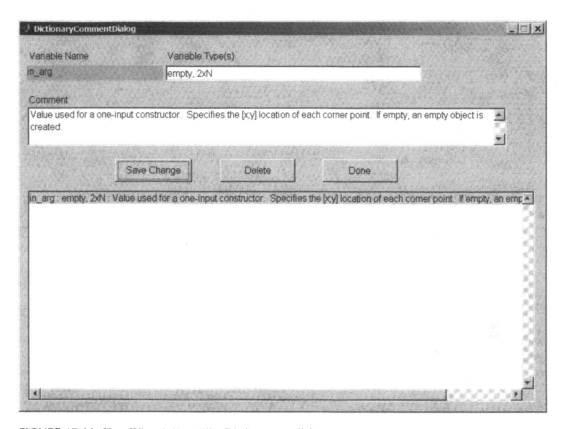

FIGURE 17.16 Class Wizard, Data File::Dictionary ... dialog.

Variable Name: displays the name of the variable. This name can't be changed because it is linked to the definition of one or more member functions.

Variable Type(s): holds a comma-separated list of types expected. Any descriptive text can be entered in this field. The text is not used to generate code, but rather it is used to comment on the variable in the header of every function where it is used. The field is intended to be a description of the allowed types.

Comment: holds a string description pertaining to the variable. This comment is copied into the header comments for each function that uses the variable in its input argument list.

The three buttons, **Save Change**, **Delete**, and **Done**, are the same three buttons used in the parent-class dialog. Refer to §17.2.1.2 for a description of their behavior. When you finish modifying the object's parent data, click the **Done** button. This will save your changes and return you to the main dialog.

17.2.1.13   Build Class Files Button

After entering class data, class files are generated by clicking the **Build Class Files** button. This button first displays the standard dialog that allows you to select the directory where the files should be written. The dialog includes a button that allows you to create a new class directory. Don't forget to include **@** in the directory name. An example view of the dialog is shown in Figure 17.17.

Selecting a directory and clicking **OK** allows Class Wizard to generate the collection of class files. In addition to generating class functions, the class definition file is also saved in the selected directory in **mat-file** format. The group-of-eight files are completely functional, and

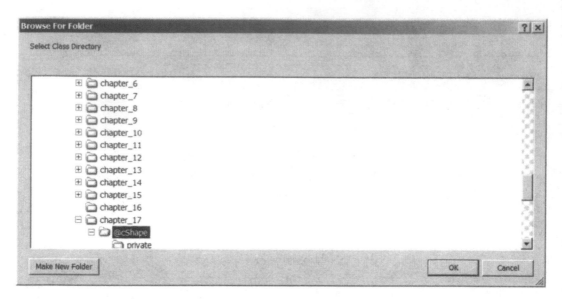

FIGURE 17.17 Class Wizard, **Build Class Files** dialog.

class-specific member functions exist as simple function stubs. If new public or private member variables need to be added, it is a simple process to reload the definition file, add the new variables, and rebuild the files. The class organization and default wizard settings make this possible.

17.3 SUMMARY

For building a robust MATLAB class, Class Wizard has no equal. The various dialog screens are organized along the same divisions used to describe an object-oriented design. This makes data entry much less of a chore. Once the design data are entered, Class Wizard builds a full implementation of the group of eight and takes care of some of the more mundane details. In short, Class Wizard allows you to focus on the design and on the application-specific aspects of the class.

There are several ways that Class Wizard can be used in a development environment. The least effective way is to use Class Wizard to generate an initial set of class functions and then never use it again. I don't recommend this approach because it is very difficult to keep all of the various files in synch. The file dependency graph in Figure 17.2 is too complicated. Some changes seem easy, but eventually, something will be omitted or updated incorrectly. It is easy and much safer to let Class Wizard manage changes to the group of eight.

One viable approach is to enter only parent, constructor, and variable information into Class Wizard. This allows Class Wizard to manage changes to group-of-eight functions while you manage private and public member functions outside of the group of eight. You lose the advantage of uniform headers and variable descriptions, but that might be an acceptable trade-off in some development environments. For a well-documented class, these data will still need to be entered; however, they do not have to be entered through Class Wizard fields. Keeping default check box and radio button selections and never entering data for private and public member variables enable this approach.

The third approach extends definition data to include names and arguments for public and private functions. Comments associated with arguments should also be documented in the data dictionary. The first time a class-specific function is generated, the header will include a complete set of comments. After that, selecting **new** will prevent the file from being overwritten. It would be nice to be able to regenerate header comments yet leave the files code intact. That way the definition would always be consistent with the Class Wizard–generated section of each file. That capability does not currently exist, but there are plans for future upgrades that will fill this and other known deficiencies.

In this chapter, we focused on the mechanics of entering data into Class Wizard. There are some idiosyncrasies due to Guide, but overall the GUI interface makes it much easier to enter data and keep the design organized. Data contained in individual dialogs mirror the implementation model discussed throughout the first two sections of this book. The functions generated from data entered through these dialogs also mirror the code developed in the first two sections. In the next chapter, we will redevelop the complete **cShape** example using Class Wizard. Differences in development time and coding accuracy will be very apparent.

17.4 INDEPENDENT INVESTIGATIONS

1. Open Class Wizard (the command is **class_wizard**) and enter a few variables and functions.
2. Practice saving and loading definition files. You can use the **.mat** files for Chapter 18 and get a preview of the next chapter.
3. Navigate into the Header Info dialog box and enter your pertinent information. Use the **Default Header Info** menu to save the data for future reference.
4. After entering some data, select **Build Class Files** and follow the process. After building the files, inspect a few of them and note their close similarity to the standard idioms.

18 Class Wizard Versions of the Shape Hierarchy

In Chapter 17, we covered Class Wizard's various input dialogs along with their general operation. In this chapter, we demonstrate the complete Class Wizard process of developing a collection of classes. To do this, we will recreate our now familiar collection of classes that includes **cLine-Style**, **cShape**, **cStar**, and **cDiamond**. Creating a collection of familiar classes is important because it allows us to spot logical errors. It also allows us to compare automatically generated files with the handcrafted versions. The collection also includes a rich hierarchy with both parent–child inheritance and composition. This is important because the hierarchy exercises most of the available options.

The primary activity in this chapter involves entering data into the various Class Wizard dialog screens. As data are entered, the lower-list box in each dialog shows a line-by-line summary of the data. To assist you in data entry, a screen shot of each completed dialog is included. That way, all variables and functions are provided as you will see them displayed on your screen. The syntax of each line in the lower-list box is easy, and converting from the display to individual fields quickly becomes obvious. If the translation isn't clear, you can always refer back to Chapter 17. In addition, a shorthand table description of the data in each field is provided.

The first step is of course entering data. The second step allows Class Wizard to generate class files. At this point, group-of-eight functions are fully functional. Objects can be created and displayed, and direct-link public variables can be accessed and mutated. Even so, this is not the final step. Some files will require postgeneration tailoring. The list of files includes most of the public and private functions that give each class their unique behavior. Enter the names and arguments for these functions, and Class Wizard will give you a head start by generating the initial version. The initial version contains full header comments but not much more. For example, a description for **draw** can be included in the **Public Functions** dialog, but until it is tailored, calling **draw** will not do anything. The implementation isn't complete until code for the application-specific member functions has been added. The example code for this chapter includes a copy of the as-generated files in a directory separate from the full solution.

18.1 CLINESTYLE CLASS WIZARD DEFINITION DATA

Begin by running the graphical interface for Class Wizard. To do this, the directory **/utils/wizard_gui** must be on or added to the MATLAB path. You can add the path in one of three ways: **cd** into the directory, use an **addpath** command, or use MATLAB's **File::Set Path** menu item. After adding the directory, the command to run Class Wizard is simply

```
>> class_wizard
```

The current version accepts no input arguments. The **class_wizard** command opens the main Class Wizard dialog with empty fields and default options. You must now fill in fields that describe your particular class definition. After doing this for **cLineStyle**, the main dialog will look like Figure 18.1. The full definition file can be found in **chapter_17/@cLineStyle/cLineStyle.mat**. You can follow along and enter data, but if data entry becomes too tedious, you can load the full **.mat** file at any time. Similarly, the definition files for the other classes are located in their respective class directories. As with the other chapters, the class directories under chapter_17

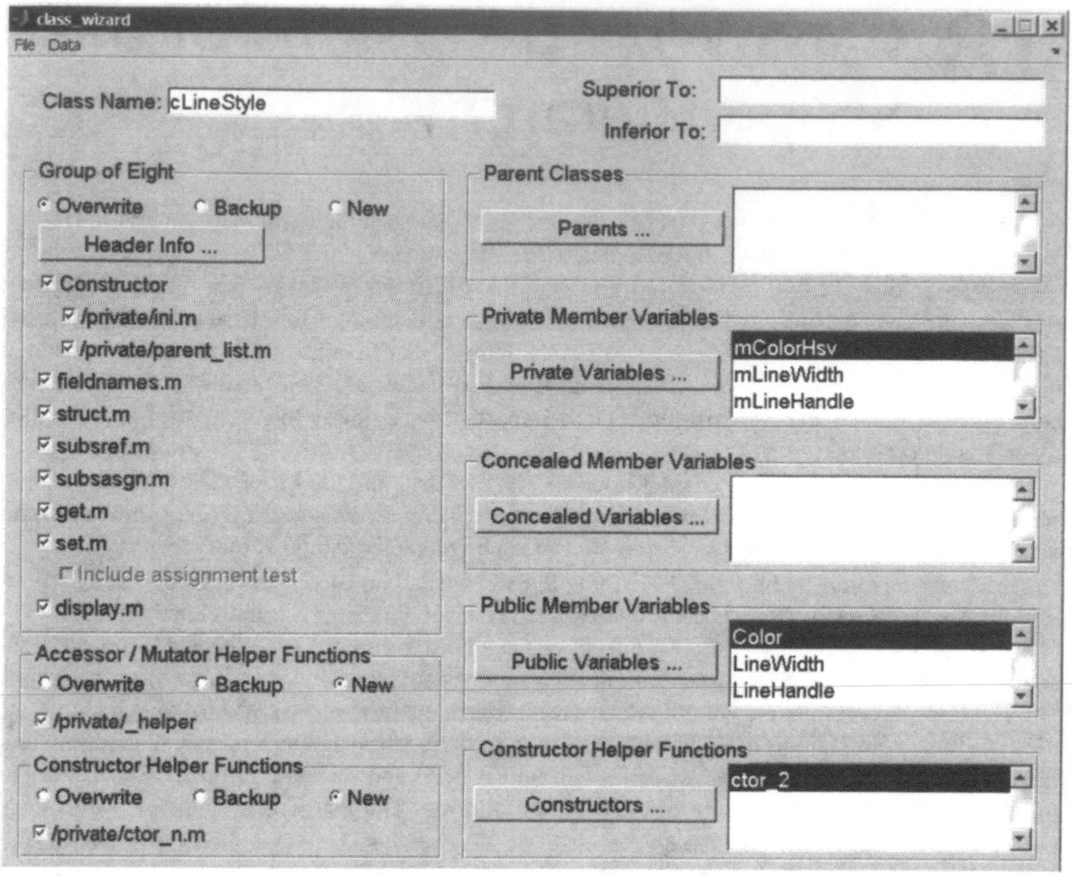

FIGURE 18.1 Class Wizard, main dialog for cLineStyle.

are fully functional. Since these directories become fully functional only after tailoring, a copy of the files prior to tailoring can be found in the class directories under **chapter_17/as_generated**.

Open a new session of Class Wizard and type in **cLineStyle** as the class name. Leave the other fields on the main dialog blank or filled with their default values. This gives Class Wizard control over the group of eight (**Overwrite**) and allows Class Wizard to generate other files only when the definition data are new (**New**). The remaining definition data are entered into each corresponding dialog. Dialog order doesn't matter, and each dialog can be opened and changed any number of times. In the text that follows, a separate subsection is devoted to each dialog.

18.1.1 cLineStyle Header Info

A good place to begin is the header info dialog. Click the **Header Info ...** button and enter the data shown in the various fields of Figure 18.2. Of course, you can replace the example text with your own name, company information, and so on. After entering all header information, save the fields for future use. Before clicking **Okay**, select the menu item Default Header Info::Save. There are no prompts; however, the fields contained in the dialog are now stored in the file **default_header.mat** located in the same directory as **class_wizard.m**. For a new class, you can recall the fields by opening the **header info** dialog and selecting **Default Header Info::Load**.

Dialog names associated with each field are merely a suggestion because Class Wizard doesn't inspect the values. All fields use a free format, and you can commandeer any field to write other

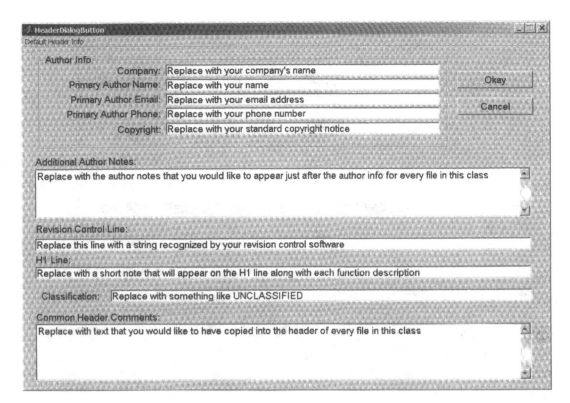

FIGURE 18.2 Class Wizard, cLineStyle header information dialog.

information into the files. In the header, each string gets a comment delimiter and the order of appearance is fixed. Once you figure out where each string is written, you will be able to bend the header information to your specific needs. A little later when we look at specific code examples, we can observe the header output. For now, simply click **Okay** to commit the data and return to the main dialog. If you click **Cancel**, you will return to the main dialog but changes will not be committed.

18.1.2 cLineStyle Private Variables

The next dialog we will visit defines the private variables. Click the **Private Variables** ... button and enter the data shown in Figure 18.3. Initially, the lower display will be empty. If the first blank line in the lower display block is not highlighted, select the first empty line by clicking on it. The data fields are active, and you can start entering private variable data. After entering **mColorHsv** data, click the **Save Change** button to commit the changes. The data are displayed in WYSIWYG format in the display box, and the selection moves to an empty line. Follow the same procedure to enter data for the other private variables. The field data are summarized in Table 18.1.

As you enter data, the contents of the lower display are almost identical to the code included in **ctor_ini.m**. Even the default-value assignment is correctly formatted. The **Initial Value** string is copied verbatim into the display and into **ctor_ini.m**. Virtually any value that can be written on the right-hand side of an assignment can be used as an initial value. For example, a function call generates the initial value for **mColorHsv**. Click **Done** to commit the changes and return to the main dialog.

When Class Wizard generates **/@cLineStyle/private/ctor_ini**, the private variable names and their default values are included in the code. The names and comments are included in the header. If you return to the main screen and click **Build Class Files**, Class Wizard will generate the file **@cLineStyle/private/ctor_ini.m** shown in Code Listing 105. Other files will also be generated, but **ctor_ini** is the current focus.

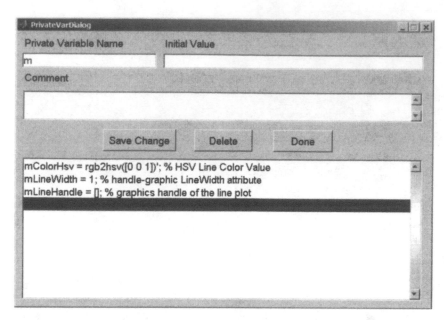

FIGURE 18.3 Class Wizard, cLineStyle private variable dialog.

TABLE 18.1
cLineStyle Private Variable Dialog Fields

Private Variable Name	Initial Value	Comment
mColorHsv	rgb2hsv ([0 0 1])'	[H; S; V] color of border; default is blue
mLineWidth	1	handle graphic LineWidth attribute
mLineHandle	[]	graphics handle of the line plot

Code Listing 105, Constructor Helper from Class Wizard, @cLineStyle/private/ctor_ini.m

```
1    function [this, superior, inferior] = ctor_ini
2    %CTOR_INI for class cLineStyle, Replace with a short note ...
3    % Replace with something like UNCLASSIFIED
4    %
5    % function [this, superior, inferior] = ctor_ini
6    %
7    % Replace with text that you would like to have copied into
     the header of
8    % every file in this class
9    %
10   % Private Member Variables
11   % mColorHsv: HSV Line Color Value
12   % mLineWidth: handle-graphic LineWidth attribute
13   % mLineHandle: graphics handle of the line plot
```

```
14  %
15  % Author Info
16  % Replace with your company's name
17  % Replace with your name
18  % Replace with your email address
19  % Replace with your phone number
20  % Replace with the author notes that you would like to
       appear just after
21  % the author info for every file in this class
22  % Replace with your standard copyright notice
23  % Replace with a string recognized by your revision control
       software
24  % A Class Wizard v.3 assembled file, generated: 20-Dec-2005
       13:23:23
25
26  % piece-meal create to avoid object and cell problems
27  this = struct([]);
28  this(1).mColorHsv = rgb2hsv([0 0 1])';
29  this(1).mLineWidth = 1;
30  this(1).mLineHandle = [];
31  this(1).mDisplayFunc = []; % class-wizard reserved field
32  % Construct the parent classes, if any
33  parents = cell(0, 1);
34  % Initialize parent_list
35  parent_list(parents{:});
36  % Return desired superior and inferior arguments
37  superior = {};
38  inferior = {};
39  % Replace with something like UNCLASSIFIED
```

Line 1 contains the function definition and lines 2–24 contain the header comments. Line 2 identifies the class and function along with a truncated one-line description. For this line to be meaningful, the header-info defined **H1 Line** field needs to be short and the first few words of the function comment should be concise. Line 3 and line 32 contain the **classification** string. Line 5 repeats the function definition because **help** does not automatically display it. Lines 7–8 contain the contents of the **Common Header Comments** field from header info. Lines 10–13 list the private variables and their comments. The remaining header comments are generated from various fields in header info. Lines 26–38 are code; here the private structure is created and private variables are added and initialized. Notice the private variable **mDisplayFunc** in line 31. This variable was not in the private variable list, but it shows up in the default constructor because **cLineStyle** has no parents. If you compare Code Listing 105 with **ctor_ini** from Chapter 16, the code lines are identical.

18.1.3 cLineStyle Public Variables

Moving down the collection of dialog buttons brings us to the public variables. Click the **Public Variables** ... button and enter the data shown in Figure 18.4. Fresh from the previous

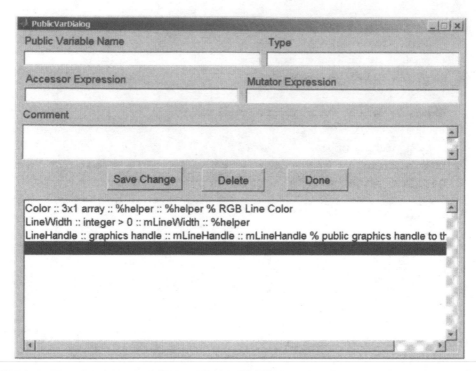

FIGURE 18.4 Class Wizard, cLineStyle public variable dialog.

exercise of entering private variables in §18.1.2, the fields **Name** and **Comment** are familiar. The **type**, **accessor**, and **mutator** fields are new.

The **type** field serves two purposes. First, with the exception of **display**, the public name and its type string are copied into all group-of-eight headers. Second, the type string is displayed as a hint when **set** is called with one argument. That also means the type string is copied into the **-possible case** inside **fieldnames**.

Accessor Expression and **Mutator Expression** fields guide the generation of public cases inside **get.m** and **set.m**. If the **Expression** field contains the name of a private variable, direct-access code syntax will be inserted into **get** or **set**. If the **Expression** field contains the string **%helper**, helper-function syntax will be inserted into **get** or **set**, and a stub for the helper will be generated. Finally, if the **Expression** field is empty, a public case for the variable is not included. The **Accessor Expression** value and **Mutator Expression** value are independent. **Accessor Expression** influences the code in **get** and **Mutator Expression** influences the code in **set**. In addition, public variables with an empty **Accessor Expression** value are not included in **fieldnames** or **struct**.

All public variables in **cLineStyle** have accessors. The accessor for **Color** uses a helper, but accessors for **LineWidth** and **LineHandle** are directly linked to **mLineWidth** and **mLineHandle**. All public variables also have mutators. In this case, the mutator for **LineWidth** is not a direct link but rather uses a helper. The table of entries for the public variables is given in Table 18.2.

The procedure for data entry follows the same procedure used for private variables. Select the first empty line in the lower display block, and enter data in the fields. After all field values have been specified, click **Save Change** to commit the data and move to the next line. In this dialog, the lower display can't be easily formatted using standard MATLAB syntax. Instead, the lower display delimits each field by putting two colons between each value. The display order is name, type, accessor, mutator, and comment. When you have finished all additions or modifications, click **Done** to commit the changes and return to the main dialog.

TABLE 18.2
cLineStyle Public Member Variable Field Values

Public Variable Name	Type	Accessor Expression	Mutator Expression	Comment
`Color`	`(3x1) array`	`%helper`	`%helper`	`RGB line color`
`LineWidth`	`integer > 0`	`mLineWidth`	`%helper`	
`LineHandle`	`graphics handle`	`mLineHandle`	`mLineHandle`	`Public graphics handle to the line plot`

If you compare the generated group-of-eight files with files from Chapter 16, the code lines are identical. Because of this, you will have no trouble relating the code to discussions in the previous chapters. Ideally, you will never need to hand tailor any function in the group of eight, but if do, you should have no trouble finding your way.

Accessor and mutator helper functions are another matter. These private functions require tailoring because the dialog data do not include any information that could be used to generate class-specific code. The functions include header information and they include code stubs that allow them to work without error. This allows group-of-eight mechanics to be tested prior to tailoring, but the class is not fully functional until afterward. We revisit the topic of helper file tailoring in §18.1.7.

18.1.4 CLINESTYLE CONSTRUCTOR FUNCTIONS

The final data-entry button on the main dialog defines constructors. The **cLineStyle** class uses a two-argument constructor to assign values for **Color** and **LineWidth**. Click the **Constructors ...** button to display the dialog shown in Figure 18.5. To define a new constructor, the

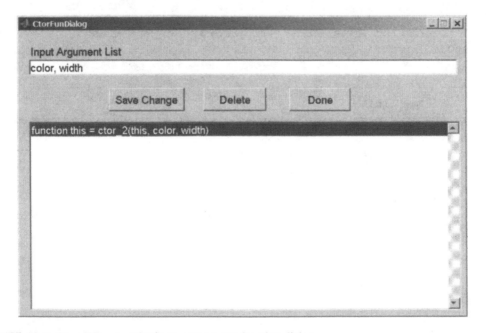

FIGURE 18.5 Class Wizard, cLineStyle constructor function dialog.

only data required are a comma-separated list of input variable names. The function name is created based on the number of variables. The comma-separated variable list is entered in the **Input Argument List** field. Any valid variable name except **this** can be used in the list.

For this example, we don't need a table of dialog values. Select the first empty line in the lower display. Then type **color, width** into the **Input Argument List** field. When you are done, click **Save Change** to commit the data. Finally, click **Done** to return to the main dialog.

During file generation, Class Wizard will use this data to generate a function stub named **private/ctor_2.m**. The stub contents are shown in Code Listing 106. The comma-separated list from the definition data shows up in the input argument list of the function definition. These variable names also show up in the header on lines 12 and 14. The comments list them as having no type info and no description because data dictionary data for these variables do not yet exist. The generated code is found in lines 27–31. The function will run; however, until it is tailored, line 29 will display a warning. The helper can be tailored by copying code from the Chapter 16 version.

Code Listing 106, Two-Input Class Wizard Constructor, @cLineStyle/private/ctor_2.m
function this = ctor_2(this, color, width)

```
1    function this = ctor_2(this, color, width)
2    %CTOR_2 for class cLineStyle, Replace with a short note ...
3    %  Replace with something like UNCLASSIFIED
4    %
5    % function this = ctor_2(this, color, width)
6    %
7    % Replace with text that you would like to have copied into
     the header of
8    % every file in this class
9    %
10   % Input Arguments::
11   %
12   % color: no type info: no description provided
13   %
14   % width: no type info: no description provided
15   %
16   % Author Info
17   % Replace with your company's name
18   % Replace with your name
19   % Replace with your email address
20   % Replace with your phone number
21   % Replace with the author notes that you would like to appear
     just after
22   % the author info for every file in this class
23   % Replace with your standard copyright notice
24   % Replace with a string recognized by your revision control
     software
25   % A Class Wizard v.3 assembled file, generated: 20-Dec-2005
     13:23:23
26
```

```
27  %  \/   \/   \/   \/
28  %  replace with your specific constructor code
29  warning('OOP:incompleteFunction', ...
30     'The function definition is incomplete');
31  %  /\   /\   /\   /\
32  %  Replace with something like UNCLASSIFIED
```

18.1.5 cLineStyle Data Dictionary

At this point in the definition, public and private variables are defined and an additional constructor is available. From the main screen, you could generate all required files for a fully functioning **cLineStyle** class. But don't click **Build Class Files** because there is one more dialog that needs attention. We need to add comments so the header inside **ctor_2** will contain meaningful comments for its input arguments.

On the menu bar of the main dialog, select **Data::Dictionary** .... This selection will display the dialog shown in Figure 18.6. These fields are similar to the same fields in the public variable dialog. Initially the lower display should include the variable names **color** and **width** but there will be no type or comments. The variable names in the lower display were collected from the argument definitions used to define constructors, public functions, and private functions. Since **cLineStyle** uses the standard set of public and private functions, the list only includes constructor arguments. The data dictionary dialog can't be used to add variables. Variables are added automatically based on function definitions.

The type and comment data you need are provided in Table 18.3. Select each variable by pointing to its line in the lower display and clicking. The field values are now active and can be modified. Click **Save Change** to commit the changes before selecting the next name. After entering all the data, click **Done** to return to the main dialog. Now if you generate the files, the header in **ctor_2** will contain meaningful comments. The affected lines now look like the following:

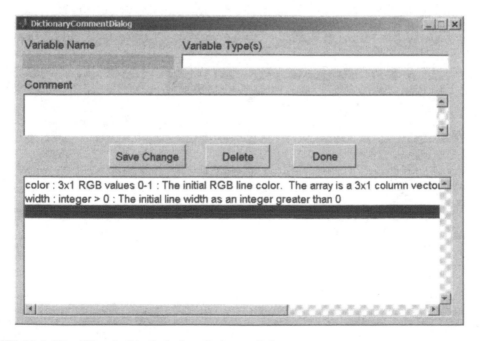

FIGURE 18.6 Class Wizard, cLineStyle data dictionary dialog.

TABLE 18.3
cLineStyle Data Dictionary Field Values

Variable Name	Type	Comment
color	3x1 RGB values 0-1	The initial RGB line color. The array is a 3x1 column vector of values and the values range from zero to one.
width	integer > 0	The initial line width as an integer greater than 0

```
%  Input Arguments::
%
%    color: 3x1 RGB values 0-1: The initial RGB line color.  The
%      array is a 3x1 column vector of values and the values
%      range from zero to one.
%
%    width: integer > 0: The initial line width as an integer
%      greater than 0
```

18.1.6 cLineStyle Build Class Files

The definition for **cLineStyle** is now complete. Click **Build Class Files** to begin class file generation. You always need to specify a destination class directory. MATLAB's standard directory-selection dialog is used. An example of the dialog is shown in Figure 18.7. Simply highlight the desired directory and click **OK.** If a suitable directory does not exist, the **Make New Folder** button on the lower left will allow you to create one. When you click **OK**, Class Wizard

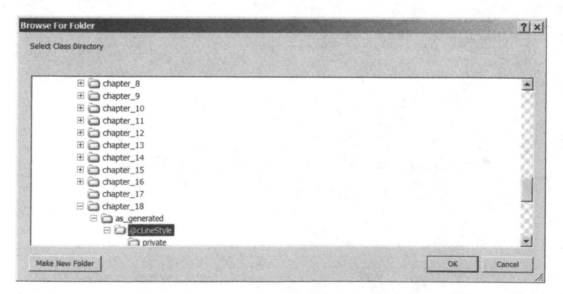

FIGURE 18.7 Class Wizard, cLineStyle directory-selection dialog.

generates class files. File generation is very fast. Click **Okay** on the confirmation dialog to return to the main Class Wizard dialog. The newly generated class should work without error; however, a couple of helper functions need to be tailored before the class will achieve full functionality. These functions are discussed next.

18.1.7 cLineStyle Accessor and Mutator Helper Functions

In **cLineStyle** three private helper functions need to be tailored. The first is **ctor_2**, a private constructor helper. The as-generated file was shown in Code Listing 106. Modifying the as-generated file is easy because we can copy the code body from the working version in Chapter 16. Refer to Code Listing 89 to see the complete function body.

Code bodies for the other two helpers, **Color_helper** and **LineWidth_helper**, can also be copied from Chapter 16. After copying the code bodies, **cLineStyle** is complete. The tailored versions of **Color_helper** and **LineWidth_helper** are also included in this chapter's source files. Before moving to the other classes, let's look at the initial helper-file stub. The as-generated version of **Color_helper** is shown in Code Listing 107. The listing consists mostly of comments, but there are some important lines of code in each **case**.

Code Listing 107, Public Variable Helper, as Generated by Class Wizard, cLineStyle::Color_helper

```
1    function [do_sub_indexing, do_assignin, this, varargout] =
     ...
2     Color_helper(which, this, index, varargin)
3    %COLOR_HELPER for class cLineStyle, Replace with a short
     note ...
4    % Replace with something like UNCLASSIFIED
5    %
6    % function [do_sub_indexing, do_assignin, this, varargout]
     = ...
7    % Color_helper(which, this, index, varargin)
8    %
9    % Replace with text that you would like to have copied into
     the header
10   % of every file in this class
11   %
12   % Author Info
13   % Replace with your company's name
14   % Replace with your name
15   % Replace with your email address
16   % Replace with your phone number
17   % Replace with the author notes that you would like to appear
     just
18   % after the author info for every file in this class
19   % Replace with your standard copyright notice
20   % Replace this line with a string for your revision control
     software
21   % A Class Wizard v.3 assembled file, generated: 18-Jan-2006
     13:18:46
```

```
22   %
23
24   switch which
25     case 'get'   % ACCESSOR
26       % input: index contains any additional indexing as a
            substruct
27       % input: varargin empty for accessor
28       do_sub_indexing = true;   % tells get.m whether to index
            deeper
29       do_assignin = false;   % leave false until you read book
            section 3
30       varargout = cell(1, nargout-3); % -3, 3 known vars plus
            varargout
31       % \/   \/   \/   \/
32       % YOUR 'GET/ACCESSOR' HELPER CODE GOES HERE
33       % e.g., [varargout{:}] = {function of public and private
            vars};
34        warning('OOP:incompleteFunction', ...
35        'The function definition is incomplete');
36       % /\   /\   /\   /\
37     case 'set'   % MUTATOR
38       % input: index contains any additional indexing as a
            substruct
39       % input: varargin contains values to be assigned into
            the object
40       do_sub_indexing = false;   % always false, mutator _must_
            index
41       do_assignin = false;   % leave false until you read book
            section 3
42       varargout = {}; % 'set' returns nothing in varargout
43       % \/   \/   \/   \/
44       % YOUR 'SET/MUTATOR' HELPER CODE GOES HERE
45       warning('OOP:incompleteFunction', ...
46       'The function definition is incomplete');
47       % below is a code template as a convenient starting point
48       % if isempty(index) % No more indexing requested, assign
            input
49       %  [this.Color] = deal(varargin{:});
50       % else  % deeper indexing requested, use subsasgn to do it
51       %  Color = [this.Color];   % Modify the assignment
52       %  Color = subsasgn(Color, index, varargin{:});
53       %  [this.Color] = Color;
54       % end
55       % /\   /\   /\   /\
56     otherwise
57       error('OOP:unsupportedOption', ['Unknown helper option: '
            which]);
```

```
58  end
59  % Replace with something like UNCLASSIFIED
```

Lines 25–36 contain the placeholder for tailored accessor code. Lines 28–29 assign typical flag values, and line 30 preallocates **varargout** based on the size of **nargout**. These three lines are usually necessary so they are automatically included. Lines 31–36 should be replaced by helper-specific accessor code. Otherwise, lines 34–35 will generate a **warning** and return empty values. If accessor syntax is direct-link, there are two options depending on how much control is desired. Either leave the warning in place or replace the warning with direct-link code.

Lines 37–55 contain the placeholder for tailored mutator code. Lines 40–41 assign typical flag values, and line 42 preallocates **varargout**. Note that the mutator code must either use all the index values or throw an error. Here **varargout** is empty because the object is returned in the output variable **this**. These three lines are usually necessary so they are automatically included. Lines 43–55 should be replaced by helper-specific mutator code. Otherwise, lines 45–46 will generate a **warning** and an unmodified **this** will be returned. The comments in lines 48–54 represent typical direct-link syntax and are included as an aid to development.

18.2 CSHAPE CLASS WIZARD DEFINITION DATA

Data entry for every class follows the same procedure used to define **cLineStyle**. During the definition of **cShape**, we will build on that procedure by spending more time discussing new areas. Open a new session of Class Wizard or select **File::New** from the menu and type in **cShape** as the class name. From an earlier chapter, we know that **cShape** needs to be superior to **double**. In the **Superior To:** field on the main dialog, add the string **double**. If **cShape** needed to be superior to more than one type, a comma separated list would be used. Keep the default values for all other main dialog data. The remaining definition data are entered using the various data-entry dialogs.

18.2.1 cSHAPE HEADER INFO

Click the **Header Info ...** button and select Default Header Info::Load from the menu. This selection loads the collection of default values previously saved during the definition of **cLineStyle**. You can change the field values or leave them as is. Click **Okay** to return to the main dialog.

18.2.2 cSHAPE PRIVATE VARIABLES

The next dialog for data entry defines the class' private variables. Click the **Private Variables ...** button and enter the data shown in Figure 18.8. The data are also summarized in Table 18.4. Data entry is the same as before. First, select an empty line in the lower display block and start entering private variable data. Click **Save Change** to commit the changes and move to the next line. Finally, when data for all variables have been saved, click **Done** to return to the main dialog.

The only noteworthy aspects of the private variables are the initial values. The initial **mPoints** array is now defined to be empty. Previous versions of **cShape** used the corner points of a star to populate **mPoints**. If you prefer star corner points, modify the initial value field for **mPoints** and rebuild the class. The initial value for **mLineStyle** calls the **cLineStyle** constructor using two arguments. This is an example of composition and demonstrates how easy it is to define a class that uses composition. Except for comments, the version of **/@cShape/private/ctor_ini** resulting from the private variable definitions is identical to the Chapter 16 version. This file and all the class files for this chapter can be found in **/oop_guide/chapter_18**.

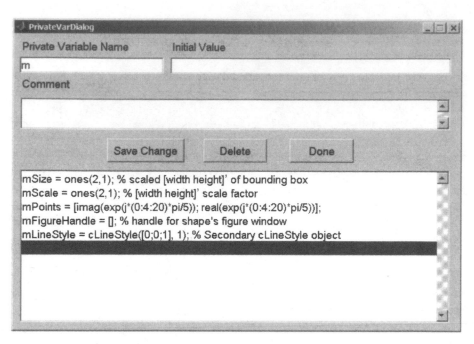

FIGURE 18.8 Class Wizard, cShape private variable dialog.

TABLE 18.4
cShape Private Variable Dialog Fields

Private Variable Name	Initial Value	Comment
mSize	ones(2,1)	Scaled [width; height] of bounding box
mScale	ones(2,1)	[width; height] scale factor
mPoints	zeros(2,0)	Columns of [x; y] shape corner values
mFigureHandle	[]	Handle for the shape's figure window
mLineStyle	cLineStyle ([0;0;1], 1)	Secondary cLineStyle object

18.2.3 cShape Concealed Variables

Moving down the collection of dialog buttons brings us to the concealed variables button. Click the **Concealed Variables ...** button and enter the data shown in Figure 18.9. The concealed variable data are also provided in Table 18.5. Fields for concealed variables are the same as the fields for public variables because there is very little difference between the two. In the generated functions, concealed variables are written into the concealed variable sections of **get** and **set**. If you examine these files, you will notice that the **mFigureHandle** shares the concealed section with another concealed variable, **mDisplayFunc**. Managed exclusively by Class Wizard, **mDisplayFunc** should never be included in the concealed variable dialog. When you are finished, click **Done** to return to the main dialog.

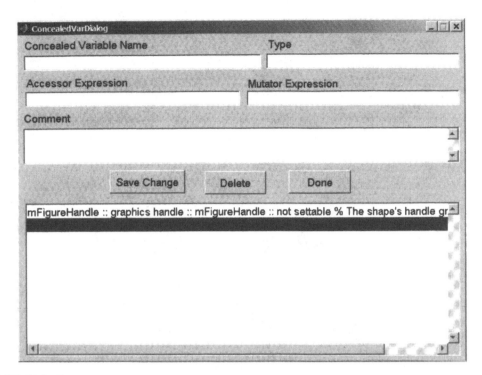

FIGURE 18.9 Class Wizard, cShape concealed variable dialog.

TABLE 18.5
cShape Concealed Variable Dialog Fields

Concealed Variable Name	Type	Accessor Expression	Mutator Expression	Comment
mFigureHandle	graphics handle	mFigureHandle		The shape's handle-graphics handle

18.2.4 CSHAPE PUBLIC VARIABLES

The next move down the collection of dialog buttons brings us to the public variables button. Click the **Public Variables ...** button and enter the data shown in Figure 18.10. The public variable data are also provided in Table 18.6. When you are finished, click **Done** to return to the main dialog.

All public variables defined for **cShape** have accessors. Accessors for **Size** and **Points** use simple, direct-link syntax, and accessors for **ColorRgb** and **LineWeight** use a helper function. Internally, **cShape** manages color and line width through a secondary object stored in **mLineStyle**. Access to the color value is simple, but it does not conform to direct-link requirements. Consequently, **ColorRgb** must specify helper-function syntax. Access to the line width is more complicated because the interface converts between strings **'normal'** and **'bold'** and integer width values.

All public variables defined for **cShape** also have mutators. In this case, the desire for a robust interface complete with input value checking means that all public variables use helper function syntax for mutation. Helper-function stubs all look similar to the **Color_helper** stub in Code Listing 107. The appropriate helper-function code for **cShape**'s private variables was developed in Chapter 16.

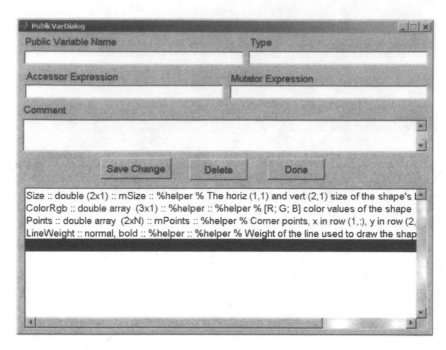

FIGURE 18.10 Class Wizard, cShape public variable dialog.

TABLE 18.6
Public Member Variable Field Values

Public Variable Name	Type	Accessor Expression	Mutator Expression	Comment
Size	double array (2x1)	mSize	%helper	The horiz (1,1) and vert (2,1) size of the shape's bounding box
ColorRgb	double array (3x1)	%helper	%helper	[R; G; B] color values of the shape
Points	double array (2xN)	%helper	%helper	Corner points: x in row (1,:), y in row (2,:)
LineWeight	normal, bold	%helper	%helper	Weight of the line used to draw the shape; either 'normal' or 'bold'

18.2.5 cSHAPE CONSTRUCTOR FUNCTIONS

The final data-entry button on the main dialog defines constructors. The **cShape** class uses a one-argument constructor to assign initial **Point** values. The one-argument constructor is a little odd because Class Wizard always generates a copy constructor. When a one-argument constructor is defined, the generated version of **ctor_1** uses the specified variable name and still includes a

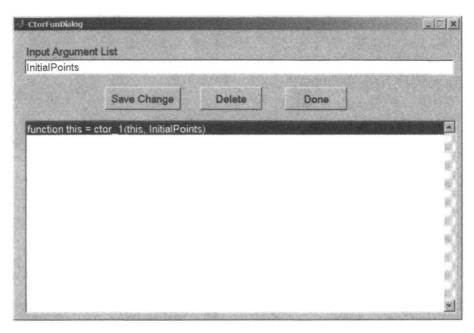

FIGURE 18.11 Class Wizard, cShape constructor function dialog.

case for copy. Clicking the **Constructors** ... button brings up the dialog shown in Figure 18.11. Select an empty line and enter **InitialPoints** as the input argument list. Now click **Save Change** to commit the list and **Done** to return to the main dialog. The function **ctor_1.m** will again be tailored using code from Chapter 16.

18.2.6 cShape Public Functions

We are done with the buttons on the main dialog, but we are not yet done entering all definition data for the class. The public interface includes three public functions, **mtimes**, **reset**, and **draw**. We are going to let Class Wizard generate the initial versions of these three files. To do that, we need to enter public-function data.

At the bottom of the main screen, click **More** .... This will open a dialog box with a button for public functions. Click the **Public Functions** ... button and enter the data shown in Figure 18.12. The public-function data are also provided in Table 18.7. When you are finished, click **Done** to return to the more dialog. In the upper right-hand corner of the more dialog, click **Done** to return to the main dialog.

The initial version of the public function will run without error, but it doesn't do anything. The code body includes a warning message, and any output variables that are not also passed into the function are assigned an empty value. To tailor these files, we will again copy code from Chapter 16.

18.2.7 cShape Data Dictionary

At this point, all the elements of **cShape** have been defined but we still need to add some comments for the function arguments. On the main dialog menu bar, select **Data::Dictionary** ... and the dialog shown in Figure 18.13 will be displayed. Enter type information and comments for each variable. The variable data are also provided in Table 18.8. When you are finished, click **Done** to return to the main dialog.

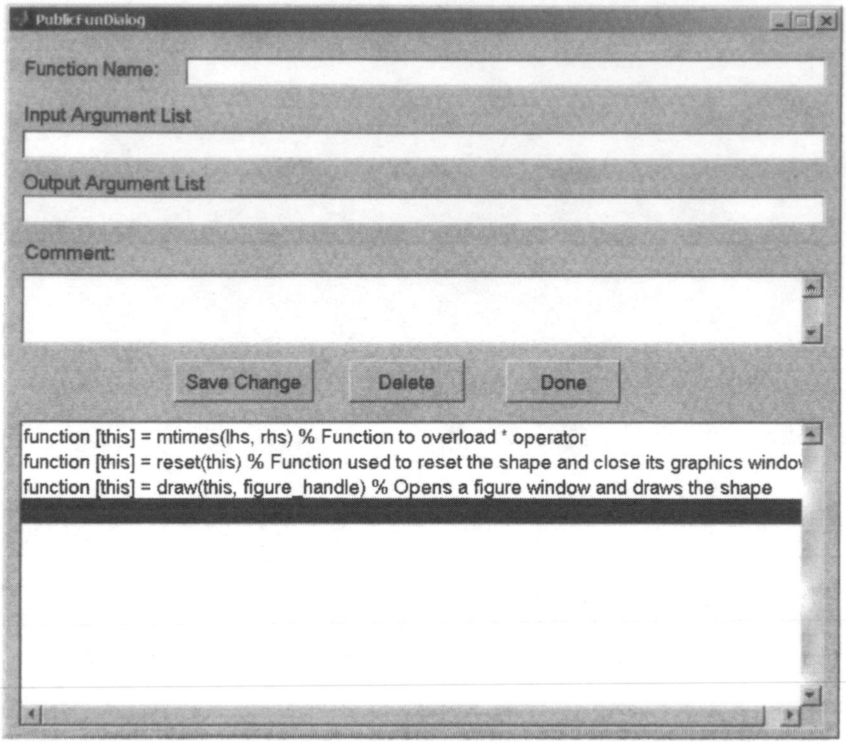

FIGURE 18.12 Class Wizard, cShape public function dialog.

TABLE 18.7
Public Member Function Field Values

Public Function Name	Input Argument List	Output Argument List	Comments
`mtimes`	`lhs, rhs`	`this`	`Function used to overload the * operator`
`reset`	`this`	`this`	`Function used to reset the shape and close its graphics window`
`Draw`	`this, figure_ handle`	`this`	`Opens the figure window and draws the shape`

18.2.8 CSHAPE BUILD CLASS FILES

The definition for **cShape** is now complete. Click **Build Class Files** to begin class file generation. You will be prompted to choose a destination directory. If you started the definition by selecting **File::New**, the initially selected directory is probably not the desired directory. Simply highlight the desired directory and click **OK**. If a suitable directory does not exist, the **Make New Folder** button on the lower left will allow you to create one. When you click **OK**, Class Wizard generates the files. Click **Okay** on the confirmation dialog to return to the main Class Wizard dialog.

The new **cShape** class should work without error; however, helper functions and public functions need to be tailored before the class will achieve full functionality. The files that require

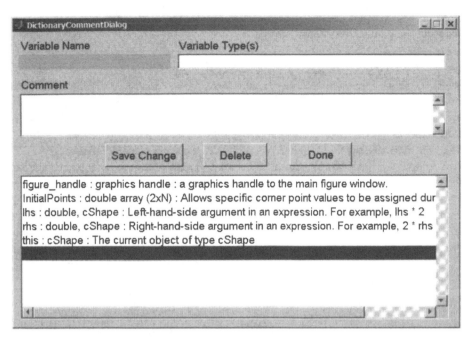

FIGURE 18.13 Class Wizard, cShape data dictionary dialog.

TABLE 18.8
cShape Data Dictionary Values

Public Function Name	Type	Comments
figure_handle	graphics handle	A graphics handle to the main figure window
InitialPoints	double array (2xN)	Allows specific corner points to be assigned during construction
lhs	double, cShape	Left-hand-side argument in an expression, for example, lhs * 2
rhs	double, cShape	Right-hand-side argument in an expression, for example, 2 * rhs
this	cShape	The current object of type cShape

more work are **draw**, **mtimes**, **reset**, **ctor_1**, **ColorRgb_helper**, **LineWeight_helper**, **Points_helper**, and **Size_helper**. The Chapter 16 versions of these files contain the correct code bodies. Instead of simply copying files, code is copied out of each Chapter 16 file and pasted into the new version. This preserves the comment information in the new files.

The **cShape** class is now completely functional. There is one difference due to a change in the initial value of **mPoints**. If you try to draw a **cShape** object, a figure window will open but there is no shape. In this chapter, the default value of **mPoints** is **zeros(2,0)**. Consequently, **draw** receives no corner points and produces an empty figure window. The constructor for **cShape** now makes no assumptions about the shape. It will now be up to each child to pass appropriate corner data via the parent-class constructor.

18.3 CSTAR CLASS WIZARD DEFINITION DATA

In previous chapters, after we developed an implementation for the parent, child development was almost trivial. The same holds true for entering child-class definitions. Most of the data entry for **cStar** and **cDiamond** occurred during data entry for **cLineStyle** and **cShape**. The definitions for **cStar** and **cDiamond** do include a new element, a parent-class definition.

Open a new session of Class Wizard or select **File::New** from the menu and type in **cStar** as the class name. Also on the main dialog, add the string **double** to the **Superior To:** field. Keep the default values for all other main dialog data. Now click the **Header Info** ... button and select **Default Header Info::Load** from the menu. This selection loads default header values. You can change the field values or leave them as is. Click **Okay** to return to the main dialog. The next step is to enter data for parents, additional member variables, and member functions.

18.3.1 cStar Parent

Click the **Parents** ... button and enter the data shown in Figure 18.14. Since there is only one parent, a table of values is not necessary. Simply read the values from fields shown in Figure 18.14. The **varargin** field value consists of a $2 \times n$ array of corner points. The default points for **cStar** line on the unit circle, and a complex exponential is one easy way to generate the values. When arrays are used as initial values, don't add commas to separate elements in the array. MATLAB can delimit array elements using a comma or a space. If you use a comma, Class Wizard will get confused because it counts commas to determine how many arguments are in the input list. In response to the parent data, Class Wizard will generate a **parent_list** function that returns a **cellstr** populated with parent-class values. After entering **cShape** parent data, click **Save Change** to commit the data. Click **Done** to return to the main dialog.

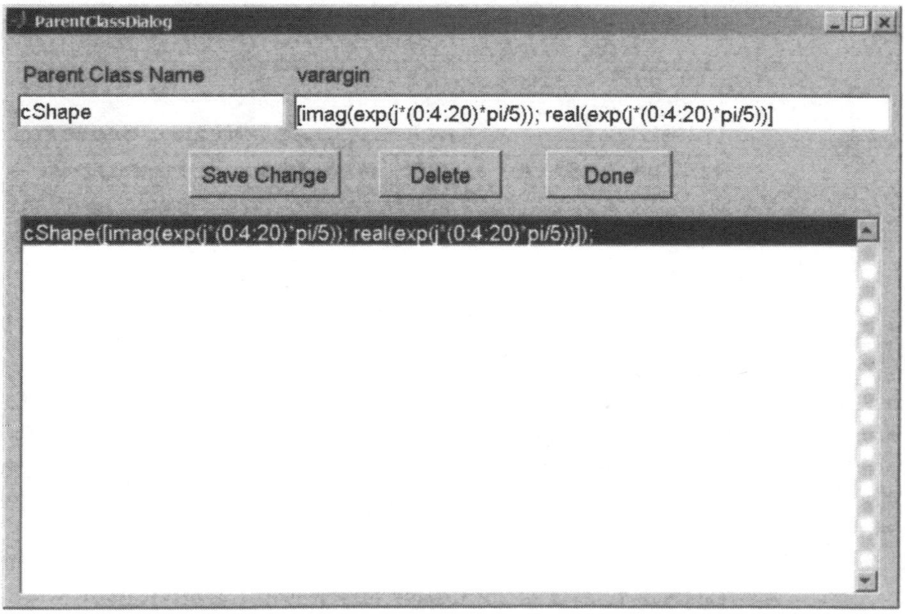

FIGURE 18.14 Class Wizard, cStar parents dialog.

TABLE 18.9
cStar Private Variable Data

Private Variable Name	Initial Value	Comment
`mTitle`	`'A Star is born'`	`Title for the figure window`

In the typical case, the child class would overload some of the parent's functions. For that situation, we would need to open the Public Functions dialog and enter function names and argument lists. Class Wizard would then generate stubs, which we would fill in with child-specific code. In the case of such a simple **cStar** class, no redefinitions are required. Default Class Wizard files are all that are needed for the test drive.

18.3.2 OTHER cStar DEFINITION DATA

In addition to inheritance, **cStar**'s definition also includes one additional private variable, one additional public variable, and three public functions. The data associated with these elements are provided in the tables that follow.

The child-class **cStar** adds a title to the figure window where the shape is plotted. To do this, **mTitle** is added as a private variable and **Title** is added as a public variable. To add the correct private variable, start at the main dialog. Click the **Private Variables** ... button and enter the data provided in Table 18.9. After entering the data, click **Save Changes** and **Done**. This will commit the data and return you to the main dialog.

For the public variable, click the **Public Variables** ... button and enter the data provided in Table 18.10. Notice that the accessor is direct-link and the mutator uses a helper function. Before the class is fully functional, code for the helper function must be copied from the Chapter 16 version. After entering the data, click **Save Changes** and **Done**. This will return you to the main dialog.

To support arrays of objects, **cStar** needs to overload the parent-class member functions. The code inside **mtimes** and **reset** simply includes a slice-and-forward operation. The code inside **draw** includes slice-and-forward code, but it also includes code to add a figure title. Of course, the code to support this functionality needs to be copied from the Chapter 16 Version, but Class Wizard will generate the initial stub. For the public functions, first click **More** ... and then **Public Functions** .... Enter the data from Table 18.11 into the public-function dialog. After entering the data, click **Save Changes** and **Done** to return to the more dialog. Clicking **Done** in the dialog's upper right-hand corner will return you to the main dialog.

Before generating the class files, the variables used in the public functions should be documented. From the main dialog, select the menu item labeled Data::Dictionary .... Enter the data shown in Table 18.12 into the data dictionary dialog. After entering the data, click **Save Changes** and **Done** to return to the main dialog.

TABLE 18.10
cStar Public Variable Data

Public Variable Name	Type	Accessor Expression	Mutator Expression	Comment
`Title`	`string`	`mTitle`	`%helper`	`A title for the figure window`

TABLE 18.11
cStar Public Member Function Data

Public Function Name	Input Argument List	Output Argument List	Comments
`mtimes`	`lhs, rhs`	`this`	`slices the parent and forwards to the parent-class version of mtimes`
`reset`	`this, varargin`	`this`	`slices the parent and forwards to the parent-class version of reset`
`draw`	`this, varargin`	`this`	`First slices the parent and forwards to the parent class draw. After the parent draws the shape, a title is added.`

TABLE 18.12
cStar Data Dictionary Values

Public Function Name	Type	Comments
`lhs`	`double, cShape`	`Left-hand-side argument in an expression`
`rhs`	`double, cShape`	`Right-hand-side argument in an expression`
`this`	`cShape`	`The current object of type cStar`
`varargin`		`a variable-length input argument list`

The definition for **cStar** is now complete. Click **Build Class Files** to begin class file generation. You will be prompted to choose a destination directory. Highlight the desired directory and click **OK**. If a suitable directory does not exist, the **Make New Folder** button on the lower left will allow you to create one. When you click **OK**, Class Wizard generates the files. Click **Okay** on the confirmation dialog to return to the main Class Wizard dialog.

As always, the helper functions and public functions must be tailored before the class will achieve full functionality. The files that require more work are **draw, mtimes, reset**, and **Title_helper**. The Chapter 16 versions of these files contain the correct code bodies. Copy and paste the code bodies from each Chapter 16 file into the **cStar** versions. This preserves the comment information in the new files. We still have to create a definition for **cDiamond**, but after all that work, you should probably create a **cStar** object and draw it. If you would prefer to wait for the test drive, that is okay with me.

18.4 CDIAMOND CLASS WIZARD DEFINITION DATA

The definition for **cDiamond** and **cStar** are almost the same. The difference is that **cStar** includes some additional member variables. If we start with **cStar**'s definition, delete a couple of entries, and change the name, we can easily arrive at a definition for **cDiamond**. This approach will also exercise dialog controls we have not yet used.

If the definition file for **cStar** is still open, leave it open. Otherwise, start Class Wizard and from the main menu select **File::Open**. Navigate into your most recent **/@cStar** directory and select the file **cStar.mat**. This is the definition file for **cStar**. The definition file is written into the class directory every time class files are generated. Click **Open** to load the definition file into Class Wizard.

On the main dialog, change the class name from **cStar** to **cDiamond**. Next, click the **Parents ...** button. In the bottom display, highlight the line that contains the **cShape** parent name. In the **varargin** field, change the corner point array to **[-1 0 1 0 -1; 0 -1 0 1 0]**. Don't add commas to separate the elements. Next, click the **Private Variables ...** button. In the bottom display, highlight the line that contains the variable name **mTitle**. Click **Delete** and **mTitle** is no longer a private variable. Click **Done** to return to the main dialog. Next, click the **Public Variables ...** button. Highlight the line that contains the variable name **Title**. Click **Delete** and **Title** is no longer a public variable. Click **Done** to return to the main dialog.

The definition for **cDiamond** is now complete. In this particular situation, starting from an existing definition proved much easier compared to starting from scratch. Click **Build Class Files** to begin class file generation. You will be prompted to choose a destination directory. Be very careful because the dialog will suggest **@cStar** as a destination. Select a more suitable directory and click **OK** to generate the files. Click **Okay** on the confirmation dialog to return to the main Class Wizard dialog.

Again, helper functions and public functions must be tailored before the class will achieve full functionality. For **cDiamond**, there are no helper functions. As with **cStar**, code bodies for the public member functions **draw**, **mtimes**, and **reset** can be copied from the Chapter 16 versions. Copy and paste code bodies from each Chapter 16 file into the **cDiamond** versions. That concludes the complete generation of all the classes in the **cShape** hierarchy. We can now exercise those classes by creating and drawing a few shapes.

18.5 TEST DRIVE

The code generated by Class Wizard is supposed to be functionally identical to the handcrafted code in Chapter 16. For helper functions and class-specific public functions, this is almost certainly true because Class Wizard–generated stub code was replaced by code from that chapter. Even so, it is important to demonstrate the proper operation of the wizard-generated group of eight along with the interfaces to helper functions and public functions. Since the classes are expected to be functionally identical, we can reuse commands from earlier chapters. Of course, drawing a shape is the most visually appealing. The following combines default construction, **mtimes**, and **draw** into one command.

```
>> star = draw([cStar 1.5*cStar]);
```

The graphical result of this command is shown in Figure 18.15. In fact, this single command exercises a significant number of member functions, both public and private. The list of executed member functions is detailed in Table 18.13. The table includes an accounting of all the member functions. All the functions executed during the **draw** command above have a gray background. The members of **cDiamond** are not exercised because there are no **cDiamond** objects involved in the command.

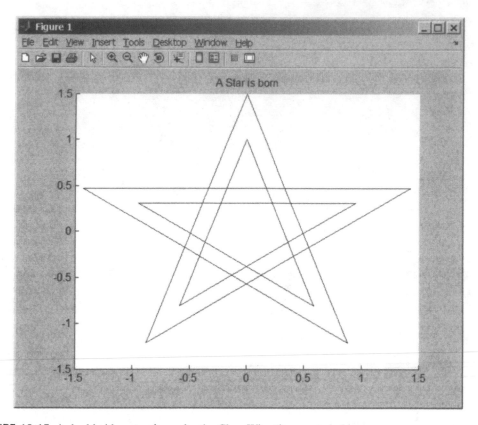

FIGURE 18.15 A double blue star drawn by the Class Wizard generated classes.

Most of the remaining member functions are exercised by the commands in Code Listing 108. These commands came directly from the test drive in Chapter 12. Refer to §12.1.3.2 for a complete description of the commands and their outputs. Except for the byte size of the objects and the new fields added to **cStar**, the outputs for the Class Wizard–generated files are identical to the outputs from the earlier handcrafted version. None of these commands tests **cDiamond**. The first independent investigation asks you to repeat the commands using **cDiamond** instead of **cStar**.

18.6 SUMMARY

In this chapter, we used Class Wizard to recreate the entire class hierarchy developed in the preceding chapters. Functions belonging to the group of eight are completely and reliably generated. The commands in the test drive demonstrate this. Functions outside the group of eight are also generated; however, the code body does not include full functionality. The code body must be independently implemented, and in this chapter, we recycled code from the Chapter 16 implementation. If you closely examine the files, you will notice that all the headers are consistently formatted and contain a rich set of comments. It takes a lot of time and effort to include the same kind of repetitive information when the files are coded from scratch.

The difficulty involved in creating classes varies from language to language. At first, creating classes in MATLAB seems easy. Indeed, it is quite easy to create a class, define some member functions, and begin using objects. Unfortunately, the bloom falls off the rose as you begin to realize all the things you can't do with a simple MATLAB object. The first step toward an improved implementation takes advantage of syntax using **subsref** and **subsasgn**. After that, the development of a truly robust class requires attention to nearly every detail. It has already taken eighteen chapters to discuss all of the details, and we are not yet done.

TABLE 18.13
Executed Member Functions Are Highlighted

@cLineStyle	@cShape	@cStar	@cDiamond
constructor	constructor	constructor	constructor
Subsref	subsref	subsref	subsref
Subsasgn	subsasgn	subsasgn	subsasgn
Display	display	display	display
Struct	struct	struct	struct
fieldnames	fieldnames	fieldnames	fieldnames
get	get	get	get
set	set	set	set
cat	cat	cat	cat
vertcat	vertcat	vertcat	vertcat
horzcat	horzcat	horzcat	horzcat
ctor_ini	ctor_ini	ctor_ini	ctor_ini
ctor_1	ctor_1	ctor_1	ctor_1
parent_list	parent_list	parent_list	parent_list
ctor_2		ctor_2	ctor_2
Color_helper	draw	draw	draw
LineWidth_helper	mtimes	mtimes	mtimes
	reset	reset	reset
	ColorRgb_helper	Title_helper	
	LineWeight_helper		
	Points_helper		
	Size_helper		

Code Listing 108, Chapter 18 Test Drive Command Listing Based on Class Wizard–Generated Member Functions

```
1    >> clear classes; fclose all; close all force;
2    >> star = cStar;
3    >> star2 = cStar(star);
4    >> whos
5     Name          Size                      Bytes    Class
6     ans           1x1                           8    double array
7     star          1x1                        1676    cStar object
8     star2         1x1                        1676    cStar object
9    Grand total is 93 elements using 3360 bytes
10
11   >> disp(star.Size')
12    1       1
13   >> disp(star.ColorRgb')
14    0       0       1
15   >> disp(star.Points)
16    0  5.8779e-01 -9.5106e-01  9.5106e-01 -5.8779e-01 -4.8986e-16
17   1.0000e+00 -8.0902e-01  3.0902e-01  3.0902e-01 -8.0902e-01
       1.0000e+00
```

```
18  >> star.Size = [2;3];
19  >> disp(star.Size')
20     2        3
21  >> star
22  star =
23          Size: [2x1 double]
24       ColorRgb: [3x1 double]
25         Points: [2x6 double]
26     LineWeight: 'normal'
27          Title: 'A Star is born'
28  >> fieldnames(star)
29  ans =
30    'Size'
31    'ColorRgb'
32    'Points'
33    'LineWeight'
34    'Title'
35  >> fieldnames(star, '-full')
36  ans =
37  ans =
38    'Size % double array (2x1)'
39    'ColorRgb % double array (3x1)'
40    'Points % double array (2xN)'
41    'LineWeight % normal, bold'
42    'Title % string'
43  >> fieldnames(star, '-possible')
44  ans =
45    'Size'
46    {1x1 cell}
47    'ColorRgb'
48    {1x1 cell}
49    'Points'
50    {1x1 cell}
51    'LineWeight'
52    {1x1 cell}
53    'Title'
54    {1x1 cell}
55  >> struct(star)
56          Size: [2x1 double]
57       ColorRgb: [3x1 double]
58         Points: [2x6 double]
59     LineWeight: 'normal'
60          Title: 'A Star is born'
61  >> star = [cStar cStar; cStar cStar];
62  >> size(star)
63  ans =
64     2        2
```

```
65  >> [star.Size]
66  ans =
67   1       1        1        1
68   1       1        1        1
69  >> {star.Size}
70  ans =
71   [2x1 double]    [2x1 double]    [2x1 double]    [2x1 double]
72  >>
73  >> disp(class(star))
74  cStar
75  >> disp(isa(star, 'cShape'))
76   1
77  >> disp(isa(star, 'cDiamond'))
78   0
```

Attending to the myriad details is something that a CASE tool can do very well. Even this is difficult unless there is a good organizational structure. The organizational structure advocated by the preceding chapters results in good class implementation, and Class Wizard is very helpful in maintaining that structure. This is particularly true when the class definition evolves. With Class Wizard, evolution is a simple matter of adding elements to the definition and rebuilding the files. Files managed by the tool are overwritten with the new definition, while handcrafted files are untouched. The best balance is always maintained between standard idioms and a developer's creativity.

18.7 INDEPENDENT INVESTIGATIONS

1. Repeat the test-drive commands using **cDiamond** objects instead of **cShape** objects.
2. Modify the class interfaces to allow shapes to be rotated by an arbitrary angle. Use Class Wizard to generate the initial versions of helper functions and public member functions.
3. Add other line-style features to **cLineStyle**, and expose these features so that clients can use them with **cStar** and **cDiamond** objects (for example, dotted vs. solid lines).
4. Add a **cCircle** class to the hierarchy. Does **cCircle** inherit **cShape** or is there a better relationship? Should **/@cCircle/draw** use **polar** instead of **plot**? How would the use of **polar** change the organization?

Part 3

Advanced Strategies

In this section, we redeploy standard object-oriented techniques in a way that allows MATLAB to create a few special-purpose classes commonly found in other object-oriented languages. These include *containers, singleton objects, functors*, and *iterators*. These classes require strong encapsulation and a flexible object-oriented language. The fact that these sophisticated classes can be created from elements that already exist pays tribute to the MATLAB design team. If these example classes make you wonder what else is possible, they have done their job. With a little imagination and creativity, anything is possible.

Some of the topics in this section are controversial because they upset the status quo. Redefining member-function syntax, adding a pass-by-reference function model, and obtaining protected visibility for variables and functions are probably the most disruptive topics. The discussions don't try to judge whether you should adopt a particular technique, but instead try to demonstrate the flexibility inherent in MATLAB objects and expand the way you think about them. Some of the techniques are worthy of adoption, while others would benefit from more support from the language and the user community. Like many disruptive technologies, it is hard to know in advance what will be embraced. Unlike many languages, MATLAB's evolution isn't restricted by an ISO standard. If enough of us adopt a few of these techniques, market forces will ultimately prevail.

19 Composition and a Simple Container Class

As a further demonstration of composition, we make an initial foray into designing and implementing a general container class. A general container is different from an array because it can hold different types. A general container is different from a cell array because all objects must descend from the same parent. For example, a general **cShape** container can hold both **cStar** and **cDiamond** objects because they both use **cShape** as a parent. A container is also different from a cell array because a container has a structure-like interface. The interface makes a container behave a lot like an object array. Rather than looping over each element in the container, clients can use vector syntax. Often the loop still exists; however, it is now hidden behind the container's interface.

Developing a set of standard containers compatible with the general computer-engineering literature* or with National Institute of Standards (NIST) definitions** would be an enormous undertaking. The goals for this chapter's container are much less ambitious. The primary goal is to demonstrate one potential use of composition. A secondary goal is to produce a container that might be useful as is, or at least produce a container that can be easily improved. The container developed for this chapter isn't perfect, but with what you already know, you can fix all of its deficiencies.

19.1 BUILDING CONTAINERS

To implement a container, several details are important. First, we need to specify the object type held by the container. Any object that passes an **isa** test for the specified type will be allowed in. Thus, objects of the specified type and objects using the specified type as a parent are okay to add to the container. For the example, we will specify **cShape** as the object type. That will allow the container to hold **cShape**, **cStar**, and **cDiamond** objects. If we want to create new shape classes, the container will hold them too. Of course, these new classes must have **cShape** somewhere in their hierarchy so that **isa(object, 'cShape')** returns **true**.

The next thing we need to decide is how the container implementation will store the objects. MATLAB will not let us use a built-in type, like **cell**, as a parent, so we must look for an alternative. There are two options but both represent compromises. The first and probably the most obvious approach stores objects in a private cell array. Cell array storage is probably the best approach because it aligns public and private indices. One potential problem with this approach is the mismatch among built-in functions like **length** and **size** and the number of objects held in the container. Of course, we will code around this problem by overloading **length** and **size**. We might also want to consider overloading **reshape**, **ndims**, **numel**, **num2cell**, and **mat2cell**, among others.

The next potential problem with a private cell array is the index value **end**. Using **end** to add a new element to the container should work the same as adding an element to an array. For example, the command syntax might look like the following:

---

* Cardelli, L., and Wegner, P. "On Understanding Types, Data Abstraction and Polymorphism," *ACM Computer Survey*, 17, 4, December 1985, 471–522.

** http://www.nist.gov/dads/.

```
shape_array(end+1) = cStar;
```

The built-in behavior of **end** returns the dimension of **shape_array**, not the dimension of the private cell array inside **shape_array**. Redefining **size** and **length** doesn't help, but thanks to the foresight of the MATLAB developers, we can code around this problem too. In this situation, **end** acts like an operator. Like any operator, MATLAB converts **end** into a function call. This behavior allows us to overload the function **end.m** to return an appropriate value.

An alternate container solution avoids **length**, **size**, **reshape**, and **end** issues by taking advantage of the way MATLAB implements structures. For example, the container class might include a private member variable named **mObject**. After several additions, **class(this(1).mObject)** might equal ‘**cStar**’ and **class(this(2).mObject)** might equal ‘**cDiamond**’. MATLAB allows different object types stored in the **mObject** element to coexist. As long as we never try to concatenate **mObject** elements (i.e., **[this.mObject]**), everything will work fine. With this solution, adding a new object simply increases the size of the private structure. The primary problem with this approach involves repeating the container's private structure and the fact that arrays of structures are memory hogs. Using **repmat** can also produce inconsistent results.

Regardless of the approach, we also need to consider concatenation with **cat**, **horzcat**, and **vertcat**. Achieving the best compatibility means supporting the concatenation of a container and an object and the concatenation of two or more containers. We usually don't want to restrict the concatenation order, and that means the container must be **superiorto** the classes it holds.

19.2 CONTAINER IMPLEMENTATION

For implementation purposes, this chapter uses the cell-array approach. With the cell-array approach, the container object itself is never empty even when the private cell array contains no objects. This eliminates the potential for empty-object memory errors that sometimes arise.* The cell-array approach requires a little more work up front, but the result seems to be more robust compared to the object-array approach. After the first container implementation, the added workload isn't a problem because most of the tailored functions can be copied, as is, to other container implementations.

The implementation example is organized into three sections. The first section focuses on our standard group-of-eight framework. The second section focuses on a set of tailored functions that overload the behavior of standard MATLAB built-in functions. The third section focuses on **cShape**-specific functions. The implementation of any container can be organized along these divisions.

19.2.1 THE STANDARD FRAMEWORK AND THE GROUP OF EIGHT

Even though a container class is quite different from the other class examples, we don't have to code everything from scratch. Instead, use Class Wizard to generate the initial set of files and modify them to suit the needs of the container. The constructor, **ctor_ini**, **ctor_1**, **display**, **parent_list**, and **struct** won't need modifications. The remaining group-of-eight functions — **fieldnames**, **get**, **set**, **subsref**, and **subsasgn** — will need container-specific changes. The changes are modest and are relatively easy since the generated code serves as a guide. The data entered into Class Wizard are provided in Table 19.1 through Table 19.4. The list of function names in Table 19.3 provides a preview of the tailoring to come. Fields not listed in the tables should remain set to their default values. The complete Class Wizard **mat** file and the unmodified

---

* Versions 7.1 and earlier are not stable when **repmat** is used to create an object array with a dimension size equal to zero. Returning a so-called empty object from a constructor is particularly bad. The fact that a default-constructed container should be empty makes the repeated-structure approach unreliable in these versions.

TABLE 19.1
cShapeArray Class Wizard Main Dialog Fields

Field	Value
Class Name	cShapeArray
Superior To	cShape, cStar, cDiamond, double

TABLE 19.2
cShapeArray Private Variable Dialog Fields

Private Variable Name	Initial Value	Comment
mType	'cShape'	Container can hold any object that passes isa(object, this.mType).
mArray	{}	Cell array for the container.
mFigHandle	[]	Figure handle where all contained shapes are drawn.

results arc included in **/chapter_0/as_generated cShapeArray**. After entering the data, generate the class.

The container itself contains no public member variables, and, as generated by Class Wizard, the public variable sections inside **fieldnames**, **get**, and **set** arc empty. These sections will not remain empty. Instead, these functions will forward public variable requests to the secondary objects stored in the container. The Class Wizard cases inside **subsref** and **subsasgn** also need some changes. The initial code assumes the container itself is an array. In reality, the container class is always scalar. Changes to **subsref** and **subsasgn** use the private cell array to make the container look like an array. The dot-reference **case** is okay because changes to **get** and **set** determine dot-reference behavior. The array-reference **case** needs to access and mutate objects held in the container's cell array. Only the highlights are included in the following sections. The fully modified files are included in **/chapter_0/@cShapeArray**.

19.2.1.1 Container Modifications to fieldnames

Since the container itself has no public variables, **fieldnames.m** doesn't initially contain a list of public names. This is correct because only the objects held by the container have public variables. The container needs to return a list of public names, but it doesn't need an explicit list. Rather than coding an explicit name list inside the container's version of **fieldnames**, we simply forward the **fieldnames** request and collect the result. There are two potential targets for the forward: the class type held in **this.mType** (see Table 19.2) and the objects held in **this.mArray** (see Table 19.2). Choosing the first returns the public members allocated to the parent. These names are guaranteed to exist for every object in the container. Choosing the latter also includes parent-class public names, but it might also include public names defined for the children. Choosing the latter also means that any particular object may or may not contain every public variable listed. This is not necessarily a problem, but it is something that must be considered when container functions are implemented.

For **cShape** and its children, most of the public variables are defined by the parent. In this situation, using the container class type held in **this.mType** is a good choice. This choice also

TABLE 19.3
cShapeArray Public Function Field Values

Function Name	Input Argument List	Output Argument List	Comment
draw	this, FigureHandle	this	Calls draw for every object in the container. If FigureHandle is not passed in, draw will manage the use or creation of a figure window.
end	this, k, n	num	Redefines built-in behavior. Returns an index value consistent with "end." If n is not equal to length(size(this.mObject)), some reshaping is done to find the correct value.
length	this	num	Redefines built-in behavior. Returns the correct length based on the number of objects in the container.
mat2cell	this, varargin		Redefines built-in behavior. Function is not supported; throws an error if called.
mtimes	lhs, rhs	this	Redefines built-in behavior for *. Allows multiplication between the container and arrays of doubles.
times	lhs, rhs	this	Redefines built-in behavior for *. Allows multiplication between the container and arrays of doubles.
ndims	this	num	Redefines built-in behavior. Returns the correct ndims value based on the shape of the container's mObject cell array.

TABLE 19.3 (CONTINUED)
cShapeArray Public Function Field Values

Function Name	Input Argument List	Output Argument List	Comment
num2cell	this, varargin	container_ cells	Redefines built-in behavior. Use this function to access the container's entire cell array. Function only supports one input argument. If you try to pass in a direction, the function will throw an error.
reset	this	this	Calls reset for every object in the container.
size	this, varargin	varargout	Redefines built-in behavior. Returns the correct size array based on the number of objects in the container.
Reshape	this, varargin	this	Redefines built-in behavior. Reshapes the object cell array.

allows the container to return a list of names even when the container is empty. Add the following command to the end of the initial version of **@cShapeArray/fieldnames.m**

```
names = [names; fieldnames(feval(this.mType), varargin{:})];
```

In this command, **feval(this.mType)** creates a temporary object and **varargin{:}** expands input arguments. The complete list of names is created by concatenating the return value with any names that already exist. To improve run time, the result could be assigned to a persistent variable. Use the profiler to determine when a persistent is warranted.

19.2.1.2 Container Modifications to subsref

For dot-reference operations, the container needs to forward the operation to the objects held in the container. The best location for the forward isn't in **subsref** but rather in **get**. Locating the forward inside **get** means no changes to **subsref**'s dot-reference case.

For array-reference operations, the input **index** value is used to return elements in the container's cell array. In the normal situation, the built-in version of **subsref** and MATLAB's assignment operator cooperate to return a subset array with the same type as **this**. The container's array-reference code can't rely on the same built-in behavior. Instead, the code first constructs an empty container and then assigns the indexed subset into the new container's **mArray** variable. Modifications to **subsref**'s array-reference case are shown in Code Listing 109.

Line 2 instantiates a new container object by calling the constructor. **Class(this)** returns the name of the constructor and **feval** executes it. No arguments are passed with the function call so the result is an empty container. Line 3 uses **index(1)** to get the correct subset out of

TABLE 19.4
cShapeArray Data Dictionary Field Values

Variable Name	Type	Comment
container_cell	cell array of objects	Cell array of objects held in the container
FigureHandle	figure handle	Used to pass around a handle-graphics figure handle
K	integer > 0	Specifies which dimension to inspect
lhs	double, container	The left-hand-side value in an expression, e.g., lhs * rhs
n	integer > 0	Total number of dimensions
num	integer >= 0	Used to return integer values associated with functions like length, end, etc.
rhs	double, container	The right-hand-side value in an expression, e.g., lhs * rhs
this	cShapeArray	The current or "active" object
varargin	cell array	Variable-length input argument list; see help varargin
varargout	cell array	Variable-length output argument list; see help varargout

Code Listing 109, Modifications to the subsref Array-Reference Case for a Container Class

```
1    case '()'
2      this_subset = feval(class(this));  % create a new container
       object
3      this_subset.mArray = this.mArray(index(1).subs{:}); % fill
       with subset
4      if length(index) == 1
5        varargout = {this_subset};
6      else
7        % trick subsref into returning more than 1 ans
8        varargout = cell(size(this_subset));
9        [varargout{:}] = subsref(this_subset, index(2:end));
10     end
```

the container's cell array. The subset is assigned into the new container's cell array. The initial commands on lines 4–10 are okay. If there is only one level of indexing, line 5 assigns the subset container object into **varargout**. If there are more indexing levels, lines 8–9 calls **subsref**.

19.2.1.3   Container Modifications to subsasgn

Container additions to **subsasgn** follow a pattern similar to the additions in **subsref**. **Subsasgn**'s dot-reference case is okay because container-related modifications to **set** forward the operation to container's objects. Commands in the array-reference case are modified to target elements of **this.mArray**. **Subsasgn**'s modified array-reference case is shown in Code Listing 110. Compared to **subsref**, there are more lines of code. Input type checking and distributing input objects into the correctly indexed locations are the primary reasons for this.

Code Listing 110, Modifications to subsasgn Array-Reference Case for a Container Class

```
1    case '()'
2      if isempty(this)
3        % due to superiorto, need to look at this and varargin
4        if isa(this, mfilename('class'))
5          this = eval(class(this));
6        else
7          this = eval(class(varargin{1}));
8        end
9      end
10
11     if length(index) == 1
12       if length(varargin) > 1
13         error('Container:UnexpectedInputSize', ...
14           'Only one input is allowed for () assignment.');
15
16       elseif isempty(varargin{1})
17         % empty input, delete elements, use builtin subsasgn
18         this.mArray = subsasgn(this.mArray, index,
           varargin{1});
19
20       elseif strcmp(class(varargin{1}), mfilename('class'))
21         % another container of the same type
22         error('Container:UnsupportedAssignment', ...
23           'Container to container assignment is not supported.');
24
25       elseif iscell(varargin{1})
26         % a cell array of objects
27         error('Container:UnsupportedAssignment', ...
28           'The assignment of cells into a container is not
             supported.');
29
30       elseif isa(varargin{1}, this.mType)
31         % an object that can indeed be held by the container
```

```
32          % might have a length > 1
33          set_val = num2cell(varargin{1});
34          this.mArray = subsasgn(this.mArray, index, set_val);
35          is_empty = cellfun('isempty', this.mArray);
36          if any(is_empty)
37            this.mArray(is_empty) = {feval(this.mType)};
38          end
39
40        else
41          % any other condition is an error
42          error('Container:UnsupportedAssignment', ...
43            ['Container cannot hold objects of type '
              class(varargin{1})]);
44        end
45
46      else
47        this_subset = feval(class(this));  % create a new
            container object
48        this_subset.mArray = this.mArray(index(1).subs{:}); %
            fill with subset
49        this_subset = ...
50        subsasgn(this_subset, index(2:end), varargin{:});   %
            assign input
51        this.mArray(index(1).subs{:}) = this_subset.mArray; % put
            subset back
52      end
```

Lines 2–9 are already okay. Lines 2–9 detect when the input variable **this** is empty and take appropriate action. When the execution reaches line 11, **this** will be a nonempty container object. When there is only one index level, lines 11–43 assign the input objects. There are several ways the input objects might be packaged: scalar object, object array, cell array, multiple inputs, and container. The example implementation supports only one, throwing an error for the others. It isn't difficult to add support for the other options. The container also supports **[]** as an input option. This allows a client to delete elements in the container using the standard syntax.

Lines 12–14 throw an error if more than one input is detected. Using the functional form of **subsasgn** is the only way this error can occur. Array-operator syntax always converts into a call with only one input. When the functional form is used, any number of inputs may be passed.

Lines 16–18 support element deletion. When the input is **[]**, the assignment removes elements from **this.mArray**. Line 18 passes **this.mArray**, the indices, and **[]** into the built-in, cell-array version of **subsasgn**. The cell array returned from the built-in call will have fewer elements. When the cell array is assigned back into **this.mArray**, the container will contain fewer objects.

Lines 20–23 detect the assignment of one container into another and throw an error. In a fully functional container class, this form of assignment should not throw an error unless a size mismatch or some other error is detected. Logically, the elements of **varargin{1}.mArray** need to replace the elements of **this.mArray(index(1).subs{:})**. Element types don't need to be checked because the containers are the same type. Of course, the number of elements in the input container must be compatible with the number of indexed elements. If a mismatch is detected, **subsasgn** is typically expected to throw an error.

Lines 25–28 detect the assignment of a cell array into the container and throw an error. In a fully functional container class, this form of assignment would also be supported. In this case, the elements in **varargin{1}{:}** are assigned into **this.mArray(index(1).subs{:})**. Unlike container-to-container assignment, the type of every element in **varargin{1}{:}** would need to be checked against **this.mType**. Unfortunately, **cellfun** coupled with **'isclass'** performs the wrong check (see **help cellfun**). The input cell array size must also be compatible with the number of indices.

Lines 30–38 allow the indexed assignment of a scalar object or an object array. Line 30 checks the input object's type to make sure it was derived from **this.mType**. After that, assigning the object should be straightforward but there are two complicating conditions. The first condition occurs with a nonscalar input object. Line 33 converts the object array into a cell array of objects, and line 34 uses the built-in version of **subsasgn** to complete the assignment. The second complication occurs when the assignment indices increase the size of **this.mArray**. We have to be careful, or we might end up with a container that contains empty cells. This is not necessarily a problem, but if allowed, it complicates the other member functions. There is nothing to prevent line 34 from adding empty cells. Lines 35–38 detect the empty cells and replace them with default objects. This behavior is consistent with normal array expansion. Line 35 uses **cellfun** to locate empty cells, and line 37 assigns a default object into each empty index.

Lines 40–44 catch all other input conditions and throw an error. The error message indicates the type that caused the error. In general, this is a good idea because cogent error messages help make debugging easier.

When more than one level of indexing is required, lines 46–51 perform the assignment. In this case, the input value doesn't end up in **this.mArray** as an object, but rather, the input value is assigned into an object that already exists in **this.mArray**. There are three steps involved. In the first step, lines 47–48 create a new container and populate it with a subset of the objects in the container. The objects in the subset are selected based on the indices in **index(1)**. In the second step, lines 49–50 call **subsasgn** to mutate the subset container according to the indices remaining in **index**. In the third step, line 51 uses **index(1)** to assign the now-mutated subset back into its original location.

19.2.1.4   Container Modifications to get

Dot-reference access is **get**'s domain. Two sections in the standard version of **get** need container-specific additions. Both the public variable section and the concealed variable section need to forward the dot-reference operation to objects in **this.mArray**. For the public forward, the desired public variable name is formatted as a **substruct**. For the concealed forward, the variable name is formatted as a string. Container-specific versions of both sections are shown in Code Listing 111. These are the only sections that need to be modified.

Code Listing 111, Modifications to the Public and Concealed Variable Sections of get.m for a Container Class

```
1    % public-member-variable section
2    found = true;   % otherwise-case will flip to false
3    switch index(1).subs
4      otherwise
5        found = false;   % look in each object
6        for k = 1:numel(this.mArray)
7          try
8            varargout{k} = get(this.mArray{k}, index, varargin{:});
```

```
9              do_sub_indexing = false; % object must sub-index
10             found = true;
11          catch
12             err = lasterror;
13             switch err.identifier
14               case 'MATLAB:nonExistentField'
15                 varargout{k} = [];
16               otherwise
17                 rethrow(err);
18             end
19           end
20        end
21   end
22
23   % concealed member variables, not strictly public
24   if ~found && called_by_name
25     found = true;
26     switch index(1).subs
27       case 'mDisplayFunc' % class-wizard reserved field
28         if isempty(this)
29           varargout = {};
30         else
31           varargout = {this.mDisplayFunc};
32         end
33       otherwise
34         found = false;   % look in each object
35         for k = 1:numel(this.mArray)
36           try
37             varargout{k} = get(this.mArray{k}, index(1).subs,
                 varargin{:});
38             do_sub_indexing = false; % object must sub-index
39             found = true;
40           catch
41             err = lasterror;
42             switch err.identifier
43               case 'MATLAB:nonExistentField'
44                 varargout{k} = [];
45               otherwise
46                 rethrow(err);
47             end
48           end
49         end
50     end
51   end
```

Instead of throwing an error, the **otherwise** cases in both the public and concealed variable sections loop over the objects in **this.mArray**, calling **get** for each object. Before entering the loop, **found** is set to **false** (lines 5 and 34). The first command in each loop is a **try-catch** statement. The first command in each **try** block forwards the **get** call to an object (lines 8 and 36). Either **get** will return a value, which is inserted in **varargout**, or **get** will throw an error. If **get** is successful, line 8 or line 38 informs the container that no further subindexing is required. This will always be correct for Class Wizard objects because **get** for every object includes subindexing code. Finally, line 9 or line 39 informs the container that a value was found.

If the object's **get** throws an error, we immediately jump to the **catch** block (line 11 or 40). There we apply standard error-processing using **lasterror**. If the error identifier is **'MATLAB:non-ExistentField'**, it means the object couldn't locate a field consistent with the **index**. For this **case**, line 15 or 44 inserts empty as the return value from the object. Assigning empty delays the evaluation of **found**. We will wait until every object is queried to make that determination. If no objects return a value, **found** will be assigned **false**, but if even one object returns a value, **found** will be assigned **true**. This logic may sound odd, but it covers the situation of a child defining additional public variables. In your container implementations, you may choose to handle this differently. If every object throws an error, line 10 or 39 will never execute, all **varargout** cells will be empty, and **found** will be **false**. If even one object returns a value, line 10 or 39 assign **found** a value of **true** and at least one **varargout** cell will contain an assigned value

The way **found** and **varargout** are managed means that not all objects in the container need an identical set of public or concealed variables. If any object in the container returns a value, **found** will be set to **true** and the corresponding cell in **varargout** will contain that value. Objects that throw an error contain empty in their corresponding **varargout** cell. This behavior makes the container a little more flexible, but it also allows inconsistent behavior. For example, if the container holds even one **cStar** object, **shapes.Title** will successfully return a value. On the other hand, if the container does not hold a **cStar** object, trying to access **shapes.Title** will cause an error. If inconsistent behavior is a problem, the collection of accessible names should be limited to the names returned from **fieldnames**.

Examine the forward calls on lines 8 and 37. The entire **index** is used in the public section, but only **index(1).subs** is used in the concealed section. Prior to lines 8 and 37, the passed-in **index** is converted into a **substruct index**; see §8.2.2. After the conversion, **called_by_name** has a value that either allows or prevents access to concealed variables. If concealed access is allowed, we can be assured that the **substruct index** will have only one level of type **'.'**. Line 37 pulls the variable name out of **index** and passes the string. By passing the string, the object's **get** will allow access to its concealed variables. Passing the **substruct index** would not allow concealed access.

19.2.1.5 Container Modifications to set

Dot-reference mutation is **set**'s domain. Like **get**, the same two sections in **set** need container-specific additions. The only difference between the modified public and concealed variable sections is the format of **index**. The public section uses a **substruct**, while the concealed section uses a string. Since the additions are so similar, only the public variable section is shown in Code Listing 112. The fully modified function can be found in the **chapter_19/@cShape-Array** directory.

Code Listing 112, Modifications to the Public Section of set.m for a Container Class

```
1    % public-member-variable section
2    found = true;  % otherwise-case will flip to false
3    switch index(1).subs
```

```
4     otherwise
5       found = false;   % look in each object
6       for k = 1:numel(this.mArray)
7         if length(varargin) == 1
8           set_val = varargin{1};
9         else
10          set_val = varargin{k};
11        end
12
13        try
14          this.mArray{k} = set(this.mArray{k}, index, set_val);
15          found = true;
16        catch
17          err = lasterror;
18          switch err.identifier
19            case 'MATLAB:nonExistentField'
20              % NOP
21            otherwise
22              rethrow(err);
23          end
24        end
25      end
26  end
```

Instead of throwing an error, the **otherwise** case beginning on line 4 loops over the objects in **this.mArray**, calling **set** for each object. Before entering the loop, line 5 assigns **found** equal to **false**. Inside the loop, lines 7–11 format the input assignment value. Line 8 supports the assignment of the same input value into the public variable of every object. Line 10 supports an array of input values by matching the input index with the container index. The **try-catch** statement in lines 13–24 performs the assignment. Inside **try**, the **set** on line 14 attempts to mutate a public variable. The object will either accept the value or throw an error. If the indexed object accepts the value, line 15 assigns **found** equal to **true**. If the indexed object throws an error, line 17 uses **lasterror** to assign the error structure to **err**. The switch statement in lines 18–23 identifies the error and takes appropriate action. If the error is **'MATLAB:nonExistent-Field'**, no further action is required. All other errors are rethrown.

The same inconsistency described for **get** also occurs for **set**. Correcting inconsistent behavior in one requires the same correction for the other. Of course, fixing the inconsistency also means limiting the set of returned public variables to those held in common by all objects in the container. Generally, that means the public variables allocated to the parent.

19.2.2 TAILORING BUILT-IN BEHAVIOR

Container-specific modifications to group-of-eight files now allow objects to be added to the container. Group-of-eight modifications also provide control over each object's public member variables. We can't get full control over the objects in the container until we tailor the behavior of several built-in functions. Most of these functions have something to do with the number of objects in the container. For example, the built-in version of **size** will return a value consistent with the container object itself, but that value isn't related to the number of objects held in the container.

Fortunately, MATLAB's object-oriented features allow us to overload and tailor the behavior for built-in functions. Here we look at **end**, **length**, **ndims**, **reshape**, and **size**.

19.2.2.1 Container-Tailored end

In §19.1, the following use of **end** was highlighted:

```
shape_array(end+1) = cStar;
```

The built-in behavior of **end** is not appropriate because it returns the wrong value. The inputs to **end** are the object **this**, the dimension of interest **k**, and the total number of dimensions **n**. Values for **n** and **k** are determined based on the total number of dimensions used in the index and the particular dimension where **end** is used. For example, **shape_array(end)** would assign **n=1** and **k=1**, while **shape_array(5, end, 3, 1)** would assign **n=4** and **k=2**. The input argument behavior drives the implementation in Code Listing 113.

Code Listing 113, Overloading end.m to Support Container Indexing

```
1   function num = end(this, k, n)
2   array_size = size(this.mArray);
3   n_size = [array_size(1:n-1) prod(array_size(n:end))];
4   num = n_size(k);
```

Obtaining the value is tricky because indexing operations do not always include values for every dimension. Line 2 gets the size of **this.mArray**. Line 3 uses this size to calculate a different-sized array based on **n** dimensions. The leading elements in **n_size** are copies of the number of elements in the **1:n-1** dimensions of **this.mArray**. The last value in **n_size** represents the number of elements in the remaining dimensions. Line 4 selects the **k**th element from the new **n_size** array.

19.2.2.2 Container-Tailored cat, horzcat, vertcat

Concatenation is a convenient alternative to inserting objects element by element. Three functions are used for concatenation: **cat**, **horzcat**, and **vertcat**. **Horzcat** and **vertcat** are particularly important because they have corresponding operator syntax. For example, **[container, star]** is converted into a call to **horzcat** and **[container; star]** is converted into a call to **vertcat**. The **cat** function has no corresponding operator, but it is the most general because it will concatenate along any dimension.

Given an implementation for **cat**, the implementation of **horzcat.m** consists of the one-line command

```
this = cat(2, varargin{:});
```

Similarly, **vertcat.m** consists of the one-line command

```
this = cat(1, varargin{:});
```

All three are important because **cat** contains the general-purpose concatenation commands, while **horzcat** and **vertcat** conveniently map to operator syntax. All three must be overloaded because built-in versions of **horzcat** and **vertcat** will not call an overloaded version of **cat**. The implementation for **cat** is provided in Code Listing 114.

Line 2 instantiates an empty container that will be used as the destination for the concatenated result. Line 3 preallocates a cell array that will eventually hold the full set of objects. Lines 5–8 call the subfunction **expand_input** to form an equivalent cell array of objects for every input

Code Listing 114, Overloading cat.m to Support Container Operations

```
1    function this = cat(dir, varargin)
2    this = feval(mfilename('class'));  % new empty container is
      destination
3    object_varargin = cell(size(varargin));  % object cells will
      go in here
4
5    for idx = 1:numel(varargin)
6      object_varargin{idx} = ...
7        expand_input(varargin{idx}, mfilename('class'),
         this.mType);
8    end
9
10   this.mArray = cat(dir, object_varargin{:});
11
12   % ---------------------------------------
13   function out_cell = expand_input(in_val, container_type,
      allowed_type)
14   if isa(in_val, container_type) % container object
15     out_cell = in_val.mArray;  % mArray is a cell array
16
17   elseif isa(in_val, allowed_type) % object array
18     out_cell = num2cell(in_val);
19
20   elseif isa(in_val, 'cell')  % cell array of objects
21     out_cell = cell(size(in_val));
22     for idx = 1:numel(in_val)
23       out_cell{idx} = ...
24         expand_input(in_val{idx}, container_type,
            allowed_type);
25     end
26     if any(cellfun('length', out_cell(:)) > 1)
27       error('Container:UnsupportedAssignment', ...
28         'The input arguments are too complicated to easily
            expand.');
29     end
30     out_cell = reshape(cat(1, out_cell{:}), size(in_val));
31   else
32     error('Container:UnsupportedAssignment', ...
33       'Container cat for specified inputs is not supported.');
34   end
```

in **varargin**. Line 10 calls the built-in version of **cat** using list expansion for the expanded cells. The concatenated result is assigned into **this.mArray** and passed back to the caller.

The subfunction **expand_input** configures the input arguments so that the **cat** command in line 10 produces the desired result. Three input types can be expanded: a container object (lines 14–15), an array of objects with a type compatible with the container (lines 17–18), and a cell array of objects (lines 20–30). For a container, line 15 returns the private cell array, **in_val.mArray**. For a compatible object array, line 18 converts the array into a cell array of objects and returns the result. Processing for a cell array is more complicated because each element in the cell array can be a container, an object array, or another cell array. Lines 22–25 loop over the cells, making a recursive call to **expand_input**. The expanded results are collected in elements of **out_cell**. Some input configurations are too complex to expand in this way, and lines 26–29 throw an error when the input is too complicated. Finally, line 30 concatenates the expanded inputs and reshapes the result so that the output size is compatible with the input size. Expanding the inputs in this way yields a container version of **cat** that can accept a wide range of inputs.

19.2.2.3   Container-Tailored length, ndims, reshape, and size

Even with all of these changes in place, a few functions in the group of eight return unexpected results. For example, regardless of how many objects are stored in the container, **struct** currently returns a scalar structure. This behavior might be **struct**'s problem but it isn't **struct**'s fault. The mismatch occurs because **struct** calls **length(this(:))** and the built-in version of **length** doesn't know about **this.mArray**. Currently, any function that relies on **length** will receive the wrong value. The same can be said for **ndims**, **reshape**, and **size**.

Putting **struct** back on the right track requires a tailored version of **length**. The code is very simple: instead of returning **length(this)**, the tailored version returns **length(this.mArray)**. The new function is shown in Code Listing 115.

Code Listing 115, Overloading length.m to Support Container Indexing

```
1  function num = length(this)
2  num = length(this.mArray);
```

For similar reasons, we also need to provide tailored versions of **ndims**, **reshape**, and **size**. **Ndims** and **reshape** are one-liners. The one-line command inside **ndims** is

```
num = ndims(this.mArray);
```

The online command inside **reshape** is

```
this.mArray = reshape(this.mArray, varargin{:});
```

A similar pattern is used to implement **size**. The difference with **size** is that more than one output might be required. Multiple outputs may be collected in the usual way. Use **nargout** to preallocate an empty cell array and assign the empty array into **varargout**. When **size** is called for **this.mArray**, the correct number of outputs will be returned. All of this requires two lines instead of one. The two-line implementation for **size** is

```
varargout = cell(1, max(1,nargout));

[varargout{:}] = size(this.mArray, varargin{:});
```

After **length**, **ndims**, **reshape**, and **size** are added to the class directory, the container looks very much like an array. With a few more additions, the array-like public interface will be complete.

19.2.3 cShapeArray and numel

The function **numel** should be in the same category as **length**, **size**, **reshape**, and **ndims**; however, **numel** requires a separate section because it exhibits some unexpected behavior. The tailored version of **numel** doesn't always seem to be called at the right time. We can implement **numel** and demonstrate what happens. Implementing the tailored version follows easily from the previous section. The one-line command inside **numel.m** is

```
num = numel(this.mArray, varargin{:});
```

First, create a **cShapeArray** container with two shapes in it. This can be done using the following commands:

```
>> shape_array = [cShapeArray cStar cDiamond];
```

Next, look at the result of dot-reference access once with and once without a container-specific version **numel**. On the disk, the class that includes **numel** can be found in **chapter_19/with_numel**. If you are following along, when you change between directories, be sure to **clear classes** and recreate the container. The result with **numel** is

```
>> shape_array.LineWeight

ans =

normal

ans =

normal
```

and the result without **numel** is

```
>> shape_array.LineWeight

ans =

 'normal' 'normal'
```

Differences are subtle, but the result with **numel** included is correct. You should expect two answers because the **length** of **shape_array** is two. Somewhere behind the scenes, MATLAB finds the correct value of **nargout** by calling **numel**. When the container class includes **numel**, **subsref** and **get** receive the appropriate value for **nargout**. When the container class does not include **numel**, the built-in version supplies the wrong value to **nargout**. Code inside **get** is trying to correct the mismatch by concatenating the **LineWeight** strings in a single cell array. If that was the end of the story, it would be easy to say, "Let's overload **numel**." If that was the end of the story, I wouldn't be putting you through all of this. Before we make a firm decision on **numel**, let's look at an example of dot-reference mutation.

Include a container-specific version of **numel** and see what happens for the following command:

```
>> [shape_array.LineWeight] = deal('bold');
```

```
??? Insufficient number of outputs from function on right hand
side of equal sign to satisfy overloaded assignment.
```

We can shed some light on the cause of the error by putting breakpoints at the beginning of the built-in version of **deal.m** and at the beginning of the container versions of both **numel.m** and **subsasgn.m**. Execute the same command, and the first break occurs inside **deal**. Checking the value of **nargout** returns 1. The value of **nargout** is incorrect even though our container carefully overloads **size**, **length**, **ndims**, and **numel**. Continue, and the next break occurs inside **numel**. Here MATLAB is trying to figure out how many elements are required by the left-hand side, and it calls **numel** to find out. As a result, the left-hand side reports that it needs two inputs but MATLAB has already determined that the right-hand side has only one to offer. The mismatch results in an error. We never even reached the breakpoint inside **subsasgn**. Try the same thing with a structure array, and **nargout** inside **deal** returns the correct value.

A slightly different syntax produces the desired result with no error. The modified command is

```
>> [shape_array(:).LineWeight] = deal('bold');
```

Here, the execution never hits the break point in **numel**. Instead, **subsasgn** performs the assignment. Unfortunately, the problem still exists; it is just hiding in the modified syntax.

The first hint that the problem still exists comes from the fact that the container's version of **numel** is never called. Knowing this, we can make the error reoccur by trying to assign two **LineWeight** values into the two elements of **shape_array**, for example:

```
[shape_array(:).LineWeight] = deal('bold', 'normal');

??? Error using ==> deal

The number of outputs should match the number of inputs.
```

This command throws an error because the value of **nargout** inside **deal** is still one. In **deal**, one output is not compatible with two inputs so the result is an error. In one case, the error appears to be occurring because **deal** is called before **numel**. In the other case, the overloaded version of **numel** isn't called at all.

The result when the container version of **numel** is not included is different but still not satisfying. In the no-**numel** situation, both versions of the single-input **deal** work, for example:

```
>> [shape_array.LineWeight] = deal('bold');

>> [shape_array(:).LineWeight] = deal('bold');
```

Both commands assign `'bold'` to all objects in **shape_array**. While this represents a small improvement in consistency, trying to **deal** more than one value still generates an error. Even so, a small improvement is better than no improvement. For this reason, the test drive uses a **cShapeArray** implementation that does not redefine the behavior of **numel**.

In reality, a container class with no **numel** function is a poor compromise. Now any command that relies on **numel** will receive one instead of the correct number of elements. To make matters worse, **numel(shape_array)** and **length(shape_array(:))** return different values. Two commands that are supposed to return the same value but don't can lead to subtle, difficult-to-find errors in client code. I think this behavior is an error that can only be corrected by changing MATLAB. In a container, the problem is masked due to support for vector syntax. The loops encapsulated inside the container use **numel(this.mArray)**, which always returns the correct value.

19.2.3.1 Container-Tailored num2cell and mat2cell

Array-reference access through **subsref** always returns a container. This is true even when the container contains only one object. Having the object versus a container with only one object usually doesn't matter because it is hard to tell the difference. The reason it is hard to tell is due to the container's ability to mimic the interface of the objects it holds. Occasionally we need to get an object out of its container. Tailoring **num2cell** for this task is a logical extension of its normal behavior. Normally, **num2cell** converts an array into a cell array. Thus, with some limits, it is perfectly natural to expect **num2cell** to convert a container into a cell array.

Some options available through **num2cell** aren't supported for this container. That does not mean they can't be supported. For example, a second input argument is supposed to organize the output by row or column. We can't use concatenation to do this, but we could return a cell array of containers, one for each row or column. Adding this ability isn't difficult, but it isn't vital to this introduction. Specifying more than one input for this container's version of **num2cell** will throw an error. For the same reasons, the container's version of **mat2cell** will always throw an error.

The code for **num2cell** is provided in Code Listing 116. Lines 3–4 throw an error when **nargin** is greater than one, and line 6 returns **this.mArray** as the converted output. Individual objects can then be accessed by indexing the returned cell array. The code for **mat2cell** includes an **error** call very similar to the code in lines 3–4.

Code Listing 116, Overloading num2cell to Support Raw Output from a Container

```
1   function container_cells = num2cell(this, varargin)
2   if nargin > 1
3     error('Container:UnsupportedFunction', ...
4       'num2cell for a container only supports one input');
5   else
6     container_cells = this.mArray;
7   end
```

19.2.4 CONTAINER FUNCTIONS THAT ARE SPECIFIC TO cSHAPE OBJECTS

With the basics out of the way, we can focus our attention on the functions that give shape objects their unique behavior. Changing the size, drawing the shapes, and resetting the figure are all important operations valid for cShape objects. We need to extend the same set of operations to **cShapeArray** containers. As with the other container functions, these member functions must make the container appear to be an array of shapes. As you would expect, the container's versions index over the objects in **this.mArray{:}** in the same way the original functions index into **this(:)**.

19.2.4.1 cShapeArray times and mtimes

Multiplication of a shape object with a **double** changes the shape's size. Multiplication of a **cShapeArray** container with a **double** changes the size of every shape in the container. MATLAB uses two operators for multiplication. Array multiplication, **times.m**, uses an operator syntax given by **x.*y**. Matrix multiplication, **mtimes.m**, uses an operator syntax given by **x*y**. The only multiplication function overloaded by **cShape** is **mtimes**. For **cShapeArray** objects, both **mtimes** and **times** are overloaded.

To be effective, **cShapeArray**'s version of **times** must closely match the expected, built-in behavior. When one input is a scalar, every object in the container must be multiplied by the scalar input. When the same input is an array of **doubles**, the behavior must be element-by-element multiplication. The code for **times** is provided in Code Listing 117.

Code Listing 117, Overloading times.m for the cShape Container

```
1   function this = times(lhs, rhs)
2   % one input must be cShape type, which one
3   if isa(lhs, 'cShapeArray')
4     this = lhs;
5     scale = rhs;
6   else
7     this = rhs;
```

```
8      scale = lhs;
9    end
10
11   if ~isnumeric(scale) || ~isreal(scale)
12     error('Container:InvalidInput', ...
13       'Multiplicand must be a real numeric value');
14   end
15
16   if length(scale) == 1
17     scale = scale * ones(size(this.mArray));
18
19   elseif any(size(scale) ~= size(this.mArray))
20     error('Container:InvalidInput', ...
21       sprintf('%s\n', '??? Error using ==> times', ...
22         'Dimensions are not correct.'));
23   end
24
25   for index = 1:numel(this.mArray)
26     this.mArray{index} = this.mArray{index} * scale(index);
27   end
```

The container is superior to **double** and that means the container can be passed into **times** as the left-hand or right-hand argument. Lines 3–9 assign the container to **this** and the other input to **scale**. Lines 11–14 restrict **scale** to real numeric values. Lines 16–17 expand a scalar value into an array the same size as **this.mArray**. Now every element in **this.mArray** can be multiplied by a corresponding element of **scale**. If the input is an array, lines 19–22 throw an error if the **size** of **scale** and the **size** of **this.mArray** don't match along every dimension. Finally, lines 25–27 loop over all objects in the container to calculate the result. The result is stored back into **this.mArray**.

In general, it is probably not possible to define matrix multiplication between objects in a container and an array because the operation depends on both multiplication and addition. For some containers it will work, and for others it will not. It is possible to define matrix multiplication between a **cShape** container and a scalar. With a scalar, array multiplication and matrix multiplication are the same. The implementation for **mtimes** reuses Code Listing 117 by replacing lines 19–22 with the following lines:

```
else
  error('Container:InvalidInput', ...
  sprintf('%s\n', '??? Error using ==> mtimes', ...
  'Matrix multiplication of container and array is not
  allowed.'));
```

As implemented, container multiplication introduces a subtle difference between a container with one object and the object. Container multiplication does not support the use of different vertical and horizontal scale factors. There are several ways to code around this difference, but since every container is different, no single solution will work in all situations. Rather than complicate the example, we will simply allow this difference to exist.

19.2.4.2   cShapeArray draw

The container's version of **draw** uses commands from both **cShape**'s version of **draw** and the
cell-array **draw** example we discussed in §13.1.3. The commands from **cShape**'s version manage
the figure handle, and commands from the cell-array example call **draw** for every object in
this.mArray. Like the cell-array example, all shapes in one container are drawn in the same
figure. The function is shown in Code Listing 118.

Code Listing 118, Overloading draw.m for the cShape Container

```
1    function this = draw(this, FigureHandle)
2    if nargout ~= 1
3      warning('draw must be called using: obj = draw(obj). Nothing
         drawn.');
4    elseif ~isempty(this.mArray)
5      if nargin < 2
6        FigureHandle = [];
7      end
8
9      shape_handles = [get(this(:), 'mFigureHandle')];
10     if iscell(shape_handles)
11       shape_handles = cell2mat(shape_handles);
12     end
13     handle_array = unique([FigureHandle shape_handles(:)']);
14     if numel(handle_array) > 1 % mismatched
15       for k = fliplr(find([handle_array ~= FigureHandle]))
16         try
17           delete(handle_array(k));   % close figures
18         end
19         handle_array(k) = [];
20       end
21     end
22
23     if isempty(handle_array)
24       handle_array = figure;   % create new figure
25     end
26     figure(handle_array);
27
28     if nargin < 2   % assume if handle passed in, clf already
         called
29       clf;     % clear the figure
30     end
31
32     hold on;   % all shapes drawn in the same figure
33     for k = 1:numel(this.mArray)
34       this.mArray{k} = draw(this.mArray{k}, handle_array);
35     end
```

```
36      hold off;
37    end
```

Lines 2–3 enforce the use of mutator syntax by warning the user to include a return argument. When **nargout** equals one, the execution skips to line 4. If the container is empty, there are no shapes to draw. The execution skips to the end and returns. If **this.mArray** has elements, line 5 begins the process of drawing them. Lines 5–7 ensure that the **FigureHandle** variable exists. Line 9 collects figure handles from all objects in the container, and lines 10–12 reformat the array just in case the **get** in line 9 returned cells. Line 13 keeps only the unique figure handles. If **FigureHandle** contained a value, that value can now be found in **handle_array(1)**. Lines 14–21 check for more than one figure handle and close the extras. When the execution reaches line 23, if **handle_array** is empty, line 24 creates a new figure.

Line 26 selects **handle_array** as the current figure. If a figure handle was passed into **draw**, lines 28–30 do nothing. Otherwise, line 24 clears the figure. Finally, lines 32–36 loop over all the objects in the array, calling **draw** for each.

19.2.4.3   cShapeArray reset

Like **draw**, the container's version of **reset** needs to loop over all objects in the array, calling **reset** for each. After the shapes are reset, the figure window can be closed. The implementation is shown in Code Listing 119.

Code Listing 119, Overloading reset.m for the cShape Container

```
1    function this = reset(this)
2    for k = 1:numel(this.mArray)
3      this.mArray{k} = reset(this.mArray{k});
4    end
5    try
6      delete(this.mFigHandle)
7    end
8    this.mFigHandle = [];
```

Lines 2–4 loop over all objects in the container, calling **reset** for each. Lines 5–7 then close the figure window by calling **delete**. Calling delete more than once with the same figure handle throws an error. The **try-catch** statement in lines 5–7 allows the error to occur with no consequences. Error handling for the command on line 6 requires no corresponding **catch**. Finally, line 8 assigns empty to the container's figure handle.

19.3   TEST DRIVE

From the outside, a **cShapeArray** container should look almost exactly like an array of **cShape** objects. The difference, of course, is that the container can hold objects with type **cShape**, **cStar**, and **cDiamond**, while an array of **cShape** objects can hold only objects of type **cShape**. This is a significant difference achieved through changes to functions in the standard group of eight, the redefinition of several built-in functions, and the redefinition of shape-dependent functions. All of these member functions work together to create an interface that mimics the simplicity of an array. The commands in Code Listing 120 demonstrate the implementation.

Code Listing 120, Chapter 19 Test Drive Command Listing: cShape Container

```
1   >> cd '/oop_guide/chapter_19'
2   >> set(0, 'FormatSpacing', 'compact')
3   >> clear classes; fclose all; close all force;
4   >>
5   >> shapes = cShapeArray
6   shapes =
7     cShapeArray object: 0-by-0
8       with public member variables:
9         Size
10        ColorRgb
11        Points
12        LineWeight
13  >>
14  >> star = cStar;
15  >> star.LineWeight = 'bold';
16  >> star = 0.5 * star;
17  >>
18  >> diamond = cDiamond;
19  >> diamond = [2 3] * diamond;
20  >> diamond = cDiamond;
21  >> diamond = [1.5 2] * diamond;
22  >>
23  >> shapes(1) = star;
24  >> shapes(3) = diamond;
25  >> shape_cell = num2cell(shapes)
26  shape_cell =
27    [1x1 cStar]      [1x1 cShape]      [1x1 cDiamond]
28  >> shapes = [shapes cStar cDiamond];
29  >> shapes(2) = [];
30  >> size(shape)
31  ans =
32    1        4
33  >> shapes = reshape(shapes, 2, []);
34  >>
35  >> shapes(1,1).ColorRgb = [1;0;0];
36  >> shapes(1,2).ColorRgb = [0;1;0];
37  >> shapes(2,1).ColorRgb = [0;0;1];
38  >> shapes(2,2).ColorRgb = [1;0;1];
39  >> shapes(1,2).LineWeight = 'bold'
40  >> shapes.ColorRgb
41  ans =
42    1        0        0        1
43    0        0        1
44    0        1        0        1
45  >>
```

```
46  >>  shapes  =  [1 1;  0.75 1]  .*  shapes;
47  >>  shapes  =  draw(shapes);
48  >>  shapes  =  reset(shapes);
```

Line 5 creates an empty **cShapeArray** container. Omitting the trailing semicolon produces the output that follows on lines 6–12. The output is a result of the container-specific version of **display** in concert with a host other member functions. The list of functions includes the constructor, **ctor_ini**, **parent_list**, **display**, **fieldnames**, **get**, **length**, and **size**. Even more important, **0-by-0** displayed on line 7 confirms that the default container contains the correct number of objects.

Lines 14–21 create a few shape objects with specifically assigned values. Lines 23–33 add, remove, and reshape container elements. Line 23 inserts **star** into index 1, and line 24 inserts **diamond** into index 3. During the command on line 24, **subsasgn** inserted a default **cShape** object into index 2. Calling **num2cell** and displaying the result (lines 25–27) confirm our expectations for object types. Line 28 uses operator notation for **horzcat** to add a default **cStar** object and a default **cDiamond** object to end of the container. The empty assignment in line 29 removes the default **cShape** object from the container. The container now contains two **cStar** objects and two **cDiamond** objects. Calling **size** (line 30) confirms that the container now holds four objects. Line 33 uses **reshape** to changes the size from 1 × 4 to 2 × 2. So far, the container acts like an array.

Lines 35–39 mutate member variables in place, and line 40 displays the RGB color values from every object in the container. Notice that the color output isn't exactly right. Instead of four separate answers, we see an array with four columns, the result of a **nargout** mismatch. Line 46 demonstrates **times**, and line 47 draws the shapes. The resulting figure window is shown in Figure 19.1. The shapes are the right line colors, and both stars are bold. The sizes are also consistent with scale values set using the **times** operator. Finally, line 48 resets the shapes and closes the figure window.

There are many other commands we could try, but the commands in Code Listing 120 provide us with a lot of confidence that the container really does act like an array. As long as we can put up with inconsistent behavior from **numel**, we can use containers to simplify the syntax for a hierarchy. Without containers, we are forced to store different object types in a cell array, and cell

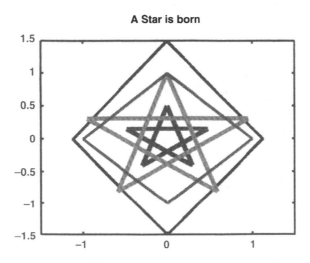

FIGURE 19.1 Shapes in a container drawn together.

array syntax isn't very convenient. This is particularly true for vector operations, where **cellfun** is as good as it gets.

19.4 SUMMARY

In many object-oriented languages, objects and containers go hand in hand. Yet, with regard to MATLAB, containers have been totally ignored. Nobody is talking about containers, and outside of the implementation in this chapter, I know of no other. I hope that this chapter will change that situation and initiate a dialog that will improve the implementation. As containers go, the container implemented in this chapter isn't perfect; however, it does achieve most of the necessary functionality. There is little doubt that over time the basic implementation in this chapter will be improved upon.

The container implementation is an excellent example of the power of object-oriented programming and an example of the flexibility provided by the group-of-eight framework. The container gives us a way to collect objects derived from the same parent into something that acts very much like a normal array of objects. With the container, a user doesn't need to remember which objects use array syntax and which use cell-array syntax. The ability to encapsulate container code behind an interface also makes it easier to use different objects in a hierarchy. This is a huge selling point because nobody will use MATLAB objects unless they are easy to use. Consistency in the group-of-eight interface makes classes easier to implement and containers make hierarchies more approachable.

19.5 INDEPENDENT INVESTIGATIONS

1. Add code to **subsasgn** that will allow a cell array of objects to be passed in and assigned to objects in the container. The operator syntax for the assignment might look something like

   ```
   shapes([1 2]) = {cStar cDiamond};
   ```

2. Add code to **subsasgn** that will allow another container of the same type to be passed in. The operator syntax for the assignment might look like the last line in the following:

   ```
   your_shapes = cShapeArray;

   shapes = cShapeArray;

   your_shapes(1:3) = [cStar cStar cStar];

   shapes([2 4]) = your_shapes(1:2);
   ```

   At first glance, you might think that **your_shapes(1:2)** is an array; but the way we implemented **subsref, your_shapes(1:2)** is another **cShapeArray** container.

3. Modify **times** or **mtimes** to support different scale values for the vertical and horizontal size elements.

20 Static Member Data and Singleton Objects

Quite often, a class needs to manage data that must be shared among all objects of the class. Every object of the class needs full and immediate access to this classwide data. When one object changes a value, this change must be immediately available to every object in the class. In other languages, such classwide data are often called *static*. So-called *static member variables* can't be stored with an object's private structure because objects maintain separate copies of their private data. Using **global** data is a possibility, but that has its own set of limitations. Under the right conditions, a **persistent** variable is perfectly suited for this application. In this chapter, we implement a static member variable strategy that uses a **persistent** variable. The implementation creates a standard location and an interface that fit nicely into the group-of-eight framework. The example implementation also includes a way to **save** and **load** static variables along with the private variables. Objects with this kind of **load** and **save** capability are often called *persistent objects*. With the introduction of static variables, we can now define a class using only static variables. Objects of an all static variable class are called *singleton objects* because all objects of the class share a single copy of their variables.

20.1 ADDING STATIC DATA TO OUR FRAMEWORK

Most object-oriented languages support a way to declare and manage data that are shared among all objects of a class. Classwide shared data represent a new data category that isn't local, nested*, global, or private. In C++, the *static* keyword is used to declare shared member variables and the term *static member variable* is widely recognized. MATLAB includes no organic support for static member variables, but that hasn't stopped us yet. Once we have a plan, adding support for static member variables is actually easy. We can take advantage of encapsulation to implement a static member interface that fits reasonably well with the group of eight. The basic implementation in this chapter hits all the highlights but probably leaves room for improvement.

Here's an outline of the plan. First, we will create a private member function named **static.m** that contains **persistent** storage for static variables and provides a simple interface for accessing and mutating values. Since all objects of the class use the same functions, any persistent variable in a member function is automatically shared by all objects of the class. Second, we will add static variable initialization commands to the constructor. These commands will assign initial values and initialize the **persistent** variables in **static.m**. Third, we will give **get** and **set** a way to access and mutate static variables. Finally, we will include **load** and **save** functionality. Before we start the implementation, we need to discuss a few issues.

Since **static.m** is a private function, static member variables have private visibility. Thus, static variables are not automatically included in the collection of public variables, and clients have no direct access to them. If we wanted to be verbose, we could call them *static private member variables*. When I use the term *static variable*, I really mean static private member variable. Like normal private variables, only member functions have direct access to static variables. Also like normal private variables, clients can be given indirect access through **subsref, subsasgn, get**, and **set**. Again being verbose, we could refer to this indirect access as a *static public member*

---

* See *Nested Functions* in the MATLAB documentation or help browser.

variable. Like normal public variables, static public variables can be implemented using direct-link or non-direct-link techniques. The only important difference between normal private variables and static variables is where the data are stored.

With no precedent, we are free to define the interface to **static.m** in any way we choose. The fact that clients can't call **static.m** allows us to be cavalier with respect to data checking. Encapsulation restricts the visibility and reduces the chance that **static.m** will be abused. We can always add error-checking code if the simple interface proves to be inadequate. The implementation for **static** is shown in Code Listing 121.

Code Listing 121, Private static.m Used to Store and Manage Classwide Private Data

```
1  function static_this = static(static_this)
2  persistent static_var
3  if nargin == 1
4    static_var = static_this; % mutator
5  else
6    static_this = static_var; % accessor
7  end
```

With one input argument and one output argument (line 1), the interface is extremely simple. Static variables are stored in the **persistent** structure declared in line 2. Lines 3–7 implement the interface. If **static** is called with one input, line 4 copies the input into the **persistent** **static_var** variable. If this seems too dangerous, add code that compares fields in the input structure to fields in the **persistent** structure. If **static** is called with no inputs, line 6 simply copies the static variable structure into the output variable. This interface forces a mutator to call static **twice**: once to get the structure of static variables, and again to assign the modified values.

20.1.1 HOOKING STATIC DATA INTO THE GROUP OF EIGHT

Now that the static variable interface is specified, we can modify the group-of-eight functions to take advantage of them. Before we can hook static data into the group of eight, we first need some classwide data. In our shape hierarchy, no existing variable would benefit from being made static. Thus, we need to invent a reason to use a static variable. Suppose we are interested in logging the way our clients use a particular function. For example, every time a client sets the line width, we want to log unique **width** values and count how many times each value is used. This information might be useful for interface design or run-time optimization. We could add a **persistent** variable in the helper function, but how would we access its value after the run? A static variable is a much better choice. We could also use a **global** variable and accept the risk of a name clash. Again, a static variable is a better choice. In fact, anytime you are tempted to add a **persistent** or **global** variable to a member function, you should always think about using a static member variable instead.

Modularity in the group of eight reduces the effort involved in adding static member variables. Static private member variable support requires only one group-of-eight change. The constructor helper needs to initialize the static variable structure and pass the structure into **static.m**. Static public member variable support requires changes to **get** and **set**. Since static variables are not stored in **this**, cases associated with static variables need to access the static variable structure. Finally, if we want the developer view option to display both private and static variables, a small addition to the **developer_view** subfunction is necessary. Saving and loading objects with static data involve two new overloads: **saveobj** and **loadobj**.

20.1.1.1 Static Variables and the Constructor

Like any private variable, the new static variable, **mLineWidthCounter**, must be declared and initialized during construction. Instead of adding **mLineWidthCounter** to the structure for **this**, the new private variable is added to a structure and passed into **static**. Inside **static**, the input structure is stored as a **persistent** variable, making it available to all objects of the class. The default module for private variable initialization is **/private/ctor_ini**. Static variable additions to **/@cLineStyle/private/ctor_ini** are shown in Code Listing 122. If the static variable list includes one or more names, Class Wizard will generate these additions.

Code Listing 122, Additional ctor_ini.m Commands for Static Variable Initialization

```
1  % initialize and assign static data
2  if isempty(static)
3    static_this = struct([]);
4    static_this(1).mLineWidthCounter = [];
5    static(static_this); % stores static_this as persistent
6  end
```

Line 2 calls **static.m** to check its status. If the return is empty, it is okay for the helper to assign initial values. Lines 3–5 create the initial structure of static variables, assign initial values, and pass the structure into **static.m** for safekeeping. If the return value in line 2 is not empty, static variables already exist and the helper should not overwrite the existing values with default values.

20.1.1.2 Static Variables in get and set

Like all private variables, static variables are only visible inside the class. Clients don't have access to static values unless they are included in the public interface. In the Class Wizard dialogs, there is no difference between a normal public variable and a static public variable. In the **Public Variables** ... dialog, fields for both **Accessor Expression** and **Mutator Expression** will accept the name of a static private member variable. When group-of-eight files are generated, **get** and **set** cases for direct-link static variables are slightly different from the nonstatic cases. The **get** and **set** cases for non-direct-link public variables don't change because helper functions are required. After generating the class, the static variable is available through direct-access code placed inside **get** or **set**. Direct-access static variable code is a little different from the direct-access code for nonstatic variables. The direct-link **case** inside **get** is shown in Code Listing 123. The corresponding direct-link **case** inside **set** is shown in Code Listing 124.

Code Listing 123, Direct-Access get case for mLineWidthCounter

```
1  case 'LineWidthCounter'
2    if isempty(this)
3      varargout = {};
4    else
5      static_this = static;
6      varargout = repmat({static_this.mLineWidthCounter},
         length(this(:)));
7    end
```

Lines 1–4 are identical to those used for any public or concealed variable. On line 1, the **case** statement uses public name, and line 3 returns nothing when the object is empty. Line 5 is new, and line 6 has been modified. Line 5 retrieves the entire structure of static variables with a single call to **static**. Line 6 gets the appropriate value and repeats the value to match the number of objects in the object array. There is only one copy of the static variables, but there may be more than one object in the array. Line 6 also assigns the repeated value into **varargout**.

```
Code Listing 124, Direct-Access set case for mLineWidthCounter
1    case 'LineWidthCounter'
2      static_this = static;   % read
3      if length(index) > 1
4        if length(this(:)) == 1
5          static_this.mLineWidthCounter = ...
6            subsasgn(static_this.mLineWidthCounter, ...
7            index(2:end), varargin{end}); % modify
8        else
9          [err_id, err_msg] = array_reference_error(index(2).
           type);
10           error(err_id, err_msg);
11       end
12     else
13       [static_this.mLineWidthCounter] = varargin{end};
14     end
15     static(static_this);   % write
```

The important differences between a normal **set** and a static **set** occur in lines 2 and 15, where static data are read and written. Lines 2 and 15 are the beginning and end of a read-modify-write cycle, and lines 3–14 perform the modification. Line 2 retrieves the entire structure of static variables with a single call to **static**. Lines 3–14 execute the standard direct-link **set** commands with one substitution: **static_this** is used instead of **this**. Finally, line 15 passes the modified value of **static_this** back to **static**.

20.1.1.3 Static Variables in display

The developer view option in **display** is a very convenient tool, particularly during development and debugging. With a couple of additions to the **developer_view** subfunction, static variables will be included in the developer view output. These additions are shown in Code Listing 125.

```
Code Listing 125, Static Variable Additions to developer_view
1    function developer_view(this, display_name)
2    disp('---- Public Member Variables ----');
3    full_display(struct(this), display_name);
4    disp('.... Private Member Variables ....');
5    full_display(this, display_name, true);
6
7    try
8      static_this = static;
9    catch
```

```
10    static_this = [];
11  end
12  if ~isempty(static_this)
13    disp('.... Private, Static Member Variables ....');
14    full_display(static_this, display_name, true);
15  end
```

The additional commands are found in lines 7–15. Lines 7–11 assign the structure of static variables into **static_this**. If the call to **static** on line 8 fails, line 10 assigns empty. If **static_this** is empty, there are no static variables to display. Otherwise, lines 12–15 display the static variables using a call to **full_display**.

20.1.2 OVERLOADING LOADOBJ AND SAVEOBJ

We haven't talked much about **load** and **save** (see Chapter 2), because up to this point they worked fine without our intervention. We now have a situation where private data are stored outside of the object's private structure. If we want to **save** and **load** static data, the standard behaviors for **save** and **load** are no longer adequate. Normally, if we want to change the behavior of a built-in function, we simply include a tailored version of the function in the class directory. In this case we can't overload **save** and **load**, but we can overload **saveobj** and **loadobj**.

We can think of **saveobj** and **loadobj** as helper functions for **save** and **load**. During a **save**, MATLAB calls **saveobj**; and during a **load**, MATLAB calls **loadobj**. By overloading **saveobj** and **loadobj**, we get an opportunity to modify values in the object's structure on its way to and from a **mat** file. There are many potential uses for this behavior. In this example, **saveobj** will copy static variables into the private structure and **loadobj** will extract static variables from the private structure and pass them into **static**. To make all of this work, we need three things: an element in the private structure where static data can be temporarily stored, a tailored version of **saveobj** that will copy static data into the private structure, and a tailored version of **loadobj** that will copy data from the private structure back into **static**.

Whenever static data are defined for a class, the class structure will include an element named **mTempStatic**. In **ctor_ini**, the **mTempStatic** variable is initially assigned an empty value. Tailored versions of **saveobj** and **loadobj** can now use **mTempStatic** during **save** and **load** calls. The tailored version of **saveobj** is included in Code Listing 126, and the tailored version of **loadobj** is included in Code Listing 127.

Code Listing 126, Tailored saveobj That Includes Static Data

```
1  function this = saveobj(this)
2  if ~isempty(this)
3    this(end).mTempStatic = static;
4  end
```

Code Listing 127, Tailored loadobj That Includes Static Data

```
1  function this = loadobj(this)
2  if ~isempty(this) && ~isempty(this(end).mTempStatic)
3    static(this(end).mTempStatic);
4    [this.mTempStatic] = deal([]);
5  end
```

Line 3 calls **static** and assigns the static variable structure into **mTempStatic** of the last object in the object array. As long as **loadobj** uses the same object, it doesn't matter which object holds the static data. Line 2 prevents us from copying static data into an empty object array.

Commands in **loadobj** simply reverse the process used by **saveobj**. Line 2 includes the same check for an empty object array, but it also includes another **isempty** check. The second check prevents **loadobj** from overwriting the static variable structure with empty. If **this** contains objects and **mTempStatic** isn't empty, line 3 passes the contents of **mTempStatic** into **static** and line 4 empties the contents of every **mTempStatic** element in **this**.

20.1.3 COUNTING ASSIGNMENTS

Static data are now integrated into the framework. Member functions can read and write static variables, public variables can be linked to static variables, and static variables can be saved and loaded. All we need now is a link between **mLineWidth** and **mLineWidthCounter**. We will add that link to the mutator section of **@cLineStyle/private/LineWidth_helper.m**. Only the modifications are shown in Code Listing 128.

Code Listing 128, A Modification to LineWidth_helper That Counts LineWidth Assignments

```
1    static_this = static;
2    for width = [varargin{:}]
3      if length(static_this.mLineWidthCounter) < width
4        static_this.mLineWidthCounter(width) = 1;
5      else
6        static_this.mLineWidthCounter(width) = ...
7          1 + static_this.mLineWidthCounter(width);
8      end
9    end
10   static(static_this);
```

The commands use the standard static variable read-modify-write cycle. Line 1 reads, lines 2–9 modify, and line 10 writes. Regardless of the code's ultimate purpose, mutating static values should always follow this cycle. The modify part of the cycle is usually the most involved, and lines 2–9 are no exception. Line 2 loops over all **linewidth** values passed in through **varargin**. The first time a particular width value is found, line 4 increases the length of the counter array and sets the count for this new width to 1. Lines 6–7 increment the count for elements that already exist. In the test drive, we will see what happens.

20.2 SINGLETON OBJECTS

With normal private member variables, every object gets its own, exclusive copy. Assigning a private value in one object does not affect the private member variables in another. With static variables, the situation is different. Assigning a value to a static variable in one object affects all objects of that type. Equally important is the fact that static values are maintained even when there are no objects of the class active in memory. Even if every object goes out of scope, static values remain in the **persistent** variable inside **static.m**. Instantiate a new object, and it immediately has access to the previously stored static values.

A class may include any combination of private and static variables. Objects that store all their data in static variables are called *singleton objects* because all objects of the class share a single copy of their variables. One potential use for singleton objects involves the creation of something we can loosely call a *name space*. For our purposes, a name space is simply a named collection of variables. For example, variables declared using the **global** keyword are stored in the global name space. Global variables can be brought into any local workspace with the **global** command. Variables stored in a singleton object represent a different name space. Singleton object variables can be brought into any local workspace with a call to the constructor. In our framework, construction is cheap, so there is no serious penalty in constructing an object simply to gain access to its static values.

Compared to global variables, singleton objects have some significant advantages. Like it or not, all modules that use the same name space are coupled. This means that all modules that declare **global** variables are coupled. Often the coupling goes unnoticed; however, the risk of a name clash and unpredictable behavior is always present. Singleton objects give us a way to reduce coupling by splitting variables in the global name space into smaller, more manageable groups. Another advantage for singleton objects is their interface. The global name space has no controlling interface, while access into a singleton object is fully controlled by the group of eight. This gives singleton objects the same public-versus-private protections enforced for any object.

20.3 TEST DRIVE

Adding static variables to **cLineStyle** should not affect previously existing behavior. The first few commands in the test drive are used to verify that the additional features do no harm. The outputs from these commands are not shown because they are identical to the outputs already shown in Chapter 18.* The test drive for this chapter focuses on the new behavior. The new commands along with their outputs are shown in Code Listing 129.

Code Listing 129, Chapter 20 Test Drive Command Listing: Static Members

```
1   >> cd '/oop_guide/chapter_20'
2   >> set(0, 'FormatSpacing', 'compact')
3   >> clear classes; fclose all; close all force;
4   >> do_chapter_18 = false;   % change to true to repeat
    Chapter 18 commands
5   >> if do_chapter_18; test_drive_18; end;
6   >> clear classes; fclose all; close all force;
7   >>
8   >> style = cLineStyle;
9   >> style = set(style, 'mDisplayFunc', 'developer_view')
10  ---- Public Member Variables ----
11  style.Color = [0   0   1]';
12  style.LineWidth = [1];
13  style.LineHandle = [];
14  style.LineWidthCounter = [];
15  .... Private Member Variables ....
16  style.mDisplayFunc = 'developer_view';
17  style.mTempStatic = [];
18  style.mColorHsv = [0.66667            1            1]';
```

---

* If you want to see the outputs, the files for this chapter include a script that will generate them. Navigate into the **chapter_20** directory and execute the command **test_drive_18**.

```
19   style.mLineWidth = [1];
20   style.mLineHandle = [];
21   .... Private, Static Member Variables ....
22   style.mLineWidthCounter = [];
23   >>
24   >> style.LineWidth = 7;
25   >> style.LineWidthCounter
26   ans =
27     0      0      0      0      0      0      1
28   >>
29   >> clear style;
30   >>
31   >> star = cStar;
32   >> star = draw(star);
33   >> star.LineWeight = 'bold';
34   >> star = reset(star);
35   >> clear star;
36   >>
37   >> style = cLineStyle;
38   >> style.LineWidthCounter
39   ans =
40     1      0      1      0      0      0      1
41   >>
42   >> save style style
43   >> clear classes; fclose all; close all force;
44   >> load style
45   >> style.LineWidthCounter
46   ans =
47     1      0      1      0      0      0      1
48   >>
49   >> shape = cShape;
50   >> save shape shape
51   >> clear classes; fclose all; close all force;
52   >> load shape
53   >> style = cLineStyle;
54   >> style.LineWidthCounter
55   ans =
56     1
```

The commands on lines 5–6 construct a **cLineStyle** object and force a developer view version of the display. Line 11 displays the new public variable, **LineWidthCounter**, and lines 18–19 display the new static variable, **mLineWidthCounter**.* These variables are empty because we haven't yet changed a line width. Line 21 assigns a **LineWidth** value of seven, and line 22 shows the updated count. **LineWidthCounter** now contains seven elements, and the value at index **(7)** is one. These values will remain available until either a **cLineStyle** object changes

---

* The Class Wizard version of **display.m** includes additional code that allows `'developer_view'` to display static private variables.

them or a **clear all** command deletes them. Deleting the only instance of **cLineStyle** (line 26) doesn't affect them. The next few commands demonstrate this.

Lines 28–32 construct a default **cStar** object, draw it, set the weight of the line to **'bold'**, close the figure, and remove **star** from the workspace. During all this activity, the constructor in line 28 uses **LineWidth** to initialize the width to 1 and the **LineWeight** assignment in line 30 calls **LineWidth** with a **'bold'** value of 3. These calls should have changed the count values in **cLineStyle**'s static variables.

To confirm this, line 34 constructs a new **cLineStyle** object and lines 35–37 display the values in **LineWidthCounter**. Index **(1)** logged the constructor's call, index **(3)** logged **LineWeight**'s call, and index **(7)** didn't change. The count values are exactly what we expect. Even more important, the static variable code appears to be working correctly.

Lines 39–44 confirm the operation of **saveobj** and **loadobj**. Line 39 saves the variable **style** in a file named **style.mat**. During **save**, MATLAB calls **saveobj**, where we copy the static variables into private variable reserved for that purpose. Line 40 clears the workspace, and line 41 loads **style** back into the workspace. During the **load**, MATLAB calls **loadobj**, where we restore the **persistent** variable in **static.m** back to its previous value. Lines 42–44 confirm that the static values were indeed restored.

Lines 46–53 demonstrate a **load and save** problem when objects are used in composition. A **cShape** object uses a **cLineStyle** object in its private structure so that line 46 constructs both a **cShape** object and a **cLineStyle** object. Line 47 saves the **cShape** object. **Save** should follow the organization of the hierarchy by calling **saveobj** on every object. Unfortunately, **@cLineStyle/saveobj.m** is never called.* As a result, static values aren't copied into the object's private structure. The static variables never had a chance.

In contrast, the **load** command appears to be correctly implemented. During the **load** on line 49, MATLAB correctly calls **@cLineStyle/loadobj.m**, but by that time, it is too late to recover. Since **save** failed to schedule a call to **saveobj**, the value stored in **this.mTempStatic** is empty. The output on line 56 displays the **LineWidth** change that occurred during **cShape** construction. We really expected to see the same vector that was previously displayed on line 47. This behavior is broken and needs to be fixed.

20.4 SUMMARY

At first, static member variables might seem like an unnecessary luxury; however, if industrial-strength classes are the goal, static member variables are a necessity. Their ready availability in other object-oriented languages encourages many object-oriented designers to include them in a design. There are many object-oriented designs that use static variables to good effect, and lack of support for static variables is a liability. Without the techniques in this chapter, implementing a design with static variables involves global variables and all the headaches associated with them. The techniques in this chapter represent a much better alternative.

Static variables also address issues related to software quality. Static variables and singleton objects can be used to reduce the module-to-module coupling that often occurs when **global** variables are used. Each singleton-object class loosely represents a unique name space separate from **global**. The object-oriented interface makes these name spaces safer to use. Subject to certain limits, it is also easier to **save** and **load** the values stored in a singleton object. Finally, with the developer view format enabled, it is certainly easier to display their values.

It is also encouraging to notice how easily we added static variables to the framework. The modular organization inherent in the group of eight and the functional-block arrangement in **get** and **set** are proving to be very extensible. From the earliest chapters, we have been taking advantage of that organization. The chapters that follow extend the organization even further.

---

* MATLAB Version 7.1.0.246 (R14) Service Pack 3.

20.5 INDEPENDENT INVESTIGATIONS

1. Use **cLineStyle** as a parent class and determine if the parent's version of **saveobj** is called when the child is saved. This will tell you whether the save process is broken for inheritance in general or only for composition and secondary objects.
2. Make **mFigureHandle** a static variable of **cShape** and draw all shapes derived from **cShape** in the same window.

21 Pass-by-Reference Emulation

You are probably aware that MATLAB always passes function arguments by value. In a structured design, pass-by-value works well. In an object-oriented design, strict adherence to pass-by-value is at best inconvenient, and at worst it compromises the quality of a design. MATLAB doesn't support pointers; however, under certain conditions, a trio of commands gives a good approximation to pass-by-reference. The three commands are **inputname**, **evalin**, and **assignin**. These commands are not limited to object-oriented programming, and the discussion in this chapter will help sort out some of the general pitfalls of using them both inside and outside an object-oriented implementation.

21.1 ASSIGNMENT WITHOUT EQUAL

In attempting to achieve pass-by-reference behavior, we are not entering entirely uncharted waters. MATLAB's handle-graphics interface apparently uses pass-by-reference. You can see this by looking at the handle-graphics set command. The syntax is defined as

```
set(H, 'PropertyName', PropertyValue, ...)
```

where **H** is a handle to a graphic object. Obviously, **set** is a mutator; however, there is no equal sign and no left-hand side. The value returned by set does not need to be assigned because **H** is assigned in place using pass-by-reference. Other graphics' functions also use pass-by-reference. The list includes, among others, **plot**, **grid**, **title**, **xlabel**, and **ylabel**. If pass-by-reference is good for handle graphics, perhaps it is also good for object-oriented programming.

The biggest difference between handle graphics and our group-of-eight MATLAB objects is the use of **subsref** and **subsasgn** vs. **get** and **set**. With handle graphics, **get** and **set** must be used because the type of a graphics handle is **double**. Dot-reference operators won't work for handles. By comparison, MATLAB objects can, and usually should, make an object look like a structure by tailoring the operation of **subsref** and **subsasgn**. Such tailoring allows clients to use objects as a more powerful type of structure. Except under special conditions, such tailoring also forces us to discourage clients from using **get** and **set** on objects.

For two reasons, investigating pass-by-reference isn't necessarily a gee-whiz, look-what-I-can-do exercise. The first reason is practical. There are some situations where the required behavior simply can't be implemented without it. These situations are rare, but when they occur, it is good to know how to deal with them. The second is a concession to interface designs and to clients converting to MATLAB from a language where references are ubiquitous. In particular, developers converting from C++ are comfortable with pass-by-reference syntax and often complain about MATLAB's exclusive use of pass-by-value. These developers don't care that pass-by-value syntax helps isolate accessors from mutators because they are already accustomed to the small ambiguity arising from pass-by-reference. Some programmers make fewer coding errors when the interface uses pass-by-reference emulation. If it weren't for the fact that these developers often contribute to the object-oriented design, we could easily dismiss their whining. The potential for errors must be balanced with the overhead inherent in the emulation.

On the other hand, many MATLAB developers are more comfortable using standard pass-by-value syntax. They typically like the fact that the standard syntax reinforces the purpose of a particular command. More importantly, MATLAB programmers are not accustomed to input arguments that mysteriously change during the course of a function call. In a MATLAB-centric environment, pass-by-reference syntax can reduce code quality and interfere with debugging. If you press me, I recommend that you use pass-by-reference very sparingly. Even so, if you decide to include pass-by-reference syntax, it's important to have a good strategy. In the examples that follow, we will implement one possible strategy.

Currently all functions in the shape hierarchy use standard pass-by-value syntax. Consequently, all mutators must return a copy of the modified object, and a user must assign the returned object to a variable. This works well whenever it is obvious that a function is a mutator. For some functions, it is difficult to decide at a glance whether the function is a mutator. In the shape hierarchy, **draw** is a mutator but this fact is easy to forget. Calling **draw** modifies **mFigureHandle**, but **mFigureHandle** is an internal implementation detail. Clients should be shielded from internal details, and pass-by-reference is another tool that can be used to help enforce the separation between public and private.

The current implementation of **draw** includes the following test:

```
if nargout ~= 1

  warning('draw must be called using: obj = draw(obj)');

else

  ...
```

Since all side effects from **draw** are private, a client might reasonably expect to call **draw** without assigning the return value. In the current implementation that would result in an error. The client doesn't get the desired result, but at least the error message tells what to do. With pass-by-reference emulation, **draw** might still perform a **nargout** test; however, the result of the test would no longer throw an error. Instead, pass-by-reference emulation would be used to modify the input object in place. The change would be immediately reflected in the client's workspace. In the examples that follow, we will modify **draw** by allowing it to be called as a mutator or with pass-by-reference syntax.

Like member functions, public member variables can include pass-by-reference capability. This allows dot-reference operations with accessor syntax to include hidden side effects. These side effects require pass-by-reference assignment of the input object. We will demonstrate this behavior by modifying a class in the **cShape** hierarchy. Rather than change the operation of an existing public variable, we will invent a new public variable called **View**. When **View** is **true**, the object will display itself using developer view format; and when **View** is **false**, normal display format will be used. To demonstrate the pass-by-reference operation, anytime **View** is accessed, the accessor will change the value stored in **developer_view**. With standard pass-by-value, this change would be lost; however, with pass-by-reference, changes to the object are preserved.

21.2 PASS-BY-REFERENCE FUNCTIONS

The three commands used to implement pass-by-reference emulation are **inputname**, **assignin**, and **evalin**. These standard MATLAB functions are described as follows:

- **inputname(argument_number)**: This function looks in the caller's workspace and returns the name of the variable associated with the input argument at position **argument_number**. Thus, we can find the name of the object in the caller's workspace by calling **inputname** for **this**.
- **assignin('caller', 'name', value)**: This function assigns a value to a variable in the caller's workspace. To do this, you have to know the name of the variable in the caller's workspace. The name can be inferred from a standard naming convention, or the name can be obtained using **inputname**.

- **evalin('caller', 'expression')**: This function evaluates an expression in the caller's workspace. Almost any expression can be evaluated. **Evalin** allows a function to gather a lot of information about the caller and the caller's workspace.

The biggest limitation in pass-by-reference emulation occurs when **inputname** returns an empty string. This happens when the input is not a pure variable but rather the result of an operation. Among others, some common syntax examples that results in an empty **inputname** are **x(1)**, **x+y**, **s.val**, and **varargin{:}**. Anytime our code uses **inputname**, we must remember to check for an empty string and take the appropriate course of action. In most cases of pass-by-reference emulation, the correct action is an error.

21.3 PASS-BY-REFERENCE DRAW

Currently **draw** throws an error when **nargout** is zero. By adding **inputname** and **assignin**, we can still assign the mutated object even when **nargout** is zero. Additions to the beginning and end of **draw** are provided in Code Listing 130. All tailored versions of **draw** must include these additions.

```
Code Listing 130, An Approximation to Call-by-Reference Behavior
1    function this = draw(this, figure_handle)
2
3    if nargout == 1
4      do_assignin = false;
5    else
6      do_assignin = true;
7      callers_this = inputname(1);
8      if isempty(callers_this)
9        error('must be called using mutator or call-by-reference
           syntax')
10     end
11   end
12
13   % The guts of draw goes here
14
15   if do_assignin
16     assignin('caller', callers_this, this);
17   end
```

The same as before, line 3 checks the number of output arguments. If **nargout** is one, line 4 sets the variable **do_assignin** to **false**. **Draw** does not need to assign the object in place because the caller is correctly using pass-by-value syntax. If there is no output argument, lines 6–10 initialize the pass-by-reference variables. Line 6 sets **do_assignin** to **true** because now we want **draw** to assign the object before it exits. Line 7 tries to get the name of the object in the caller's workspace. If **inputname** returns an empty string, lines 8–10 throw an error.

The comment in line 13 is a placeholder for the body of code normally included in **draw**. We have listed those commands before and don't need to list them again. At the end of **draw**, if **do_assignin** is **true,** line 16 performs the pass-by-reference assignment. The value of **callers_this** is the name of the object in the caller's workspace found on line 7.

Draw now supports mixed use of either call-by-value or call-by-reference syntax. The normal call-by-value syntax doesn't change. It still looks like the following:

```
shape = draw(shape);
```

The new call-by-reference syntax omits the assignment. Call by reference syntax looks like the following:

```
draw(shape);
```

Supporting both methods is not a requirement, but it is usually the right thing to do.

21.4 PASS-BY-REFERENCE MEMBER VARIABLE: VIEW

If one member function can benefit from pass-by-reference behavior, maybe others can benefit too. Functions outside the group of eight can use the same technique demonstrated for **draw**. Functions included in the group of eight follow a different approach. For these functions, **do_assignin** isn't assigned based on **nargout**, but rather it is passed from a helper function into **get** or **set**. The helper function must be the controlling source because MATLAB already uses syntax to decide whether to call **subsref** or **subsasgn**.

The other wrinkle in pass-by-reference emulation involves the number of function calls typically found between a client's use of operator syntax and the helper. For example, dot-reference syntax is converted into a call to **subsref**, which calls **get**, which potentially calls a parent version of **get**, which finally calls the helper. If the helper needs to specify pass-by-reference operation, that request must travel all the way back into **subsref**. The helper-function interface described in Chapter 16 gives the helper a way to kick off the process. The intervening functions must now accept the arguments and make the correct assignments.

As always, anchoring the example to some particular requirement makes the discussion easier to follow. As previously described, we will create a new public member named **View**. When **View** is **true**, the object displays using developer view format; and when **View** is **false**, the normal display format is used. Like all public variables, the logical value of **View** may be assigned using a dot-reference operator, by calling **subsasgn**, or by calling **set**.

Unlike other public variables, we are going to add pass-by-reference behavior to **View** and do something that makes pass-by-reference relatively easy to observe. In this example, except for the fact that it demonstrates pass-by-reference mechanics, the behavior is pointless. When **View** is accessed, the helper will appear to use the ~ operator to reverse value of a private logical variable. The helper returns this new value, the modified object, and **do_assignin** with a value of **true**. Ultimately, the modified object is assigned into the client's workspace. The assignment relies on pass-by-reference code inserted into **get** and **subsref** by Class Wizard.

21.4.1 Helpers, get, and subsref with Pass-by-Reference Behavior

The helper initiates pass-by-reference by mutating the object and passing back a **true** value in **do_assignin**. Inside **get**, the **do_assignin** value triggers pass-by-reference commands similar to those added to **draw**. There are a few differences because **get** is usually an intermediate function. That is, **get** is usually called indirectly through **subsref**, not directly by the client. In this situation, the proper assignment of **do_assignin** uses **assignin**. This is where code organization in the group of eight proves its worth. The block organization in **get** and **subsref** makes it easier to support a general method for call-by-reference emulation. The following example code demonstrates the general implementation.

21.4.1.1 Pass-by-Reference Behavior in the Helper

Earlier versions of **cShape** did not include a public variable named **View**. The example files in this chapter's directory include **View** as an addition. From previous experience, we know we can add a new public variable without introducing unexpected side effects. In the Class Wizard **Public Variables** ... dialog, add a new public variable named **View** and enter **%helper** in both the **Accessor Expression** and **Mutator Expression** fields. No further changes are required because the value of **View** relies on private variables that already exist. Save the change and rebuild the files. Class Wizard writes an initial version of **View_helper.m** into **/@cShape/private/**. The initial version must always be tailored to match the desired behavior. The tailored version is shown in Code Listing 131.

```
Code Listing 131, Enabling a Helper with Call-by-Reference Behavior
1    function [do_sub_indexing, do_assignin, this, varargout] =
     ...
2     View_helper(which, this, index, varargin)
3
4    switch which
5     case 'get'   % ACCESSOR
6       % input: index contains any additional indexing as a
         substruct
7       % input: varargin empty for accessor
8       do_sub_indexing = true;   % tells get.m whether to index
         deeper
9       do_assignin = true;   % !!! call-by-reference behavior
10      varargout = cell(1, nargout-3); % 3 known vars plus
         varargout
11
12      % before the toggle [] means standard, load after-toggle
         values
13      developer_sieve = cellfun('isempty',
         {this.mDisplayFunc});
14      % toggle the display function, remember false means standard
15      [this(developer_sieve).mDisplayFunc] =
         deal('developer_view');
16      [this(~developer_sieve).mDisplayFunc] = deal([]);
17
18      % fill varargout with the "requested" data
19      varargout = num2cell(developer_sieve);
20
21     case 'set'   % MUTATOR
22       % input: index contains any additional indexing as a
         substruct
23       % input: varargin contains values to be assigned into
         the object
24       do_sub_indexing = false;   % mutator _must_ do deep indexing
```

```
25      do_assignin = false;   % leave false until you read book
        section 3
26      varargout = {}; % 'set' returns nothing in varargout
27
28      if ~isempty(index)
29        error('Deeper levels of indexing is not supported');
30      end
31      % true in varargin means developer view
32      developer_sieve = logical([varargin{:}]);
33      % set the display function
34      [this(developer_sieve).mDisplayFunc] =
        deal('developer_view');
35      [this(~developer_sieve).mDisplayFunc] = deal([]);
36
37   otherwise
38      error('OOP:unsupportedOption', ['Unknown helper option: '
        which]);
39   end
```

First, let's tackle `get`, the accessor. On line 8, accepting the value of **true** allows code that already exists in **get** to handle any additional indices. On line 9, the value returned via **do_assignin** controls pass-by-reference emulation. Here, the normal return value of **false** has been changed to **true**. When **get** receives this **true** value, it will trigger a series of pass-by-reference commands. Next, the helper implements the desired behavior.

Line 10 preallocates **varargout**. Lines 13–19 use vector syntax to both toggle the value and fill **varargout**. Vector syntax is always preferred because it is more efficient when **this** is nonscalar. The value associated with the public variable **View** is determined by the value of the private variable **mDisplayFunc**. Line 13 uses **cellfun** and `isempty` to determine the logical **View** values returned through **varargout**. Lines 15–16 toggle the view state by assigning `developer_view` into the empty elements and empty into the others. This is where the mutation occurs. In an ordinary accessor, this change would never make it back to the client; however, the value returned due to change on line 9 means that this accessor is no ordinary accessor. Line 19 assigns the public **View** values into **varargout**.

Mutator code is conventional. Lines 24–26 accept the code provided by Class Wizard. In each object, **View** is scalar, so lines 28–30 throw an error if indexing deeper than the first dot-reference level is detected. Nonscalar public variables often require a block of code to handle deeper indexing levels. Line 32 converts the input cell array into a logical array, and lines 34–35 use the logical array to assign either `developer_view` or empty into the proper elements.

21.4.1.2 Pass-by-Reference Code in get.m

Commands in **get** are organized into blocks that represent public variables, concealed variables, and parent slice and forward. Variables in each block are also classified as either direct-link or non-direct-link. Direct-link variables associate one-to-one with private member variables, while non-direct-link variables use a helper function. The distinction is important because pass-by-reference behavior can only be initiated by a helper. Since direct-link variables don't use a helper, they cannot initiate pass-by-reference behavior. This is not a serious limitation because any direct-link variable can be easily converted into a non-direct-link variable. There are no side effects, and Class Wizard automatically generates most of the non-direct-link code.

Inside **get**, each non-direct-link **case** includes a properly configured call to a helper function. Values returned by the helper function may trigger pass-by-reference behavior. The primary pass-by-reference code block can be found in **chapter_0/@cShape/get.m** beginning on line 175. The pass-by-reference block has been copied into Code Listing 132.

Code Listing 132, Pass-by-Reference Code Block in get.m

```
175  if do_assignin == true
176    var_name = inputname(1);
177    if isempty(var_name)
178      warning('OOP:invalidInputname', ...
179        ['No assignment: pass-by-reference can only be used ' ...
180        'on non-indexed objects']);
181    else
182      assignin('caller', var_name, this);
183      caller = evalin('caller', 'mfilename');
184      if isempty(strmatch(caller, {'struct'}))
185        assignin('caller', 'do_assignin', true);
186      end
187    end
188  end
```

The test in line 175 guards entry into block. Pass-by-reference commands execute only when **do_assignin** is **true**. The first pass-by-reference command, line 176, uses the **inputname** command to obtain the client's name for the object. If **inputname(1)** returns an empty string, pass-by-reference assignment cannot be completed and lines 178–180 issue a warning. The conditions that lead to an empty **inputname** value were discussed in §21.3. If **inputname(1)** is not empty, lines 182–186 use the now familiar **assignin** command. As in **draw**, line 182 uses **assignin** to assign the modified object in the caller's workspace. Different from **draw** are the additional commands found in lines 183–186. These additional lines indirectly forward **do_assignin** to every caller except **struct.m**. Line 183 uses **evalin** to get the name of the calling module. Line 184 uses **strmatch** to check for the string `'struct'`, and line 185 performs the indirect assignment of **do_assignin**.

When a child class forwards **get** to a parent, the object is sliced and only the parent part is passed. When a pass-by-reference operation is required, the parent's **get** uses Code Listing 132 to assign both the mutated parent and **do_assignin**. The child must detect a change to its own **do_assignin** variable and reattach the mutated parent. The parent forward block is shown in Code Listing 133; only lines 151–154 are new.

Code Listing 133, Pass-by-Reference Parent Forward Assignment Commands

```
116  % parent forwarding block
117  if ~found
118
119    if called_by_name
120      forward_index = index(1).subs;
121    else
122      forward_index = index;
```

```
123    end
124
125    if nargout == 0
126      varargout = cell(size(this));
127    else
128      varargout = cell(1, nargout);
129    end
130
131    for parent_name = parent_list'  % loop over parent cellstr
132      try
133        parent = [this.(parent_name{1})];
134        [varargout{:}] = get(parent, forward_index,
             varargin{:});
135        found = true;  % catch will assign false if not found
136        do_sub_indexing = false;  % assume parent did all sub-
             indexing
137        found = true;  % catch will assign false if not found
138        break;  % can only get here if field was found
139      catch
140        found = false;
141        err = lasterror;
142        switch err.identifier
143          case 'MATLAB:nonExistentField'
144            % NOP
145          otherwise
146            rethrow(err);
147        end
148      end
149    end
150
151    if do_assignin
152      parent = num2cell(parent);
153      [this.(parent_name{1})] = deal(parent{:});
154    end
155
156  end
```

Line 117 guards entry into the parent forward block so that line 151 is skipped if the variable has already been found. If the execution reaches line 151 and **do_assignin** is **true**, it means the parent forward operation returned a mutated parent. Lines 152–153 assign the parent slice back into the child. The **true** value that remains in **do_assignin** allows the commands in Code Listing 132 to complete the task of indirectly assigning the mutated object into the caller's workspace. The complete process can be difficult to follow and thus difficult to debug and maintain. Class Wizard takes care of the heavy lifting. All you need to do is return the correct value of **do_assignin** from the helper.

21.4.1.3 Pass-by-Reference Code in subsref.m

Pass-by-reference additions in **subsref** follow a similar pattern. The commands listed for **get** in Code Listing 132 are also included in **subsref**. These commands can be found in **chapter_21/@cShape/subsref.m** on lines 63–75. These commands give **subsref** the ability to assign the object in the caller's workspace. These commands take care of client workspace assignments, but we aren't quite finished with the array-reference case.

We need to add some commands that will ensure that an indirect assignment into **this_subset** will be correctly copied back into **this**. To do this, we need to check the value of **do_assignin** and take action when the value is **true**. The modified array-reference case is shown in Code Listing 134.

```
Code Listing 134, Array Reference Case in subsref.m with Pass-by-Reference Commands

40    case '()'
41      this_subset = this(index(1).subs{:});
42      if length(index) == 1
43        varargout = {this_subset};
44      else
45        % trick subsref into returning more than 1 ans
46        varargout = cell(size(this_subset));
47        [varargout{:}] = subsref(this_subset, index(2:end));
48        if do_assignin
49          % the value of this_subset has also changed
50          this(index(1).subs{:}) = this_subset;
51        end
52    end
```

Lines 48–51 are the additional commands that support pass-by-reference emulation. Like normal, line 47 forwards **this_subset** along with all remaining index values to **subsref**. When the execution returns to line 48, the value of **do_assignin** is checked. If the value of **do_assignin** is **true**, it means that the values now stored in **this_subset** were indirectly assigned into **subsref**'s workspace. Line 50 copies the subset array back into its original indices. This captures the change and allows the subsequent commands in lines 63–75 to assign the mutated object into the client's workspace.

21.4.2 OTHER GROUP-OF-EIGHT CONSIDERATIONS

Now that **get** and **subsref** have been modified to support pass-by-reference emulation, we are in a good position to consider the potential impact on the remaining group-of-eight functions. There is no impact on the mutators **set** and **subsasgn** because they already assign **this**. There is also no impact on the constructor because it isn't involved in pass-by-reference emulation. That leaves **display**, **struct**, and **fieldnames**.

Display and **struct** both rely on the **cellstr** value returned by **fieldnames** and on the operation of **get**. We already know that **get** is involved in pass-by-reference emulation, so there might be an interaction among **display**, **struct**, **fieldnames**, and **get**. We explore this interaction at the end of the test drive description.

21.5 TEST DRIVE

There aren't as many new items in this chapter as you might have expected. Pass-by-reference support commands were discussed in this chapter; however, they have been lurking in the group-of-eight functions since Chapter 18. Thus, all preexisting functions and variables have been well tested with the pass-by-reference additions. New to this chapter are the **View** public variable and the execution of pass-by-reference commands. The test drive commands in Code Listing 135 limit their scope to test only these new elements.

Code Listing 135, Chapter 21 Test Drive Command Listing: Pass-by-Reference Emulation

```
1    >> cd '/oop_guide/chapter_21'
2    >> set(0, 'FormatSpacing', 'compact')
3    >> clear classes; fclose all; close all force;
4    >>
5    >> star = cStar;
6    >>
7    >> get(star, 'mFigureHandle')
8    ans =
9       []
10   >> draw(star);
11   >> get(star, 'mFigureHandle')
12   ans =
13      1
14   >>
15   >> get(star, 'mDisplayFunc')
16   ans =
17      []
18   >> star
19   star =
20          Size: [1 1]
21      ColorRgb: [0 0 1]
22        Points: [1x12 double]
23    LineWeight: 'normal'
24          View: 1
25         Title: 'A Star is born'
26   >> star.View
27   ans =
28      1
29   >> get(star, 'mDisplayFunc')
30   ans =
31   developer_view
32   >>
33   >> star
34   ---- Public Member Variables ----
35   star.Size = [1   1  ];
36   star.ColorRgb = [0   0   1  ];
37   star.Points = [ values omitted ];
```

```
38    star.LineWeight = 'normal';
39    star.View = [0];
40    star.Title = 'A Star is born';
41    .... Private Member Variables ....
42    star.mTitle = 'A Star is born';
43    star.cShape.mDisplayFunc = 'developer_view';
44    star.cShape.mSize = [1   1   ]';
45    star.cShape.mScale = [1   1   ]';
46    star.cShape.mPoints(1, :) = [ values omitted   ];
47    star.cShape.mPoints(2, :) = [ values omitted   ];
48    star.cShape.mFigureHandle = [];
49    star.cShape.mLineStyle.mDisplayFunc = [];
50    star.cShape.mLineStyle.mTempStatic = [];
51    star.cShape.mLineStyle.mColorHsv = [0.666666666666667  1  1  ]';
52    star.cShape.mLineStyle.mLineWidth = [1];
53    star.cShape.mLineStyle.mLineHandle = [];
54    >>
55    >> star.View = false;
56    >> star
57    star =
58              Size: [1 1]
59          ColorRgb: [0 0 1]
60            Points: [1x12 double]
61        LineWeight: 'normal'
62              View: 1
63             Title: 'A Star is born'
64    >>
65    >> get(star(1), 'View')
66    Warning: No assignment: pass-by-ref. can't be used on indexed
      objects
67    > In cStar.get at 124
68    ans =
69       0
```

Line 5 constructs a default **cStar** object, and line 7 displays the handle to **star**'s figure window. Since **star** has not yet been drawn, its figure handle is empty (lines 8–9). Line 10 uses pass-by-reference syntax to draw the **star**. A figure window opens and a blue star is drawn. Now the figure handle has a value (lines 12–13). Pass-by-reference emulation code assigned the mutated object into the command window's workspace even though line 10 contains no explicit assignment.

Next, we look at the pass-by-reference behavior added to **View**. The initial value of **star**'s **mDisplayFunc** is empty (Lines 16–17), and the expected display format is normal. This can be seen in lines 19–25. Now things start to get interesting. Line 26 accesses **View** and displays the value. What isn't so obvious is the fact that the access operation on line 26 also changed the object. Lines 29–31 display the value of **mDisplayFunc**, and we see that it has changed. With this value, we expect developer view format from **display**. That is exactly what we get in lines 34–53.

We should also be able to assign **star.View** using mutator syntax. Line 55 uses a dot-reference operator to assign **false** into **View**. Internally, **false** is converted into an **mDisplayFunc** value of empty. The assignment changes the display format back to normal. Indeed, the display in lines 57–63 uses normal format. Finally, lines 65–69 demonstrate the warning that occurs when **inputname** can't resolve the name.

That ends the test drive, but before moving to the next chapter, we need to explore a subtle interaction that occurs during the command on line 18 among **display**, **struct**, and **field-names**. Recall what happens when we enter the command **star** without a trailing semicolon. MATLAB converts the syntax into a call to **display**. **Display** calls **struct(this)**, **struct** calls **get**, and **get** calls the helper function. If the helper function requests pass-by-reference behavior, what happens?

To answer that question, work from the helper function back toward **display**. The helper function sets **do_assignin** to **true**, and **get** receives the value. A **true** value will cause the execution to enter the block of commands added to **get** earlier in this chapter. In Code Listing 132, line 183 finds that the caller is `'struct'` and thus skips the **assignin** command on line 185. The mutated object is assigned into **struct**'s workspace, but the **true** value in **do_assignin** is not assigned. Thus, the mutated object is not passed from **struct** into **display**. In most situations, this is the right behavior because we usually don't expect a command like **struct** or **display** to change the object. In the next chapter, we will examine an even more perilous pass-by-reference situation.

21.6 SUMMARY

Under the right set of circumstances, pass-by-reference emulation can make up for certain limitations in MATLAB's pass-by-value architecture. Prime candidates for pass-by-reference emulation are mutator functions for which the mutation is hidden or at least not immediately obvious. In the **cShape** hierarchy, **draw** represents one of these functions because mutations occur only within the private variables. It is easy to forget the assignment and annoying to receive an error. As the class designer, you can choose to use pass-by-reference emulation or you can halt the execution and throw an error. The overhead involved in both options are comparable, but handling the error is a lot more user-friendly.

Pass-by-reference emulation with public variables yields a public variable syntax that is more familiar to many object-oriented programmers. The trade-offs between risks and benefits aren't clear. The benefit side includes a command syntax that is less verbose and easier to use. The risk side includes lack of support for certain variable names and uncertainty about the return from **display**, **struct**, and **fieldnames**. Either way, Class Wizard already generates the support commands for pass-by-reference emulation. Changing one logical value in the output of a helper function triggers the emulation. The behavior is rather adaptable. In the next chapter, we will look at a different twist for the combination of member variables and pass-by-reference.

21.7 INDEPENDENT INVESTIGATIONS

1. Edit **fieldnames** and remove **View** from the list of public variable names. Rerun the test drive and note any differences. After you finish, add **View** back to the **fieldnames** list.
2. Modify **struct** and **display** so they operate using pass-by-reference behavior. (Hint: you probably need to change the way **get** assigns **do_assignin**.)
3. How would you set up pass-by-reference conditions so that a client, rather than the helper, is in control? (Hint: suppose the existence of a **do_assignin** variable in the caller's workspace somehow makes its way into the helper.) Can **struct** and **display** use this approach to determine when to perform **assignin**?
4. Modify **set.m** so that when **nargout == 0**, the function will use pass-by-reference emulation to assign the mutated **this** in the caller's workspace.

5. Modify other mutator functions so that when **nargout == 0**, they assign the mutated **this** into the caller's workspace. Is the modification better or worse than throwing an error when **nargout == 0**? Can you think of examples where throwing an error would be more appropriate?

6. Add a non-direct-link public member variable named **Reset**. Inside **Reset_helper**, call the **reset** public member function. For this exercise, it doesn't matter if **Reset** uses pass-by-reference emulation, but in an industrial-strength class, it probably would. Create a shape and draw it. Access the **Reset** variable and confirm that it does the same thing as the member function. Redraw the shape. Display the contents of the shape variable by typing the variable name without a trailing semicolon. Did the shape figure disappear? What can you do to change this behavior?

7. Change the visibility of all **reset.m** modules from public to private by moving the modules into private directories. What other changes are necessary to allow this change to work? Does every child class still need a private **reset.m** module?

8. Create another public member variable named **Draw** and link its helper function to **draw.m**. Can you make **draw.m** private as **reset.m** was made private in investigation 7? How does the fact that **cStar** objects' **draw** method changes the figure title make the implementation of public variable **Draw** different from the implementation of public variable **Reset**?

22 Dot Functions and Functors

In the previous chapter, we introduced a member variable with unusual behavior. The behavior was unusual because the variable didn't really behave like a variable. Instead, it seemed like **View** was really a member function dressed up to look like a variable. In this chapter, we explore how dot-reference member variable syntax might be used to call a member function. The first thing we need to investigate is operator conversion. We need to understand what happens to the arguments when MATLAB converts operator notation into a function call. We already have a good understanding of **substruct**, but we don't really know the variable types supported. Armed with this knowledge we will be able to tear down the wall that currently exists between member variables and member functions. This will allow us to investigate another common object-oriented specialty class, the functor.

22.1 WHEN DOT-REFERENCE IS NOT A REFERENCE

Strictly speaking, MATLAB dot-reference operators aren't true references because MATLAB always converts the operators into a function call, either to **subsref** or to **subsasgn**. These functions are usually configured to give the appearance of a reference, but such an appearance is not required. The operators convert into **subsref** or **subsasgn**, but what happens to the operator's arguments and indices? In general, we know that arguments are packaged into a special structure called a **substruct** and passed into the function as an index. Some of the indices are used inside **subsref** or **subsasgn**, some are used inside **get** or **set**, and some are passed into a helper function. Typically, the helper function has little use for the indices and simply passes them back to the calling function for further evaluation. So far, we haven't made much use of the fact that the helper function can elect to use these indices. In this chapter, the indices are the central theme.

Suppose we want to redeploy dot-reference syntax so that, in addition to accessing public member variables, it can be used as the public interface to a member function. Of course, this is already the case. The difference in appearance is the behavior of the helper function. Currently, helper functions are implemented with a behavior that makes them look like variable references. We could just as easily implement helper functions with general member-function behavior. **Draw** is a good function to investigate because it has no arguments. Consider the **draw** syntax used in the following, functionally equivalent commands. Both use pass-by-reference emulation.

```
>> draw(shape);
```

```
>> shape.draw;
```

While both examples are functionally equivalent, there is an important difference with respect to ambiguity. For functions with two or more arguments, the relative superiority among the arguments can introduce ambiguity. Recall that "standard" syntax doesn't demand that the object be the first argument. As long as an object has the highest relative priority, it can occur anywhere in the argument list. Among like-named functions, we aren't certain which will be selected until the relative superiority of all arguments is sorted out. By convention, we always try to place the object first in the argument list and we try not to modify the relative superiority through **superiorto** and **inferiorto**. This convention has allowed us to sidestep many issues related to superiority. Operator overloading is the only place where superiority was an issue. With dot-reference syntax (e.g., **shape.draw**) there is no ambiguity. MATLAB always calls the version of **draw_helper** associated with **shape**. The conversion from dot-reference syntax guarantees it. This fact alone helps justify the new syntax.

Gauging run-time performance between member functions using normal syntax and those using dot-reference syntax is a complicated matter. For a flat hierarchy with little or no inheritance, the run-time difference is not significant. With inheritance, run time is better for the normal syntax only when the class restricts itself to scalar objects. In the face of both inheritance and nonscalar objects, both versions must implement parent–child slicing at every level. It doesn't matter whether this slicing occurs inside **get** or inside another member function; the effect on run time is the same. The fact that **get** already includes slice-and-forward code is another good argument for dot-reference syntax.

For convenience, we need a name for dot-reference function syntax. It doesn't fit the definition of a public member variable, and it doesn't fit MATLAB's definition of a public member function.* Until someone invents a better name, I will refer to member functions invoked using dot-reference syntax as *dot member functions*. Generically, a dot member function is simply a member function. Thus, it is okay to use the generic term as long as the context is clear or the context doesn't matter.

Earlier, I said, "**Draw** has no arguments." Of course, that isn't exactly true because the object itself must be an argument so that MATLAB can find the function. When **draw** is called using dot-operator syntax, MATLAB packages arguments into a **substruct** index. These indices are passed from the command line, into **subsref**, into **get**, and finally into the helper function. When **shape.draw** reaches its helper, the index array is empty. What I should have said is "**Draw** has no *indices*." As we will soon see, for dot member functions, arguments and indices refer to exactly the same thing.

Operator conversion and the group-of-eight implementations support indexing to any level. This also means that helper function associated with a dot member function can receive any number of indices. We know we can construct indices using integers and logicals; however, if the same limits are placed on the indices passed into dot member functions, they won't be very useful. Since there is virtually no documentation on operator syntax conversion, we have to build a class that contains a dot member function and experiment.

Let's start with a new class so we can better focus on the important details. The complete class implementation is included on the companion disk in **/chapter_22**, or you can create the new class from scratch. If you want to create one from scratch, open Class Wizard and create a class named **cBizarre**. In the **Public Variables** ... dialog box, give **cBizarre** one public member variable named **show_arg**. Give **show_arg** in both the **Accessor Expression** and **Mutator Expression** fields the value **%helper**. Click **Done** to return to the main Class Wizard dialog. Click **Build Class Files** and navigate to an appropriate location. Make sure you name the new class directory **@cBizarre**. Exit Class Wizard and try out the class. See line 5 in Code Listing 137 for an example. At this point, receiving a warning is normal because the helper function is still a stub.

To support our investigation of **substruct**, modify the content of **show_arg_helper.m**. We are only interested in the **'get'** case. The complete function is quite simple and is shown in Code Listing 136.

Code Listing 136, Helper Function to Experiment with input–substruct Contents

```
1    function [do_sub_indexing, do_assignin, this, varargout] =
     ...
2      show_arg_helper(which, this, index, varargin)
```

---

* Outside of MATLAB, it would be very common to find **shape.draw** classified as a member function and **shape=draw(shape)** classified as a friend function. This can sometimes lead to confusion when discussing object-oriented designs.

```
3
4    switch which
5      case 'get'   % ACCESSOR
6        do_sub_indexing = false; % tells get.m not to index deeper
7        do_assignin = false;  % no reason to use pass-by-reference
8        varargout = cell(1, nargout-3); % [] okay for return
9        full_display(index); % simply displays the full syntax
10       if nargin > 3
11         full_display(varargin);
12       end
13     case 'set'   % MUTATOR
14       do_sub_indexing = false; % always false in 'set'
15       do_assignin = false; % mutator usually isn't pass-by-
          reference
16       varargout = {}; % mutator return is in this, not varargout
17       full_display(index); % simply displays the full syntax
18       if nargin > 3
19         full_display(varargin); % displays full syntax
20       end
21     otherwise
22       error('OOP:unsupportedOption', ['Unknown helper option: '
          which]);
23   end
```

In line 6, **do_sub_indexing** has been changed from **true** to **false**. This change prevents errors due to unexpected values in the **substruct** index. In line 7, the value of **do_assignin** stays set to **false**. Change the value to **true** if you want to use pass-by-reference emulation. Line 8 sets the helper's return values to **[]**. In this case, returning empty is perfectly acceptable because we are only interested in the display. Line 9 gives us the functionality we desire. Here we are reusing **full_display** to write the entire contents of **substruct index** to the screen. This will let us experiment with the input syntax because **full_display** gives us a complete picture of the indices. In case **varargin** isn't empty, lines 10–12 display the full content of a nonempty **varargin**. Lines 17–20 repeat the same commands for the **'set'** case.

Sample commands and their outputs are shown in Code Listing 137. In short, MATLAB does not check the variable type when it converts from operator syntax to **substruct**. The responsibility for checking lies with the function that ultimately uses the indices. This means we can use dot-reference syntax to pass virtually any input into the member function.

Code Listing 137, Chapter 22 Test Drive Commands for Dot Member Functions

```
1    >> cd '/oop_guide/chapter_22'
2    >> set(0, 'FormatSpacing', 'compact')
3    >> clear classes; fclose all; close all force;
4    >>
5    >> b = cBizarre
6    index = [];
7    b =
8      show_arg: []
```

```
9    >> b.show_arg;
10   index = [];
11   >>
12   >> struct(b);
13   index = [];
14   >>
15   >>get(b, 'show_arg');
16   index = [];
17   >>
18   >>b.show_arg.name;
19   index.type = '.';
20   index.subs = 'name';
21   >>
22   >> b.show_arg(1:3, 5);
23   index.type = '()';
24   index.subs{1, 1} = [1   2   3   ];
25   index.subs{1, 2} = [5];
26   >>
27   >> b.show_arg{1:3, 5};
28   index.type = '{}';
29   index.subs{1, 1} = [1   2   3   ];
30   index.subs{1, 2} = [5];
31   >>
32   >> b.show_arg{1:3, 5}(1, 2);
33   index(1, 1).type = '{}';
34   index(1, 1).subs{1, 1} = [1   2   3   ];
35   index(1, 1).subs{1, 2} = [5];
36   index(1, 2).type = '()';
37   index(1, 2).subs{1, 1} = [1];
38   index(1, 2).subs{1, 2} = [2];
39   >>
40   >> b.show_arg(pi);
41   index.type = '()';
42   index.subs{1} = [3.14159265358979];
43   >>
44   >> b.show_arg(1.5, exp(1), @whos, 'a string');
45   index.type = '()';
46   index.subs{1, 1} = [1.5];
47   index.subs{1, 2} = [2.71828182845905];
48   index.subs{1, 3} = @whos;
49   index.subs{1, 4} = 'a string';
50   >>
51   >> b.show_arg(0:0.25:1, struct('a', 1.1, 'b', 'a string'),
     {1 'another'});
52   index.type = '()';
53   index.subs{1, 1} = [0   0.25   0.5   0.75   1   ];
54   index.subs{1, 2}.a = [1.1];
```

```
55  index.subs{1, 2}.b = 'a string'
56  index.subs{1, 3}{1, 1} = [1];
57  index.subs{1, 3}{1, 2} = 'another';
58  >>
59  >> get(b, 'show_arg', substruct('()', {1.5   0:0.25:1}));
60  index.type = '()';
61  index.subs{1, 1} = [1.5];
62  index.subs{1, 2} = [0   0.25   0.5   0.75   1  ];
63  >>
64  >> get(b, substruct('.', 'show_arg', '()', {1.5   0:0.25:1}));
65  index.type = '()';
66  index.subs{1, 1} = [1.5];
67  index.subs{1, 2} = [0   0.25   0.5   0.75   1  ];
68  >>
69  >> b.show_arg(0:0.25:1, 'option') = 10;
70  index.type = '()';
71  index.subs{1, 1} = [0   0.25   0.5   0.75   1  ];
72  index.subs{1, 2} = 'option';
73  varargin{1} = [10];
74  >>
75  >> b.show_arg(0:0.25:1, 'option') = {10   'a string'   @whos};
76  index.type = '()';
77  index.subs{1, 1} = [0   0.25   0.5   0.75   1  ];
78  index.subs{1, 2} = 'option';
79  varargin{1}{1, 1} = [10];
80  varargin{1}{1, 2} = 'a string';
81  varargin{1}{1, 3} = @whos;
```

Line 5 constructs an object of type **cBizarre**, leaving off the trailing semicolon. The display shows that **show_arg_helper** received an empty **index** value. An empty index also occurs when **show_arg** is accessed with no arguments (line 9), when **struct(b)** is called (line 12), and when **show_arg** is accessed with **get** (line 15). As a rule, all dot member functions must be able to handle the empty-input case.

The syntax on line 18 indexes **show_arg** as a structure. As the output on lines 19–20 shows, structure indexing is okay as long as the dot member function expects it. The function can determine the index operator by examining **index.type**. Any number of strings may be passed by using additional levels of dot-reference syntax. Experiment with the syntax and examine the organization in the output.

Lines 22, 27, and 32 display the conversion for normal integer indices. With a single set of array- or cell-reference operators, the indices for each dimension are organized into a separate cell. In this way, each element of **index.subs{}** represents an input. Think about the way **varargin** is organized because **index.subs** is the same. Again, experiment with different command syntax and observe the organization. You can even use **end** and '**:**' syntax, but you may not get the results you expect. See the independent investigations at the end of this chapter for more detail.

We didn't expect any trouble with integer indices, and lines 40 and 44 demonstrate that trouble-free conversion extends to noninteger scalar values. In line 44, a real, the result from a function call; a function handle; and a string are all converted and packaged into separate cells (lines 45–49). Line 51 demonstrates the same trouble-free conversion of complicated types. Here a real vector, a

332 A Guide to MATLAB Object-Oriented Programming

structure, and a cell array are all successfully packaged into separate cells. This is good news because it means MATLAB places no restrictions on the type of input converted from operator syntax.

Lines 59 and 64 demonstrate an alternate but more cumbersome syntax. This syntax must be used when normal operator syntax is not available, for example, when trying to call a dot member function from another member function. The syntax on line 59 can be used to access public dot member functions, and the syntax on line 64 extends access to concealed dot member functions (which, strictly speaking, are not really dot member functions because they can't be called using a dot).

Indexing for access is no different from indexing for mutation. MATLAB converts and packages indices the same way for both. Group-of-eight implementations of **subsasgn** and **set** use the same method of index passing used by **subsref** and **get**. When the dot member function is called for **'set'** versus **'get'**, the biggest difference is a nonempty **varargin**. Lines 69–73 show an example with one input. Lines 75–81 show an example with three inputs. The mutator case has to manage the index values passed through **index** and the input values passed through **varargin**.

Much is possible, and you are the final judge concerning the options supported by your classes. The same is true regarding the functionality included in dot member functions versus normal member functions. Aside from how they are invoked, there is virtually no difference in functionality. As a starting point, consider the following guidelines.

- Don't use nonstandard index values in the left-hand side of an assignment (e.g., lines 69 and 75 above). Standard index values are integers. Everything else is nonstandard. One notable exception might occur when a string is used like an enumerated value. Another notable exception might occur when the index is a single, fixed-range, floating-point value.
- Don't use operator-function, mutator syntax if more than one input value must be passed. For this guideline, a matrix, structure, or cell array can often be considered as a single input. If you implemented the operator-member function as a normal member function, would the input value be passed as one argument or more than one? If the answer is more than one, don't use operator-function, mutator syntax.
- Don't use operator-member-function syntax for complicated functions. Here, *complicated* can mean a lot of input values or an algorithm that is computationally intensive.
- Don't use operator-member-function syntax for functions that return more than one output for a scalar object. It is okay for a function to return N outputs for an object array containing N objects.
- Use operator-member-function syntax rather than resorting to calls to **superiorto** or **inferiorto**.

These guidelines encourage the use of relatively simple dot member functions.

22.2 WHEN ARRAY-REFERENCE IS NOT A REFERENCE

If you look at MATLAB's object-oriented requirements in Chapter 2, there is no mention of **subsref** or **subsasgn**. These functions are critical to the object-oriented implementation but they are nothing more than the functional form of an operator. Our classes achieve a structure-like interface because of the way we elected to implemented **subsref** and **subsasgn**. As long as we can live with the constraints imposed by their arguments, we are free to define the behavior of **subsref** and **subsasgn** to be anything we want.

When **subsref** and **subsasgn** implement a structure-like interface, array-reference index values are limited to integers or logicals. Based on results from §22.1, we realize that this is a self-imposed limit. MATLAB passes all index types into **subsref** and **subsasgn**, and it is up to us to define the behavior. We already know how to achieve structure-like indexing behavior, but it is also easy to make array-reference behave like a function call. Simply treat the indices as arguments and use them to calculate a value or perform some operation. You can even include pass-by-reference emulation.

22.2.1 FUNCTORS

In this section, we examine classes that overload the array-reference operator to execute a function. Using the array-reference syntax as a function call changes the central focus of the class. Normally, this focus divides evenly between states (a.k.a. the data) and behavior (a.k.a. the functions). Redefining array-reference syntax so that it evaluates an expression tilts the focus in favor of behavior, so much so that everything about the class centers on the evaluation of the principal function. In computer science, an object that can be used as a function is called a *functor*.

Recall that the main difference between a structure and a class is the class' close association between data and function. A functor has the same close association between data and function; however, the functor's main function is the one associated with the array-reference operator. Much of the data associated with the evaluation of the main function are stored in private member variables of the class. The data are very similar to persistent data used by a normal function except that every instance of the functor gets its own unique copy. Compared to persistent data, functor data are also easier to assign because variables are accessed through the public interface. The data are also easier to load and save. In a functor, all the advantages of a class come along for free.

Let's implement a functor so we can experiment with its syntax. We can get Class Wizard to provide us with the bulk of the implementation, but a few last-minute tweaks to **subsref** will be required. The functor example will calculate a polynomial based on private variable coefficients. The coefficient array will have a public interface, and array-operator syntax will request an evaluation. Build the functor using Class Wizard or use the files available on the companion disk in **/chapter_22/@cPolyFun**.

Open Class Wizard and create a class named **cPolyFun**. In the private variable dialog, add **m_coef** as a variable and set its initial value to **zeros(1,0)**. In the public variable dialog, add **coef** as a variable and set both the **Accessor Expression** and **Mutator Expression** to **m_coef**. Build the class in a new **@cPolyFun** directory and exit Class Wizard. Now open **@cPolyFun/subsref.m** and replace the **case '()'** commands with those shown in Code Listing 138. After making this change, be careful if you need to regenerate the class because, by default, Class Wizard overwrites **subsref**. Uncheck the **subsref** box in the "Group of Eight" button group to prevent this.

Code Listing 138, cPolyFun Array-Reference Operator Implementation

```
1  case '()'
2    if numel(index) > 1 || numel(index.subs) > 1
3      error('cPolyFun:invalidInput', 'Only one input argument is
       allowed');
4    end
5    x = reshape(index.subs{1}, [], 1);   % x reshaped as a col
6    coef = repmat(this.m_coef(:)', numel(x), 1);
7    power = repmat((0:numel(this.m_coef)-1), numel(x), 1);
```

```
8    x = repmat(x, 1, size(coef, 2));
9    varargout = {reshape(sum(coef .* x.^power, 2),
     size(index.subs{1}))};
```

The polynomial function evaluation takes place in line 9. The equation for the right-hand expression can be written as

$$y_{i,j} = C_1 + C_2 x_{i,j} + C_3 x_{i,j}^2 + C_4 x_{i,j}^3 + \cdots + C_N x_{i,j}^{N-1} = \sum_{k=1}^{N} C_k x_{i,j}^{k-1}$$

The other lines check inputs, copy values, reshape matrices, and allow the expression on line 9 to be written in vectorized form. Line 2 checks the number of inputs against the number supported by the functor. The first check, **numel(index) > 1**, throws an error if the function call includes index operators beyond the initial **'()'**. This check is usually acceptable. The second check, **numel(index.subs) > 1**, limits the number of input arguments to 1. In general, functors can accept any number of arguments, and **numel(index.subs)** serves the same purpose as **nargin**. Line 5 reshapes the input argument as a column. Line 6 duplicates the vector of coefficients, one row for every element in the column of **x**. Line 7 performs the same duplication for the array of powers. Line 8 repeats the column of **x** values, one column for every column in **coef**. The local variables **x**, **coef**, and **power** are now the same size. Line 9 uses element-by-element operators to produce a value for every input and then resizes the result to match the input size.

22.2.2 FUNCTOR HANDLES

Now that we have something that behaves a lot like a function, it is natural to wonder where appearances give way to reality. For example, you can't use the **@** character to create a function handle to the functor function. The commands

```
p = cPolyFun;

p_func = @p;
```

result in an error because MATLAB will not allow **p** to be both a variable and a function. By this point in our object-oriented odyssey, you might look at the second command above and wonder whether you can overload the **@** operator and return the correct handle. Sadly, as far as I have been able to determine, you can't overload the **@** operator. Anonymous functions provide a solution, albeit with a small increase in syntax complexity. The following commands yield the desired handle:

```
p = cPolyFun;

p_func = @(x)p(x);
```

Anonymous function syntax forces us to declare the number of inputs, so it isn't as flexible as a general function handle. Anonymous function syntax also forces us to assign all private member variables prior to creating the anonymous handle. During handle construction, MATLAB makes a copy of the object and associates the copy with the handle. MATLAB does not give you a handle to **p** but rather a handle to a *copy* of **p**. Even with these limitations, an anonymous function handle allows us to use commands that require a function handle. For example, the command **quad(@(x)p(x), 1, 0)** will integrate a **cPolyFun** object over the limits [0 1]. As in this example, if you need to pass a function handle, it is safer to create the anonymous handle on the fly. It is too hard to remember where the handle points, and that can lead to errors that are very difficult to diagnose. For many situations, there is another option that is more elegant: overload **feval**.

22.2.3 Functor feval

Many commands in the **quad** category allow you to pass the function as a handle, a string, or an **inline** object. In fact, when a function's help text demands a function handle, you can usually pass a handle, a string, or an object.* For the object-input option, the intended type is **@inline**; however, an object of any class that overloads **feval** will usually work just as well. If we write a **cPolyFun**-specific **feval**, we can sidestep most of the problems related to anonymous function handles. The commands for **feval** are provided in Code Listing 139.

Code Listing 139, Functor feval Listing

```
1  function varargout = feval(this, varargin)
2  varargout = cell(1, max([1 nargout]));
3  [varargout{:}] = subsref(this, substruct('()', varargin));
```

The lines in Code Listing 139 implement **feval** so that any functor can reuse it as is. In line 1, **varargin** and **varargout** support reuse. Line 2 preallocates **varargout** with the correct number of outputs. We have used this technique before. Line 3 forwards the input arguments to the array-reference operator and collects return values in the elements of **varargout**. Line 3 highlights the relationship between **subsref index** and the function's input arguments. With **feval** in place, we can integrate a **cPolyFun** object using simple syntax. For example, the command would be **quad(p, 0, 1)**, a big improvement over the anonymous handle syntax described in the previous section. In the test drive, we will demonstrate some of these commands.

22.2.4 Additional Remarks Concerning Functors

As a group, functors represent a special-purpose class with a relatively narrow scope. Similar to **inline**, everything defined for a functor should support the principal, array-referenced function. As a starting point, the following guidelines help keep functors lean and mean.

- Always overload **feval** so that it performs the same operation as the array-reference operator. This will guarantee the same behavior regardless of how the primary function is called.
- Nonscalar functors are difficult to manage, and they don't work particularly well as an extension of **inline**. Prevent the inadvertent creation of nonscalar functor objects by overloading **horzcat**, **vertcat**, **cat**, and **repmat**.
- Don't allow nonstandard function-call syntax. For example, don't support indexing syntax beyond the required '()'.
- All member variables (public and private) and all member functions (public, dot, and private) should relate to the evaluation of the primary function. Instead of adding elements unrelated to the principal function, think about using a functor in composition.
- Avoid using **subsasgn** syntax for functors. We didn't discuss the possibility of putting the functor on the left-hand side of an assignment. While possible, the syntax is probably too bizarre to be useful.

---

* Any function that processes the function handle input with **fcnchk** will accept a function handle, a string, or an object. See **help fcnchk** for more information. Functions that use **isa(x, 'inline')** to look for **inline** objects will usually throw an error when passed an object of any other type. Functions in this category include **fminbnd**, **fminsearch**, **fzero**, **ezgraph3**, and **ezplot**.

23.3 TEST DRIVE

The test-drive commands used to discover how MATLAB collects and passes index arguments were shown in Code Listing 137. The commands in Code Listing 140 demonstrate functor syntax using **cPolyFun**.

```
Code Listing 140, Chapter 22 Test Drive Command Listing: functor
1    >> cd '/oop_guide/chapter_22'
2    >> set(0, 'FormatSpacing', 'compact')
3    >> clear classes; fclose all; close all force;
4    >>
5    >> p = cPolyFun;
6    >> p.coef = [0 0 1];   % y = 0 + 0*x + 1*x^2
7    >> p_func = @(x)p(x);
8    >>
9    >> x = -5:0.1:5;
10   >> plot(x, p(x));
11   >> ezplot(@(x)p(x), -5, 5);
12   >>
13   >> [quad(p_func, 0, 5)  quad(@(x)p(x), 0, 5)  quad(p, 0, 5)]
14   ans =
15     41.6667    41.6667    41.6667
16   >>
17   >> p.coef(3) = 2 * p.coef(3);
18   >> [quad(p_func, 0, 5)  quad(@(x)p(x), 0, 5)  quad(p, 0, 5)]
19   ans =
20     41.6667    83.3333    83.3333
21   >>
22   >> objectdirectory
23   cPolyFun (3 instances)
24   >>
25   >> p2_func = @(x)p(x);
26   >> objectdirectory
27   cPolyFun (4 instances)
```

Line 5 constructs a **cPolyFun** object. Line 6 initializes the polynomial coefficients with values that yield a polynomial equal to **x^2**. Line 7 generates an anonymous function handle using a copy of **p**. Lines 10 and 11 plot the function, and the result of both commands is a very recognizable parabola. I didn't include the plots as figures. If you want to see the resulting plots, you'll have to enter the commands.

The expression **p(x)** on line 10 also demonstrates that the functor can accept a range of inputs and produce an equal number of outputs. On line 11, **ezplot** is an example of a function that demands a function handle but will actually accept an **inline** object. Unfortunately, **ezplot** will not accept any object type, forcing us to create an anonymous handle. As we will soon see, it is safer to create the handle as it is needed.

Line 13 uses **quad** to integrate the functor from zero to five. We expect the answer to be

$$\tfrac{1}{3}x^3\Big|_0^5 = \tfrac{1}{3}\left(5^3 - 0^3\right) = 41.667$$

and this value matches the values displayed on line 15. Calling quad with a precomputed anonymous handle, an anonymous handle created at the time of the call, or a functor object produces the same result. Using the unadulterated functor object produces the easiest syntax. Line 17 doubles the **x^2** coefficient, and as a result, the integration of **p** over the same limits should double. Values from the repeated **quad** commands are displayed on line 20. The value associated with the previously saved anonymous handle didn't change. The assignment in line 17 didn't affect **p_func**.

The next few lines provide some insight into this behavior. Lines 22–23 display a complete summary of all objects in the workspace. Chapter 24 discusses **objectdirectory** in more detail. Line 25 explicitly created an anonymous function handle, and behind the scenes, line 25 created a copy of **p**. Lines 26–27 display the evidence. The anonymous function handle isn't connected to **p**, but rather to a copy of **p**. That's why the first value in line 20 didn't change. That is also why it is dangerous to create anonymous function handles to functor objects before they are needed.

22.4 SUMMARY

We are approaching the end of our journey, and this chapter provides some of the tools you will need to survive on your own. The examples in this chapter push the syntax beyond current convention. Dot member functions have certain advantages over typical member-function syntax and very few disadvantages. The primary advantage is that dot-member-function syntax helps eliminate ambiguity. The function selected is always associated with the referenced object independent from the superiority of the input arguments. The primary disadvantage is that MATLAB doesn't officially recognize dot-member-function syntax. Because of this, dot-member-function syntax doesn't match with MATLAB's call-by-value model. This is particularly true when a member function takes advantage of call-by-reference emulation.

Functors are a very convenient way to create functions that rely on many parameters. A non-object-oriented implementation might store the parameters as a global or persistent variable. Stored as a global or persistent, every function evaluation uses the same parameters. Functors are not subject to this limitation because every functor has its own set of values. In the conventional implementation, evaluation with different parameters requires passing the parameters along with the input variables. This leads to overly complicated input checking code that all too often is inadequate. Functors can get around this problem by creating a set of atomic, orthogonal public member variables. The values are checked when they are assigned; and once checked, the principal function can use them without checking them again. Not only does this reduce complexity; it also often improves run time. This is particularly true for parameters that are set once, because once assigned into the functor, they don't need to be checked during every function call. The danger in using functors is the potential lack of support inside built-in functions. If built-in functions alter their interface to accept only **inline** objects, the syntax becomes more cumbersome, and existing calls that use functors would break.

22.5 INDEPENDENT INVESTIGATIONS

1. Input the commands **b.show_arg(1:end)** and **b.show_arg{1}(end)**, and observe the output. Did you get the index values you expected? Put a breakpoint at the beginning of **subsref** and repeat the commands. How many times is **subsref** called for each command? Examine the value of **index** passed into **subsref**. Based on the indices, what is the initial call to **subsref** trying to obtain? What would happen if

show_arg didn't support an empty-input call? (Hint: how does MATLAB convert **end** to a numeric value?)

2. Input the commands **b.show_arg{:}** and **b.show_arg{1}(:)**, and observe the output. Did you get the index values you expected? How many times is subsref called in this investigation? How are the index inputs **':'** and **end** different?

3. Add a *concealed* member variable named **cshow_arg** with an "accessor expression" and a "mutator expression" of **%helper**. Copy the contents of **show_arg_helper** into **cshow_arg_helper**. Repeat the command examples from Code Listing 137, but replace **show_arg** with **cshow_arg**. Do all the commands work without error? Why?

4. Modify **cPolyFun** so that you can optionally pass in the coefficient array during construction.

5. Add a member function to **cPolyFun** named **fc_handle** that will return an anonymous function handle to the class' primary function. For this investigation, use either normal member function or operator-member-function syntax. After adding the function, try the following commands:

   ```
   p = cPolyFun;

   p_func = fc_handle(p);

   feval(p_func, 1)
   ```

   The answer should be zero. If the answer instead lists **coef** as an element, you assigned the wrong handle. (Hint: inside a **cShape** member function, think about the difference between **this.color** and **subsref(this, substruct('. ', 'color'))**. Why does the first return an error and the second return a value?)

6. Use the command **which inline** to locate the directory. Look at the list of files defined for **@inline**. Some of these names will look very familiar, and some unfamiliar. Open some of these files and examine their content. Are there any modules we should tailor for every functor? You can create a functor that uses **inline** as the parent class. Is this a good idea? What would you need to overload to make everything work correctly?

7. Change the indexing behavior for **cPolyFun.coef**. Match the index to the power of **x** in the polynomial. That is, **p.coef(0)** is the constant, **p.coef(1)** multiplies **x**, **p.coef(2)** multiplies **x^2**, and so on. You will need to use a helper function, and the helper function will need to remap the indices.

8. Add a constructor to **cPolyFun** that accepts as inputs a coefficient array and "x" values, for example, **cPolyFun([0 0 1], 1)**. Ordinarily the **cPolyFun** constructor returns a **cPolyFun** object. Is that the correct return type for this constructor? If you decide to return something other than a **cPolyFun** object, can you implement the constructor? Try it and see if there are any showstoppers.

9. Create a class named **cF2C** and overload **times** so that the following command correctly converts degrees F into degrees C:

$$deg\_c = [32\ 212]\ .*\ cF2C;$$

Is **cF2C** a functor? Does this syntax have any benefit vs. a function call?

23 Protected Member Variables and Functions

In trying to bring MATLAB's object-oriented capability in line with conventional object-oriented theory, some areas are easy, some are difficult, and some are like trying to fit a square peg into a round hole. Coercing MATLAB to supply protected visibility fits into the latter category. This is mostly because MATLAB has no organic support for protected visibility. If you apply enough pressure, you can push a square peg through a round hole. Similarly, with a reasonably small increase in complexity, the group of eight can be extended to provide protected visibility. Every class must first include a pair of private functions that support protected variables in the same way **get** and **set** support public variables. Next, the child and its parents must exchange a set of function handles corresponding to the set of member functions with protected visibility. The best time to execute this exchange occurs during construction. Finally, the child's member functions must be able to locate and use the appropriate function handles.

23.1 HOW PROTECTED IS DIFFERENT FROM OTHER VISIBILITIES

Public and private visibilities enable a class to create an impregnable interface. Objects of the class have access to both public and private members, but clients are restricted to public members only. Introducing parent–child inheritance also introduces a level of visibility between public and private. Protected visibility is the name for this middle ground where a child class has access but clients do not. Visibility restrictions for public and private don't change but the visibility of protected members changes depending on the user. For a client, protected means the same as private; and for a child, protected means the same as public. Here we lay out a prescription for protected visibility and investigate its implementation. The implementation is difficult because it relies on the correct organization of function handles across an inheritance hierarchy. Often it hardly seems worth the effort. This is particularly true when you consider that concealed visibility already provides much of the needed functionality and that protected visibility adds quite a lot of code and complexity.

Currently, Class Wizard does not include the ability to build class hierarchies with protected functions or protected variables. Even so, Class Wizard–generated files may be modified to include some level of protected visibility. The classes implemented on the companion disk in **oop_guide/chapter_23** provide a working example. The highlights are examined below.

23.2 CLASS ELEMENTS FOR PROTECTED

Before we can design a solution for protected access, we need to understand what we are dealing with. Some of the considerations include the following:

- Both member variables and member functions may have protected visibility.
- Multiple inheritance means a child may have more than one parent. Any parent may define a protected member, and if more than one parent defines the same protected member, there is ambiguity.

- In a hierarchy with multiple levels of inheritance, any particular protected member may be defined at any level. If more than one level defines the same protected member, there is ambiguity.
- To a child, public and protected members should exhibit the same behavior. This means the implementation strategy must consider both direct-link and non-direct-link protected variables.
- Ideally, it would be impossible for a client to gain direct access to protected members.

For public variables, **get** and **set** represent an implementation strategy that already considers issues related to multiple inheritance, multilevel hierarchies, and direct-link vs. non-direct-link variables. We can avoid an entirely new design pattern by reusing this strategy. The implementation for protected variables centers on two protected functions: **pget** and **pset**. The contents of **pget** and **pset** closely mimic the contents of **get** and **set**, respectively. The differences are small and include the following:

- A protected-variable block instead of a private-variable block
- No concealed-variable block
- A slice-and-forward block that calls **pget** or **pset** instead of **get** or **set**

23.2.1 PROTECTED FUNCTIONS AND ADVANCED FUNCTION HANDLE TECHNIQUES

MATLAB provides two built-in levels of visibility: public and private. Protected visibility is neither. If we locate protected functions in the public area, they become part of the public interface. There are other reasons why this location is a bad choice, but keeping the public interface simple is chief among them. The only other choice is to locate protected functions in the private directory. Functions located in the parent's private directory are not usually available to the child; however, function handles can be used to circumvent the usual restrictions.

One function-handle feature, often overlooked, is the relationship between a function handle and the function search path. A function handle uses the function path that was in effect at the time the handle was created, not at the time the handle is evaluated. For example, a parent class can create a function handle to one of its private functions and pass the handle to a child. When the child evaluates this handle, MATLAB executes the module located in the parent's private directory. The function handle already knows the path to its function, so it goes there with no exception.

23.2.2 PASSING PROTECTED HANDLES FROM PARENT TO CHILD

A protected function-handle strategy hinges on one detail: passing an array of protected functions from the parent to the child. The function used to pass the protected function-handle array must be public, otherwise the child would not be able to call it. On the other hand, we don't want to use a public function because we don't want to give clients an opportunity to access the protected handle array. To avoid giving a client too many opportunities to grab the handle array, we will return the protected handle array only during object construction. Code inside the constructor will check a very strict set of conditions before populating the array. Returning the array from the constructor requires a second output argument. The modified prototype is

```
function [this, handles] = constructor(varargin)
```

Since all current code expects the constructor to provide only one output, this change will not trigger any errors. The commands in Code Listing 141 are also added to the end of the current constructor.

In Code Listing 141, line 6 assumes that Class Wizard created the child class so that the child-class constructor calls each parent-class constructor from **private/ctor_ini**. This allows the

Code Listing 141, Protected Function Modifications to the Constructor

```
1   if nargout == 2
2     stack = dbstack('-completenames');
3     caller = stack(end-1);
4     [call_path, call_name] = fileparts(caller.file);
5     [dc, private_name] = fileparts(call_path);
6     if strcmp(call_name, 'ctor_ini') && strcmp(private_name,
        'private')
7       % omit pget and pset handles for any parents
8       handle_str = cellfun(@func2str,
          this.m_protected_func_array, ...
9        'UniformOutput', false);
10      omit = [strmatch('pget', handle_str, 'exact')  ...
11        strmatch('pset', handle_str, 'exact')];
12      include = setdiff(1:numel(handle_str), omit);
13      % include pget and pset for this class
14      handles = {@pget; @pset;
          this.m_protected_func_array{include}};
15    else
16      handles = {};
17    end
18  end
```

protected handle test to use the strings **`ctor_ini`** and **`private`**. If the constructor is called from any **`private/ctor_ini.m`**, it is okay to return the set of protected function handles. This assumption is the only place where this implementation is less secure compared to language-enforced protected visibility. Lines 7–14 assign the function handles into the output argument. Lines 7–12 find all handle references to **pget** and **pset** for parents of this class. Line 14 adds references to this class' **pget** and **pset** functions and adds all parent handles except **pget** and **pset**. This substitution must occur or we risk the possibility of sending the wrong slice to a parent function. It is now up to the child-class constructor helper to call parent-class constructors with two output arguments and save the protected function handles. For an example, see the code in

`chapter_23/@cChild/private/ctor_ini.m`

23.2.3 Accessing and Mutating Protected Variables

From inside a member function we are already familiar with the use of **get** or **set** to access or mutate public member variables. Protected variables require the same treatment except that **pget** and **pset**, respectively, substitute for **get** and **set**. Following this approach, let's use the same indexing techniques for both public and protected variables. Doing so also allows us to reuse large sections of **get** and **set** in the implementations of **pget** and **pset**. The only significant changes occur inside the parent slice-and-forward blocks. The implementation for the slice-and-forward block inside **pget** is shown in Code Listing 142. The complete class implementations can be found on the companion disk in the **chapter_23** directory.

Many of the commands in **pget**'s slice-and-forward block are identical to the commands already detailed for **get**. The first difference occurs in lines 11–13, where indices for the parent handles to **pget** are found. Lines 11–12 use **cellfun** to loop through the handles in

Code Listing 142, Parent Forward Inside Protected pget

```
1    % parent forwarding block
2    if ~found
3      if nargout == 0
4        varargout = cell(size(this));
5      velse
6        varargout = cell(1, nargout);
7      end
8
9      % get the indices of all parent pget functions they should
       be in the
10     % same order as parents in parent list.
11     handle_str = cellfun(@func2str,
       this(1).m_protected_func_array, ...
12       'UniformOutput', false);
13     pget_index = strmatch('pget', handle_str, 'exact');
14
15     parent_name = parent_list';
16     for pk = 1:numel(parent_name)
17       try
18         parent = [this.(parent_name{pk})];
19         parent_pget_index = pget_ index(pk);
20         pget_func = this(1).m_protected_func_array
           {parent_pget_index};
21         [varargout{:}] = feval(pget_func, parent, index);
22         found = true; % catch will assign false if not found
23         do_sub_indexing = false; % assume parent did all sub-
           indexing
24         break; % can only get here if field was found
25       catch
26         found = false;
27         err = lasterror;
28         switch err.identifier
29           case 'MATLAB:nonExistentField'
30             % NOP
31           otherwise
32             rethrow(err);
33         end
34       end
35     end
36     if do_assignin
37       parent = num2cell(parent);
38       [this.(parent_name{1})] = deal(parent{:});
39     end
40   end
41
```

m_protected_func_array and turn them into equivalent strings. Line 13 then finds the indices using **strmatch** with the **'exact'** option. During construction, as long as every parent returns a handle to **pget**, the indices in **pget_index** will line up with the parent classes returned from **parent_list**. An improvement to this implementation would store the protected handles as a **persistent** variable inside **parent_list**. That way, the handles and parent classes would always be synchronized.

Lines 16–35 are similar to the parent-class loop in **get**. Instead of looping over the names directly, line 15 gets the list of parent names and the loop beginning on line 16 uses indices. Line 18 uses dynamic field-name syntax to slice off the parent class and uses **assignin** to shove it into **parent**. Lines 19 and 20 get the corresponding handle to **pget** from the protected function array. Line 21 uses **feval** to call the parent version of **pget**, passing it both the parent class and the index. Here is where the function-handle magic occurs. The fully qualified path to **pget** is stored in the function handle. Since this path was established from inside the parent-class constructor, the fully qualified path points to the parent-class private directory. After the function handle is established, MATLAB does not reapply path search rules.

The call to **pget** in line 21 will either return a value or throw an error. If it returns a value, the remaining lines in the try block set some logical flags and break out of the loop. As with **get**, potential ambiguity is handled by keeping only the value from the first parent that provides one. Also similar to **get**, if **pget** throws an error, the catch block in lines 25–34 checks the error and either continues the parent-class loop or rethrows the error. Lines 36–39 are identical to those in **get**.

Modifications to **pset** proceed along a similar path. First, copy **set.m** to **private/pset.m**. The public-variable section becomes the protected-variable section, the concealed-variable section is deleted, and the parent-forward block uses **feval** on each parent version of **pset**. Code on the companion disk includes a full example.

23.2.4 CALLING PROTECTED FUNCTIONS

The parent-forward block in Code Listing 142 demonstrates the general procedure for calling protected functions. First, find the index into **this.m_protected_func_array** that corresponds to the desired function. As in the parent-forward code, converting handles into strings with **cellfun** and then using **strmatch** to find candidate indices is a good idiom. Next, use **feval*** to call the protected function. The example function, used later in the test drive, can be found in

/chapter_23/cChild/call_parent_protected.m

This public member function of **cChild**, calls the protected function located in

/chapter_23/cParent/private/protected_function.m

The potential for ambiguity enters into this general procedure because the **strmatch** command may find the same protected function defined by more than one parent. One way to avoid this problem is by not allowing the same protected function to be defined by more than one parent. This approach can't be universally applied because there are certain protected functions that require the object as an input. If the class hierarchy supports object arrays, the same slicing issues we encountered in public member functions also occur for protected functions.

Recall that object slicing adds certain limitations to inheritance. Ideally, we should be able to include a class, without modification, anywhere in a hierarchy. With scalar objects, we can achieve this goal. With nonscalar objects, however, we are forced to include some additional functions. Each child class needs to include a public slice-and-forward function for public member functions

---

* Newer versions of MATLAB support a syntax that allows you to call the function without using **feval**. See **help function_handle** for details.

defined by the parent. The same rule applies to protected functions except that the function is placed in the child's private directory and is typically included in the list of protected function handles. Dot member functions are exempt because **pget** already includes slice-and-forward code in the parent-forwarding block.

23.3 TEST DRIVE

In this test drive, we make use of two classes in **/chapter_23**: **cParent** and **cChild**. After Class Wizard generated the initial set of files, the constructors were modified to pass protected handles from parent to child. The child class also includes three public member functions that demonstrate accessing protected variables, mutating protected variables, and calling a protected function. The test drive (Code Listing 143) demonstrates results from these functions.

```
Code Listing 143, Parent Forward Inside Protected pget

1    >> cd '/oop_guide/chapter_23'
2    >> set(0, 'FormatSpacing', 'compact')
3    >> clear classes; fclose all; close all force;
4    >>
5    >> child = cChild;
6    >> objectdirectory
7      cParent (2 instances)
8      cChild (2 instances)
9    >>
10   >> private_struct = builtin('struct', child);   % use only
     for debug
11   >> private_struct.m_protected_func_array
12   ans =
13     @pget
14     @pset
15     @protected_function
16   >>
17   >> functions(private_struct.m_protected_func_array{1})
18   ans =
19     function: 'pget'
20         type: 'scopedfunction'
21         file: 'C:/oop_guide/chapter_23/@cParent/private/pget.m'
22    parentage: {'protected_function'}
23   >>
24   >> access_parent_protected(child)
25   ans =
26     NaN
27   >>
28   >> child = mutate_parent_protected(child, 'It Worked!');
29   >> access_parent_protected(child)
30   ans =
31     It Worked!
32   >>
```

```
33  >> call_parent_protected(child, ['Copies input to output'])
34  ans =
35  Copies input to output
```

After changing directories and clearing the workspace, line 5 instantiates an object of type **cChild**. Calling **objectdirectory** on line 6 shows us that the instantiation created two **cParent** objects and two **cChild** objects. The local variable **child** contains one pair of **cParent** and **cChild** objects, and the other objects are stored as persistent variables in the constructor.

Lines 10–22 display some of the internal details and allow us to confirm that the construction process worked as we expected. Line 10 uses the dangerous **builtin** command to return a copy of the private structure. Lines 11–15 display the list of function handles passed into the child-class constructor from the parent. This list resulted from code added to the end of **/@cParent/cParent.m**. Lines 17–22 provide more detail on the **@pget** handle. The important field to note is the **file** field. When the handle is used, this is the module that will be executed; no function search is involved. Use **functions** if you want to examine the other handles in the array.

Lines 24–35 use public member functions of **cChild** to demonstrate protected variable access, protected variable mutation, and protected function execution. The protected variable is stored in the **cParent** private structure, and the protected function is stored in the **cParent** private directory. The techniques discussed in this chapter give **cChild** visibility into these otherwise private members. Clients, however, do not have visibility into these private members. To demonstrate their use, public member functions in **cChild** provide an interface to the protected members.

Line 24 calls **access_parent_protected**, which uses **pget** to access the direct-link protected variable named **protected_var**. To get a feel for the way the child forwards the request to the parent, set a break point inside **access_parent_protected** and single-step through the various functions. The value shown in line 26 is the initial value assigned to **m_protected_var** in **ctor_ini**. Line 28 changes the value from **NaN** to 'It Worked!' by calling **mutate_parent_protected**. Lines 29–30 confirm the change. The command in line 33 forwards the input to **/@cParent/private/protected_function.m**, where it is simply echoed to the output. The result on line 35 is a direct result of this behavior.

23.4 SUMMARY

The techniques in this chapter can be used to give member variables and member functions protected visibility. For variables, using protected visibility seems very natural because **pget** and **pset** access and mutate protected variables the same way **get** and **set** access and mutate public variables. While we didn't demonstrate the use of helper functions and protected variables, protected helper function syntax is the same as their public counterparts. This is true for the functions themselves and for the case commands inserted in **pget** and **pset**. The complexity involved in accessing and mutating the private variables corresponding to each protected-variable case is encapsulated inside **pget** and **pset**. Potential ambiguity in protected variables is also manageable because a set of rules can be established in advance. The implementation for protected member variables is a good fit.

Protected member functions, on the other hand, have several issues that are more difficult to resolve. The first issue involves slicing with scalar versus nonscalar objects. This issue comes down to the fact that MATLAB will not slice a nonscalar object. This limitation forces us to face some difficult trade-offs. If we want to take advantage of both inheritance and nonscalar objects, child-class functions must be responsible for slicing. While this issue affects both public and protected functions, it is more critical for protected functions because MATLAB does not automatically select a function based on type. After slicing, we are responsible for matching the slice with the correct

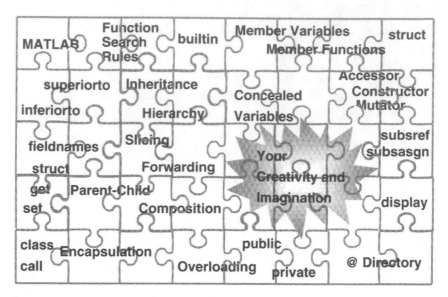

FIGURE 23.1 The complete picture.

protected handle. The second issue involves ambiguity. Adopting the same first-found rule used for protected variables is simple; however, it isn't always the correct choice. At the risk of making a complex implementation even more complicated, we could design and implement a way to disambiguate the calls.

It has been a long time since we last added pieces to our object-oriented puzzle. The last time we added a piece, the puzzle was almost complete. Since then, we have investigated object-oriented elements and investigated various techniques that would not have been possible without the final pieces. Your creativity and imagination complete the puzzle shown in Figure 23.1. Writing software is inherently a creative process, and inventing meaningful object-oriented relationships takes a great deal of imagination. I hope that the implementation mechanics discussed in this book help you focus less on writing code and more on creating solutions.

23.5 INDEPENDENT INVESTIGATIONS

1. Instead of storing protected function handles in the private structure, store them as a **persistent** variable inside **parent_list.m**. Would it also be a good idea to convert the function handles to strings and store the array of strings with the handles?
2. Add a protected dot member function to **cParent** and try to access it from inside a **cChild** member.
3. Try to obtain the list of protected function handles without actually inheriting **cParent**. Can you do it without defining a class? What additional checks could you add to the constructor to close the holes you find?

24 Potpourri for $100

Focusing on the big issues has allowed some smaller items to go unnoticed. In this chapter, we try to correct that situation by mentioning a few of the more obscure commands and techniques. The fact that these topics weren't included in the examples implies nothing about their general importance. What it does imply is that MATLAB includes object-oriented tools and capability beyond what we have already discussed. Some of the topics are only useful during debug, while others are only useful under very specific conditions. The brief discussion for each topic provides a starting point. The help browser and other third-party resources help fill in the gaps.

24.1 A SMALL ASSORTMENT OF USEFUL COMMANDS

During development and debug, it is often convenient to observe features associated with classes and objects. Class Wizard–generated classes provide some online help by calling **get** and **set** with one argument. From time to time, we have also used **builtin** with **'struct'** to examine the values in otherwise inaccessible private variables. The commands that follow are a few more that might be useful. The help browser offers additional detail on most of them.

24.1.1 OBJECTDIRECTORY

The **objectdirectory** command may be used to obtain a full accounting of all objects in the workspace. It is different from **whos** because it also accounts for objects stored in global variables, in persistent variables, and in an inheritance hierarchy. As a side note, **objectdirectory** also accounts for Java objects. Apparently, **objectdirectory** takes no input arguments and can return only one output. The output is a structure with element names corresponding to instantiated types and element values corresponding to the number of instances. Called with no output argument, **objectdirectory** will display types and instances even if you include a trailing semicolon.

Above, I use the word "apparently" because there is no help for **objectdirectory**. In trying to locate the command, MATLAB generates the following response:

```
>> which objectdirectory

built-in (undocumented)
```

24.1.2 METHODS AND METHODSVIEW

The **methods** command returns a complete list of an object's public member functions. Even when the public member functions are spread over several directories, **methods** finds them all. The input can be the name of a class or an instantiated object, and the output is a cell array of strings, for example:

```
star_methods = methods('cStar')

star_methods = methods(star)
```

Adding the string **'-full'** as a second argument causes methods to include inheritance information along with the function names. See **help methods** for more information. This option is useful for scalar-object hierarchies where member functions exist only in the appropriate parent class. Slice and forward functions in nonscalar hierarchies will cause **methods** to return an incomplete picture of inheritance.

The **methodsview** command is a graphical version of **methods**. Instead of returning a cell array, **methodsview** opens a window and displays function information. The **methodsview** display is tailored for Java objects but the command will also work for MATLAB objects. See **help methodsview** for more information.

24.1.3 FUNCTIONS

The **functions** command returns detailed information on a function handle. Many advanced object-oriented techniques use function handles, and the information provided by **functions** is useful during development. The input is a function handle and the output is a structure with fields that list a handle's **name**, **type**, **path**, and **parentage**. See **help functions** for more information. When the **path** element contains a fully qualified module name, the search path is not reevaluated when the handle is used. When the path element is empty or contains something other than a fully qualified name, search path conditions at the time of **feval** are used.

24.2 OTHER FUNCTIONS YOU MIGHT WANT TO OVERLOAD

Along with the group of eight, concatenation, and overloaded operators, there are a few other built-in overload candidates. The first topic discusses a technique you can use to tailor the behavior of any function normally associated with a built-in type. The fact that MATLAB treats built-in types as objects makes this possible. The remaining topics discuss several special-purpose functions that support the implementation of unique, narrowly focused classes.

24.2.1 FUNCTIONS FOR BUILT-IN TYPES

If you search the directory tree where MATLAB is installed, you will find many directories that begin with **@**. All of these are class directories. There are two notable features of these directories. The first notable feature is the number of class directories with the same name. §2.2.1.1 discussed the use of multiple class directories, and between then and now it wasn't discussed further. By now, you have developed a very good understanding of how MATLAB orders the function search path. With multiple class directories, the search order is essentially the same except that more than one class directory must be included. Since class directories are not included on the path, their order is determined based on the order of the directory that contains the class directory. A class directory in **pwd** has higher priority than a class directory in a directory on the path. The example below capitalizes on this behavior.

The second notable feature is the fact that all standard built-in types appear to be associated with class directories. The list includes **/@double**, **/@char**, **/@logical**, and all the rest. Does this mean that all MATLAB data types are objects? It's a question with no easy answer; however, in at least one important way they act like objects: the function search path includes the class directories associated with built-in types. Searching proceeds the same as if built-in types were objects; the type of a function's leftmost input argument determines the class directory searched. This behavior makes it very easy to redefine the behavior of almost any built-in function. The following example demonstrates when redefinition might be useful.

Suppose you are plotting the result of a long run and see the following warning,

```
Warning: Imaginary parts of complex X and/or Y arguments
ignored.
```

Your software isn't designed to use complex numbers, so there is an error somewhere. You are reasonably sure the square root of a negative number is causing the problem. It would be time-consuming to find the error by setting break points on every **sqrt** call, and stepping through line by line is out of the question. Instead, you can temporarily redefine the behavior of **sqrt** so that in addition to performing the square root, it uses **isreal** to inspect the result. Create a **@double** directory in **pwd** and add to it the **sqrt.m** function shown in Code Listing 144. Rerun the program and line 4 will display the call stack every time the square root result is complex.

Code Listing 144, Redefined Behavior for sqrt

```
1   function x = sqrt(x)
2   x = builtin('sqrt', x);
3   if ~isreal(x)
4     dbstack
5   end
```

In an equally important way, built-in types don't act like objects: built-in types can't be used as a parent.

24.2.2 SUBSINDEX

The built-in versions of **subsref** and **subsasgn** call **subsindex** when an object is used as an array-reference index or as a cell-reference index. For example, if **x** is an array of doubles and **k** is an object, the syntax **x(k)** attempts to convert **k** into an integer index by calling **subsindex**.

There are two odd things about **subsindex**. At least in versions 6.5, 7.0, and 7.1, the input is odd because the only argument passed in is the object. Without access to both the object and the array being indexed, it is difficult to create index values compatible with the size of the array being indexed. Since the built-in versions of **subsref** and **subsasgn** appear to pass in only one argument, **subsindex** is not very useful for indexing built-in types. The output required by the built-in versions of **subsref** and **subsasgn** is also odd because the first index is zero instead of one.

Another way to use **subsindex** is to create a pair of dependent classes. One class is an array class and the other is a so-called *iterator* class. The classes depend on one another because the array class needs an iterator object as the array-reference index. Inside the array-reference case, the command

```
array_index = subsindex(index.subs, this);
```

can be used to calculate the correct integer index. Here the inputs aren't odd because both the iterator object and the object being index are passed into **subsindex**. The output isn't odd because **subsindex** is designed to return a suitable value.

24.2.3 ISFIELD

A close relative of **fieldnames** is **isfield**. With respect to objects, testing for the presence or absence of a public member variable should never be necessary. Objects of a particular type always have the same set of public variables, and either **class** or **isa** may be used determine the type. Even so, you sometimes need to yield to client demand. If you want to enhance an object's structure-like interface, overload **isfield**.

24.3 SUMMARY

Contrary to much of the conventional wisdom, MATLAB has a wealth of object-oriented features and commands. It is obvious from the help text that certain features are intended for Java object support; however, they work just as well with MATLAB objects. It is also interesting to note the current similarity between built-in types and user-defined types. The number of object directories in MATLAB continues to grow with every new release. There is no reason to believe that this trend will change. Even though it is not universally recognized as such, MATLAB is a very complete, extremely capable, object-oriented programming environment. The expertise required to create a robust MATLAB class and run-time concerns are partially to blame for the lack of recognition. By capturing much of the required expertise, Class Wizard goes a long way toward making the implementation of MATLAB classes much less of a burden. The use of vectorized, nonscalar objects and object-oriented designs tailored to MATLAB's peculiarities answers many of the run-time complaints. For the future, we can expect that MATLAB's organic support for object-oriented programming will increase. This will allow more users to migrate toward object-oriented techniques and increase the chance for internal changes that will improve run time.

24.4 INDEPENDENT INVESTIGATIONS

1. Change into the **chapter_18** directory and instantiate a **cStar** object. Enter the **objectdirectory** command and observe the output. Call **methods** and **methodsview** on the **cStar** object and observe the output.
2. Look at the difference between **functions(@draw)** and **functions(@ver)**. Both handles are simple, but for one the **file** element is empty. What does that mean?
3. Instantiate a **cStar** object and a **cDiamond** object. Save the function handle for **@draw** in a variable, for example, **draw_func = @draw**. Use this handle to draw both shapes, for example, **star = feval(draw_func, star)**. If the function path is stored with the handle, how can the same handle be used to call member functions from different classes? Does the output from **functions(draw_func)** provide any clues?
4. In the §24.2.1 example, suppose that **sqrt** isn't the source of the complex value. What other functions can produce a complex value? What about **x^(1/2)** and **x.^(1/2)**? Can you redefine the behavior of these operators so that they too check for a complex result? (Hint: **help ops**.)
5. In the **@double** directory, temporarily redefine **rand** so that instead of returning random numbers from 0 to 1, it always returns 0.5. Can you think of a debugging scenario where this might be useful?
6. Build a simple class named **cIterator** and overload **subsindex**. Inside the overloaded **subsindex** function, display the value of **nargin** and add a **keyboard** command. Enter the following commands and confirm that **nargin** is one and that the only input is the **cIterator** object.

```
>> x = 1:5;
>> iter = cIterator;
>> x(iter);
```

Index

A

Accessing private variables, 52
Accessing protected variables, 344
Accessor, 30, 50, 56, 57, 63, 100, 109, 111, 158, 160, 217, 222, 234, 235, 236, 261, 323, 327, 332
Accessor/Mutator
  Combining, 41, 42, 221
Array-reference Operator, 29, 57, 62, 64, 68, 71, 79, 176, 283, 333, 335, 349
Arrays of Objects, 34, 57, 74, 85, 94, 103, 120, 124, 172, 175, 180, 197, 202, 222, 287, 306, 308
assignin command, 36, 216, 217, 220, 313, 314, 315, 316, 319, 320, 321, 324, 343

B

Base class, 154, 156, 165, 192
Basili, Victor, 12
Boehm, Barry, 12
builtin command, 32, 48, 63, 64, 69, 74, 79, 81, 82, 85, 86, 89, 95, 96, 98, 116, 118, 139, 159, 160, 176, 177, 178, 285, 344, 345, 347, 348, 349, 350
built-in functions, 45, 46, 74, 77, 113, 177, 182, 183, 198, 279, 280, 290, 299, 307, 337
Built-in types, 17, 20, 21, 22, 28, 47, 56, 57, 89, 124, 137, 139, 191, 348, 349

C

Call by reference, 316, 337
cat command, 177, 182, 273, 280, 291, 292, 293, 335
cChild class, 341, 343, 344, 345, 346
cellfun
  isclass, 177, 287
  isempty, 59, 67, 84, 106, 115, 117, 127, 164, 211, 215, 286, 287, 317, 318
  length, 292
cellfun command, 59, 67, 84, 85, 106, 115, 117, 127, 164, 177, 178, 180, 182, 211, 215, 286, 287, 292, 302, 317, 318, 341, 342, 343
Cell-reference operator, 29, 48, 49, 62, 65, 66, 68, 74, 331, 349
cellstr command, 59, 91, 92, 96, 195, 268
child class (see also, Hierarchy), 139, 154, 156, 158, 160, 161, 162, 168, 172, 175, 183, 184, 193, 269, 319, 325, 339, 340, 343, 344
class developer roles, 31, 78, 96, 111, 150
class functions, 33, 142

class structure, 33, 37, 71, 154, 160, 307
Class Wizard
  Data Dictionary, 244
  inheritance, 268, 269
  static-variable, 239, 240
clear command, 24, 25, 27, 30, 41, 71, 86, 87, 93, 97, 110, 119, 136, 169, 184, 187, 198, 203, 223, 273, 294, 300, 309, 310, 311, 322, 329, 336, 344
Client Roles, 14
Client Roles Versus Developer Roles, 8, 53, 77, 118, 120, 154, 295
Code Maintenance, 77, 210
Code Modularity, 31, 93, 98, 99, 209
Code Reuse, 3, 8, 13, 14, 137, 150, 156, 157, 160, 181, 212, 271, 335
Concatenation, 34, 46, 59, 71, 97, 175, 177, 179, 182, 205, 273, 280, 291, 292, 301, 335
concealed variable access, 103, 106, 109, 289
Concealed Variables, 100
Concealed Visibility, 339
Construction
  Helper functions, 145, 146, 155, 197, 199, 228, 229, 238, 240, 244, 259, 304, 341
  Input arguments, 141, 144, 146, 152, 155, 257
Constructor, 23, 36, 155, 231, 268, 340, 343
  child class, 154, 171, 184, 340, 345
  constructor helper (ctor_ini.m), 146
Constructor helper, 23, 198, 256
Containers, 175, 280, 283, 284, 286, 290, 292, 293
cParent class, 343, 344, 345, 346

D

decomposition (see also, Object-Oriented Design), 10
Developer View Display Option, 78, 83, 84, 86, 87, 88, 160, 304, 306, 310, 311, 314, 316, 323
Development
  code evolution, 4, 6, 7, 8, 121, 139, 154, 189, 193, 198, 226, 275, 277
  direct-link public variables, 210, 211, 212, 213, 216, 220, 223, 234, 235, 236, 249, 261, 263, 269, 304, 305, 306, 318, 340, 345
display
  overloaded, 321
display command, 17, 77, 79, 80, 81, 83, 84, 88, 93, 94, 98, 116, 117, 136, 192, 310
do_assignin pass-by-reference control, 213, 214, 215, 216, 217, 218, 220, 221, 222, 259, 260, 315, 316, 317, 318, 319, 320, 321, 324, 328, 329, 342

dot-reference operator, 50, 55, 63, 64, 66, 102, 110, 120, 172, 179, 235, 316, 323, 327

E

empty object array, 55, 64, 116, 128, 280, 308
Encapsulation
    interface, 1, 7, 8, 14, 15, 29, 31, 32, 33, 34, 35, 42, 48, 51, 52, 53, 54, 70, 74, 78, 83, 92, 93, 99, 113, 128, 142, 146, 150, 183, 191, 198, 203, 204, 206, 209, 212, 222, 226, 240, 265, 275, 293, 302, 305, 309, 327, 333, 339, 340
    member variables, 31, 78
end command, 46, 280
evalin command, 216, 220, 313, 314, 315, 319
Extreme Programming, 6
extreme-programming lifecycle, 4

F

fcnchk command, 335
feval command, 1, 48, 84, 86, 117, 142, 144, 145, 157, 283, 284, 286, 292, 334, 335, 338, 342, 343, 348, 350
fieldnames
    overloaded, 97, 199, 321
fieldnames command, 17, 32, 91, 92, 93, 126, 137, 161, 183, 184, 192, 194, 199, 281, 283
filesep, 2
Function Handle, 1, 85, 88, 89, 337, 339, 340, 341, 343, 344, 345, 346, 348
    Anonymous Function, 334, 335, 336, 337, 338
Function overloading, 348
    struct, 80, 113
    subsref, 159, 160
Function Search Path, 47, 56, 113, 142, 161
functor, 277, 327, 333, 334, 335, 336, 337, 338

G

George, Michael, 12
get command, 17, 43, 99, 104, 111, 126, 136, 158, 162, 172, 183, 185, 192, 193, 195, 198, 200, 210, 213, 227, 234, 236, 254, 260, 287, 317, 318, 319, 329
get.m, 185
getfield command (deprecated), 43, 50, 91, 99, 102
global variables, 304, 309, 311, 347
Goldratt, Eliyahu, 13
Group of eight
    framework, 156, 280, 302, 303
    functions, 101, 113, 121, 140, 158, 160, 167, 172, 173, 177, 182, 183, 217, 225, 226, 229, 242, 246, 249, 280, 304, 321

H

handle-graphics, 191, 193, 197, 204, 206, 252, 263, 284

Helper function
    Color_helper, 212, 214, 218, 221, 222, 259, 263, 273
    ColorRgb_helper, 267, 273
    LineWidth_helper, 218, 222, 259, 273, 308
    Reset_helper, 325
    Title_helper, 270, 273
    View_helper, 317
Helper Function
    Accessor/Mutator, 239, 240
    Interface, 212, 223, 316
horzcat command, 46, 71, 97, 175, 177, 179, 182, 205, 273, 280, 291, 301, 335
hsv color, 43, 54, 80
hsv2rgb command, 43, 53, 54, 55, 60, 61, 66, 68, 105, 108, 127, 129, 195, 196, 221
Humphrey, Watts, 3, 4

I

IEEE, 4, 12
inferiorto command, 36, 47, 49, 74, 116, 143, 144, 146, 157, 228, 327, 332
Inheritance, 15
    child class, 35, 139, 153, 154, 155, 159, 160, 161, 162, 164, 167, 168, 169, 175, 182, 184, 187, 189, 191, 193, 339
    Composition/Aggregation, 139, 191, 192, 193, 198, 201, 202, 203, 205, 206, 249, 261, 279, 311, 312, 335
    hierarchy, 1, 7, 14, 15, 139, 150, 153, 154, 160, 162, 165, 169, 171, 183, 205, 228, 249, 279, 301, 311, 328, 339, 343, 347
    overloaded function, 139, 153, 160, 172, 183
    parent-child, 139, 157, 183, 191, 193, 198, 205, 206, 226, 249, 339
inline objects, 335, 336, 337, 338
inputname command, 81, 82, 84, 117, 216, 220, 313, 314, 315, 319, 324
Instantiation (see also Construction), 87, 283, 291, 345, 347, 350
isa command, 69, 70, 116, 131, 146, 158, 159, 168, 169, 171, 176, 206, 275, 279, 281, 285, 292, 296, 335, 349
ischar command, 43, 59, 104, 106, 107, 109, 126, 129, 162, 166, 213, 218
isnumeric command, 43, 146, 297
isreal command, 297, 349

L

lasterror command, 114, 116, 144, 145, 157, 164, 167, 215, 219, 288, 289, 290, 320, 342
length command, 293
Lifecycle Models, 10
List Expansion, 71, 97, 103, 119, 144, 146, 210, 231, 238, 256, 261, 292
loadobj command, 46, 304, 307, 308, 311
lookfor command, 7

M

mat2cell command, 54, 55, 66, 105, 108, 127, 130, 195, 196, 221, 279, 282, 295, 296
methods command, 347, 348
methodsview command, 347, 348, 350
Meyer, Bertrand, 13
Module Coupling, 10, 226, 311
mtimes command, 46, 54, 69, 70, 73, 123, 124, 131, 135, 139, 167, 168, 169, 198, 202, 265, 266, 267, 269, 270, 271, 273, 282, 296, 297, 302
Multiple inheritance, 154, 156, 160, 162, 167, 185, 340
Mutator, 30, 31, 33, 36, 40, 116, 212, 213, 220, 221, 222, 261, 299, 323, 332

N

nargin command, 34
nargout Workaround, 64
ndims command, 48, 279, 282, 291, 293, 294
non-direct-link public variables, 210, 212, 216, 222, 235, 236, 304, 305, 318, 319, 325, 340
num2cell command, 40, 60, 68, 108, 129, 166, 168, 169, 187, 201, 202, 215, 219, 221, 279, 283, 286, 292, 295, 296, 300, 301, 317, 320, 342
numel command, 48, 59, 279, 287, 288, 290, 292, 294, 295, 297, 298, 299, 301, 333, 334, 341, 342

O

object (definition), 9
objectdirectory command (undocumented), 336, 337, 344, 345, 347, 350
Object-Oriented Design, 1, 3, 9, 11, 30, 33, 34, 47, 150, 246, 311, 313, 328, 350
Object-Oriented Programming, 291, 350
objects, 1, 30, 91, 277, 302, 313, 348, 350
Overload
    subsasgn, 48, 49, 50, 51, 53, 61, 62, 63, 65, 69, 70, 71, 74, 79, 91, 99, 101, 102, 110, 111, 118, 160, 198, 235, 272, 281, 313, 332, 333, 349
    subsref, 48, 49, 50, 51, 53, 61, 62, 63, 65, 69, 70, 71, 74, 79, 91, 99, 101, 102, 110, 111, 118, 160, 198, 235, 272, 281, 313, 332, 333, 349
Overloading
    cat, 175
    class-specific tailoring, 21, 23, 36, 45, 46, 47, 48, 56, 59, 63, 64, 65, 69, 70, 74, 77, 78, 79, 80, 83, 86, 91, 92, 93, 95, 96, 98, 106, 109, 113, 114, 115, 118, 121, 139, 143, 145, 155, 156, 157, 160, 167, 168, 171, 198, 238, 240, 241, 242, 243, 246, 255, 259, 271, 293, 294, 307, 315, 317
    display, 81, 82, 88, 91
    fieldnames, 91, 95
    functions, 46, 47, 61
    get, 101
    getfield, 99

operators, 45, 46, 47, 48, 74
    struct, 95

P

parent class (see also, Hierarchy), 35, 153, 154, 155, 156, 175, 186, 225, 227, 231, 253, 270, 312, 338, 340, 343, 348
parent helper (parent_list.m), 155, 156, 157, 158, 160, 161, 162, 163, 164, 165, 166, 173, 184, 189, 192, 194, 195, 199, 205, 215, 219, 226, 231, 240, 253, 268, 273, 280, 301, 320, 342, 343, 346
pass by reference emulation, 36, 277, 313, 314, 315, 316, 318, 319, 321, 322, 323, 324, 325, 327, 329, 333
pass by value, 36, 313, 314, 315, 324
pass-by-reference emulation, 313, 314, 315, 316, 318, 321, 322, 323, 324, 325, 327, 329, 333
Paulk, Mark, 4
Polymorphism
    argument superiority, 37, 47, 54, 69, 143, 144, 227, 327, 337
Poppendieck, Mary and Tom, 5
private visibility, 26, 31, 303
Protected
    function, 340
Protected function, 340
protected visibility, 35, 277, 339, 341, 345
Public interface, 7, 8, 15, 32, 34, 35, 51, 74, 93, 99, 142, 146, 150, 183, 191, 198, 203, 206, 209, 222, 265, 293, 305, 327, 333, 340
public visibility, 100

Q

Quality
    bug-free, 11, 13

R

read-only public varaiables, 41, 53, 78, 100, 186, 191
reference operator syntax, 29
reshape command, 34, 96, 97, 279, 280, 283, 291, 292, 293, 294, 300, 301, 333, 334
rgb2hsv command, 43, 53, 54, 60, 61, 68, 87, 108, 130, 196, 221, 252, 253
Rittel, Horst, 5

S

saveobj command, 46, 304, 307, 308, 311, 312
search path, 153, 340, 350
search path ambiguity, 31
search path priority, 142
set command, 17, 43, 99, 107, 110, 128, 136, 165, 183, 186, 192, 193, 196, 198, 201, 202, 211, 217, 227, 235, 236, 254, 289, 324, 343

setfield command (deprecated), 43, 50, 91, 99

singleton objects, 277, 303, 308, 309, 311

size command, 75

Slicing, 159, 160, 161, 164, 167, 168, 172, 173, 183, 184,
        185, 186, 187, 189, 206, 269, 318, 319, 328,
        340, 341, 343, 345

Software Engineering Institute, 4

Stahl, L., 4

static data, 303, 304

static helper function (static.m), 239, 303, 304, 305, 308,
        311

static keyword, 303

strmatch command, 216, 220, 319, 341, 342, 343

Stroustrup, Bjorne, 10

struct
    overloaded, 321

struct command, 17, 32, 95, 96, 97, 137, 192, 319, 344

Sub-index control, 213, 214, 215, 216, 217, 218, 220, 221,
        222, 259, 260, 288, 317, 320, 328, 329, 342

subsasgn command, 17, 45, 46, 48, 49, 68, 115, 136, 192,
        294

subsindex command, 46, 349, 350

subsref command, 17, 45, 46, 48, 49, 56, 63, 66, 114, 136,
        172, 192, 201, 211, 230, 321, 333

substruct structure, 49, 50, 55, 56, 58, 62, 63, 74, 81, 82,
        85, 96, 99, 102, 105, 106, 107, 109, 110, 111,
        126, 129, 162, 163, 166, 201, 212, 213, 217,
        218, 260, 287, 289, 317, 327, 328, 329, 331,
        335, 338

superiorto command, 36, 47, 49, 54, 74, 87, 116, 125, 143,
        144, 146, 157, 176, 228, 280, 285, 327, 332

T

taxonomy (see also, Hierarchy), 10, 153

times operator, 301

try-catch error handling, 1, 115, 145, 289, 290, 299

U

UML
    static-structure diagram, 150

untyped variables, 3, 37

User-defined Types, 9, 20, 47, 56, 57, 89, 350

V

varargin, 284

varargout, 284
    work around, 210

vectorization, 1, 8, 34, 74, 158, 168, 175, 180, 205, 279,
        295, 302, 318

vertcat command, 34, 46, 175, 177, 182, 273, 280, 291, 335

visibility, 26, 32, 206, 340

W

Webber, Melvin, 5

whos command, 19, 20, 25, 27, 28, 78, 169, 190, 273, 330,
        331, 347

Wicked Problems, 4, 5

write-only public variables, 53, 78